Law and Private Life
in the Middle Ages

Cover image: Detail from the base panel of the fourteenth-century tomb of King Christopher II (d. 1332) and Queen Euphemia in the church of Sorø (Zealand, Denmark). The bronze relief depict scenes from various popular tales that illustrate the theme 'amor vincit omnia'. The third to the right shows the humiliating subjugation of Aristotle by the woman Phyllis, whom the philosopher becomes infatuated with in Henri d'Andeli's Lai d'Aristote.

Per Andersen, Mia Münster-Swendsen
& Helle Vogt (eds.)

Law and Private Life in the Middle Ages

Proceedings of
the Sixth Carlsberg Academy Conference
on Medieval Legal History 2009

DJØF Publishing
2011

Per Andersen, Mia Münster-Swendsen & Helle Vogt (eds.)
Law and Private Life in the Middle Ages
Proceedings of the Sixth Carlsberg Academy Conference
on Medieval Legal History 2009

First edition 2011

© 2011 DJØF Publishing Copenhagen
Jurist- og Økonomforbundets Forlag
DJØF Publishing is a company of the
Association of Danish Lawyers and Economists

All rights reserved.
No part of this publication may be reproduced, stored in a retrieval system,
or transmitted in any form or by any means – electronic, mechanical, photocopying,
recording or otherwise – without the prior written permission of the Publisher.

Cover photo: Mia Münster-Swendsen
Cover: Bo Helsted
Printing: Scandinavian Book, Aarhus

Printed in Denmark 2011
ISBN 978-87-574-2159-5

The publication of this volume is funded by
The School of Law, Aarhus University, and
The Ernst Andersen and Tove Dobel Andersen Foundation

Sold and distributed in North America by
International Specialized Book Services (ISBS)
Portland, OR 97213, USA
www.isbs.com

Sold in Scandinavia by
DJØF Publishing
Copenhagen Denmark
www.djoef-forlag.dk

Sold in all other countries by
The Oxford Publicity Partnership Ltd
Towcester NN12 6BT, UK
www.oppuk.co.uk

Content

INTRODUCTION Per Andersen, Mia Münster-Swendsen and Helle Vogt	1
WERE THE ENGLISH ECCLESIASTICAL TRIBUNALS COURTS OF LAW? Richard H. Helmholz	11
THE APOSTOLIC PENITENTIARY AND DOMESTIC VIOLENCE *The Apostolic Penitentiary in the Middle Ages and its Historical Records* Kirsi Salonen	29
MARITAL ECONOMY AND FEMALE NAMING PRACTICES *IN LATE MEDIEVAL GERMANY* Christof Rolker	49
CANONICAL LEGISLATION ON INCEST AND EXCOMMUNICATION *IN SIXTH-CENTURY GAUL* Frederik Keygnaert	61
PRIVATES ON PARADE: IMPOTENCE CASES AS EVIDENCE *FOR MEDIEVAL GENDER* Frederik Pedersen	81
SCHOOL OF LIFE: LEARNED LAW AND THE SCHOLASTIC HABITUS Helge Dedek	105
PROSECUTING AND PROVING SEXUAL INFIDELITY AT THE COURT *OF KING ARTHUR: THE CASE OF GUINEVERE V. LANVAL* Stephen D. White	123

Introduction

PRIVATE LIFE IN CANON LAW COLLECTIONS   149
ATTRIBUTED TO BISHOP IVO OF CHARTRES
Bruce C. Brasington

CIVIL CUSTODY AS COERCIVE MEASURE IN MEDIEVAL LAW   165
Harry Dondorp

CANON LAW AND CELIBACY: THE SEXUAL URGES   181
OF THE SECULAR CLERGY IN FIFTEENTH-CENTURY BRUGES
Hendrik Callewier

SEXUALITY IN EARLY CHURCH LAWS IN NORWAY AND ICELAND   191
Bjørn Bandlien

VOREMUNDE HEBBEN: CHILDREN, ELDERLY AND IMPAIRED PEOPLE   205
IN EIKE VON REPGOW'S SACHSENSPIEGEL
Chiara Benati

FAMILY FROM A PERSPECTIVE OF DYING – EVALUATING THE POWER   219
OF TESTAMENTS
Jakub Wysmułek

PRIVATE CITIZENS BETWEEN LAW AND POLITICS IN A TUSCAN TOWN   229
Siena from the Early Thirteenth Century to the Early Fourteenth Century
Mario Ascheri

MARITAL CASES OF TOWN INHABITANTS IN THE CHURCH COURTS   245
OF MEDIEVAL POLAND
Łukasz Truściński

CONTRIBUTORS   255

Introduction

From 29 April to 1 May 2009 an interdisciplinary group of international scholars convened for the sixth in a series of conferences on medieval legal history at the Carlsberg Academy in Copenhagen. With nine sessions, accommodating thirty speakers and moderators from thirteen countries, the conference was the largest and most ambitious in the series so far.

The conference theme, 'Law and Private Life', was deliberately chosen to enable as many potential speakers as possible to respond to our call for papers, since the intention was to explore from a variety of angles the conjunction of private life and public legal systems and practices within medieval societies, this time covering Byzantium as well. Equally, from the outset the editorial principle has been to give the authors maximum liberty to choose their particular approach to the overall subject within their fields of specialisation. The result is a collection that stretches from the early to the late Middle Ages, covering a wealth of subjects from the perspectives of both civil and canon law. These include marriage, naming practices, incest, domestic violence, the distinction between public and private spheres, the urban space, the function and practices of medieval courts, adultery, sexuality, celibacy, transgender, identity formation, imprisonment, life-cycles, and age groups such as children, the elderly, and the dying. In its diversity, the anthology thus reflects the proceedings of the conference and the editors have made no attempt to establish a consensus or reach a final conclusion. Instead, we asked authors to provide brief abstracts of their essays to be embedded in an introductory chapter, which will hopefully give the reader an overview of the content.

In the opening essay, based upon his keynote lecture, Richard H. Helmholz asks: *Were the English Ecclesiastical Tribunals Courts of Law?* Using the example of the diocesan courts of England, the essay addresses a question much discussed in today's scholarly literature: Did local courts in the Middle Ages act as courts of law, applying the formal law found in legal formularies and texts? Or is their action better described as 'dispute resolution', dependent more upon social mores and the desires of the parties and their friends than the formal law? The essay makes use of the records of the courts, assessing what they reveal in six areas of the law; marriage and divorce, testamentary succession, tithes and ecclesiastical dues, defamation, assaults upon the clergy, and heresy. Its conclusion is that the English ecclesiastical courts did both. They applied the law as written, sometimes in the face of public opinion. In some areas, however, they also bent to allow popular attitudes and the realities of life a dominant place in the outcome of cases. The evidence by which we can discern the motivation of the judges and lawyers is not thick, but they acted as if this apparently contradictory attitude was quite compatible with the legitimate fulfilment of their responsibilities and even with the intent of the *ius commune* itself.

Professor Helmholz's contribution is followed by two essays dealing with aspects of late medieval marriage. Kirsi Salonen's essay, *The Apostolic Penitentiary and Domestic Violence*, discusses the petitions regarding violence between husbands and wives or close relatives brought before the Apostolic Penitentiary during the pontificate of Pius II (1458–1464), thus engaging with source material that has never before been used for studying domestic violence. During these years, the office handled approximately 16,000 petitions for an apostolic absolution (and dispensation), of which only thirty-six cases involved domestic violence. Thus domestic violence appears not to have been a major issue for the Church, still in certain cases Christians seem to have turned to the highest ecclesiastical authorities for resolving problems connected to domestic violence. The corpus consists of different types of violent crimes, from assault with no permanent injury to the victim to intentional homicide, the latter forming the majority since the ecclesiastical norms did not make distinction between different degrees of violence but condemned all violent behaviour as sin that had to be confessed and satisfied through penance. The present essay analyses the main details of the thirty-six petitions. It starts by examining the provenance of the petitions in order to see whether domestic violence was more of an issue in certain areas of Christendom than in others. The article then concentrates on the persons involved: Who were the violators and who were their victims, and how were they related to each other? The last question analysed concerns the motives behind the violent behaviour. Why did the violent acts take place, and were there common denominators for domestic violence?

In his essay, *Marital Economy and Female Naming Practices in Late Medieval Germany*, Christof Rolker deals with female naming practices in fifteenth-century Germany in relation to the various marital economy regimes of a number of towns and cities. One of the most difficult questions concerning the marital economy of medieval Europe is the question of who could actually dispose of property, rather than who owned it. The evidence from normative sources, 'marriage contracts' and related documents, gives important clues but the evidence is often very sketchy and comparison remains very difficult. Here, the study of names can provide valuable additional evidence. Rolker proposes that gender-specific naming practices (as found in testaments, 'marriage contracts', and other documents) can be used as a proxy for the economic position of married women. Patterns of naming were commonly very consistent in the sense that the same form of name would be used in the same context over a long time and by different scribes in any given town. Both comparative studies and individual case studies suggest that family names were a symbolic good the use of which coincided with the access to economic goods.

Frederik Keygnaert's essay investigates *Canonical Legislation on Incest and Excommunication in Sixth-Century Gaul*. From the beginning of the Middle Ages the main ecclesiastical weapon to punish violations of church law was excommunication. Observance of the penalty by the powerful was critical to enforce Church authority. However, the canons of sixth-century Merovingian councils and some narrative texts by Gregory of Tours together seem to imply that obedience to excommunication was not easy to achieve. In all likelihood, the political power that came with the privilege to excommunicate was a frequent cause for concern among lay rulers. Moreover, the ongoing process of judicialising the procedure of excommunication probably complicated enforcement of the sentence, as it became harder to implement excommunication without a proper trial. This paper aims to show how early medieval conflicts might not be properly understood without fully grasping the function and mechanism of excommunication as an instrument of power. This is particularly true for some sixth-century conflicts which initially merely seemed to concern incest law. A dispute between the Burgundian King Sigismund and his bishops serves to demonstrate this. The quarrel involved Sigismund's treasurer, Stephanus, who was excommunicated for contracting an incestuous marriage to Palladia, the sister of his dead wife. All the indications are that the Burgundian bishops focused on the importance of respecting the Church's main weapon rather than seeking a fight with the king over violation of incest law. Sigismund refused to accept the ecclesiastical sentence, as it would have meant the religious and social exclusion of his treasurer, rendering him unable to perform his duties. The bishops reacted with a threat to go on strike, while Sigismund took advantage of the loopholes in the incest laws, which were still inconclusive about the appropriate penalty for transgressions. In the end, a compromise was reached, through which Stephanus and Palladia probably incurred a eucharistic excommunication, without further exclusion from social contact. To conclude, this case study may serve as a stepping stone to reveal in what way the impact of incest laws was related to the canonical prescriptions regarding excommunication throughout the sixth century.

Introduction

From the early Middle Ages we move forwards in time to Frederik Pedersen's essay, *Privates on Parade: Impotence Cases as Evidence for Medieval Gender*. The practice of English medieval church courts examining a man for impotence by means of a group of 'good and honest women' who attempted to excite the man sexually to give him an erection has become a commonplace of medieval social history, whether it is intended for academics or a more general audience. There have been many attempts to contextualise and explain this English practice, all of which have considered it surprising and unusual. Common to these studies has been the suggestion that medieval church courts took some pleasure or had some ulterior motive in exposing men to this kind of examination: among the more idiosyncratic explanations it has been suggested that these expert witnesses must have been prostitutes or that the courts were involved in producing pornography. Few, if any, modern commentators have taken the surviving evidence as a serious attempt by the medieval church courts to solve unusual, but still not uncommon, problems affecting marriage and few studies have seriously considered the evidence as descriptions of real medical conditions. This chapter argues two points: firstly, that although English court practice does differ from French practice in its use of women as expert witnesses, the English practice meets canon law's requirement that expert witnesses examine the man, and, secondly, that all but one of the English medieval impotence cases can be shown to involve men with severe genital malformations which occur naturally in any human population. Furthermore, in one specific case it may be argued that the defendant, who grew up as a man and whose masculine identity would never have been challenged by medieval English society, was genetically a woman who would now be classified as being in an inter-sex state--most likely suffering from congenital adrenal hyperplasia, a disease that blocks the infant's metabolism, causing a range of symptoms including abnormal sex organs and early death.Thus we must conclude that, though the practice of the medieval English courts may appear to be incomprehensible to a modern observer, it was a rational and sensible solution to biological problems that are as prevalent today as they were then.

Helge Dedek's essay, *School of Life: Learned Law and the Scholastic Habitus*, deals with the mindset of the learned lawyers, seeing the origins of the learned law as inextricably interwoven with the origins of the Western university: the school, this peculiar space of 'studious leisure'. Despite the early legal academics' involvement in legal practice and their integration into the environment of the newly flourishing urban space, it is obvious that legal texts produced by 'learned' authors also bore the marks of what Pierre Bourdieu has called the 'scholastic point of view'. The 'scholastic point of view', Bourdieu has argued, is related to the specific and completely unique quality of thinking that takes place in academic space. Starting from this abstract conceptualisation of this 'scholastic' condition, the paper focuses on the role of its concrete medieval incarnation, the phenomenon known as Scholasticism, as a structure that shaped the views of medieval jurists and therefore the character of medieval learned law. Scholasticism, according to Dedek, could be understood not merely as a philosophy or a methodology, but, as Erwin Panofsky put it, as a 'mental habit'. This (again in the words of Bourdieu) habitus grew out of the 'daily life' of the academy: academia constituted a 'world apart', a particular life-world in which the scholar was completely immersed. To illustrate that Scholasticism, thus perceived as habitus, did not only operate on a rational and conscious level, the essay highlights one of the irrational aspects of the discourse of the learned law that can hardly be explained in functional or rational terms: drawing mainly on the works of Umberto Eco and Erwin Panofsky, and legal theorists such as Pierre Schlag, attention is drawn to what could be called the 'legal aesthetics' of the Scholastic jurists.

Stephen D. White's essay, *Prosecuting and Proving Sexual Infidelity at the Court of King Arthur: The Case of Guinevere v. Lanval*, deals with adultery and concubinage in Arthurian romance. In Marie de France's *Lai de Lanval* (c.1170), Guinevere falsely accuses Lanval of shaming her by seeking her love and of insulting her, when she rejected him, by comparing her unfavourably to the lowliest serving-maid of his own love, a fairy princess who had given him her love on condition that he not speak of her. Lanval denies that he had sought the queen's love. He also expresses regret for having spoken the words that had indeed insulted the queen. But what Lanval says he regrets about the words is not that they were insulting to the queen, but rather that by speaking those words and thus speaking of his own love, he had broken the condition under which his love had given herself to him and had therefore lost her. The judges of Arthur's court dismiss the first charge and allow him to rebut the second by proving the truth of what he said about the queen. The fairy princess and her serving-maids provide the proof necessary to secure the acquittal of Lanval, who rides off to Avalon with her. Whereas previous commentators have argued that Marie de France constructed Lanval's case so as to reveal the inadequacies of the courts of her own day, this essay demonstrates that strict adherence to traditional judicial procedures is what saves Lanval and that, in this respect, his case closely resembles many other literary law cases of the late twelfth and early thirteenth centuries, in which an honourable man or woman is falsely accused of sexual treason by a male or female accuser who is truly a traitor, is tried in accordance with traditional procedures virtually identical to those depicted in Lanval's case, and ultimately acquitted.

Regarding lay people in the collections of canon law, Bruce Brasington, in his essay, *Private Life in Canon Law Collections Attributed to Bishop Ivo of Chartres*, notes that it is only in the eleventh century,

Introduction

specifically in the *Decretum* of Bishop Ivo of Chartres, that we encounter a section of canon law specifically devoted to the laity. This section, *De causis laicorum*, collected older canons that treated issues as diverse as lay infringement on ecclesiastical property and sexual behaviour. Due to the antiquity of these texts, however, it is difficult to ascertain what they might say about clerical attitudes towards the laity's private life. Fortunately, some manuscripts of the *Decretum* augment this section by the addition of canons. These additional canons, products of a compiler's particular interest in 'updating' or 'refining' this section of the compilation, concern adultery, marriage, and burial practices.

Harry Dondorp's essay, *Civil Custody as Coercive Measure in Medieval Law*, highlights the differences between Dutch law and that of neighbouring countries in enforcing specific performance through confinement. Dondorp states that nowadays in the Netherlands all obligations and legal duties other than to pay a sum of money can be enforced through civil imprisonment. As William de Groot, Hugo Grotius' younger brother, attested, this was already the case in seventeenth-century Holland: 'In our country there is a system unknown to other nations, called gyzeling, by which judgements condemning a person to do something are executed'. *Gyzeling* was a compulsatory measure, not be confused with imprisonment for debt, for it began as a – more or less voluntary – confinement in an inn. Only debtors who stubbornly refused to follow the court's order were imprisoned after fourteen days. Even though *gijzeling* is rooted in the medieval indigenous German practice of *leisten* (Latin: *obstagium*), an extra-judicial compulsory measure, traces can be found in the learned law of the Middle Ages. Referring to a decretal of Alexander III, the canonists taught that the agreement of bailsmen to confine themselves to a certain place was legally binding. Hence, they could (if needed) be apprehended. Customary law legitimised the use of foot-irons, according to William Durandus. Many glossators, however, considered this to be contrary to Roman law. Firstly, because as a rule specificies that a debtor could discharge his obligation to do something through a payment of damages. Secondly, they read in the *Corpus iuris* that free men were not to be enslaved because of their debts. Debtors and bailsmen who were restrained in their movement were, according to this line of thought, comparable to slaves. Public interest, however, viz. that of the university, could legitimise the use of foot-irons. A scribe who had promised a student to copy (law) books could thus be forced to finish his work.

The next two essays treat legal aspects of celibacy and sexuality. In *Canon Law and Celibacy: The Sexual Urges of the Secular Clergy in Fifteenth-Century Bruges*, Hendrik Callewier confronts the late medieval popular image of lecherous clerics, as expressed in a fifteenth-century Flemish chronicle: 'Are really all of them arrogant and lecherous whore-hoppers and ravishers of virgins?'. In Bruges there were hundreds of secular clerics connected to the town's numerous religious institutions. Archival sources do indeed confirm that many of these clerics were guilty of living in concubinage, of visiting brothels, of committing rape, paedophilia, sodomy, and adultery with married women, despite the fact that canon law forbade clerics who had taken orders to engage in sexual activities. This prohibition, which would repeatedly appear in synodal statutes, was ignored by large numbers of the clergy. The *privilegium fori* stipulated that members of the clergy could only be tried in an ecclesiastical court. The episcopal courts, the officialities, limited their activities to collecting fines, which should be regarded as taxation rather than punishment. Moreover, from the sources one gains the distinct impression that clerics received a milder punishment for criminal offences than lay persons. In the second half of the fifteenth century, however, a stricter approach towards priests living in concubinage becomes noticeable. This was, on the one hand, a consequence of initiatives by the ecclesiastical authorities who tried to fight concubinage in the provincial councils. On the other hand, the stricter adherence to canon law seems to have reflected the mood of the laity, who had become increasingly intolerant of the clergy's sexual escapades.

Bjørn Bandlien's essay, *Sexuality in Early Church Laws in Norway and Iceland*, deals with the effects of the legal changes following the the introduction of Christian laws in Norway and Iceland shortly after Christianisation in the early eleventh century. The essay examines how these early Christian laws constructed a Christian identity, and especially a Christian sexual identity. It is argued that the two main structuring principles are those of space and time. The spatial orientation is oriented towards Jerusalem on a macro-level, and the local church as a holy place on a local level. Time is important both in the cases of the annual cycle of feast and fast days, as well as structuring the life of Christians through baptism, marriage, and death. In the case of sexuality, the Christian laws regulate especially the time when believers are allowed to marry or to have sexual intercourse. In the regulation of time, eating of meat was as much regulated as sexual conduct. In a spatial context, the criteria of baptism and burial were more emphasised than sexuality. Thus, it can be concluded that changing sexual relations was not of the highest priority in the early Icelandic and Norwegian churches. Early Christian law did not fundamentally challenge the traditional Norse attitudes towards sex and sexual identities as foremost linked to social power and honour. A new paradigm of Christian identity based upon sexuality was only introduced in the late twelfth century. This is most clearly seen in the penitential of Bishop Þorlákr of Skálholt and the writings of the Archbishops Eysteinn and Eiríkr of Nidaros. Here, the sexual transgressions can be said to define the individual as a Christian, thus constructing a more distinct Christian discourse of sexuality.

Two essays deal with the legal aspects of age groups and life cycles. Chiara Benati's essay, *'Voremunde hebben': Children, Elderly and Impaired People in Eike von Repgow's Sachsenspiegel*, is a study of categories of age as represented in one of the oldest private *Rechtsbücher* in the German language area and certainly the most popular in the Middle Ages. Thanks to its prominent role within the German medieval legal tradition, Eike von Repgow's lawbook appears to be particularly suitable for a research study aimed at describing the regulation of private life in that specific phase of German legal history. In this article, the status of all those people who, in contemporary Northern Germany, were not considered because of their age or health conditions to be able to act as adults and needed to undergo guardianship (*voremund*) is taken into consideration. A lexical analysis conducted on the main Low German manuscript of the text (Codex Picturatus Oldenburgensis, CIM I 410, Landesbibliothek Oldenburg) of the terms and phrasemes used to describe this institution, provides a picture of this particular aspect of legislation in regard to private life.

The first part of Jakub Wysmulek's essay, *Family from a Perspective of Dying – Evaluating the Power of Testaments*, focuses on the process of the appearance of wills in the Kingdom of Poland. The essay describes how the old rules of inheritance, based on the law that was common in Poland as well as in German towns, were eroded due to the influence of wills. This new, alien element, introduced and spread by the Church, became a way of controlling the testator's property and the family even after his or her death, which became very widespread among the wealthy burghers of the time. Furthermore, the popularisation of wills in the dynamically changing society had an impact upon the evolution of that particular type of document. Having a religious origin, the will was gradually secularised during the fifteenth century. Moreover, the pious bequest eventually stopped playing the decisive role in making the last will. The second part of the essay is devoted to analysing the authors of the wills and their families. The prosopographical study of the people writing the wills helps us to picture the social group we are dealing with, which appears to be the prosperous or reasonably well-off urban dignitaries in the majority of the cases. By analysing the bequest itself, unique information about the burgher's family emerges, such as its composition, number of members, and the relationships among them. Although enlarged by the group of close associates, such as servants, confessors, fellow traders etc., these families often appear to be small, almost nuclear, ones. The essay also attempts to describe the strategies of the testators regarding how and among whom the estate should be divided. The abovementioned aspects, it is argued, might be interpreted as indicators of the processes of individualisation and 'modernisation' that marked late medieval urban society.

The final two contributions both concern the function of law in the urban space. Mario Ascheri's essay, *Private Citizens between Law and Politics in a Tuscan Town*, deals with Siena in the early thirteenth to the early fourteenth centuries. The essay provides an introduction to the many legal problems that inhabitants of an important Italian commune faced during the late Middle Ages, when the city developed its own law based on Roman law and Lombard customary law. Citizens and foreigners, men and women, married or single, adults and minors, laity and clergy, merchants and nobles, were among the many different categories that had specific norms for many aspects of their daily life. Taxes, procedures in the courts, political rights, marriages, sumptuary laws, crimes, and so on were to be reconsidered in the effort to ensure the freedom and independence of the city. The main aim of the essay is to highlight the complexity of the legal life in a period which may seem distant, but is closer to us than is normally recognised. Many 'modern' needs were equally felt by common people then, but it was not always possible to reach a solution for these problems. This is, for example, the case of the translation of Siena's statutory law into the vernacular to make it easier for ordinary citizens to understand the law, as part of a polemic against the legal experts, who were regarded as the true enemies of justice. What was equally crucial to these legislative processes was the interaction between law and politics as internal conflicts and foreign relations forced legislators to discriminate between categories of citizens.

In his article, *Marital Cases of Town Inhabitants in the Church Courts of Medieval Poland*, Łukasz Truściński attempts to show the character of marital cases filed with the ecclesiastical courts by the inhabitants of towns in medieval Poland. This is done by analysing registers from the episcopal courts of Cracow and Lublin during the period from 1410 to 1489. According to these sources, marital cases predominantly concerned the breaking of the marital oath and separation from the spouse as well as so-called 'obstacles' preventing the continuation of matrimony. Regarding the latter aspect, the parties sought annulment of a marriage for a variety of reasons; the husband's impotence or the wife's infertility, or the claim that the marital oath was taken against one's will. The people who most frequently had their cases tried in ecclesiastical courts were predominantly the less affluent or only moderately wealthy residents of towns; journeymen and craftsmen, such as tailors, cobblers, furriers, bakers and butchers, as well as apprentices and (especially with regard to women) domestic servants. Significantly, the cases analysed do not involve representatives of the wealthiest social strata of medieval towns, such as merchants and town council members.

Introduction

The conference and the publication of this volume were made possible through generous funding from The Carlsberg Foundation, Knud Højgaard's Foundation, Ernst Andersen's Foundation, and last, but not least, The School of Law, Aarhus University, who stepped in to cover the printing costs. As organisers and editors we wish to express our gratitude to the Carlsberg Academy for providing us once again with the spectacular venue that gives the conference series its special ambience, namely the mid-nineteenth century villa of the founder of the Carlsberg Breweries, I. C. Jacobsen. As usual, our thanks also go to the caretaker of the estate, Svend Rasmussen, for his patience and invaluable help in making the event run smoothly.

Aarhus and Copenhagen
December 2010

Per Andersen   Mia Münster-Swendsen   Helle Vogt

WERE THE ENGLISH ECCLESIASTICAL TRIBUNALS COURTS OF LAW?

R. H. Helmholz

Introduction

Legal historians assume that the highest courts in medieval Europe applied the formal law in the cases that came before them. Not without good reason. It is self-evident that professional lawyers and judges in courts of law would wish to do more than provide an arena for dispute resolution. So they had been trained. So they acted. Of course, there were sometimes practical impediments to enforcement of the law – bribery of witnesses, corruption of judges, or pressure from above, for example. However, the goal of the officials who controlled litigation in the courts was to put the law into practice, and usually they did so. If they left some room for equitable considerations to come into play, even that fell into regular patterns capable of legal statement.

There is more disagreement among historians, however, about what happened in lesser tribunals. The aims and aspirations of the men who administered justice in local courts have long been open to debate. Their knowledge of the law itself has also been doubted. In English legal history, the question has been raised with particular acerbity for the many manorial courts that existed during the Middle Ages and whose records have now been examined in some detail. Did they apply rules of law, or were they guided instead by the interests of the lord and the personal preferences of the suitors in the court? The opinions of scholars have differed.[1] The

---

1. Compare Lloyd Bonfield, 'The Nature of Customary Law in the Manor Courts of Medieval England', *Comparative Studies in Society and History* 31 (1989), 514-34, with John S. Beckerman, 'Toward a Theory of Medieval Manorial Adjudication:

answer matters to our understanding of the character of medieval justice in England, and it takes on an additional relevance in a wider European context. It affects our understanding of the reasons for a growing acceptance of Roman and canon law in the courts of northern lands.

The same question has been asked about the subject of this paper: the ecclesiastical courts. With the law of the church, it is undeniable that the men who practised it had considerable legal resources upon which to draw if they wished. The *Corpus iuris canonici* contained a sophisticated body of legal rules; some say it was the first modern legal system.[2] The commentators of the *ius commune*, drawing upon the *Corpus iuris civilis* as well as the canons, provided a procedural law that encouraged formality and fidelity to legal rule. Appeals to the papal court in Rome were available to secure conformity to the law.

However, as one reads through the historical literature on the subject, it is not so clear that these resources dictated what actually happened in the diocesan courts of the church. The question is whether they dealt with the conflicts that came before them by applying the rules of law found in the formal sources of law. Or did they do something else? Did they pay more attention to factors like honour, emotion, private interest, and community harmony than to the law's requirements? There is a body of literature that tends toward the latter point of view.[3] Except at their very highest level,

---

The Nature of Communal Judgments in a System of Customary Law', *Law and History Review* 13 (1995), 1-22. See also Paul R. Hyams, 'What did Edwardian Villagers Understand by "Law"?' in *Medieval Society and the Manor Court*, eds. Zvi Razi and Richard Smith (Oxford: 1996), 69-116, and Maureen Mulholland, 'Trials in Manorial Courts in Late Medieval England' in *Judicial Tribunals in England and Europe 1200–1700*, eds. Maureen Mulholland and Brian Pullan (Manchester: 2003), 81-101.

2. Harold J. Berman, *Law and Revolution: The Formation of the Western Legal Tradition* (Cambridge, MA: 1983), 199-254.

3. See the careful statement by F. D. Logan, *The Medieval Court of Arches* (Canterbury & York Society 95, 2005), pp. vii-viii. On the general subject, including some use of ecclesiastical material, see Daniel Lord Smail, *The Consumption of Justice: Emotions, Publicity, and Legal Culture in Marseille, 1264–1423* (Ithaca, NY: 2003); *Communities and Courts in Britain, 1150–1900*, eds. Christopher Brooks and Michael Lobban (London: 1997); *The Moral World of the Law*, ed. Peter Coss (Cambridge: 2000); Richard Firth Green, *A Crisis of Truth: Literature and Law in Ricardian England* (Philadelphia, PA: 1999); Marjorie K. McIntosh, *Controlling Misbehavior in England, 1370–1600* (Cambridge: 1998); *Expectations of the Law in the Middle Ages*, ed. Anthony Musson (Woodbridge, Suffolk, England: 2001); *The Letter of the Law: Legal Practice and Literary Production in Medieval England*, eds. Emily Steiner and Candace Barrington (Ithaca, NY: 2002).

the courts of the church were local courts, and they may have acted as such. This appears to be an unsettled question.

It is also a question that has interested many participants in these Conferences. Reading through the proceedings of the Fourth Carlsberg Academy Conference, a copy of which Professor Helle Vogt was kind enough to give to me, I was impressed by the frequency and the seriousness with which participants had approached the question of whether courts dealt with dispute resolution through the application of formal law or instead by more informal means. Many of them asked: Do we see action in courts being taken on the basis of 'conceptions of law as an autonomous sphere enforced by a coercive power?'[4] Or was the law more accurately characterized as one way among many of legitimizing behaviour, so that most disputes were settled by non-legal considerations, by compromise, force, and societal pressure?[5] Power can be exercised in different ways, and the essays brought the alternatives into clear contrast. They contributed to understanding of a legitimate question.[6] The Proceedings of the Fifth Conference, devoted to custom and law, raised the same subject in a different way.[7] They moved me to ask the question of the courts that I have studied over the years. Did they belong to one sphere or to the other? This question seemed especially appropriate for a conference devoted to law and

---

4. Hans Jacob Orning, 'The Interplay between Law, Sin and Honour', in *Law and Power in the Middle Ages*, eds. Per Andersen, Mia Münster-Swendsen and Helle Vogt (Copenhagen: 2007), 28.
5. Ibid. 33. In the same volume, see John G. H. Hudson, 'Power, Law, and the Administration of Justice in England 900–1200', ibid., 153-70; and Gerd Althoff, 'Nobility in Court', ibid., 11-25.
6. Most famous is the work of Alan Watson; see, e.g., his *Society and Legal Change* (Philadephia, PA: 2001). This seems also to be the attitude of James A. Brundage, 'Legal Learning and the Professionalization of Canon Law', in *Law and Learning in the Middle Ages*, eds. Helle Vogt and Mia Münster-Swendsen (Copenhagen: 2006) 5-27, at 27. A particularly good example of how sharp the difference can be, even using the same sources, is provided by the scholarly disagreement about the nature of practice in the local and manorial courts in England. Compare Lloyd Bonfield, 'The Nature of Customary Law in the Manor Courts of Medieval England', *Comparative Studies in Society and History* 31 (1989), 514-34, with John S. Beckerman, 'Toward a Theory of medieval Manorial Adjudication: The Nature of Communal Judgments in a System of Customary Law', *Law and History Review* 13 (1995), 1-22. An introduction to the state of understanding among American legal historians is Peter Hoffer, *Law and People in Colonial America* (Baltimore, MD: 1998), pp. xii-xv.
7. See several of the essays in *Custom: The Development and Use of a Legal Concept in the Middle Ages*, eds. Per Andersen, Mia Münster-Swendsen and Helle Vogt (Copenhagen: 2009).

private life, where the intimate nature of many of the disputes seemed to invite informality. Let's look at the evidence. I have taken six different subjects, perhaps not quite at random, but the choice is wide enough to include the major aspects of the spiritual jurisdiction exercised by the ecclesiastical courts in England. The period covered here runs from the late thirteenth to the early sixteenth century.

Marriage and Divorce

The first topic is marriage and divorce, a much studied subject. My own conclusion here is that in this sensitive area, embracing the most personal kinds of family relationships, the English courts did act as courts of law. The formal canon law here was, to say the least, out of step with the attitudes of many of the people affected by it – that the exchange of words of present consent alone made a full and indissoluble marriage was not, as I read the medieval evidence, what most lay people desired or thought.[8] Until consummation, or at least solemnization, they regarded the verbal exchange as a contract to marry, not as a completed and full marriage. It might therefore still be open to negotiation. Whatever the opinions of the theologians, most people had no difficulty in distinguishing the marriage of Mary and Joseph from their own.

In the face of this attitude, however, the canon law courts in England enforced the canonical definition, ordering couples who had gone no further than exchanging *verba de praesenti* to solemnize their unions and to live together as man and wife. In other words, they decided these cases based upon the formal canon law. It may be true that parties to litigation used various 'strategies' involving false testimony and sought to take advantage of other procedural 'devices' involving delay and compromise. It may be that informal meetings were commonly held in order to avoid having recourse to the courts.[9] It is a certainty that the parties sometimes disobeyed the sentences issued. Reliable evidence on all these points has appeared in

---

8. See. e.g., Frederik Pedersen, 'A Matter of Choice: Spiritual and Secular Jurisdiction in Two English Marriage Cases in the Early Fourteenth Century', in *Law and Learning* (above note 6), 223-34. The classic work on this point is Georges Duby, *Le chevalier, la femme et le prêtre; le mariage dans la France féodale* (Paris: 1981); new vistas were opened on it by Mia Korpiola, *Between Betrothal and Bedding: Marriage Formation in Sweden 1200–1600* (Leiden and Boston, MA: 2009).
9. Frederick Pedersen, *Marriage Disputes in Medieval England* (London: 2000), 105-18.

print.[10] But none of it challenges the conclusion about what the courts themselves did. In this most controversial area of the law, they conformed their sentences to the matrimonial law of the church.

The regulation of sexual activity, sometimes involving divorce *a mensa et thoro* within a marriage, sometimes involving the punishment of sexual relations outside of marriage or otherwise in violation of the marriage bond, was handled a little differently. This subject was usefully investigated by Professor Larry Poos; he reached the conclusion that in their disciplinary jurisdiction over the laity, the English lower ecclesiastical courts adopted a more informal stance towards marriage. In them, 'the formal law, community scrutiny, and the messy reality of private life' came together.[11] What he found was that the courts acted more to preserve the harmony of villages and peace among the villagers than to enforce the letter of the canon law. If a married couple could not live together peaceably, the courts either granted them a divorce *a mensa et thoro* or winked at their living separately. If local scandal had brewed because of the suspicion of sexual relations between a man and a woman, the courts would order them to keep apart, that is, to avoid coming within each other's company in private. Such an order was not contrary to the canon law, but neither was it driven by the law; no requirement of the law I know of suggested that such an order be issued. The driving force, according to Professor Poos, was community opinion. The courts worked within the realm of the possible, and this meant paying more attention to what men and women, the leaders of the local community or sometimes the parties themselves, wished than it did to texts of the canon law. It was his finding that much of the church's matrimonial jurisdiction in disciplinary matters depended in large part upon the desires and opinions of the laity.

Much of the abundant literature devoted to the history of the church's matrimonial law in recent years seems in accord with the approach taken by Professor Poos. The authors have concentrated on the social side of things.[12] However, it is not always clear how far this attitude was shared by the lawyers who staffed the medieval courts. Much of the evidence is equivocal. Take, for example, the most sensational aspect of practice in the medieval courts in England – the appointment of a group of women to

---

10. Charles Donahue, Jr., *Law, Marriage, and Society in the Later Middle Ages* (Cambridge: 2007), 46-62.
11. L. R. Poos, 'The Heavy-Handed Marriage Counsellor: Regulating Marriage in some Later-Medieval English Local Ecclesiastical Court Jurisdictions', *American J. Legal Hist.* 39 (1995), 291-309, at 309.
12. The literature is usefully surveyed in Conor McCarthy, *Marriage in Medieval England: Law, Literature and Practice* (Woodbridge, Suffolk, England: 2004), 1-18.

attempt to arouse a man's sexual desires in causes brought to secure a divorce on the grounds of sexual impotence.[13] Not found in the canonical texts or anywhere in the law of proof, this method of proving impotence seems as 'lawless' as it was crude. Criticism of it was surely warranted; in practice it was abandoned soon enough. However, when examined closely, the writing of the canonists make its use less surprising than it would otherwise be.[14] Not that they endorsed it, but they do make it apparent that the law of proof in the *ius commune* was not meant to be a strait jacket. It left room for judicial choice. More importantly, the canonists stated repeatedly and emphatically that the impediment of impotence should never be allowed to serve as a means of undoing valid marriages. They worried about the possibility. The danger was real. Litigants might 'deceive' the church. That must not be allowed to happen. Fearful men, even lawyers, sometimes endorse silly things. They see no inconsistency with the law in so doing. To my way of thinking, this is exactly what happened in this situation. It was a mix of law and compromise.

Probate Jurisdiction

A second test is provided by the law of succession, principally last wills and testaments. The English courts Christian exercised probate jurisdiction over movable property, including that of the laity, but not over most rights in land, throughout the Middle Ages and long after. On which side of the line did the exercise of this jurisdiction fall? Here one has to confess that a firm answer is impossible. We know too little; not enough careful spadework has yet been done with the records.[15] I count myself partially at fault for this. Nonetheless we do know some things, enough to reach a tentative conclusion.[16]

---

13. See Jacqueline Murray, 'On the Origins and Role of "Wise Women" in causes for annulment on the grounds of male impotence', *Journal of Medieval History* 16 (1990), 235-49.
14. The early canonists found the impediment of impotence a particularly difficult subject; see James Brundage, 'Impotence, Frigidity and Marital Nullity in the Decretists and the Early Decretalists', in *Proceedings of the Seventh International Congress of Medieval Canon Law*, ed. Peter Linehan (Vatican City: 1988), 407-23.
15. The only comprehensive work attempted so far is Michael M. Sheehan, *The Will in Medieval England* (Toronto: 1963); its coverage runs only to the end of the thirteenth century, unfortunately a period before English ecclesiastical court records survive in any number.
16. See, e.g., Ralph Houlbrooke, *Church Courts and the People during the English Reformation 1520–1570* (Oxford: 1979), 89-116.

The formal law applied in the English courts itself is worthy of note. The Gregorian Decretals contained a section on testaments.[17] However, almost all of it was devoted either to the testamentary capacity of the clergy or to securing enforcement of charitable bequests in favour of the church. Roman law contained little about the former and it was in the special interest of the church to promote the latter. Decretal law was obviously needed for both. Otherwise, however, the canon law on this subject was slight. Ordinarily succession was treated as a secular matter and subject to secular law. This left something of a gap in England, and the principal law on the subject in England was contained in several provincial constitutions, most of them enacted during the thirteenth century. These local laws sought to guarantee the right to make a will to a very large group of people indeed – including laymen and secular clerics, married women, slaves and serfs.[18] The bishop or his representative was to supervise the process of estate administration in order to see that the last wishes of decedents were fully carried out. The constitutions called for a regime of testamentary freedom. That was the law meant to be applied in practice.

What do the records show about its realization? They show that the English church established a system administered by the consistory courts to test the authenticity of wills, to name competent administrators to collect the decedent's assets and to pay his debts, and to supervise the payment of his legacies. The provincial legislation itself did not require creation of this special jurisdiction, but formal organization was found to be the best way to secure conformity with the provincial legislation's dictates. It was not contrary to the Decretal law. And indeed, in the records we find many examples showing that the courts did in fact attempt to carry out the terms of last wills proved before them. It extended even to verbal directions made after written wills had been completed, so that a man who said on his death bed, 'I forgot to include my servant William in my written testament, I want him to have £10,' would have found an ally in the spiritual tribunals. The courts would require the executor to pay that amount to William. This, I would say, was acting as a court of law. It meant enforcing the applicable law. The regularity of proof of last wills and testaments, noted in many, many probate act books, is the external manifestation of that aspect of ecclesiastical jurisdiction.

Even here, however, the English ecclesiastical courts were not impervious to non-legal influence – What shall we call it? – perhaps the

---

17. X 3.26.1-20.
18. This is stated clearly and commented upon in William Lyndwood (d. 1446), *Provinciale (seu Constitutiones Angliae)* (Oxford: 1679), 172-73, esp. 173, gl. v. *propriarum uxorum*.

force of opinions widely shared among the people subject to the law. It played a determinative role, however, in a slightly different way than occurred in the law of marriage. As just noted, the law held that married women had the full capacity to make a valid testament. On this point, however, sentiment among the property-owning classes in England had long stood against this rule. Men thought that married women should not have this right; all their property belonged by right to their husbands while the marriage lasted. Michael Sheehan has shown that during the thirteenth and fourteenth centuries the spiritual courts sought with some success to enforce the canon law's position. Subsequent investigation has shown, however, that by the fifteenth century, they had given up the effort.[19] In practice, married women had lost the right; only with the express consent of their husbands could they make a valid testament. Probate records produce so few that it is evident that the courts had stopped trying to make the canonical position effective, whatever the formal law. The same, I think, can be said of the testaments of the unfree, the English villeins, although there more serious research is needed. The courts also allowed many estates to go unadministered; the effective rate of probate was only something between thirty and forty per cent even though the law required all men to provide for their successors and to prepare themselves for death. In other words, this is a situation where the courts seem to have given up trying to swim against a tide of lay sentiment. They still acted as courts of law in the testamentary matters that were brought before them, but they did not go beyond that. They did not attempt to impose a system of succession on the people.

Tithes and Ecclesiastical Dues

The monetary duties of the laity towards church and clergy provide a third test of the question about the nature of ecclesiastical jurisdiction. Many such duties existed. The tithe, the tenth of the fruits of the earth and of men's labour that was owed to the clergy under the canon law, was probably the most important, but there were others – church rates to keep the parish church in repair, the mortuary fee collected by the incumbent of each parish on the death of a member of his flock, customary offerings to pay for bread and wine or for candles, annual salaries paid to the sexton and parish clerk,

---

19. Evidence on this point is collected in R. H. Helmholz, 'Married Women's Wills in Later Medieval England', in *Wife and Widow in Medieval England*, ed. Sue Sheridan Walker (Ann Arbor, MI: 1993), 165-82; see also Joseph Biancalana, 'Testamentary Cases in Fifteenth-Century Chancery', *Tijdschrift voor Rechtsgeschiedenis* 76 (2008), 283-306, at 298.

and some others. The subject is not covered in any detail in most treatments of English ecclesiastical jurisdiction – other than to say it was a 'festering sore' between clergy and laity.[20] These dues were not a matter of choice. On this account, a look at them provides a way of evaluating the nature of the church's jurisdiction as it was in practice.

The pattern here is different from that of the first two subjects, but equally suggestive, in thinking about whether the courts acted as courts of law. They certainly did in one sense. If a layman failed to pay his tithes, the courts would enforce the obligation, and they used the law of proof of the *ius commune*, as found in the many existing *ordines judiciarii*, to determine which party had the better argument on his side. A great many of the medieval cases found in the English records involved disputes between different claimants of the tithe, as between a monastic house and the vicar of a parish church or two monastic houses, and here too the disputes seem to have been decided along the lines laid out in the formal law.[21] The distinction between praedial tithes and personal tithes endorsed in the canonical texts, and leading to quite different levels of clerical taxation, was maintained in practice throughout the medieval period,[22] and the difficult question of monastic tithes seems also to have been dealt with according to the book.[23] It would be quite wrong to suppose that the law of tithes was abandoned in favour of a model of informal conflict resolution or a surrender to the force of public opinion.

This said, it would nonetheless be mistaken to treat it as a full or satisfactory description of the reality. One reason is that the tithe, although in some ways like a modern tax on income, was also different in one important sense. It was not collected by a state (or church) bureaucracy. Collection was left to the incumbent of each parish church, and he was allowed to agree with his parishioners about what they owed. Any such agreement might not bind his successor, but it would bind him. In litigation over tithes, parishioners, as defendants, often pleaded that the plaintiff, their vicar, 'had compounded with this parishioners that, receiving the sum of £5 from them, he would demand no tithes'.[24] If this was so, that amount was all they

---

20. E.g., Richard Wunderli, *London Church Courts and Society on the Eve of the Reformation* (Cambridge, MA: 1981), 109.
21. Some of the evidence is presented in R. H. Helmholz, *Oxford History of the Laws of England, Volume One: The Canon Law and Ecclesiastical Jurisdiction from 597 to 1640* (Oxford: 2004), 456-60.
22. X 3.30.20-22.
23. X 3.39.4; the legal position is well stated in Giles Constable, *Monastic Tithes: From Their Origins to the Twelfth Century* (Cambridge: 1964).
24. Taken from Ayres c. Crowe (Court of Arches 1582), Lansd. MS. 135, f. 6v, British Library, London.

owed. It is not often that we can see much of the bargaining that took place. Not enough depositions in tithe causes have survived. We can see only the result. We see that result clearly enough, however, to know that individual choice and the social pressures that went with life in a village played a role in tithe collection.

A second reason for thinking that formal rules of law were not always determinative in court practice is that a large part of the law of tithes and oblations was itself based upon local custom. Local custom depended on the conduct of the people. Most of the oblations due to the clergy came from local habit that had hardened into legal obligation, rather than from the Decretal law. And even in the formal law of tithes, the obligation to pay a tenth had been so widely commuted into a duty to pay a fixed sum of money that sometimes the formal law of the church seems almost to have faded into the background. What had to be proved in much of the litigation was the existence of a valid local custom.[25] True enough, the law of custom was a part of the canon law; but enforcement of the monetary obligations still depended largely upon immemorial usage among the laity. The relevant evidence came from what men and women had done in the past, and such a standard required the courts to become involved with social attitudes and habits. It is of course impossible to look inside the minds of the judges who decided the cases, but we can see much of the evidence that was presented to them as the basis for decision, and much of that evidence turns out to have concerned local custom.

Defamation

A fourth test is provided by the law of defamation – libel and slander in modern law. Almost all of it was oral before the invention of printing, and this is what appears in the act books. The wrong would have been classed as *iniuria* under Roman law, but in England more often it was given the special name *diffamatio*, perhaps to separate it from the physical attacks that were the exclusive province of the secular courts. As was true for the example of testamentary law, the English law on the subject was found in provincial legislation, chiefly an enactment of the Council of Oxford in 1222. One of its constitutions proclaimed a sentence of excommunication against any person who maliciously imputed a crime to another person – thus, if I were to say 'Smith is a thief or an adulterer' this would be actionable, but if I

---

25. See, e.g., Case of Tithes of Ewerby (Lincoln 1517), in *An Episcopal Court Book for the Diocese of Lincoln 1514–1520*, ed. Margaret Bowker (Lincoln Record Society 61, 1967), 42.

were to say 'Smith is a blockhead or a miser' it would not be. To be a 'blockhead' or 'a miser' is not a crime. This feature of the law had the advantage of screening out many of the simple insults that are part of our daily lives and that we learn to tolerate. Rightly so it seems. The English constitution had the advantage of confining litigation to situations where someone stood in danger of prosecution under the criminal law because of the words of another person – that is, in danger of real and serious harm.

When we look at the evidence from the medieval records, it is apparent that the courts did enforce this formal law. Virtually all the actionable defamation cases in the thirteenth and fourteenth centuries involved imputations of crimes, always remembering that adultery, fornication and scolding were treated as crimes in the law of the time. To say, therefore – 'Maud Smith is a whore and I will prove it' or 'Cuthbert Smith is a quarrelsome scold and everyone knows it' came within the legal definition of the Oxford constitution of 1222, because prostitution and scolding were then criminal offences. The courts could not entirely escape having to deal with some seemingly trivial insults, as these examples suggest, but at least the law offered them a way to escape the worst of it, and they seized the opportunity. Defamation in England during the first two centuries after 1222 involved imputations of crimes. That meant that the courts were in fact acting as courts of law, not as a forum for the encouragement of social harmony.

This is not the complete story, however. The English constitution did not match the Roman law perfectly, and it did not match the desires of many potential plaintiffs. To be called 'a blockhead' might be tolerable, but to be called 'a bastard' or 'a leper' might not, even though neither of the latter amounted to a crime. Both of them could have serious consequences, indeed more serious practical consequences than being called 'a whore'. The one might cause the loss of one's inheritance; the other the loss of one's friends. On this account, there was social pressure to expand the remedy for defamation.

Already by the time of William Lyndwood (the mid fifteenth century), the courts were beginning to yield to that pressure.[26] Once they had done so, it was impossible to go back, and thereby they had involved themselves in resolving some quite petty quarrels.[27] They were almost inevitably moved into the arena of promoting social harmony. To say, for example,

---

26. See Lyndwood, *Provinciale* (above note 18), at 346, gl. v. *crimen*.
27. Sandy Bardsley, *Venomous Tongues: Speech and Gender in Late Medieval England* (Philadelphia, PA: 2006), 82-89: Martin Ingram, 'Scolding Women Cucked or Washed: A Crisis in Gender Relations in Early Modern England?', in *Women, Crime and the Courts*, eds. Jenny Kermode and G. Walker (London: 1994), 48-80.

'There is no good man or women' in this parish became enough to call forth ecclesiastical proceedings against the speaker.[28] Where the potential of words for disrupting the harmony of a community becomes the test of actionability, as it did in English practice, any line between strict law and public opinion disappeared. This is what happened.

The remedies at the disposal of the spiritual tribunals – public apologies and public penance – were well suited for dealing with petty quarrels and disruptive language. The ecclesiastical lawyers worked with what they had. Where they considered public punishment inappropriate, they might 'sentence' one party to having to make an apology to the other.[29] The apology could even be made in private. To characterize this as applying the formal law requires a considerable stretch of the imagination. It seems closer to pure dispute resolution. Of course, it did not mean that the courts acted lawlessly. The judges continued to cite and look to the provisions of the 1222 Oxford constitution and also to the Roman law of *iniuria*. Apparently, they felt no conflict between fidelity to the law and embrace of informal dispute resolution. The subject seemed to call for both approaches.

Assaults on the Clergy

The fifth subject concerns assaults on the clergy, incorporated into the canon law from a decree of the Second Lateran Council (1139) and commonly known by its incipit, *Si quis suadente* (C. 17 q. 4 c. 29). The canon enacted that anyone who laid violent hands on a cleric or monk incurred an automatic sentence of excommunication. It further provided that except where the offender was in danger of death, he could be absolved only by presenting himself at the apostolic see and receiving papal remission. The canon was thus a part of the contemporary movement to separate the clerical order from the secular world by creating a special immunity from violence in favour of the clergy.

Again, when we look at the court records it quickly becomes apparent that the English ecclesiastical courts enforced this canon. In some sense, they did so with effect. It might be thought that there would have been objection from the English royal courts, which otherwise claimed an exclusive jurisdiction over serious violence. Here however, they did not;

---

28. Ex officio c. Alyn (London 1509), Act book, MS. 9065/10, f. 69, Guildhall Library, London.
29. E.g., Forse c. Whytton (Canterbury 1519), Act book Y.2.10, f. 46, Canterbury Cathedral Archives: 'Postea iudex monuit eam quod petat ei veniam coram duobus testibus vel tribus'.

the common law judges carved out an exception for *Si quis suadente*.³⁰ The spiritual courts took advantage of it. Cases brought by clerics against men and women said to have laid violent hands upon them figured regularly in the act books of the English church. The judges who administered the law gave the canon an expansive reading, so that a man who had thrown a glass of beer at a cleric was subjected to prosecution even though the canon spoke only of 'laying violent hands'. Also culpable under this canon was throwing a stone at the head of a cleric, even though the stone missed. So too was intentionally starting a fire that burned a cleric.³¹ Interpretative questions like those raised in these cases are bound to occur with any legal text, and I would myself say that the English courts sought to resolve them according to the purpose that underlay *Si quis suadente*. They enforced the spirit as well as the letter of the canon.

There were limits, however. It turns out that the requirement of resort to the papal court for absolution became a dead letter in practice; the courts regularly ignored it. A trip to Rome would have been highly inconvenient for most ordinary people, and I doubt it could have been enforced as written. The canonists themselves recognized the difficulties that would have attended strict enforcement. Agricultural workers had neither the time nor the resources to undertake a trip to Rome. Thieves and bullies would have caused more trouble along the way than they would have profited from apostolic absolution.³² Hence, the power to absolve was sometimes delegated to a local bishop or assumed, as if by default, in a local ecclesiastical court.

Probably more significant for present purposes, the pedestrian nature of most cases found in the records – involving quarrels and disputes among local people, one of whom happened to be in holy orders – seems to have been the most common reason for deviation from the canon's text. The English judges allowed, even sought, compromise and settlement of many of the disputes that came before them. No penitential trip to Rome would have come into the picture. No sentence of excommunication would have ensued. Doing this may seem contrary to the letter of the canon law, but it became a regular feature of court practice. In a fifteenth-century case from the diocese of Rochester, for instance, the act book records that 'the official

---

30. See the writ 'Circumspecte agatis' (1286), in *Councils & Synods with other Documents relating to the English Church II, A.D. 1205–1313*. eds. F. M. Powicke and C. R. Cheney (Oxford: 1964), Pt. II, 974-75.
31. The case law on the subject is discussed in my paper, '*Si quis suadente* (C.17 q.4 c.29): Theory and Practice', in *Proceedings of the Seventh International Congress of Medieval Canon Law*, ed. Peter Linehan (Vatican City: 1988), 425-38.
32. See, e.g., Hostiensis, *Summa aurea*, tit. *De sentencia excommunicationis*, no. 4 (Venice: 1574).

[himself] sought to induce the parties to concord, whereupon they agreed to arbitration'.[33] The act books record many cases where the injured cleric's consent was sought and given as part of settlement of the dispute. In other words, in exercising this jurisdiction, the English judges had the authority to act according to strict law and under some circumstances they did just that. In other situations, however, they themselves chose not to do so.[34] They were more intent on settling quarrels.

Heresy and Religious Dissent

Sixth and last in this brief survey comes religious dissent, in particular its most serious form, heresy. According to the medieval canonists, heresy was a *crimen gravissimum*. It was a crime that offended God and brought ruin upon society. They thought it right to visit the most awful punishment on the guilty, and they developed a system of inquisitorial justice that was designed in part to do just that. That is why it was a *crimen exceptum*.

Heresy raises a subject of importance in the context of this inquiry. Were the courts in which accused heretics were tried acting as courts of law? Or were they doing something else, something that reflected the church's panicky reaction to dissent? If we accept the conclusions of H. A. Kelly, who has made a study of the subject, they were doing the former.[35] His survey of the printed heresy trials convinced him that due process was regularly afforded to English men and women accused of heresy, though of course the nature of that due process depended upon a canon law that regarded heresy as the most dangerous of crimes. The laws by which they were convicted did not accord with modern standards of fairness – denial of a right to a lawyer, for example – but as the term was then understood, due process was accorded to men and women accused of heresy. The careful attention given to the subject by English bishops of the time lends credence to his conclusion.[36]

---

33. Ex officio c. Wike (Rochester 1451), Act book, ms DRb Pa 1, f. 157v, Kent Archives Service, Maidstone: '[Officialis] induxit eos ad concordiam et compromiserunt in arbitratores'.
34. Another example is given in Eldbjørg Haug, 'The Conflict in the Stavanger Church around 1300 and the Intervention of Håkon Magnusson', in *Law and Power* (above note 4), 109-44, esp. at 144.
35. H. A. Kelly, 'Thomas More on Inquisitorial Due Process', *English Historical Review* 123 (2008), 862-70. See also the balanced account in John Tedeschi, *The Prosecution of Heresy: Collected Studies* (Binghamton, NY: 1991), 127-203.
36. See, e.g., Anne Hudson, 'The Examination of Lollards', *Bulletin of the Institute of Historical Research* 46 (1973), 145-59.

However, the trials surveyed by Professor Kelly were matters of importance – 'show trials' we might call them without great risk of anachronism. What of the ordinary ecclesiastical courts – those of the diocesan bishops, archdeacons, and even rural deans? Do they show the same concern for legal form and the same determination to prosecute heresy to the full extent permitted under the law? Or were defendants left to the system of compurgation used for other spiritual crimes in the courts of the church, a system that left a good deal of room for local opinion and informal settlement?

Over the years, I have made notes of heresy causes that appeared in the act books. Five conclusions have gradually emerged. First, the total number of prosecutions in them was very small. They were hard to find. The most serious cases must have gone to the bishops rather than to the ordinary courts. Second, when a prosecution for heresy did appear in an act book, it very often turned out that the defendant had fled. At least he did not appear. That points to a problem common to all medieval criminal prosecutions – not entirely overcome today – but contumacy seems to have been even more common than in prosecutions for, say, adultery or unlawful usury. Little wonder, considering the possible penalties. Third, the courts were willing to undertake prosecutions on the basis of suspicious behaviour alone – a London man who did not allow his daughter to hear Mass or Matins in church, for example, was prosecuted for heresy.[37] So was a Canterbury woman who had incautiously denied the efficacy of pilgrimages to the site where relics or statutes of saints were to be found.[38] The possession of an English Bible was also treated as suspicious enough to require explanation.[39] Fourth, the judges in these cases did not regularly leave guilt or innocence to compurgation, as they did for more routine ecclesiastical offences.[40] They normally questioned the persons suspected of heresy, requiring them to state their opinions in detail,[41] and also calling

---

37. Ex officio c. Thomas Crawe (1500), Act book, ms. 9064/1, f. 33v, Guildhall Library, London.
38. Ex officio c. Joan Daye (Canterbury 1450), in Act book X 1.1, f. 19v, Cathedral Archives, Canterbury.
39. Ex officio c. Landesdale (Lichfield 1511), in Act book, ms. B/C/13, f. 6, Joint Record Office, Lichfield.
40. E.g., Ex officio c. William Nicholl (London 1497), Act book, ms. 9064/7, f. 41v, Guildhall Library, London: the defendant offered to undergo compurgation, but this was apparently refused, and he was later assigned public penance. Attempts to use compurgation seem normally to have been choked off in practice; see, e.g., Ex officio c. Shelley (London: 1497), in William Hale, *A Series of Precedents and Proceedings in Criminal Causes 1475-1640* (London: 1873), no. 206.
41. Ex officio c. George Hodgeson (Lincoln 1527), Act book, ms. Cj/3, f. 39v, Lincolnshire Archives Office, Lincoln. In it the defendant was found in possession

upon witnesses to appear and testify to what they knew about the conduct and beliefs of the person accused.[42] Fifth, upon findings of guilt, the courts did not usually proceed to license the death penalty by handing defendants over to the secular arm. They allowed an initial abjuration and they normally assigned public penance, though penance of a serious kind, to convicted but penitent offenders.[43] What this all means is that proceedings for heresy were being treated according to the canon law, leaving little room for bargaining, community sentiment, or any of the informal and mitigating devices that are found in the court records for the first five subjects covered in this paper. Heresy seems to have been a *crimen exceptum* in that sense too.

Conclusion

What should one conclude from the accumulation of evidence? Can the causes behind the decision to apply the law as written in some cases and to bend to social forces in others be discerned? And can it be said that one or the other predominated in practice? These are the important questions. The evidence presented here suggests two possible answers, or at least two points that can be made on the basis of this survey.

One point is that the spiritual courts did both, and apparently without any sense of incongruity. They enforced the letter and spirit of the canon law in litigation over the formation and dissolution of marriage, in testamentary matters, in the law of tithes, in defamation practice, in enforcing the canon *Si quis suadente*, and in heresy trials. In each, several features of the formal law were 'out of step' with views shared by most of the community, but the courts followed the former. *Populus docendus est, non sequendus*.

At the same time, other aspects of practice were influenced, and sometimes even determined, either by an informal style of dispute

---

of heretical books and was quizzed, apparently at some length, about his ability to read English and Latin. He claimed that he could only read a few words of English and none at all of Latin.

42. Sometimes the records of heresy trials were kept in separate act books, perhaps because of their perceived special character. See, e.g., Act book B/C/13 (Coventry and Lichfield 1511-12), Joint Record Office. Lichfield. Its contents have been examined in detail by John Fines, 'Heresy Trials in the Diocese of Coventry and Lichfield, 1511–12', *Journal of Ecclesiastical History* 14 (1963), 160-74.

43. E.g., Ex officio c. Elizabeth Sculthorp (1519), in *An Episcopal Court Book for the Diocese of Lincoln 1514–1520*, ed. Margaret Bowker (Lincoln Record Society 61, 1967), 84-85. See also the evidence in *Heresy Trials in the Diocese of Norwich, 1428–31*, ed. Norman Tanner (Camden Society, 4th ser. 20, 1977), 22-25.

resolution or by a societal consensus that ran along a different track from the formal law of the church. The disappearance of the married woman's will is perhaps the best example of the latter; the treatment accorded to quarrelling husbands and wives the best example of the former. They show that one cannot treat anything that happens in a court as automatically belonging to the legal sphere.[44] This was the conclusion of Gerd Althoff, and the evidence from the ecclesiastical courts supports it. Except for the *crimen exceptum* of heresy, the English court records show the contrary. The courts of the church sometimes moved in accord with a societal consensus that was contrary to the formal law.

The second point requires discussion of the probable reasons for the difference in treatment. Why were some things treated more formally and legally than others? It is hard to be certain, but one part of the answer to this question must lie in the nature of the disputes themselves. Cases involving the formation of marriage, for example, required a direct answer. Men and women cannot live at peace for very long if they do not know to whom they are married. By contrast, relations between husband and wife within an existing marriage can be left more fluid, usually without danger to their souls or to society.

Another part of any likely answer must lie in the strength of public opinion. In some areas, the spiritual courts could not act as courts of law because secular rules or societal attitudes stood in the way. They proved just too strong to be resisted, and the church was not directly concerned enough to make that effort worthwhile. Married women's wills are perhaps the best example. Perhaps the ecclesiastical courts in England would like to have acted as courts of law in dealing with them, but it proved difficult, even impossible, for them to do so.

A further answer must lie in the canon law itself and in the attitudes of the canonists. In some respects, the canon law itself encouraged the use of informal norms to settle disputes. Local norms might influence the interpretation of the law itself.[45] The strong role allowed for custom in tithing matters and the regular endorsement of informal compromise in defamation cases show this. Even the very impracticality of some of the canon law's rules – as in the requirement that anyone laying violent hands on a cleric undertake a long and penitential trip to Rome – turned out to encourage informal settlement of disputes. The spiritual courts had to adjust to the possible. Perhaps all courts have to do so.

---

44. Gerd Althoff, 'Nobility in Court', in *Law and Power* (above note 4), 11-25, at 11-12.
45. Norman Tanner, *The Church in the Later Middle Ages* (London and New York: 2008), 86.

The short of it is that whatever the desires of the judges and lawyers who practised in them, the ecclesiastical courts were moved in many circumstances by considerations of expediency and practicality. They did not ignore the desires of the people governed by the law. The expansion of the scope of the English remedy for defamation towards the close of the Middle Ages provides a fitting example of one of the ways the interests of litigants had an effect on the law as applied. Change happened because litigants pushed the courts in that direction. True, the civilians found legal justification for it in the Roman law, but it must have been the pressure of demand that drove the change, more so than the texts of the Digest. They had been there all along. I do not believe this made the courts operate without regard for the law. The courts did act as courts of law but, with the exception of the contentious subject of doctrinal heresy, they also acted as an arena for informal dispute resolution. In short, the English ecclesiastical courts served both functions, and I at least think they did so naturally and without any consciousness that their authority was thereby being impaired. Doing the one did not keep them from also being the other.

THE APOSTOLIC PENITENTIARY AND DOMESTIC VIOLENCE

The Apostolic Penitentiary in the Middle Ages and its Historical Records

Kirsi Salonen

Introduction

This essay analyses the petitions regarding violence between husbands and wives or close relatives brought before the Apostolic Penitentiary during the pontificate of Pius II (1458–1464).[1] Since some readers might not be familiar with the Apostolic Penitentiary and its medieval sources, I will begin by explaining briefly what the Penitentiary was and what kinds of documents its archives can offer us in respect of domestic violence.

The Apostolic Penitentiary is usually classified as one of the three medieval papal tribunals. Since the office dealt with all matters concerning sins, it has been called 'the supreme tribunal in matters of conscience'. Defining Penitentiary as a 'tribunal', however, is slightly misleading because the office did not hold court sessions or make decisions about the guilt or innocence of the litigant persons. The Penitentiary simply granted – on the request of people from all over Christendom in the form of a petition (*supplicatio*) – graces to those who had some problem they needed to solve

---

1. The study is limited to one pontificate for the sake of proportionality. This essay is a result of my earlier research project 'The Apostolic Penitentiary and the Local Church' financed by the Academy of Finland, to which I wish to express my gratitude.

at the papal curia.[2] The powers given to the office by the popes allowed it to grant four kinds of grace:

(1) Special absolutions for those who had broken the regulations of canon law in such severe matters that the local father confessors or even the local bishops did not have the power to absolve them. Such crimes were, for example, killing or assaulting an ecclesiastic, simony, escaping from a monastery, or selling forbidden products to infidels.

(2) Dispensations that allowed Christians to act against the regulations of the Church. With a dispensation from the Penitentiary, Christians could, for example, marry a close relative, receive priestly ordination despite an impediment like illegitimacy, minority, or bodily defect, or change from one monastery to another.

(3) Special licences that allowed Christians not to observe certain ecclesiastical norms in matters concerning the exercise of religion. For example, to confess to a priest other than one's own parish priest, to commute ecclesiastical vows to another kind of pious works, or to make a pilgrimage to the Holy Land.

(4) Official declarations. For example, it could declare that a cleric was not guilty of murder despite being (unjustly) accused of murder. Furthermore, it could declare a marriage annulled or a monastic profession void, if the supplicants could show that there was something canonically wrong in the contracting of the marriage or in making the profession.

The medieval records of the Penitentiary consist of register volumes that contain (abbreviated) copies of petitions directed to and approved by the office. The complete series of the registers begins from the middle of the fifteenth century. The register volumes are relatively practical to use because they are divided internally into several different categories of which each contains cases related to one specific matter. The main petition categories are the following: *de matrimonialibus* (about marriages), *de*

---

2. About the history and functioning of the Penitentiary, see Emil Göller, *Die päpstliche Pönitentiarie von ihrem Ursprung bis zu ihrer Umgestaltung unter Pius V.*, 2 vol. in 4 parts, Bibliothek des Königlich Preußischen Historischen Instituts in Rom 3, 4, 7 and 8 (Rome: 1907, 1911), passim, as well as Ludwig Schmugge, Patrick Hersperger and Béatrice Wiggenhauser, *Die Supplikenregister der päpstlichen Pönitentiarie aus der Zeit Pius' II. (1458–1464)*. Bibliothek des Deutschen Historischen Instituts in Rom, Band 84 (Tübingen: 1996), 4-56; Kirsi Salonen, *The Penitentiary as a Well of Grace in the Late Middle Ages. The Example of the Province of Uppsala 1448–1527*. Suomalaisen Tiedeakatemian Toimituksia – Annales Academiae Scientiarum Fennicae 313 (Saarijärvi: 2001), 40-56; Kirsi Salonen and Ludwig Schmugge, *A Sip from the 'Well of Grace'. Medieval Texts from the Apostolic Penitentiary*. Studies in Medieval and Early Modern Canon Law 7, Catholic University of America Press (Washington DC: 2009), 13-16, 69-83.

diversis formis (concerning various types of cases), *de declaratoriis* (about declarations), *de defectu natalium* and *de uberiori* (matters related to illegitimacy), *de promotis et promovendis* (about ordinations), and *de confessionalibus* (licence to choose a personal confessor).[3]

The Penitentiary and Graces Related to Violence

The petitions related to the theme of violence can be found in two categories in the Penitentiary registers; *de diversis formis* and *de declaratoriis*.[4] The Penitentiary normally handled such cases of violence in which at least one of the parties (assailant or victim) was an ecclesiastic, while cases involving violence between laypersons were generally taken to the civil courts. If cases of pure lay violence were brought to the Penitentiary, there was usually a question of violence between close relatives, because that was considered as an especially severe form of violence. In such cases, the local father confessors or bishops sometimes refused to absolve the guilty people and sent them to the papal curia to obtain absolution from their sin. Domestic violence was, however, not always purely lay business, because among the Penitentiary petitions we find cases in which clerics too were guilty of violence against their close relatives.

Before analysing more closely the content of these cases, a few words about how the Penitentiary could help those men and women who had sinned by committing a violent act. There is a fundamental difference depending on whether the violent act was committed by a layman or by a cleric.

According to Constitution 15 of the Second Lateran Council, known as the constitution *Si quis suadente diabolo*, anyone who assaulted or murdered an ecclesiastic was subject to an immediate and automatic excommunication from which only the pope could absolve the sinner.[5] Thus

---

3. About the faculty of the Penitentiary, see Schmugge, Hersperger and Wiggenhauser, *Die Supplikenregister*, 68-217; Salonen, *The Penitentiary*, 58-77, 103-210; Salonen and Schmugge, *A Sip*, 17-68.
4. Since the entries in the Penitentiary registers are abbreviated copies of the original petitions they have the form of supplication, but the syntax of the phrases has often been damaged when they were registered in an abbreviated form. The entries are edited here as they appear in the registers (even if some words are in a non-conventional form, for example *actingente* and not *attinente*) without linguistic comments. Only evident errors have been corrected. In a few cases words have been added in order to make incomplete phrases better understandable. The additions are indicated by angle brackets < >. The variation between v/u has been normalized so that "u" is used for the vowel.
5. C. 17 q. 4 c. 29, edited in Friedberg I, col. 822-823.

a layperson who had violated an ecclesiastic had to seek pardon from the papal curia. If a layperson violated another layperson, he incurred excommunication as well, but the local father confessors had the power to absolve him from this excommunication. Only in very special cases would local father confessors refuse to absolve the sinners and send them to the papal curia for absolution. For laypeople who were guilty of a violent act it was enough to be absolved and they were free of the burden of sin.

The case of offending clerics was more complicated. They incurred the same automatic excommunication, but in addition to that they became irregular (that is, unworthy to act in ecclesiastical office) and could no longer carry out their priestly duties. In order to cleanse their conscience, the clerics (like any layman) needed an apostolic absolution. In addition to that, they needed a dispensation that would free them from the irregularity and allow them to continue in their office. The Penitentiary had the power to grant guilty clerics both graces. The petitions for absolutions (and dispensations) both for clerics and laypeople are usually registered in the *de diversis formis* category and in these cases there is always a question about a supplicant who had admitted his guilt in committing a violent act.

There are petitions related to violent behaviour in the *de declaratoriis* category too. There we find mostly petitions of clerics or aspirant ecclesiastics who had been unjustly accused of a murder and who petitioned for a declaration of innocence. In these cases the question of being 'guilty' or 'not guilty' is quite complicated and a person could demonstrate his innocence by making use of the various attenuating circumstances that can be found in canon law. For example, if a person had killed another accidentally or in self-defence, canon law did not consider him guilty of a murder.

The reason for the declarations was to ensure that a clergyman could carry out his duties without problems. A declaration of innocence was necessary for clerics because, according to canon law, a murderer could not act as father confessor or in altar service – both things that belonged to the duties of a parish priest. Thus a parish priest who had murdered someone could not continue in his office, which meant in practice that he lost his job and income. Therefore it was especially important for a priest who had killed someone to receive a declaration stating that he was not guilty of murder. If the circumstances were such that the killer was clearly guilty of a premeditated murder, he could not receive a declaration, but he was obliged to ask for a normal papal absolution from his sin and dispensation. The absolution and dispensation did not, however, grant him the right to return to his benefice.[6]

---

6. More about Penitentiary and violence cases in the *de diversis formis* and *de declaratoriis* categories, see Schmugge, Hersperger and Wiggenhauser, *Die*

In order to give a general idea of the cases related to violence in the Penitentiary documentation, let us have a look into what kinds of cases, and how many, the office handled during the pontificate of Pius II (1458–1464) which is my example period. Table 1 shows how many petitions were classified into each petition category. We are here dealing with a quite significant corpus of cases; 15,729 petitions from the six-year period. The most numerous petitions can be found in the *de matrimonialibus*, the *de confessionalibus* and the *de diversis formis* categories, followed by those regarding illegitimacy (*de defectu natalium* and *de uberiori*). The *de promotis et promovendis* category is relatively small and the *de declaratoriis* category contains only a few petitions. The supplications related to domestic violence are all registered in the *de diversis formis* category and they total thirty-six, which is only one per cent of the *de diversis formis* cases.[7]

Case type	Cases	%
De matrimonialibus	4195	27%
De diversis formis	3650	23%
De declaratoriis	334	2%
De defectu natalium	2698	17%
De uberiori	483	3%
De promotis et promovendis	1008	6%
De confessionalibus	3361	22%
Total	15729	100%

Table 1. Penitentiary cases during the pontificate of Pius II (1458–1464)
Source: ASV, *Penitenzieria Ap.*, *Reg. Matrim. et Div.*, Vols. 7-11, 13.

The church did not normally make a distinction between different kinds of violent crimes in the sense that all those who were guilty of violent behaviour were excommunicated and needed to be absolved from their crimes – no matter whether they had hit someone, caused someone's death accidentally or committed a premeditated murder. In practice, however, the church obviously made a distinction about whether a violent act was or was not a severe one.

Supplikenregister, 98-116; Salonen, *The Penitentiary*, 128-138, 103-210; Salonen and Schmugge, *A Sip*, 30-31, 52-53.

7. The number of petitions related to violence in general is quite large as a proportion of the Penitentiary material. In the *de diversis formis* category we find 1305 supplications related to violence (36%) and in the *de declaratoriis* category as many as 225 (67%). Thus a very small part of them concern domestic violence or violence between close relatives.

In the thirty-six cases I have analysed for this article, three different types of violent crimes committed between relatives can be distinguished. In five cases there was a question of an assault (with the Latin terminology: *percussit, vulneravit*) which did not cause permanent injuries to the victim, while in three cases the violators assaulted their victims so badly that they died afterwards. The most numerous cases were those of manslaughter (with the Latin terminology: *interfecit*), twenty-eight altogether. Thus, thirty-one cases resulted in the death of someone and in five cases there were no fatal consequences.

Provenance

Let us now proceed to analyse in more detail the petitions related to domestic violence and start by examining the provenance of the petitions to find out whether domestic violence was more common in certain regions of Christendom than elsewhere. For the analysis of the provenance, I have divided Christendom into seven larger territories[8] and counted how many cases come from each of them.

Provenance	Cases
British Isles	0
Eastern Europe	5
Empire	4
France	7
Iberian Peninsula	6
Italian Peninsula	14
Scandinavia	0
Total	36

Table 2. Provenance of the cases.
Source: ASV, *Penitenzieria Ap., Reg. Matrim. et Div.*, Vols. 7-11, 13.

As it appears from Table 2, fourteen petitions come from the Apennine Peninsula, four from the territory of the Empire, seven are from France and six from the Iberian Peninsula, while five come from the Eastern parts of Europe. There are no such cases from the British Isles or Scandinavia. What can be said on the basis of these numbers? Since the corpus is as small as

---

8. The division of Christendom into seven territories is the same which Ludwig Schmugge and I have used when composing the general statistics concerning the entire Penitentiary material. For example, Salonen and Schmugge, *A Sip*, 27, 48, 57, 61, 64, and 68.

thirty-six cases, drawing further conclusions about the provenance is not wise. However, these numbers demonstrate that petitions concerning violence between close relatives came from different parts of Christendom, except from the furthest North, from where usually very few petitions of any type were brought to the curia. These numbers thus show that such crimes were committed all over Christendom and it cannot be said that domestic violence or violence between relatives (and turning therefore to the Penitentiary) would have been a phenomenon limited only to certain territories. It seems that these were individual cases in which the supplicants left for Rome to settle their problem.

Violators and Victims

Let us then proceed to see who were the assailants in the Penitentiary petitions and who were their victims. I will start by discussing first briefly those five cases in which there was not question of the death of a person. They are actually all 'regular Penitentiary cases' which were brought to the curia because at least one priest was involved in the situation.

In three of these cases we find a priest who had assaulted his relatives who were also in ecclesiastical offices – thus in these cases there was a question about violence between two ecclesiastics. In one of them, the victim was a priest who was also the *nepos* of the violator,[9] and in another case the victim was a cleric and brother of the violator.[10] In the third case the supplicant was a Benedictine monk who had violated the abbot of his monastery who happened to be his uncle as well.[11] In the other two cases

---

9. ASV, *Penitenzieria Ap., Reg. Matrim. et Div.*, Vol. 10, fol. 147r-v (5.5.1462): Rodericus Petri de Cerezeda presbyter Burgen. dioc. quendam nepotem suum presbyterum in ecclesia existentem percussit et vulneravit quare excommunicationis sententiam in tales generaliter latam incurrit. Et cum dictus presbyter nepos de premissis convaluerit, petit idem /147v/ exponens a sententiis quas ex premissis incurrit absolvi ac secum super irregularitate, quam contraxit ex eo quia dictis sententiis ligatus missas et alia divina officia celebravit, dispensari. Fiat de speciali. Phi. Sancti Laurentii in Lucina.
10. ASV, *Penitenzieria Ap., Reg. Matrim. et Div.*, Vol. 11, fol. 160r (5.3.1463): Ludovicus le Picart presbyter rector parrochialis ecclesie de Perzquen Veneten. dioc. quosdam clericos duos in numero videlicet unum suum fratrem et alium percussit et vulneravit quare excommunicationis sententiam in tales generaliter latam incurrit a quibus petit absolvi, attento quod dicti presbyteri convaluerunt. Fiat de speciali, Phi. S. Laurentii in Lucina.
11. ASV, *Penitenzieria Ap., Reg. Matrim. et Div.*, Vol. 13, fol. 162v (21.5.1464): Frater Franciscus Hugonis monachus professus monasterii Sancti Augustini ordinis sancti Benedicti extra muros Lemovicen. quendam abbatem dicti monasterii eius

concerning violence, the violator was a layman who had assaulted his brother. In one of the cases the assaulted brother happened to be a priest[12] and in the other case he was a Dominican friar.[13]

In all these cases there was a question about an assault which did not cause permanent injuries to the victim. Furthermore, the assailants did not give the Penitentiary any kind of reason for their violent behaviour, they just admitted that they had offended against the regulations of canon law by assaulting someone and asked for absolution for their crime and sin.

The five cases mentioned above with very little details are less interesting for this essay and hence I will proceed with the other more interesting cases, namely those thirty-one cases in which there is the issue of killing someone close.

Violator	Victim	Cases
Husband	Wife	20
Priest	Concubine	1
Wife	Husband	1
Man	Brother	3
Man	Sister & her child	1
Father	Child	1
Mother	Child	3
Couple	Child	1

Table 3. Violators and victims
Source: ASV, *Penitenzieria Ap.*, *Reg. Matrim. et Div.*, Vols. 7-11, 13.

---

avunculum percussit et vulneravit quare excommunicationis incurrit sententiam et deinde divinis se inmiscuit. Petit a premissis absolvi ac secum super irregularitate ex premissis contracta dispensari, actento quod dictus abbas convaluit de premissis. Fiat de speciali et expresso et commictatur dicto abbati, Phi. S. Laurentii in Lucina.

12. ASV, *Penitenzieria Ap., Reg. Matrim. et Div.*, Vol. 11, fol. 193v (24.5.1463): Eckardus Suanhart laicus Treveren. dioc. quendam presbyterum eius fratrem carnalem percussit et vulneravit quare excommunicationis sententiam in tales latam incurrit a qua petit absolvi, actento quod dictus presbyter convaluit. Fiat de speciali, G. prothon. de Oddis, regens.

13. ASV, *Penitenzieria Ap., Reg. Matrim. et Div.*, Vol. 13, fol. 152r (17.4.1464): Guidetus Cauterii de Peceto laicus Taurinen. dioc. quendam fratrem professum ordinis predicatorum eius fratrem carnalem percussit et vulneravit quare excommunicationis incurrit sententiam in tales generaliter promulgatam a qua petit absolvi, actento quod dictus frater convaluit. Fiat de speciali, Jo. abbas S. Bernardi, regens.

In Table 3 the violators and their victims are distinguished on the basis of the relationship between them. In the three first rows are cases related to domestic violence that led to someone's death (22 cases) while in the last five lines are cases involving fatal violence between close relatives (9 cases). In twenty-six cases the supplicant is a man, in four cases a woman and in one case a couple together. That women were in minority among the petitioners was an expected result because, according to canon law, women were usually excluded from the obligation to seek pardon at the Holy See. The representatives of the weaker sex could usually gain such absolutions at home from their diocesan bishops, for example, while men were more often obliged to get a papal pardon.

Concerning the cases of domestic violence, we find out that in the majority of cases, the husbands were guilty of the death of their wives. In one case there is question of a priest who had killed his concubine – a case that can be considered as parallel to a case of a husband killing his wife. In just one case a woman was guilty of killing her husband. Even though a rare example, this case demonstrates, however, that domestic violence was not only committed by men – even though male violators formed the great majority.

In all the remaining nine cases the violent act took place between close relatives. Four cases concern fatal violence between siblings: three men killed their brothers and one man his sister and her child. In five cases, instead, parents were guilty of causing the death of their own children. Once a couple did that together, while once the guilty person was the father and in three cases a mother had killed her child.

Why Violence?

What circumstances led to the violent behaviour and why did these violent crimes take place? In principle, six main reasons could be distinguished in the Penitentiary cases. I will now present each of them with the help of some examples, to show concretely what kinds of documents there are in the Penitentiary registers. In the analysis are included both cases of violence and cases with fatal consequences.

1. No Explanation
As the first category of motivation behind violent behaviour we have 'no explanation', since as many as thirteen supplicants did not give any explanations for their violent behaviour, but just admitted their guilt and asked for absolution from the excommunication they had incurred by assaulting or killing their victims.

We already had the five above-mentioned cases concerning simple assaults in which the supplicants did not explain their violent behaviour in any way. An additional eight persons who were guilty of killing someone turned to the Penitentiary for absolution but none of them gave any reason for their act. All the supplicants petitioned for (and received) absolution for the crime they had committed. What is interesting in these petitions is that all of them were laymen, seven male and one female.

The only female supplicant, Margarita Vernia, widow of a certain Petrus Reginaldi, from the diocese of Clermont, confessed to the Penitentiary that she had killed her son because of which her diocesan bishop had excommunicated her and she had travelled to Rome for receiving absolution. She did not give any reason for her crime but explained further that she had no safe access to the bishop of Clermont. For the same reason she asked if the resolution of her case could be referred to the bishop of Le Puy or his vicar – which was agreed.[14]

Two of the supplicants, Petrus de Sclafina from the diocese of Messina[15] and Bonifilius from the village of Pretoli in the diocese of Perugia,[16] were guilty of beating their wives so badly that they died within a short while from the attack. Furthermore, Petrus's wife had even been pregnant, which meant that Petrus killed his unborn child together with his wife. Both supplicants received absolution from the Penitentiary together with a dispensation to remarry. Nicolaus de Busco from the diocese of Catania[17] and Georgius Wembachter from the archdiocese of Estergom[18]

---

14. ASV, *Penitenzieria Ap., Reg. Matrim. et Div.*, Vol. 11, fol. 181v (21.4.1463): Margarita Vernia relicta quondam Petri Reginaldi mulier Claromonten. dioc. quendam filium suum interfecit ac demum super premissis excommunicata per ordinarium ad curiam venit. Et cum ad dictum ordinarium tutum accessum non habeat, petit absolvi a dicto homicidii reatu ac excommunicationis sententiam per episcopum Anicien. vel eius vicarium. Fiat de speciali, Phi. S. Laurentii in Lucina.
15. ASV, *Penitenzieria Ap., Reg. Matrim. et Div.*, Vol. 13, fol. 146v (23.3.1464): Petrus de Sclafina laicus Messanen. dioc. quandam eius uxorem adeo percussit et vulneravit quod post certum temporis spacium diem suum clausit extremum. Et de morte ipsius doleat. Petit idem exponens a reatu uxoricidii huiusmodi absolvi ac secum, ut matrimonium cum aliqua alia muliere sibi in nullo gradu actingente contrahere possit, dispensari. Fiat de speciali, Phi. S. Laurentii in Lucina.
16. ASV, *Penitenzieria Ap., Reg. Matrim. et Div.*, Vol. 7, fol. 126v (12.2.1459): Martinus Bonifilii ville Pretoli dioc. Perusine uxorem suam non pregnantem cum bacculo percussit non animo interficiendi, ex quo vulnere intra quinque dies obiit, a reatu homicidii absolvitur et peccatis suis omnibus. Fiat in forma, Phi. S. Laurentii in Lucina. Et eidem conceditur posse cum alia non sibi coniuncta non obstante homicidio contrahere licite et legitime. Fiat de speciali, Phi. S. Laurentii in Lucina.
17. ASV, *Penitenzieria Ap., Reg. Matrim. et Div.*, Vol. 11, fol. 172r (13.4.1463): Nicolaus de Busco laicus Cathanien. dioc. suam propriam uxorem interfecit quare

were guilty of killing their wives too and received absolution and dispensation for marrying someone else.

Not all victims of unexplained violent acts were female. Guillelmus Sorel, a layman from the French diocese of Saint Malo, had killed his brother,[19] while Petrus Jacobi from the diocese of Gnesna had killed his son who was a priest too.[20] Johannes de Villalpaudo from the diocese of Zamora in his turn was guilty of killing two persons: his brother and a priest.[21] These men did not give any kind of justification for their acts in the supplication but just stated that they had killed the men, and asked for absolution because of their sin – which the Penitentiary granted to them.

2. Instigated by the Devil

The second motivation for violent acts we could find among the Penitentiary records was that the violator's act had been instigated by devil, *diabolo instigante*. This wording refers to the constitution of the Second Lateran Council forbidding violence against clerics (*Si quis suadente diabolo*) and it is a kind of attempt to explain why the supplicant had acted violently. In fact, referring to the instigation of the devil makes the supplicant sound a bit less guilty of the violent act, because it indicates that the violator did not act of his own free will or did not commit a premeditated act, but that something else (in this case the Devil) made him do so.

---

uxoridicii reatum commisit a quo petit absolvi ac sibi licentiam, ut cum alia muliere sibi in nullo gradu actingente contrahere possit, concedi. Fiat de speciali, Phi. S. Laurentii in Lucina.

18. ASV, *Penitenzieria Ap., Reg. Matrim. et Div.*, Vol. 11, fol. 207r (28.6.1463): Georgius Wembachter laicus Strigonien. dioc. quandam suam mulierem interfecit certis ex causis quare petit absolvi ab uxoricidii reatu ac sibi licentiam concedi, ut cum alia contrahere possit. Fiat de speciali, G. prothon. de Oddis, regens.
19. ASV, *Penitenzieria Ap., Reg. Matrim. et Div.*, Vol. 7, fol. 233v (28.8.1459): Guillelmus Sorel laicus Maclovien. dioc. fratrem suum carnalem interfecit. Supplicat igitur dictus exponens quatenus placeat ipsum ab huiusmodi homicidii reatu ac peccatis suis aliis absolvi. Fiat in forma, M. Alexan.
20. ASV, *Penitenzieria Ap., Reg. Matrim. et Div.*, Vol. 11, fol. 207r (30.6.1463): Petrus Jacobi laicus Gneznen. dioc. quendam suum filium presbyterum interfecit quare excommunicationis sententiam incurrit et filicidii reatum commisit a quibus petit absolvi. Fiat in forma, G. prothon. de Oddis, regens.
21. ASV, *Penitenzieria Ap., Reg. Matrim. et Div.*, Vol. 10, fol. 142r (30.4.1462): Johannes de Villalpaudo laicus Zamoren. dioc. quendam fratrem suum presbyterum et alium fratrem laicum interfecit quare homicidii reatum commisit et excommunicationis sententiam incurrit a quibus petit absolvi. Fiat de speciali, Phi. S. Laurentii in Lucina. Et committatur uni ex minoribus penitenciariis propter metum persone sue, Fiat, Phi.

Three supplicants refer to the instigation of devil. One of them is Perigrinus Falsinaro, a layman from the Italian diocese of Bologna. He had killed his wife 'because of the instigation of the devil' – and then after a while married another woman without a dispensation (which would have been necessary because according to canon law those who had killed their spouses could not remarry). He petitioned for absolution from the murder and a dispensation so that he could legally continue in his new relationship and to legitimise his offspring.[22]

Another was Jacominus Anthoni from the diocese of Como in Italy. He had not only killed his wife, who was pregnant, but had committed other crimes as well, such as participating in robbery, arson and other crimes, even in holy places. Furthermore, he had married another woman, whom he had later left with the excuse that their relationship was not legitimate because he had not obtained a dispensation to marry her after killing of the first wife. He, too, petitioned for absolution and dispensation from the Penitentiary but in his petition there was no mention of a legitimisation for his possible future offspring.[23]

The third, Nicolaus Knupsysen from the Hungarian archdiocese of Estergom had, according to the text of his petition, killed his wife *diabolo instigante* and afterwards married another woman. Just like the two other men, he petitioned for absolution from the excommunication he had

---

22. ASV, *Penitenzieria Ap., Reg. Matrim. et Div.*, Vol. 7, fol. 150r (21.5.1459): Perigrinus Falsinaro laicus Bononien. dioc. exponit quod ipse diabolo instigante uxorem suam propriam interfecit et deinde post lapsum temporis cum quadam alia muliere sibi in nullo gradu prohibito matrimonium publice contraxit absque aliqua dispensatione obtenta illudque carnali copula consumavit et prolem procreavit, quare reatum uxoricidii contraxit. Supplicat igitur quatenus ipsum ab huiusmodi uxoricidii reatu absolvere secumque, ut in dicto suo matrimonio remanere possit libere et licite, prolem subceptam et subcipiendam legitimam decernentes dispensare misericorditer dignemini de gratia speciali. Fiat de speciali, Phi. S. Laurentii in Lucina.

23. ASV, *Penitenzieria Ap., Reg. Matrim. et Div.*, Vol. 7, fol. 148r (12.6.1459): Jacominus Anthoni laicus Corman. [Recte: Cumen. ?] dioc. exponit quod ipse alius spoliis, rapinis, incendiis et homicidiis in locis sacris et non sacris etiam in terris ecclesie cum effractione dictorum locorum pluries interfuit ea etiam manu propria perpetravit et monasteria monialium diversorum ordinum intravit et diabolo instigante uxorem propriam impre<g>natam interfecit. Postmodum alteri nubsit quam postea dimisit propter assercionem nonnullorum iuris peritorum asserencium hoc absque dispensatione sedis apostolice fieri non posse, quare dictus exponens excommunicationum sententias in tales promulgatas incurrit. Supplicat igitur quatenus ipsum ab excommunicationis sententiis ac excessibus et aliis maleficis per eum perpetratis absolvi et dispensari mandare dignemini. Fiat de speciali dum tamen dicta monasteria non fuerint ordinis sancte Clare, Ste. eps Lucan., regens.

incurred when he murdered his wife and for dispensation so that he could remarry as well as for legitimisation for his future children.[24]

3. New Relationship

As we have already seen from the previous examples, some supplicants who turned to the Penitentiary because of killing their spouses, had committed the murder because they wanted to marry someone else. This was not necessarily the case in the three cases referred to above, because the supplicants explained that they had remarried afterwards, which does not indicate directly that the other woman was the reason for killing the first wife.

Killing one's wife or husband in order to be free to remarry was, however, the motive in seven other cases. Seven supplicants explain that they had killed their wives or husbands and then married someone else. Hence, we may assume that the idea was to kill the partner to get rid of him or her and then remarry.

This is quite clearly the case of Benerina de Satira, a woman from the Italian diocese of Pavia. She and 'another man' had together killed her husband after which she had married 'another man'. Even if this is not said explicitly, it is quite probable that she had married the same man with whom she had killed her husband. She too, needed absolution from the homicide and dispensation for remaining legally in her new marriage.[25]

A similar kind of crime was committed by Bartramus Petri, layman from the diocese of Bergamo,[26] Petrus Spanner from the diocese of Basel,[27]

---

24. ASV, *Penitenzieria Ap., Reg. Matrim. et Div.*, Vol. 9, fol. 139r (9.3.1461): Nicolaus Knupsysen laicus Strigonien. dioc. diabolo instigante uxorem suam interfecit. Et demum matrimonium cum alia contraxit. Petit igitur absolvi ab uxoricidio et peccatis suis aliis ac secum dispensari ut in suo sic contracto matrimonio libere <et> licite remanere possit et valeat cum legitimatione prolis exinde subcipiendis. Fiat de speciali, Phi. S. Laurentii in Lucina.
25. ASV, *Penitenzieria Ap., Reg. Matrim. et Div.*, Vol. 8, fol. 101v (16.12.1459): Benerina de Sartira Papien. dioc. maritum suum interfecit unacum quodam alio viro. Postmodum matrimonium cum quodam alio viro contraxit et consumavit. Cum de premissis doleat et sint occulta, supplicat quatenus ipsam a reatu homicidii absolvi et cum eadem dispensare dignemini. Fiat de speciali et expresso, Phi. S. Laurentii in Lucina.
26. ASV, *Penitenzieria Ap., Reg. Matrim. et Div.*, Vol. 7, fol. 228r (13.9.1459): Bartramus Petri laicus Bergamen. dioc. exponit quod ipse uxorem suam interfecit, postmodum tamquam simplex sine aliqua dispensatione matrimonium cum quadam alia contraxit et illud carnali copula consumavit. Quare supplicat quatenus secum ut premissis non obstantibus in suo matrimonio sic contracto remanere possit prolem subceptam et subcipiendam legitimam decernentes. Fiat de speciali, Phi. S. Laurentii in Lucina.

Zitzo Stopler from the diocese of Augsburg,[28] Georgius de Canonica de Lugano from the diocese of Como,[29] Antonius Guarischi de Casarco Valsasine from the diocese of Brescia,[30] and Johannes Constancii de Monhano from the diocese of Perugia.[31] All of them received from the Penitentiary an absolution from the excommunication they had incurred when committing homicide as well as a dispenstion for remaining legally in their new relationship. Most of the supplicants obtained a legitimisation for their future children as well.

4. Adultery

Another relatively frequent reason for killing one's spouse – and here especially one's wife – was adultery committed by the victim. In the corpus there are six such cases. One very laconic petition is that of Johannes Blasii from the Polish diocese of Gniesna, who explained that he killed his wife because she had committed adultery. Johannes himself had then married another woman and asked for absolution from the Penitentiary because of

---

27. ASV, *Penitenzieria Ap., Reg. Matrim. et Div.*, Vol. 8, fol. 153r-v (without date, 1460): Petrus Spanner laicus Basilien. dioc. quandam suam primam suam uxorem interfecit et matrimonium /153v/ cum altera contraxit. Supplicat quatenus ipsum ab uxoricidio absolvi mandare dignemini. Fiat de speciali, A. eps Aprutinus, regens.
28. ASV, *Penitenzieria Ap., Reg. Matrim. et Div.*, Vol. 10, fol. 160v (2.6.1462): Zitzo Stopler laicus Augusten. dioc. uxorem suam interfecit et demum <matrimonium> cum alia contraxit et consumavit. Petit igitur absolvi ab uxoricidio ac secum dispensari ut cum secunda remanere possit cum legitimatione prolis. Fiat de speciali, Jo. eps Castellanus, regens. A summary of this text is edited in RPG IV, 1471.
29. ASV, *Penitenzieria Ap., Reg. Matrim. et Div.*, Vol. 13, fol. 138r (4.5.1464): Georgius de Canonica de Lugano Cuman. dioc. uxorem propriam interfecit et demum matrimonium cum alia muliere contraxit et consumavit. Petit absolvi igitur ab uxoridicio et secum dispensari ut cum secunda remanere possit. Fiat de speciali si secunda uxor non fuerit machinata in mortem prime uxoris, Phi. S. Laurenti in Lucina.
30. ASV, *Penitenzieria Ap., Reg. Matrim. et Div.*, Vol. 13, fol. 138v (6.5.1464): Antonius Guarischi de Casarco Valsasine dioc. Brixien. quandam suam uxorem interfecit et demum cum alia muliere contraxit et consumavit. Petit igitur absolvi ab uxoricidio ac secum dispensari ut eo non obstante in suo matrimonio libere remanere possit cum legitimatione prolis. Fiat de speciali si 2a uxor non est machinata in morte prime, Phi. S. Laurentii in Lucina.
31. ASV, *Penitenzieria Ap., Reg. Matrim. et Div.*, Vol. 13, fol. 166r (7.6.1464): Johannes Constancii de Monhano laicus Perusin. quandam suam uxorem interfecit et cum alia matrimonium contrahere desideret. Petit ab uxoricidio absolvi ac secum ut cum alia contrahere matrimonium possit dispensari. Fiat de speciali, Phi. S. Laurentii in Lucina.

the homicide and dispensation so that he could remain in his second marriage.[32]

Some other petitioners reveal a bit more detail concerning the circumstances of the adultery that led to the killing. For instance, in the corpus there are four cases in which the petitioner had killed or asked someone else to kill the man who had seduced his wife. Petrus Blanci de Minolinibus, a citizen of Capua, had, together with his friends, killed his wife and the man with whom he had found her. He asked for absolution as well as for dispensation so that he could remarry, because he wanted to have children. The Penitentiary granted him the grace with the condition that he had killed them in the moment when he found them in the act.[33]

Unlike in the previous case, where the seducer was a layman, three other supplicants were guilty of killing priests with whom their wives had committed adultery. One of them was Johannes Sancii from the village of Ristero in the diocese of Palencia who together with his friends had killed the priest who had committed adultery with his wife. After that Johannes killed his wife too. His petition is a bit peculiar, because he had personally come to Rome and asked to be absolved by someone there because, as he claimed, he did not have safe access to his diocesan bishop.[34] Alfonsus de Villagomes from the same diocese was guilty of a similar crime – he too had killed his wife and the priest who was her lover, but he did not have to

---

32. ASV, *Penitenzieria Ap., Reg. Matrim. et Div.*, Vol. 9, fol. 178v (1.7.1461): Johannes Blasii laicus Gneznen. dioc. uxorem suam propter adulterium per eam commissum interfecit. Et demum matrimonium cum alia muliere contraxit et consumavit. Petit absolvi ac secum ut cum secunda libere remanere possit dispensari. Fiat de speciali, Phi.
33. ASV, *Penitenzieria Ap., Reg. Matrim. et Div.*, Vol. 10, fol. 198r (11.1.1462): Exponit Petrus Blanci de Minolinibus civis Capuanus et eius in hac parte complices quod ipse uxorem suam quam in adulterio cum quodam viro reperit necnon dictum virum de consilio dictorum complicum interfecit quare uxoricidii reatum commisit. Et cum pater liberorum effici desideret petit se et dictos complices a premissis absolvi ac secum, ut matrimonium cum alia muliere sibi in nullo gradu actingente contrahere possit, dispensari mandare. Fiat de speciali et expresso si interficerunt eos in actu, Phi. S. Laurentii in Lucina.
34. ASV, *Penitenzieria Ap., Reg. Matrim. et Div.*, Vol. 9, fol. 127v-128r (30.1.1461): Johannes Sancii laicus ville de Ristero Palentin. dioc. et quidam Johannes eius familiarius quendam presbyterum ex eo quia uxorem dicti Johannis cognoscebat interfecerunt ac dictus Johannes suam uxorem interfecit quare presbytericidii reatum et /128r/ sententias excommunicationis incurrerunt ac idem Johannes uxoricidium commisit. Et cum in curia presenti existant et de premissis doleant et ad eorum ordinarium accedere non valeant, petunt absolvi hic in curia. Fiat de speciali, Phi. S. Laurentii in Lucina. Et committatur uni ex minoribus penitentiariis. Fiat Phi.

travel to the papal curia to receive the absolution he needed – he just sent his petition to the Penitentiary, which granted him the requested grace.[35]

The petition of Henricus Kuelmans alias Boyes, a layman from the diocese of Cambrai, was even more generous with the details of his cause. He told that he had once married a woman who had left him for another man but who had later returned home. The couple had, however, kept quarrelling all the time (probably because of what she had done) so that in the end he had killed her. He stated in his petition too that he had settled the case with her friends and her secular lord (*dominus temporalis*) and had been absolved by a local penitentiary. But since the local father confessor had absolved him with the condition that he could not remarry, he turned to the Penitentiary and asked for dispensation so that he could remarry nevertheless. The Penitentiary agreed with his request with the condition that he is of such an age that he could not live chastely.[36]

5. Quarrel
The fifth explanation behind violent behaviour was a quarrel. This is a very usual explanation in violence cases in general, but here we only find three references to such cases – in addition to the previously mentioned case from Cambrai.

One of the supplicants, Radixius de Grassetis, a citizen of Dubrovnik, stated very laconically that he had asked two servant women to kill his wife because of her bad government (*malum regiminem*). We can interpret this in many ways, but it probably refers to constant quarrels between the couple. He also married another woman afterwards and needed absolution and dispensation.[37]

---

35. ASV, *Penitenzieria Ap., Reg. Matrim. et Div.*, Vol. 9, fol. 128v-129r (6.2.1461): Alfonsus de Villagomes laicus Palentin. dioc. /129r/ ad interficiendum quendam presbyterum et eius uxorem auxilium et favorem prestitit, quare reatum presbytericidii et homicidii commisit ac sententiam excommunicationis incurrit a quibus petit absolvi. Fiat de speciali, Phi. S. Laurentii in Lucina.
36. ASV, *Penitenzieria Ap., Reg. Matrim. et Div.*, Vol. 9, fol. 126r (23.1.1461): Henricus Kuelmans alias Boyes laicus Cameracen. dioc. exponit quod cum alius cum quadam muliere matrimonium contraxisset eadem mulier cum alio viro adulterando recessit quam iterum recuperavit et propter nonnulla verba interfecit et cum amicis ac domino temporali eiusdem mulieris satisfecerit et ab uxoricidio absolutus fuerit qua penitentiarius qui eum absolvit sibi iniunxit, ut matrimonium cum alia muliere non contraheret. Petit secum dispensari, ut aliam mulierem ducere possit. Fiat de speciali et expresso si sit talis etatis quod verisimiliter suspectus sit de incontinentia, Phi. S. Laurentii in Lucina.
37. ASV, *Penitenzieria Ap., Reg. Matrim. et Div.*, Vol. 9, fol. 199v (14.10.1461): Radixius de Grassetis civis Ragusin. propter malum regiminem sue uxoris eandem per duas mulieres suas ancillas interfici fecit quare reatum homicidii commisit et

The Apostolic Penitentiary and Domestic Violence

The other two petitioners instead explain in much more detail what led to their violent behaviour. Sancius Johannis de Laniciis, a priest and *perpetuus beneficiatus* in the parish church of saint Mary of Laquetio in the diocese of Calahorra, told the Penitentiary that he had once had a concubine, but because he wanted to live better, he had told the woman that she should go home and not visit him anymore. The dumped woman was not happy with what Sancius had said and started to visit the house of his mother often. When Sancius came to know of this, he went to his mother's house and started to drive her away, threatening her with a big stick. He threw the stick towards the woman and when she suddenly bent down, the stick accidentally hit her head and caused her death. Since Sancius did not intend to kill or hurt her, but just wanted to warn her to keep away from his mother, he asked for absolution from the homicide and for a dispensation that would allow him to serve in minor orders.[38]

Nicolaus Dubut, a priest from the archdiocese of Rouen, told in his turn that he had once had his 10-year-old nephew staying with him but the boy did not feel at home with him and decided to escape and return home to his parents, the supplicant's brother. Nicolaus had been worried about the escape of the boy, and he wanted to punish him in the presence of the father of the boy, his brother. The brother became unhappy and attacked Nicolaus in order to defend his son. While the men were fighting, Nicolaus's brother fell to the ground and hit himself on a cistern so badly that he died some days later. Nicolaus, obviously, did not mean to hurt his brother, so he petitioned to the Penitentiary and asked, just like Sancius, for absolution from the homicide as well as for a dispensation that would allow him to serve in minor orders. This time the petition was not handled and approved

---

demum matrimonium cum altera muliere contraxit et consumavit. Petit absolvi ac secum, ut eadem remanere possit, dispensari. Fiat de speciali, A. prothon. Pisanus, regens.

38. ASV, *Penitenzieria Ap., Reg. Matrim. et Div.*, Vol. 10, fol. 158v-159r (20.5.1462): Sancius Johannis de Laniciis presbyter et perpetuus beneficiatus in parrochiali ecclesia sancte Marie de Laquetio Calaguritan. dioc. exponit quod cum ipse alius quandam mulierem in concubinam tenuisset melius vivere volens eidem mulierii dixit, quod ad domum suum iret et amplius ad domum suam non veniret. Dicta mulier de premissa non contenta ad domum matris eiusdem exponentis pluries venit quibus ad notitiam dicti exponentis deductis /159r/ ad domum matris ivit et unum baculum versus dictem [sic] mulierem que de domo exiebat, ut eam in cruribus verberaret, iactavit que mulier dum fugeret se inclinavit ad eo quod baculus ipse eandem in capite percussit ex qua suum diem clausit extremum. Et cum dictus exponens baculum ipsum animo ut eam panesteret tamen proicierit et de morte ipsius doluerit petit idem exponens a reatu homicidii si quod commisit absolvi ac secum ut premissis non obstantibus in minoribus ordinibus ministrare possit dispensari. Fiat de speciali in forma, A. electus Balneoregien., regens.

by the officials of the Penitentiary but by Pope Pius II himself, who agreed with the request and ordered that the letter of grace should be expedited through the Penitentiary (and not through the much more expensive Apostolic Chancery) because of the poverty of the supplicant.[39]

6. Disgrace

The sixth type of motivation expressed for killing someone was disgrace or shame. This explanation never appears explicitly in the texts of the petitions, but it can be clearly understood from the circumstances in which the homicide took place, namely that the mother/parents needed to liberate themselves from the evidence of an unwanted pregnancy. The corpus of this essay contains four such cases.

In two cases it was the mother who was guilty of the murder. One of them was sister Blasina de la Roca, a Benedictine nun, who told the Penitentiary that she had killed two of her children and then sent her sister-in-law to bury them. She needed an absolution because of what she had done. In her case it is very clear why she wanted to get rid of the children who would have caused problems for her: the nuns were bound by the vow of celibacy and they were not supposed to give birth to children. The Penitentiary granted the requested grace, even in a form that she could go

---

39. ASV, *Penitenzieria Ap., Reg. Matrim. et Div.*, Vol. 10, fol. 167r-v (8.7.1462): Nicolaus Dubut presbyter Rothomagen. dioc. exponit, quod cum ipse quendam suum nepotem minorem decem annis secum nutriret dictusque nepotis illicenciatus plures ad domum patris suis eiusdem exponentis fratris inivisset, ipse exponens dubitans de dicto puero qui per quendam nemus quem antequam ad dictam domum patris iungere posset pertransire habebat, eundem in presencia sui patris castigare voluit de quibus pater male contentus contradixit et eundem puerum deffendere voluit. Quod videns idem exponens eundem supra quoddam staminum vim vi repellendo cadere fecit qui quidam pater in eodem stamino adeo se lesit quod post paucos dies <diem> suum clausit extremum. Et cum pater sancte idem exponens de morte sui fratris ab intimis doleat et ea ut dictum nepotem ne in nemore predicto dampnum haberet fecerit et aliter de morte eiusdem sui fratris culpabilis non sit, supplicatur e.s.v. pro parte eiusdem exponentis quatenus ipsum a premissis absolvi ac secum ut in omnibus suis ordinibus ministrare possit non obstantibus supradictis dispensari mandare dignemini. Fiat quod ordinarius provideat supplicantem prout sibi videbitur. E. /167v/ Et in altaris ministerio ut prefertur; Et quod littere de super conficiende per officium sacre penitentiarie actenta prefate exponentis paupertate. Fiat ut supra, E.
Concerning other petitions approved by Pius II and expedited by the Penitentiary, see Kirsi Salonen, 'The Decisions of Pope Pius II in the Penitentiary Registers', in: Andreas Meyer, Constanze Rendtel and Maria Wittmer-Butsch (eds.), *Päpste, Pilger, Pönitentiarie. Festschrift für Ludwig Schmugge zum 65. Geburtstag.* (Tübingen: 2004), 515-530.

and confess to Brother Petrus de Sancto Germano of the Cistercian monastery of Locedii – and not to her regular father confessor – because the case was handled in secrecy and was meant to remain so.[40] The other mother who wanted to liberate herself of an unwanted pregnancy was Barbara Kindersferin, a woman from the diocese of Salzburg, who did not kill her child but terminated her pregnancy – a crime that in canon law is understood as homicide. She too obtained an absolution from the Penitentiary but did not explain her act in a more precise way.[41]

In one case an unwanted child was killed by both of the parents, but only the father, Stephanus Gerardi, priest of the parish church of Saint Gemeniani in the diocese of Brieux, turned to the Penitentiary. He explained in his supplication that he had had a concubine who had given birth to their child. Stephanus then had baptized the child after which they had suffocated it. The crime had come to the attention of the local bishop who had sent Stephanus to the papal curia to obtain absolution. The Penitentiary granted him absolution together with a dispensation that allowed him to serve in minor orders notwithstanding his crime.[42] Also in this case we see immediately the relation to disgrace: a priest was supposed to live chastely and should not father children.

---

40. ASV, *Penitenzieria Ap., Reg. Matrim. et Div.*, Vol. 10, fol. 156r (20.5.1462): Soror Blasina de la Roca monialis professa monasterii eiusdem de la Raqua ordinis sancti Benedicti Vercellen. dioc. duos suos pueros absque babtismo interfecit et ipsos per quandam ipsius fratris uxorem sepellari mandavit quare homicidii reatum et gravem excessum commisit a quibus petit absolvi. Fiat de speciali. A electus Balneoregien., regens.
Et quia occultum est et alteri dicta mulier coniceri non vult committatur fratri Petro de Sancto Germano professo monasterii Locedii ordinis cistercien. Fiat. A.

41. ASV, *Penitenzieria Ap., Reg. Matrim. et Div.*, Vol. 8, fol. 112r (12.1.1462): Barbara Kindersferin mulier Salczburgen. dioc. fetum suum in ventre suo scenciens [recte: sentiens] interfecit quare supplicat quatenus ipsam a reatu et homicidii et feti ac peccatis suis aliis absolvi mandare dignemini. Fiat in forma, G. prothon. de Oddis, regens.

42. ASV, *Penitenzieria Ap., Reg. Matrim. et Div.*, Vol. 10, fol. 156v (14.5.1462): Stephanus Gerardi presbyter Briocen. dioc. quandam mulierem in parrochia Sancti Gemeniani cuius curam tunc gerebat pluries carnaliter cognovit ac eandem in concubinam tenuit et demum prolem ab ea susceptam babtisavit et tandem prolem ipsam ipse et dicta mulier suffocarunt de quibus quidam idem exponens coram suo ordinario convictus per eundem pro absolucione ad curiam Romanam remissus fuit, propter que idem exponens excommunicationis sentenciam in tales tam per constitutiones sinodales quam alius latam incurrit et homicidii reatum commisit a quibus petit absolvi ac secum ut in minoribus suis ordinibus ministrare possit. Fiat de speciali de absolucione et quod possit ministrare in minoribus, Jo. eps. Castellanus, regens.

In the fourth case there is a somewhat different kind of matter. The supplicant, Samuel Daffreta, a layman from the diocese of Scala in Italy, had killed his sister, a Benedictine nun, and her child. Here also we see the clear reason for disgrace that has led to the homicide: a nun should not have children. Samuel too was absolved by the Penitentiary.[43]

Conclusions

In conclusion, what have we learned from these documents?

Firstly, most of these cases were such that they ought actually not to have been brought before the Penitentiary. The local bishops should have had the authority to deal with such cases because clerics were not involved in them. The fact that these cases can be found in the pages of the Penitentiary registers indicates that they were considered such severe violations that the local father confessors or bishops did not want to absolve the sinners but sent them to Rome. The intervention of the local authorities in normal cases is the explanation why there were so few such petitions in the Penitentiary material, only thirty-six out of nearly 16,000.

Secondly, no particular region or diocese was especially well represented by these cases, but the supplicants came from almost all over Christendom.

Thirdly, we find all kinds of violent acts in the cases, from assault to murder. Most of the violators were male, but in the material there were also women as supplicants, though in the minority.

Fourthly, six explanations for the violent behaviour could be determined; no explanation at all and instigation of devil were the most common. When it comes to killing one's spouse, we found two main explanations; the wish to marry someone else or the infidelity of the murdered spouse. Furthermore, we found some cases where a quarrel had been the cause of violent behaviour, and finally there were cases when someone was killed because the violator could not face the disgrace an illegitimate child could have caused.

---

43. ASV, *Penitenzieria Ap., Reg. Matrim. et Div.*, Vol. 11, fol. 173v (15.4.1463): Samuel Daffreta laicus Scalen. dioc. quandam suam sororem religiosam professam tacite ordinis sancti Benedicti necnon eiusdem sororis filium interfecit, quare excommunicationis sententiam in tales latam incurrit et sor<or>icidii reatum commisit a quibus petit absolvi. Fiat de speciali, Phi. S. Laurentii in Lucina.

MARITAL ECONOMY AND FEMALE NAMING PRACTICES IN LATE MEDIEVAL GERMANY

Christof Rolker

Introduction: Names as Symbolic Goods

Scholars of the marital economy in the later Middle Ages have long recognised that there was a wide variety of local customs and laws in the late medieval towns, and that normative sources, if they are extant at all, fail to provide a detailed picture of these practices. Instead, historians have to take into account the actual transfer of property in the context of marriage; property exchange between the spouses and their families before and at the actual marriage, the various forms of separate or joint property, the right of disposal over this property, including acts of last will, and finally the status of the surviving partner after the death of their spouse.[1]

In this paper, a different approach will be taken. Comparing female naming practices in a number of late medieval towns I will argue that certain uses of the surname in marriage can be linked to differences in the marital economy regimes. Similar claims concerning the link between naming practices and marital economy systems have already been made in

---

1. For the recent literature, see M. C. Howell, 'The Properties of Marriage in Late Medieval Europe: Commercial Wealth and the Creation of Modern Marriage', *Love, Marriage, and Family Ties in the Later Middle Ages*, eds. I. Davis, M. Müller and S. R. Jones (Turnhout: 2003), 17–61, and A. L. Erickson, 'The Marital Economy in Comparative Perspective', *The Marital Economy in Scandinavia and Britain, 1400–1900*, eds. M. Ågren and A. L. Erickson (Aldershot, UK: 2005), 3–20. An excellent case study is B. A. Hanawalt, *The Wealth of Wives: Women, Law, and Economy in Late Medieval London* (Oxford: 2007).

the context of large-scale comparisons between pre-modern England and the Scandinavian regions.[2] In this paper, I will limit myself to the German-speaking regions in the fourteenth and fifteenth centuries. The fundamental assumption of any such study is the idea that the use and transmission of the surname can be compared to property transfer in a meaningful way. Indeed, the surname itself can be and has been described as 'symbolic' or 'social capital'.[3] As this metaphor implies, names in some respects function like material property. They can have more or less value, they can serve to accumulate prestige, and they can be used to substantiate certain claims, namely family loyalty or privileges conferred on the respective family. Having a certain surname allows the individual therefore to access and mobilise resources in various fields, including economy and politics. In other words, surnames are a form of social capital.

In addition to these rather general remarks, there are two principal reasons to treat pre-modern surnames very much like immaterial property. First, from the time of their emergence in the high Middle Ages, surnames were closely related to property rights, as is most evident with the toponymic surnames of the nobility. In the time the surname established itself, there was no clear distinction between 'surname' and 'title',[4] and this link was still perceived as powerful when toponymics were legally suppressed in the French Revolution.[5] Secondly, surnames in the Middle Ages were not only customarily transmitted along the same lines as material possessions, but often treated as an asset that could be transferred by will just like other property. The *names and arms clause* popular in eighteenth-century England is a well known example of the transmission of surnames by testament,[6] but similar phenomenona are also known from medieval times. The clearest parallel to the modern *names and arms clause* is perhaps

---

2. Erickson, 'Marital Economy', 11. For England, see also D. Postles, *Naming the People of England, c.1100–1350* (Cambridge: 2006), 125–40 (Chapter 8: 'Describing women').
3. Most concepts arguing along these lines ultimately can be traced to P. Bourdieu, *Esquisse d'une théorie de la pratique* (Paris: 1972), translated as *Outline of a Theory of Practice* (Cambridge: 1977). See, for example, P. Besnard, 'Pour une étude empirique du phénomène de mode dans la consommation des biens symboliques: le cas des prénoms', *Archives européennes de sociologie* 20 (1979), 343–51, on first names.
4. J. C. Holt, *What's in a Name? Family Nomenclature and the Norman Conquest* (Reading: 1982).
5. See A. Lefebvre-Teillard, *Le nom: droit et histoire* (Paris: 1990), 113–24.
6. W. T. Gibson, '"Withered branches and weighty symbols": Surname Substitution in England, 1660–1880', *British Journal of Eighteenth-Century Studies* 15 (1992), 15–33, and E. Spring, *Law, Land, and Family: Aristocratic Inheritance in England, 1300 to 1800* (Chapel Hill, NC: 1993), esp. 94–6.

found in acts of last will from thirteenth-century Provence by which testators bequeathed their names and arms to non-relatives.[7] Indeed comparable, if more informal arrangements are also known to have been made in fairly low-status families in late medieval towns.[8]

All in all, transferring one's surname to a non-relative was nothing exotic in the later Middle Ages; this practice of creating kinship confirms the idea that the surname, like a coat of arms, was an asset that in many ways was treated like (family) property. Very commonly, it was passed on along the lines of legitimate kinship, often also to illegitimate offspring, and sometimes it was transferred by testament or given in more informal ways to non-relatives.

The 'Married Name' in Late Medieval Germany

Surnames were not only transmitted from one generation to the next, but also very commonly from husband to wife. This practice of the 'married name' is so familiar from modern practice that it is rarely asked what exactly happened in medieval times when married women 'changed' their surname. Indeed, while there is a considerable body of scholarly literature on the (medieval) origins of the surname, we know relatively little about female uses of the surname in the Middle Ages. In the context of polemic debates concerning German legislation prescribing female name-change at marriage for most part of the twentieth century (1900–1976), it has sometimes been claimed that the married name was an age-old practice and part of the cultural heritage of the Middle Ages.[9] Opponents of this legal enforcement of the married name have branded it 'medieval' in a clearly pejorative sense, a symbol of the suppression of women.[10] The scholarly literature is equally divided. Most frequently, it is assumed rather than

---

7. See R. Aubenas, 'L'adoption en Provence au Moyen Âge', *Revue de droit historique de droit français et étranger* 13 (1934), 700–726, and more recently C. Maurel, 'Un artifice contre l'extinction des familles? La substitution de nom et d'armes à Marseille (fin XIVe siècle – fin XVIe siècle)', *Liens de famille. Vivre et choisir sa parenté* (St Denis: 1990), 29–35.
8. G. Signori: '"Family Traditions". Moral Economy and Memorial "Gift Exchange" in the Urban World of the Late Fifteenth Century', in: *Negotiating the Gift. Premodern Figurations of Exchange*, eds. G. Algazi, V. Groebner and B. Jussen (Göttingen: 2003), 295–328, here at 301–11.
9. See S.-J. von Spolena-Metternich, *Namenserwerb, Namensführung und Namensänderung unter Berücksichtigung von Namensbestandteilen* (Frankfurt: 1997), 78–81 on the German political debates of the 1950s and 1970s.
10. An early example is M. Weber, *Ehefrau und Mutter in der Rechtsentwicklung: eine Einführung* (Tübingen: 1907), esp. 420–1.

proven that married women in the Middle Ages dropped their maiden name at marriage; sometimes, however, the practice of the married name is seen as a rather late development.[11]

This all serves as a warning to establish carefully the actual naming practices before trying to link them to other phenomena. In a first step, therefore, female naming practices will be studied without any reference to the different marital economy systems. I will study 'naming practices' rather than names, asking which, if any, of the names a person 'had' were actually used in certain situations. In present day society, for example, almost everyone has at least one 'given name' and one 'surname'. Using the surname plus perhaps the given name in most public situations but the given name only in more private communication would be an example of using different names. The practices at the centre of this paper are the various ways women in a late medieval society used (or chose not to use) surnames when referring to themselves by name.

Evidently, naming practices vary greatly in different genres of sources, and it may also play a role who is describing whom. The names as they appear in charters, narrative sources and tax rolls, for example, may well be different even when referring to the same persons. For this reason, I have focussed on testaments only, and more specifically, the way married women or widows referred to themselves in their own wills.[12] In principle, a similar analysis could be done with all charters issued by women, but testaments have several advantages over other documents. First, they are fairly common, surviving in large numbers from many medieval towns, and second, despite all differences in the legal culture between various towns, they are relatively uniform. In addition, as the main question is whether the women used a name acquired by marriage rather than by birth, it is crucial to establish at least the name of the husband in all cases. This indeed is the reason why women's testaments are particularly useful for such an enterprise; not only are they issued predominantly by widows and wives, but they almost invariably mention the husband (dead or alive) by first

---

11. I. Schwenzer, 'Namensrecht im Überblick: Entwicklung – Rechtsvergleich – Analyse', *Zeitschrift für das gesamte Familienrecht* 35 (1991), 390–7, esp. at 392 and N. Arndt, *Die Geschichte und Entwicklung des familienrechtlichen Namensrechts in Deutschland unter Berücksichtigung des Vornamensrechts* (Munich: 2004), here at 37, both claim that married women in pre-modern urban societies did not adopt their husbands' surnames.

12. Indeed, I have also studied how men in their testaments referred to their wives or other women, and the patterns are very much the same. Likewise, the way women referred to themselves and the naming forms they used to refer to other women are largely the same. For a detailed study of this question, see C. Rolker, 'Namensführung und weibliche Identität im späten Mittelalter', *L'Homme. Europäische Zeitschrift für feministische Geschichtswissenschaft* 20 (2009), 17–34.

name and surname. Very commonly indeed, the testaments also mention both blood-relatives and in-laws. Thus, it is almost always clear whether or not the family name used by the testatrix is the married name or not.

My sources are acts of last will from ten late medieval towns and cities in the German-speaking regions, namely from Basle, Bern, Braunschweig, Cologne, Constance, Hamburg, Lübeck, Lüneburg, Regensburg and Zurich. Due to the different legal culture, and also the hazards of transmission, there are of course differences both in the production and the preservation of the sources that have to be taken into account. The documents from Basle are a special case; testaments in the narrow sense are rarely extant as the right to make a testament was restricted to childless testators; however, mutual arrangements known as *Mächtnis* and *Widem* have survived in very large numbers. In many aspects, these contracts fulfilled similar functions as joint testaments did elsewhere, and I rely on Gabriela Signori's minute analysis of these documents for my own study.[13] For the remaining towns and cities, I was able to use testaments in the proper sense, which have survived in hundreds and sometimes thousands from all these places. In the case of Bern, Constance and Zurich, my findings are based on the medieval registers kept by the city councils of these places.[14] The testaments of Braunschweig, Cologne, Hamburg, Lübeck and Lüneburg are transmitted in a similar fashion; very many of them can be consulted in convenient editions. The edition of the Braunschweig testaments does not provide the full texts, but the purpose of the present study, this is made up by the editor's observations on female naming practices in these documents.[15] While the Lüneburg testaments from the fourteenth and fifteenth centuries are all edited,[16] the mass of later testaments from medieval Hamburg and Lübeck is a veritable deterrent for the edition of the fifteenth-century material. This is especially true for Lübeck, which boosts over 3000 pre-

---

13. G. Signori, *Vorsorgen – vererben – erinnern: kinder- und familienlose Erblasser in der städtischen Gesellschaft des Spätmittelalters* (Göttingen: 2001). My thanks are to Gabriela Signori (Konstanz) for help and advice on these matters.
14. My thanks are to the archivists at the Staatsarchiv Bern, the Stadtarchiv Konstanz and the Staatsarchiv Zürich. For the transmission of the testaments from late-medieval Zurich and Constance, see W. Bosshard, 'Krieg und Todesvorbereitung: Zürcher letztwillige Verfügungen 1428–1445', *Ein "Bruderkrieg" macht Geschichte: neue Zugänge zum Alten Zürichkrieg*, ed. P. Niederhäuser (Zurich: 2006), 99–110, and C. Rolker, '"Eine Behörde – ein Buch"? Studien zu den Konstanzer Gemächtebüchern', *Zeitschrift für Geschichte des Oberrheins* 157 (2009), 44–62, respectively.
15. D. Mack, *Testamente der Stadt Braunschweig*, 5 vols. (Göttingen: 1988–95), here at i, 11–7.
16. Mack, *Testamente Braunschweig*; *Lüneburger Testamente des Mittelalters (1323 bis 1500)*, ed. U. Reinhardt (Hanover: 1996).

1500 testaments. On the plus side, I was able to use the extensive literature on this material.[17] Both for Hamburg and for Lübeck, I have used the available editions for the fourteenth-century material,[18] and a selection of original documents from the fifteenth century.[19] Unfortunately, such a comparison is no longer possible for the testaments from medieval Cologne, and I rely on the editions and studies made before the disaster that largely destroyed the municipal archives in March 2009.[20] For Regensburg, I was able to consult the text established for the forthcoming edition.[21]

My sample thus covers a very large number of testaments both from the Hanseatic cities of the north and the numerous towns in the south-west,

17. K. Arnold, 'Frauen in den mittelalterlichen Hansestädten Hamburg, Lübeck und Lüneburg. Eine Annäherung an die Realität', *Frauen in der Ständegesellschaft*, eds. B. Vogel and U. Weckel (Hamburg: 1991), 69–88; B. Noodt, *Religion und Familie in der Hansestadt Lübeck anhand der Bürgertestamente des 14. Jahrhunderts* (Lübeck: 2000); S. Rüther, 'Zwischen Stand und Geschlecht. Weibliches Selbstverständnis im Spiegel lübeckischer Testamente des Spätmittelalters', *Der Blick auf sich und die anderen. Selbst- und Fremdbild von Frauen und Männern in Mittelalter und früher Neuzeit: Festschrift für Klaus Arnold*, eds. S. Prühlen, L. Kuhse and J. Sarnowsky (Göttingen: 2007), 67–93; B.-J. Kruse, 'Eine Treppe in den Himmel bauen: die Stiftungspraxis Lübecker Witwen in Text, Bild und Architektur', ibid., 39–65. On the surname in Lübeck, see also A. Reimpell, *Die Lübecker Personennamen unter besonderer Berücksichtigung der Familiennamenbildung bis zur Mitte des 14. Jahrhunderts* (Lübeck: 1928).

18. For the fourtenth century, see *Hamburger Testamente 1351 bis 1400*, ed. H.-D. Loose (Hamburg: 1970) and A. von Brandt, *Regesten der Lübecker Bürgertestamente des Mittelalters*, 2 vols. (Lübeck: 1964/73), respectively. As von Brandt covers the time from 1278 to 1361 only, I have also used the 1000-odd testaments printed in Jacob a Melle, *De itineribus Lubecensium sacris* (Lübeck: 1711).

19. My thanks are to the Staatsarchiv Hamburg and Lübeck for providing microfilms of women's testaments from the second half of the fifteenth century. See also R. Rogge, *Zwischen Moral und Handelsgeist: weibliche Handlungsräume und Geschlechterbeziehungen im Spiegel des hamburgischen Stadtrechts vom 13. bis zum 16. Jahrhundert* (Frankfurt: 1998).

20. B. Kuske, 'Testamente und andere Vermögensauseinandersetzungen der Kölner Bürger (14. bis 16. Jahrhundert)', *Quellen zur Geschichte des Kölner Handels und Verkehrs im Mittelalter, Band 3: Besondere Quellengruppen des späteren Mittelalters*, ed. idem (Bonn: 1923), 189–365.

21. Olivier Richard (Mulhouse) kindly let me use his working text. On the testaments and their edition, see O. Richard and T. Paringer, 'Die Testamente der Reichsstadt Regensburg aus Spätmittelalter und Früher Neuzeit: Entstehung – Überlieferung – Quellenwert', *Archivalische Zeitschrift* 88 (2005), 197–234.

while the east is not very well represented.[22] As it turned out, the naming practices are fairly stable over time in all these places, but of course I have tried to compare contemporary material only, concentrating on the second half of the fifteenth century. The social background is relatively homogenous; most testaments were set up by women belonging to the well-to-do and indeed often rich families of their hometown. Broadly speaking, the social selectivity is less extreme in cities that encouraged or at least facilitated the making of wills, as was the case with Zurich and apparently also with Lübeck. In any case we are dealing with women who could dispose of some property at least, and as far as names are concerned, with a milieu in which the surname was a well-established institution in the fifteenth century. Even in Lübeck the surname was common already in mid-fourteenth century,[23] and for the other places an earlier date is plausible for the establishment of the surname, certainly so for the milieu we are concerned with.

Me, Myself and My Name: Female Naming Practices

Let us first consider which naming forms can be found in these sources as far as female self-designation is concerned. There are principally three different ways married women referred to themselves in medieval testaments; by first name only, by first name and married name, or by first name and a family name different from that of their husband (commonly, but not always, the 'maiden name'). In all three cases, a woman may or may not additionally refer to her husband or male relatives. Thus, if a Grethe Müller married a Hans Schmid, in her own will we may find her as 'Grethe', 'Grethe Müller' or 'Grethe Schmid'. In many other sources, references may completely do without her name, often instead referring to male family members by name (e.g. 'Hans Schmid and his wife, the daughter of Heinrich Müller'); however, while testatrices may refer to other women in this way, they always refer to themselves in one of the three ways

---

22. The reason for this imbalance is not due to a lack of testaments but to the absence of published sources, and of course my own ignorance of the Eastern vernaculars, as not all of these testaments were written in German or Latin. The number of extant documents is indeed impressive. According to T. Krzenck, 'Böhmische Bürgertestamente des 15. Jahrhunderts: Regestenverzeichnis', *Archiv für Diplomatik* 44 (1998), 141–86, there are no less than 1200 extant testaments from Prague from the years 1434–1494. J. Majorossy, 'Archives of the Dead: Administration of Last Wills in Medieval Hungarian Towns', *Medium Aevum Quotidianum* 48 (2003), 13–28, mentions more than 900 testaments from Bratislava, to quote only example from this region.
23. Reimpell, *Lübecker Personennamen*.

mentioned before. A last practice that has to be taken into account is the combination of two or more naming forms; not only may women use different names in different situations, but even within one single document the author may refer to herself by different surnames. In the following, the distinction is therefore drawn between women referring to themselves by first name only (not using any surname), by married name (not using any other surname) and by other surnames (using at least once a surname different from that of the husband).

For the second half of the fifteenth century, the results are fairly straightforward. The first result is a negative one. Perhaps surprisingly, one does not find major differences between married women and widows. In places where testaments of married women are common enough to make meaningful comparisons between wives and widows, no significant difference in the naming patterns can be discerned. Women who commonly referred to themselves by their married name apparently continued to so after the husband's death; *vice versa*, wives using different surnames in addition to or instead of the married name would also continue to do so when they were widowed. While this may be difficult to prove in every individual case, it is clear from the overall pattern that wives and widows in any given city followed the customs in their self-reference.

If, however, we compare the female practices of all towns in our sample, it becomes clear that while marital status has little if any role to play, naming practices differed significantly from one town to the other. In all towns, there is one dominating model in the sense that 70–90% of the testaments display this model, almost all others a second, and only a handful if any the third. Indeed, there is a clear geographical pattern as to which model is prevalent in which town:

In Basel, Bern, Constance and Zurich, almost all women making a will use their family name, and very commonly husband and wife can be seen to use different family names. Cologne belongs to this group as well, though the use of 'maiden name' is less frequent here.

In Braunschweig, Hamburg, Lübeck and Lüneburg women refer to themselves commonly by first name only, although the use of family names becomes more common over the time. Nonetheless, the use of *different* surnames by both spouses remains exceptionally rare, and widows consistently refer to themselves by their married name only, if they use a surname at all. More commonly, they define themselves by first name and reference to the deceased husband.

The odd case is Regensburg, where the vast majority of married women and widows refer to themselves by first name only; if they use a family name, it is the married name.

How can this geographical pattern be explained? Two explanations seem plausible to me: First, the pattern for females to use or not to use surnames in my sources by and large corresponds to the spread of the surname in the male population. Very broadly speaking, in medieval Germany the surname spread from the west to the east and from the south to the north; as a number of local studies (almost exclusively concerned with male naming practices) have shown, the surname in the fifteenth century was more common in the west and the south of the German-speaking regions than it was towards the east and the north.[24] In the milieux from which the testaments studied here are predominantly drawn, the surname was well-established in all towns, but many scholars assume that there always was a considerable delay as far as female naming practices were concerned.[25]

However, this 'delay theory' is not entirely satisfactory to explain the differences in female naming practices. Even if there were a general rule that female naming practices were simply lagging behind by a century or two, this would fail to explain the differences found in my sources. For example, the three places where family names were established very early in the thirteenth century were Cologne, Regensburg and Zurich, yet in the late fifteenth century the female use of family names is completely different in these three places. On the other hand, the use or non-use of the maiden name does not change much over time: in the south, it is found in the very first extant testaments, in the north, even in the early sixteenth century there is nothing of this sort. Geographical differences between the north and the south are in general greater than differences between the beginning and the end of the period studied here, and the differences among women from different towns are greater than those between men in the same period of time.

The key differences, in my view, are the diverging marital property regimes in general and the different role of guardianship in particular. The marital economy systems differed in many respects, sometimes even between neighbouring regions; the wide variety both in the legal systems and in actual female testamentary practices found in Flanders serves as a warning.[26] However, for the German-speaking towns and cities under consideration here, it is also clear that certain aspect were fairly similar in some places while others were more diverse. In all of Germany, for

---

24. For an overview, see K. Kunze, *Atlas Namenkunde. Vor- und Familiennamen im deutschen Sprachgebiet* (Munich: 2004).
25. See the articles in *Persistances du nom unique, vol. 2: désignation et anthroponymie des femmes: méthodes statistiques pour l'anthroponymie*, eds. M. Bourin and P. Chareille (Tours: 1992).
26. P. Godding, 'Dans quelle mesure pouvait-on disposer de ses biens par testament dans les anciens Pays-bas méridionaux?', *Tijdschrift voor rechtsgeschiedenis* 50 (1982), 279–96.

example, married women were legally able to possess property of their own and did so frequently. It is also true for all towns and cities studied here that real estate owned by the wife was better protected than movable property, in the sense that the explicit consent of the wife was necessary if the husband wanted to dispose of it. In practice, this also meant that real estate was more likely to return to the family of origin than was movable property, and that the family of origin tended to have a say in transactions of land and houses. The area where one finds the largest differences between individual urban societies concerns the actual disposal over movable property by women.

This, in turn, is closely linked to the institution of guardianship over women, which in the area of the Lübeck, Magdeburg and related city laws was more important than it was in the south and west. As a result, the marital economy regime of the Hanseatic cities in the late medieval period (and indeed also in early modern times) gave the husband almost unlimited control over the movable goods the wife brought into marriage, and sometimes even her real property.[27] In addition, the families of origin were clearly less likely to regain much of this property than was the case in the south and south-west.

In this sense, therefore, the use of the husband's name both in marriage and afterwards seems to reflect some of the differences between the marital property systems in late medieval Germany. The use or non-use of surnames, and in particular of a surname different from the 'married name' correlated with the right of disposal over property by married women. Again, Regensburg seems to be an exception to this rule as the legal and economic position of married women seems to have been much better than in the Hanseatic cities of the north, yet the use of the married names prevails in women's testaments. However, while guardianship in practice did not play a significant role in fifteenth-century Regensburg, it may be significant that, from the late fourteenth century onwards, the local statutes presuppose a joint marital property system, whereas the other towns in the German south stress separate property.[28] It may well be that legal doctrine influenced the modes of speech.

Given the complexity of the marital economy regimes and our limited knowledge of the practice of guardianship over women, it may seem daring

---

27. In late-medieval Hamburg, the husband was allowed to dispose of the real property the wife had brought into marriage since at least 1301, see Rogge, *Zwischen Moral und Handelsgeist*, esp. 95–6. On the legal situation in Braunschweig and Lübeck, see H. Piper, *Testament und Vergabung von Todes wegen im braunschweigischen Stadtrecht des 13. bis 17. Jahrhunderts* (Braunschweig: 1960) and W. Ebel, *Forschungen zur Geschichte des lübischen Rechts, Teil I: dreizehn Stücke zum Prozess- und Privatrecht* (Lübeck: 1950), respectively.

28. My thanks to Olivier Richard (Mulhouse) for valuable advice in these questions.

to explain the differences in female naming practices of various German towns by the local marital property system. Certainly marital property was not the only factor at work here, and in any case it did not completely determine the use of this or that name in every single case.[29] Nonetheless, the idea that the overall pattern of naming practices is related to the local marital economy regime is further supported if we look at the kind of testaments extant from the different towns.

Two supporting arguments can be found by analysing the corpora of last wills (not only women's testaments). Quite clearly, the use and non-use of separate surnames correlates both with the sex ratio of the testators and the existence or non-existence of joint testaments. In the west and the south-west, women's wills make up between a third and half of the extant testaments, while in the north, just 15 to 20 per cent of the testaments were made by women. Joint testaments – i.e., wills that are jointly or at least simultanously issued by husband and wife – are very common in Cologne, common in the south-west but unheard of in the north. The higher ratio of women's testaments, but also the institution of the joint testament can be taken as indicators of a stronger economic position of (married) women in the sense that they did not only legally own property but also had the right of disposal over it. The legal position of married women was similar in the sense that they all owned property but could only make wills with the consent of their husbands; however, there are marked differences in how often this consent was given. In some places it was very rare – hardly any testament of a married woman has survived from medieval Braunschweig – while in Cologne it was so common that the necessity of consent of the husband seems to have been largely a formality. Generally speaking, women in late medieval Basel, Bern, Cologne, Constance and Zurich more frequently disposed of property by last will than women in the Hanseatic cities. The almost complete absence of joint testaments in the north seems to indicate that husbands could dispose of the joint movable property of the couple relatively easily while in the west and the south the explicit consent of the wife was more frequently required.

Conclusions

One of the most difficult questions concerning the marital economy of medieval Europe is the question who could actually exercise the right of disposal over property (not who owned it). The evidence from normative sources, 'marriage contracts' and related documents gives important clues but the evidence is often very sketchy and comparison remains very

---

29. For further discussion, see Rolker, 'Namensführung und weibliche Identität'.

difficult. Here, the study of names can provide valuable additional evidence. While the marital economy system of every single town under consideration here deserves much more detailed study, it seems legitimate to conclude from the evidence quoted above that the female use of surname on the whole corresponds to women's access to movable property in marriage. Not the legal capacity to own property but the actual ability to dispose of it (or at least to veto the husband's actions in this area) was the key difference that is also reflected in the naming patterns. Therefore, I propose that gender-specific naming practices (as found in 'marriage contracts', testaments and related documents) can be used as a proxy for the economic position of married women in the sense that the maiden name is indicative of the shared interest of these women and their natal families. Names are used to earmark property and persons at the same time, and the continued use of the maiden name in marriage settlements and testaments is strongly indicative for a marital economy where it did matter which property came from which family.

Comparative studies on this basis are seriously hampered by the fact that for most places neither the naming system nor the marital economy regime have been studied in detail, and also by the fact that naming practices were influenced by other developments as well, for example, scribal routine. A comparative study between, say, German and Italian towns may well be impossible. It may be easier, and safer, to use names in the context of local studies and to study changing naming patterns over time. However, the comparative studies at least strengthen the general idea that the transfer of economic goods and family names is closely interrelated.

Legal historians have seldom restricted themselves to the study of normative sources, and in the case of marital property law we are used to relying heavily on charter evidence to understand legal institutions. My modest suggestion is that the exchange and use of symbolic goods such as family names should be studied alongside the transfer of economic goods in marriage. If properly understood, naming systems can be used by scholars interested in legal and social history alike.

CANONICAL LEGISLATION ON INCEST AND EXCOMMUNICATION IN SIXTH-CENTURY GAUL

Frederik Keygnaert

Introduction

In the year 516 the Catholic King Sigismund ascended the throne of Burgundy, bringing an end to the Arian tradition of his predecessors.[1] The following year a council was held in Epaon to discuss the collaboration between the Burgundian leadership and the Church. During the council, there was a remarkable emphasis on illicit incestuous behaviour by denying sinful couples any kind of pardon unless they separated.[2] Six years earlier, the first Merovingian council, held at Orléans (511), had already stated that no man was allowed to marry his brother's widow, or his dead wife's sister.[3] At Epaon, the list of prohibited degrees was significantly expanded,

---

I am most grateful to the organizers of this conference, Per Andersen, Mia Münster-Swendsen and Helle Vogt, and to the participants for their valuable comments on this paper. Many thanks as well to Brigitte Meijns for her in-depth advice.

1. R. Kaiser, 'Der Burgunderkönig Sigismund († 523/524): erster heiliger König des Mittelalters und erster königlicher Romfahrer, Bußpilger und Mönch', *Päpste, Pilger, Pönitentiarie. Festschrift für Ludwig Schmugge zum 65. Geburtstag*, ed. A. Meyer (Tübingen: 2004); Idem, *Die Burgunder* (Stuttgart: 2004); J. Favrod, *Histoire politique du royaume burgonde (443–534)* (Lausanne: 1997).
2. Epaon (517), c. 30, *Concilia Galliae, A. 511–A. 695*, ed. C. de Clercq (Corpus Christianorum, Series Latina 148 A) (Turnhout: 1963), 31-2: 'Incestis coniunctionibus nihil prorsus veniae reservamus, nisi cum adulterium separatione sanaverint'.
3. Orléans (511), c. 18, *Concilia Galliae*, ed. de Clercq, 9-10.

revealing a determination to ban incest that would soon put the Church at odds with the interests of the lay aristocracy. Importantly, two months prior to the council of Epaon, King Sigismund himself had issued a prohibition on incest, as part of the secular legislation of the *Liber Constitutionum*.[4] Nevertheless, shortly after the council of Epaon, another council was held at Lyon (518-19) because Sigismund had ignored his own laws on incest and those of the Epaon council. One of Sigismund's courtiers, the royal treasurer Stephanus, had contracted an illicit marriage to Palladia, the sister of his deceased wife. For this, the couple had been excommunicated before the council of Lyon took place.[5] However, Stephanus and Palladia seemed to have opposed their sentence, and so had Sigismund. The king aggressively intimidated the bishops to have them withdraw the penalty, which prompted them to meet in Lyon. During the council, in a seemingly desperate act, they threatened to suspend religious services if Sigismund did not change course. An addendum to the canons of Lyon, attached at an unknown date, states that a compromise between Church and king was eventually reached.[6] The penalty against Stephanus and Palladia was mitigated 'in line with the king's *sententia*'. The couple were now allowed to attend Mass, on the condition of leaving church before Communion was distributed.[7] From that moment onwards, Stephanus and Palladia disappear from the sources.

The nature of the couple's initial sentence and its subsequent mitigation raise some questions, as do the aggressive actions of both king and bishop. To be sure, the attempt to dissolve Stephanus's marriage, may have been part of the Church's campaign to increase its political influence.

---

4. *Liber Constitutionum*, 36, ed. R. de Salis, MGH, Leges nat. Germ. 2.1 (Hannover: 1892), 69. The imposed penance was redeemed by a financial contribution. I.N. Wood, 'Disputes in Late Fifth- and Sixth-Century Gaul: Some Problems', *The Settlement of Disputes in Early Medieval Europe*, eds. W. Davies and P. Fouracre (Cambridge: 1986), 7-22, here 10.
5. Lyon (518-523), c. 1 (1-3), *Concilia Galliae*, ed. de Clercq, 39. Pontal dates the council between 518 and 519: O. Pontal, *Histoire des conciles mérovingiens* (Paris: 1989), 71-3. Biblical quotations concerning incest are to be found in Levit. 18.18 and Deut. 25.5. According to 1 Cor. 16, husband and wife became 'one flesh' (the principle of *unitas carnis*) upon their marriage. As such, Stephanus was related through his marriage to his wife as well as to his wife's sister. E. Archibald, *Incest and the Medieval Imagination* (Oxford: 2001), 29.
6. On the textual transmission of the addendum, see Pontal, *Conciles mérovingiens*, 73.
7. Lyon (518-523), *Concilia Galliae*, ed. de Clercq, 41: 'Domni quoque gloriosissimi regis sententia secuti id temperamenti praestitimus, ut Stephano praedicto vel Palladiae usque ad orationem plebis, quae post evangelia legitur, orandi in locis sanctis spatium praestaremus'.

Throughout the Middle Ages, the authority to recognize or refuse to accept the validity of marriages among the aristocracy gave the Church considerable political power.[8] Scholars such as Paul Mikat, Ian Wood and most recently Karl Ubl have already hinted at a similar explanation for the Stephanus case.[9] However, it remains difficult to fathom why the Burgundian Church would have endangered its relationship with the first Catholic king, especially when Merovingian bishops generally displayed some flexibility with regard to the Germanic tradition on incest.[10] Similarly, the king's harassment of the bishops, mentioned at the council of Lyon, contradicted his own recent rapprochement to the Burgundian Church. To explain such contradictions, this paper will focus on one aspect which has received little attention thus far, but which probably determined the conflict's political importance. In all likelihood, the relations between Church and king quickly deteriorated because the Church excommunicated Sigismund's treasurer, removing him from the community of the faithful.

It is important to keep in mind that the observance of the ecclesiastical excommunications by the powerful must have been critical for the enforcement of Church laws. Indeed, this particular punishment accompanied just about every of the canons issued by early medieval Church councils. At a council in 567, the bishops complained that they had no other weapon to defend themselves and their property other than excommunication.[11] Of course, despite canonical prohibitions, clerics were known to resort to weapons of a more worldly nature as well – Bishop Nicetius of Trier (†566/585) was hardly defenceless in his fortified castle,

---

8. Archibald, *Incest*, 41-52; P. Mikat, *Die Inzestgesetzgebung der merowingisch-fränkischen Konzilien (511–626/27)* (Rechts- und Staatswissenschaftliche Veröffentlichungen der Görres-Gesellschaft. Neue Folge 74) (Paderborn: 1994), 41-83; K. Ubl, *Inzestverbot und Gesetzgebung. Die Konstruktion eines Verbrechens (300–1100)* (Millennium Studies 20) (Berlin and New York: 2008), 174-5, *passim*; M. de Jong, 'An Unresolved Riddle: Early Medieval Incest Legislation', *Franks and Alamanni in the Merovingian Period. An Ethnographic Perspective*, ed. I.N. Wood (Studies in Historical Archaeoethnology 3) (Woodbridge: 1998), 107-40; R.H. Helmholz, *Marriage Litigation in Medieval England* (London: 1974).
9. Mikat, *Inzestgesetzgebung*, 116-117; Ubl, *Inzestverbot*, 133-137; I.N. Wood, 'Incest, Law and the Bible in Sixth-Century Gaul', *Early Medieval Europe* 7 (1998), 291-304, esp. 299-301.
10. Mikat, *Inzestgesetzgebung*, 51-54; Ubl, *Inzestverbot*, 153, 172-3.
11. Tours (567), c. 25, *Concilia Galliae*, ed. de Clercq, 192-3: 'quia arma nobis non sunt altera [...] qui res pervadit ecclesiae, psalmus CVIII dicatur [...] ut non solum excommunis, sed etiam anathema moriatur et coelesti gladio feriatur...'.

which allegedly counted thirty towers and a catapult.[12] Violence, however, could not solve everything, nor would it enhance the credibility of an exclusion from God's Grace. Therefore, it was essential that the ruling class obeyed the ecclesiastical penalties if church leaders were to firmly establish themselves as members of that class. Only if the accompanying penalties instilled fear could church law successfully be implemented. However, from the perspective of the lay leadership, the ecclesiastical power to excommunicate – if not jointly employed to maintain political order – needed to be held in check.

With this in mind, I will reconsider the dispute between King Sigismund and his bishops. I will argue that the incest conflict might not be properly understood without fully grasping the importance and function of excommunication as an instrument of power. Particularly, this paper aims to explain how King Sigismund exploited the inconclusive nature of the laws on excommunication imposed as a punishment for incest, in order to question the legitimacy of the sentence against Stephanus. In conclusion, the case will serve as a stepping stone to reveal in what way the implementation of incest laws was related to the canonical prescriptions regarding excommunication throughout the sixth century.[13]

---

12. F. Prinz, *Klerus und Krieg im früheren Mittelalter. Untersuchungen zur Rolle der Kirche beim Aufbau der Königsherrschaft* (Monographien zur Geschichte des Mittelalters 2) (Stuttgart: 1971), 1-73. On Nicetius: R. Van Dam, 'Bishops and Society', *The Cambridge History of Christianity, II, Constantine to c. 600*, eds. A. Casiday and F.W. Norris (Cambridge: 2007), 343-66, here 362.

13. Early medieval scholarship has focused mainly on the function of excommunication in Church rituals and its relation to penance; see especially articles by S.M. Hamilton, most recently her '*Absolvimus vos vice beati petri apostolorum principis*: Episcopal Authority and the Reconciliation of Excommunicants in England and Francia c.900–c.1150', *Frankland. The Franks and the World of the Early Middle Ages. Essays in Honour of Dame Jinty Nelson*, eds. P. Fouracre and D. Ganz (Manchester and New York: 2008), 209-241; L.K. Little, *Benedictine Maledictions: Liturgical Cursing in Romanesque France* (Ithaca NY: 1999); R. Reynolds, 'Rites of Separation and Reconciliation in the Early Middle Ages', *Segni e riti nella chiesa altomedievale occidentale* (Settimane di studio del Centro italiano di studi sull'alto medioevo 33) (Spoleto: 1987), I, 405-33; C. Vogel, 'Pénitence et excommunication dans l'Eglise ancienne et durant le Haut Moyen Age', *Concilium* 107 (1975), 11-22; R. Mathisen, 'Les pratiques de l'excommunication d'après la législation conciliaire en Gaule (Ve–VIe siècle)', *Pratiques de l'eucharistie dans les églises d'Orient et d'Occident (Antiquité et Moyen Age)*, eds. N. Bériou, B. Caseau and D. Rigaux (Collection des Etudes Augustiniennes. Série Moyen Age et temps modernes 45) (Paris: 2009), I, 539-560. On excommunication in general, see, among others: V. Beaulande, *Le malheur d'être exclu? Excommunication, réconciliation et société à la fin du Moyen Âge* (Paris: 2006); E. Vodola, *Excommunication in the Middle Ages* (Berkeley CA, Los

Enforcing Incest Law: From Excommunication to an Episcopal Strike

Apart from the council records of Epaon and Lyon, just one other source sheds additional light on the story of Stephanus, namely the *vita* of Bishop Apollinaris of Valence. Apollinaris attended both the council of Epaon and that of Lyon. His *vita* was written by an anonymous, but probably contemporaneous, author who might have been Apollinaris's travel companion. The same story was copied *verbatim* in the *vita* of Avitus of Vienne, brother of Apollinaris and a key figure at the council of Epaon.[14] Although the text only survives in versions composed during the Carolingian period, Frederick Paxton has convincingly argued that the *Vita Apollinaris* still bears witness to a sixth-century tradition.[15] According to the anonymous hagiographer, the initial excommunication of Stephanus and Palladia was fulminated in the presence of Avitus.[16] This may have happened at the council of Epaon, or at an unknown gathering soon thereafter.[17] At any rate, the assembly must have predated the council of Lyon, since Avitus was dead by then.[18] Moreover, the bishops declared at Lyon that they were 'once more gathered together to discuss the case of Stephanus': *congregati iterato in unum in causa Stephani*.[19] A second meeting is also mentioned in the *vita*, explained by its author as a result of King Sigismund's disrespect for episcopal authority. According to the *vita*, Sigismund had been 'infuriated with madness' upon receiving news of the ecclesiastical sentence. When the king started making threats to the bishops,

---

Angeles and London: 1986); P. Hinschius, *System des katholischen Kirchenrechts, mit besonderer Rücksicht auf Deutschland*, 5 vol. (Berlin: 1888-1893, repr. Graz: 1959), IV/V, 691-864/1-492; H.C. Lea, *Studies in Church History, the Rise of the Temporal Power, Benefit of Clergy, Excommunication* (Philadelphia: 1869), 223-487.

14. *Vita Apollinaris*, ed. B. Krusch, MGH Scriptores rer. Merov. 3 (Hannover: 1896), 194-203; *Vita Aviti*, ed. R. Peiper, MGH Auctores ant. 6.2 (Berlin: 1883), 177-81.
15. F.S. Paxton, 'Power and the Power to Heal. The Cult of St. Sigismund of Burgundy', *Early Medieval Europe* 2 (1993), 95-110, esp. 99, 103.
16. *Vita Apollinaris*, ed. Krusch, 198: 'Avitus et Apollinaris [...] cum reliquis pontificibus simul in unum congregati ipsum Stephanum sacra communione privari sanxerunt'.
17. Mikat, *Inzestgesetzgebung*, 106-107, 109, notes 314 and 322.
18. The canons of the council were signed by Avitus's successor, Julianus. Avitus died in February 518. Favrod, *Histoire politique*, 425-6.
19. Lyon (518-523), c.1 (1), *Concilia Galliae*, ed. de Clercq, 39.

they decided to meet up again – *tamquam exilio* – in an *oppidum* called *Sardinia*, in the *civitas* of Lyon.[20]

At first sight, it is difficult to identify *Sardinia* with any known place in the Lyonnais area. Bruno Krusch, the editor of the *vita* in the *Monumenta Germaniae Historica*, even considered this fragment to be a rephrasing of African history, in which the Vandal king Trasamond was said to have exiled 220 bishops to the island of Sardinia.[21] However, a copying error could have turned *Sabiniacum* (now Savigny, near Lyon) into *Sardinia*.[22] The *oppidum* of Savigny may have offered the necessary shelter for the obstinate bishops, who defied their king. Although there is no certainty that there was an important church or monastery located within the fortified town,[23] it may have been at Savigny that further actions against Sigismund and his treasurer were discussed, which eventually resulted in the canons of Lyon.

It seems indeed that the small group of bishops was not feeling at all secure. First of all, only eleven bishops of a total of twenty-eight signed the canons of Lyon, a small number compared with the twenty-five bishops who attended the council of Epaon. This impression is further enhanced by the bishops' desperate appeal to remain united in the face of ongoing royal retaliations. The bishops urged each other not to give in to any kind of power display, an encouragement which was perhaps also meant for their absent colleagues.[24] They warned that, if Sigismund refused to return to the bosom of the Church, they would all retreat into the confinement of a monastery of their choice.[25] The exact wording of this menace is important,

---

20. *Vita Apollinaris,* ed. Krusch, 198: 'Tunc rex dirae insaniae furore permotus beatissimos pontifices acerrime insidias praetentendo iniuriare non desinebat [...] Visum enim illis est, ut in oppido civitatis Lugdunensis, quod nuncupatur Sardinia, pariter tamquam exilio deputati auxiliante Deo comitarentur'.
21. *Vita Apollinaris,* ed. Krusch, 195. Cf. B. Krusch, 'La falsification des vies des saints burgondes', *Mélanges Julien Havet: Recueil de travaux d'érudition dédiés à la mémoire de Julien Havet (1853–1893)* (Paris: 1895), 51-5, here 53-4.
22. For references on this discussion, see: Mikat, *Inzestgesetzgebung*, 108, note 319; Favrod, *Histoire politique*, 426, note 58.
23. Gregory of Tours mentions no religious places at Savigny; M. Vieillard-Troiekouroff, *Les monuments religieux de la Gaule d'après les œuvres de Grégoire de Tours* (Paris: 1976). No further information is found in J. Moreau, *Dictionnaire de géographie historique de la Gaule et de la France*, Paris, 1972-1983, nor in B. Beaujard, P.A. Février and J.-C. Picard, *La topographie chrétienne des cités de la Gaule des origines au milieu du VIIIe siècle. 4: Province ecclésiastique de Lyon (Lugdunensis prima)*, Paris, 1986.
24. Lyon (518-523), c.1 (2), *Concilia Galliae*, ed. de Clercq, 39.
25. Lyon (518-523), c.1(3), *Concilia Galliae*, ed. de Clercq, 39: 'Quod si se rex praecellentissimus ab ecclesiae vel sacerdotum comunione ultra suspenderit, locum

since it reveals the bishops' main concern. Indeed, the non-compliance with incest law seems to have been only the indirect reason for the threat. The rather difficult wording '*si se rex ... ab ecclesiae vel sacerdotum comunione ultra suspenderit*', directed at Sigismund, is crucial to understand the bishops' motivations. As Cyrill Vogel pointed out in his typological study of Gallo-Roman and Merovingian excommunications, to be 'suspended from ecclesiastical Communion' was a frequently-used formula in canon law to denote an excommunication.[26] Sigismund's own disrespectful conduct, the bishops implied, had rendered him liable to religious exclusion as well. If the adverb *ultra* means 'further', as Gaudemet and Basdevant implied in their French translation of the Merovingian canons, an excommunication had already been issued and Sigismund was warned not to ignore his sentence any longer.[27] If the king still refused to return to the bosom of the Church, the bishops would retreat in a monastery of their choice.

However, no further comment is made concerning the king's possible excommunication in the *vita* or in the canons of Lyon. The already mentioned addendum attached to the canons of Lyon even cites the moderation of the sentence of Stephanus and Palladia 'in accordance with the king's opinion'.[28] Perhaps, though, Sigismund was merely cautioned not to render himself liable to an excommunication in the future. This would be in accordance with an alternative translation of *ultra* as 'subsequently/thereafter'.[29] If we accept the translation of Gaudemet and Basdevant, it seems that Sigismund refused to pay heed both to Stephanus's excommunication and to his own. If the king was merely threatened with

---

ei dantes ad sanctae matris gremium veniendi, sancti antistites se in monasteriis absque ulla dilatione, prout cuique fuerit oportunum [...] ita ut non unus quicunque prius de monasterio, in quo elegerit habitare, discedat, quam cunctis generaliter fratribus fuerit pax promissa vel reddita.'

26. C. Vogel, 'Les sanctions infligées aux laïcs et aux clercs par les conciles gallo-romains et mérovingiens', *Revue d'histoire canonique* 2 (1952), 5-29, 171-94, 311-28, esp. 314-5.
27. *Les canons des conciles Mérovingiens (VIe – VIIe siècles). Texte Latin de l'édition C. de Clercq, introduction, traduction et notes*, eds. J. Gaudemet and B. Basdevant (Sources Chrétiennes, 353), 2 vol. (Paris: 1989), I, 129: 'Et si le très excellent roi rompait plus longtemps avec la communion de l'Eglise et des évêques, que, tout en lui offrant la possibilité de revenir dans le sein de la Sainte Mère, les saints prélats se retirent sans aucun délai dans des monastères...'. The same translation of the adverb is given by Blaise in: 'Ultra', *Dictionnaire latin-français des auteurs chrétiens*, eds. A. Blaise and H. Chirat (Turnhout: 1954), 855.
28. Lyon (518-523), *Concilia Galliae*, ed. de Clercq, 41: 'regis sententia secuti'.
29. Both translations are offered in: 'Ultra', *Oxford Latin Dictionary*, V, ed. P.G.W. Glare (Oxford: 1976), 2086.

excommunication, we are left with the impression that the bishops expected the warning to add to the king's vexation. Indeed, this would ultimately explain why they issued their startling ultimatum to withdraw behind cloister walls, which was no doubt just as good a safety precaution against Sigismund's anticipated wrath. We do not know whether the threat was actually carried out, but the phrase in the *Vita Apollinaris*, saying that the remaining bishops were hiding out in Savigny '*tamquam exilio*', may indicate that it was. If so, the retreat to Savigny did not precede the council of Lyon, as was suggested above, but could have been a consequence of the episcopal measures taken during this meeting.

The threat of an episcopal strike – by withdrawing to a monastery – bears many resemblances to a penalty that would develop in the context of the peace councils at the start of the eleventh century: the interdict. An interdict could be pronounced against an individual, but often it entailed a collective religious ban, closing all churches in a certain area in order to pressure lay potentates into complying with Church decrees. It affected the innocent faithful as much as the actual culprits and, significantly, it compensated for the deficiencies of individual excommunications in the struggle for political power.[30] Some of the earliest sources for the development of the interdict are the sermons and council reports by the Aquitanian monk Ademar of Chabannes. Recent historiography has not been kind to Ademar as far as his credibility as a historian is concerned, but his description of the peace councils offers many reliable insights on Aquitanian society.[31] According to Ademar, the council of Limoges (1031) stated that 'a new medicine was necessary to fight the general disease': *decernere oportet medicinam quam contra generalem morbum adhibeatis.*[32]

---

30. H. Zapp, 'Interdikt', *Lexikon des Mittelalters*, V (Berlin: 1991), 466-7; E. Vodola, 'Interdict', *Dictionary of the Middle Ages*, VI (New York: 1985), 493-7; E. Jombart, 'Interdit', *Dictionnaire de droit canonique*, V (Paris: 1953), 1464-75.

31. M. Frasetto, 'The Art of Forgery: the Sermons of Ademar of Chabannes and the Cult of Saint-Martial of Limoges', *Comitatus, A Journal of Medieval and Renaissance Studies* 26 (1995), 1-15; R. Landes, *Relics, Apocalypse and the Deceits of History. Ademar of Chabannes 989–1034* (Harvard Historical Studies 117) (Cambridge MA and London: 1995). On Ademar and the peace councils: F. Callahan, 'Adémar de Chabannes et la paix de Dieu', *Annales du Midi* 89 (1977), 21-43; Idem, 'Adémar de Chabannes. Apocalyptism and the Peace Council of Limoges of 1031', *Revue Bénédictine*, 101 (1991), 32-49; R. Landes, 'Between Aristocracy and Heresy: Popular Participation in the Limousin Peace of God, 994–1033', *The Peace of God. Social Violence and Religious Response in France around the Year 1000*, eds. T. Head and R. Landes (Ithaca and London: 1992), 184-218.

32. Limoges (1031), *Sacrorum conciliorum nova et amplissima collectio*, 19, ed. J.D. Mansi (Paris: 1902, repr. Graz: 1960), 541.

Interestingly, the disease to which Ademar referred was a twofold one: first, the disrespect of the *principes militiae* for Church laws such as the peace agreements, and, more importantly, a blatant contempt for the excommunications which were fulminated to punish such disrespect.[33]

Admittedly, the bishops' strike, meant to force Sigismund to accept an ecclesiastical excommunication, could never have the same impact as a local interdict, as a result of which all religious services would be suspended. Nevertheless, the canons of Lyon made it clear that the bishops' intent was indeed to disrupt ecclesiastical rites as much as possible, much as an interdict would have done. Indeed, the second canon issued at the council, immediately following the episcopal threat to withdraw to a monastery, explicitly forbade clerics to celebrate Mass or perform ordinations in the absence of their bishop, even if this was deemed necessary by them.[34] While the canon did not specifically refer to the Sigismund conflict, there is no doubt that it was influenced by the affair. In sum, the quarrel about incest was quickly escalating into a fight over the Church's right to excommunicate lay potentates. First, Sigismund tried to rescind the exclusion of Stephanus and his wife, then he made light of the possibility that he himself might be excluded from the Church. As a consequence, the Burgundian bishops threatened to suspend religious services.

Avoiding Incest Law: Excommunication and Its Canonical Legitimation

According to the author of the *Vita Apollinaris*, the bishops were summoned to appear before Sigismund one by one, eventually putting an end to their

---

33. I hope to investigate this subject further in another paper. Since A.C. Howland's doctoral thesis, *The Interdict, its Rise and Development to the Pontificate of Alexander III* (unpublished doctoral thesis, University of Pennsylvania) (Philadelphia: 1897) little attention has been paid to the origins of the local interdict. See also Howland's article, 'The Origin of the Local Interdict', *Annual Report of the American Historical Association* 1 (1899), 429-48. The most recent bibliography on interdict is found in P.D. Clarke, *The Interdict in the Thirteenth Century, A Question of Collective Guilt*, Oxford, 2007. Also, while many aspects of Ademar's reliability as a historian have been examined, his opinions on excommunication and interdict have not yet been studied in detail.
34. Lyon (518-523), c. 2, *Concilia Galliae*, ed. de Clercq, 39-40: '...nec quisquam sub hac necessitate absentante episcopo in eius qui afuerit loco aut sacrificiorum aut ordinationum audeat ministeria caelibrare. Quod si in hac temeritate vel audacia quisque proruperit [...], comunioni fratrum futurum noverit alienum'.

resistance.[35] Only Apollinaris remained steadfast and ended up curing Sigismund from a life-threatening fever with which the king had been afflicted, by divine intervention. After his miraculous recovery, Sigismund humbly begged the bishop's forgiveness and obtained absolution.[36] A different story is given in the addendum which was signed by the majority of bishops attending the council of Lyon. According to this short and unfortunately undated text, a *temperamentum* or 'moderation' of the sentence was eventually granted. Also to be translated as 'a middle way', the *temperamentum* implies that a compromise between Church and king was eventually reached.[37] Stephanus and Palladia were once more allowed to attend Mass, on the sole condition of leaving church after the reading of the gospel. In other words, they could not partake in the Eucharist.[38] The assertion of Apollinaris's hagiographer that the bishop was the only one not to give in to Sigismund's pressure sounds implausible, since Apollinaris was one of those who signed the addendum. If there were still bishops who refused to observe the compromise, it must have been Florentius of Orange/Saint-Paul-Trois-Châteaux and Viventiolus of Lyon, who were present at the council of Lyon but whose names are conspicuously missing among the signatures at the end of the addendum.[39]

Most commentators have interpreted the compromise as proof of the Church's victory over lay politics. They believed that Stephanus and Palladia were forced to divorce and perform penance. In this view, the *temperamentum* is seen as a mitigation of public penance.[40] However, as Vogel pointed out, only one Merovingian council made penance obligatory to obtain absolution from excommunication.[41] In general, culprits do not seem to have been obliged to enter the *ordo paenitentium* in order to be readmitted to Communion.[42] Moreover, such an interpretation contradicts the content of the addendum itself, which merely stated that a moderation of

---

35. *Vita Apollinaris*, ed. Krusch, 190.
36. On the political motivations of the sixth-century hagiographer to present King Sigismund as a penitent, in order to promote his cult as a saint: Paxton, 'The Cult of St. Sigismund', 95-110, esp. 105.
37. 'Temperamentum', *Oxford Latin Dictionary*, V, ed. P.G.W. Glare (Oxford: 1976), 1912-3.
38. Lyon (518-523), *Concilia Galliae*, ed. de Clercq, 41.
39. Mikat, *Inzestgesetzgebung,* 113.
40. Lyon (518-523), *Concilia Galliae*, ed. de Clercq, 41, note by the editor: 'est mitigatio paenitentiae publicae cui Stephanus et Palladia ut incestuosi se submittere debeant'; Pontal, *Conciles mérovingiens*, 73; Wood, 'Incest', 299; Paxton, 'The Cult of St. Sigismund', 102.
41. Mâcon (581-583), c. 19, *Concilia Galliae*, ed. de Clercq, 228.
42. Vogel, 'Sanctions', 315-8.

the incestuous couple's punishment was granted; nowhere does the addendum mention a divorce, nor an explicit penance.[43]

The absence of the demand for penance was in accordance with canon law, as laid down in the canons of Epaon. This policy was probably influenced by Archbishop Avitus of Vienne, who played a prominent role in the organization of the council.[44] Leading up to the gathering, Avitus had been consulted by a colleague of his, Bishop Victorius of Grenoble, on a case of incest similar to that of Stephanus. It had come to the attention of Victorius that a nobleman, named Vincomalus, had been married for thirty years to his dead wife's sister.[45] Offering his advice in a letter to Victorius, Avitus had initially told him to excommunicate the couple until they separated. After performing public penance, they would be absolved from their sentence.[46] However, when Vincomalus strongly opposed his punishment, Avitus reconsidered, and he now wrote to his colleague that public penance – which at the time could only be performed once in a lifetime[47] – was 'advisable', but should not be forced upon the couple.[48] A divorce would suffice.

The bishops, gathered at Epaon, accepted Avitus's reconsideration, for they refrained from imposing penance for the sin of incest.[49] It therefore seems unlikely that the *temperamentum* entailed a moderation of public penance. Rather, it appears that the bishops offered Stephanus and Palladia a particular type of excommunication that was less severe than their original religious exclusion. Indeed, according to Vogel's terminological study,

---

43. Cf. Mikat, *Inzestgesetzgebung*, 112-13.
44. Wood, 'Incest', 297-8. On Epaon: P. Mikat, 'Die Inzestverbote des Konzils von Epaon. Ein Beitrag zur Geschichte des fränkischen Eherechts', *Rechtsbewahrung und Rechtsentwicklung. Festschrift für H. Lange*, ed. K. Kuchinke (Munich: 1970), 64-84.
45. Avitus, *Epistularum ad diversos libri tres. Liber primus*, Ep. 16, ed. R. Peiper, MGH Auctores ant. 6.2 (Berlin: 1883), 48.
46. Avitus, Ep. 17, ed. Peiper, 49.
47. C. Vogel, *La discipline pénitentielle en Gaule des origines à la fin du VIIe siècle* (Paris: 1952), 26-8, 112.
48. Avitus, Ep. 18, ed. Peiper, 49-50: '...sufficiat censurae vestrae separatio personarum. Scindatur infelix coniugium innocentiore divortio [...] De cetero autem, quod ad paenitentiam spectat, moneatur interim agere, accipere non cogatur.' Translation: '...let the fact that the two are separated be sufficient punishment in your eyes. Let the ill-omened marriage be broken by a more innocent divorce. As far as penance is concerned, let him be advised in the meantime to do it, but not be forced to accept it.' Avitus of Vienne, *Letters and Selected Prose*, ed. and transl. D. Shanzer and I.N. Wood (Translated Texts for Historians 38) (Liverpool: 2002), 290.
49. Epaon (517), c. 30, *Concilia Galliae*, ed. de Clercq, 31-32.

there were four types of excommunication. The most severe punishment entailed both religious and social exclusion. Three other types of excommunication were only partial prohibitions, allowing the punished to be present at some predefined religious gatherings or rites, while generally refusing them admission to Communion. The sinners, though, remained part of the social community.[50]

The type of excommunication pronounced against Stephanus and Palladia is not made explicit. In the *Vita Apollinaris* the couple is said to have been 'deprived of sacred Communion', without reference to any social prohibition.[51] The canons of Lyon are equally vague when restating the couple's initial '*damnatio*'.[52] However, the course of events does suggest that Stephanus and Palladia were punished with the severest form of excommunication. The addendum's 'middle way' offered by the bishops, resembles what Vogel classified as a 'eucharistic excommunication': a prohibition against taking Communion without additional social segregation. Indeed, the text stated that the couple could remain in church until the celebration of the Eucharist. It leads us to the supposition that they initially did receive a full, social excommunication, which was then 'tempered' and changed into a eucharistic exclusion.

It now becomes possible to comprehend fully King Sigismund's indignation upon hearing of Stephanus's excommunication. Stephanus was Sigismund's treasurer, mentioned in the *Vita Apollinaris* as 'the head of administration of all royal domains'.[53] Stephanus's exclusion from social and, hence, also political dealings would have effectively prevented him from fulfilling this important function. If Sigismund was unwilling to replace his treasurer – who might have been an important Gallo-Roman noble, considering his position – he had to find another solution.[54]

In view of this, Sigismund's fear that his administration would be crippled by Stephanus's full excommunication ultimately explains the king's forceful opposition. What is more, at the time of Stephanus's excommunication, there was not yet a sufficient canonical basis for this sentence. No Merovingian canon had proclaimed that incestuous bonds were to be punished with full religious and social exclusion. The first Frankish council in Orléans (511) simply prescribed 'ecclesiastical punishment' against those who were guilty of incest, without further

---

50. Vogel, 'Sanctions', 311-20.
51. *Vita Apollinaris*, ed. Krusch, 198: '...Stephanum sacra communione privari sanxerunt.'
52. Lyon (518-523), c.1 (1), *Concilia Galliae*, ed. de Clercq, 39.
53. *Vita Apollinaris,* ed. Krusch, 198: '...Stephanus, qui super omnem dominationem fisci principatum gerebat.'
54. On the discussion regarding Stephanus's origins: Wood, 'Incest', 300.

explanation.[55] At the next Merovingian council in Epaon (517), the first Burgundian council, the bishops were content to 'prohibit' incestuous marriages, again without further clarification.[56] The subsequent councils in Orléans (533) and Clermont (535) revealed a less ambiguous episcopal stance regarding the appropriate punishment.[57] In Orléans the biblical *anathema* or divine malediction was prescribed, while the council of Clermont was clear in imposing a fully-fledged social excommunication: the sinner was barred from Christian community (*a christianu coetu atque convivio...*) as well as from attending Mass (*...vel ecclesiae matris communione privabitur*).[58]

These canons do render it plausible that even before this case, excommunication had been considered as a punishment for incestuous practices. This is of course confirmed by Avitus's initial advice to Victorius of Grenoble to excommunicate the incestuous Vincomalus. However, the lack of canonical clarity on this matter until the councils of Orléans and Clermont in the 530s made it possible for King Sigismund to fight the sentence imposed upon his treasurer on canonical grounds. A complete annulment of the punishment inflicted upon the couple would have compromised the power of the Church, as well as that of Sigismund, since he himself had condemned this specific kind of incestuous bond in his *Liber Constitutionum*. Removing the social stain from the king's treasurer was an ideal way to settle the dispute. By mitigating the initial fully-fledged excommunication to a eucharistic exclusion, the Church conformed to the

---

55. Orléans (511), c. 18, *Concilia Galliae*, ed. de Clercq, 9-10: '...si fecerint, ecclesiastica districtione feriantur'.
56. Epaon (517), c. 30, *Concilia Galliae*, ed. de Clercq, 31-2: 'Quod ut a presenti tempore prohibemus...'.
57. Orléans (533), c. 10; Clermont (535), c. 12, *Concilia Galliae*, ed. de Clercq, 100, 107-8.
58. On the Latin terminology of a full social excommunication, see Vogel, 'Sanctions', 313-4. The difference between *excommunicatio* and *anathema* remains problematic, evidently because a clear distinction was unknown, even during the Middle Ages. In general, it seems as if an *anathema* implied the same consequences for the afterlife as a full excommunication (later called an *excommunicatio maior*). Still, due to its biblical sound, the *anathema* may have been a way of instilling additional fear in the hearts of the condemned. Cf. P. Hinschius, *System des katholischen Kirchenrechts, mit besonderer Rücksicht auf Deutschland*, IV (Berlin: 1888-1893, reprint Graz: 1959), 691-864, here 800, note 6; J. Gaudemet, 'Note sur l'excommunication', *Cristianesimo nella storia. Ricerche storiche* 16 (1995), 285-306, here 298. Little, *Benedictine Maledictions*, 30-51; K. Hein, *Eucharist and Excommunication: A Study in Early Christian Doctrine and Discipline* (Europäische Hochschulschriften, Reihe 23,19), 2nd edn. (Bern: 1975), 4-5.

king's wishes (*regis sententia secuti*) without having to rescind the excommunication. As such, the variable nature of excommunication was used as a means of conflict resolution in an area where canon law had yet to come into its own.[59] However, the conflict also reveals that obedient observation of the penalty was never a given.

The Stephanus Case in Perspective: Understanding Incest Conflicts in the Sixth Century

The Stephanus case is an example of an incest conflict turning into a political fight over the Church's power to excommunicate lay potentates. Other sixth-century incest conflicts might be interpreted accordingly. For instance, it has been stated that the reaction of Gregory of Tours (538–594) with regard to violations of the incest laws, were in no way consistent.[60] His views on the subject are definitely hard to pin down. However, behind his seeming undecidedness, one might distinguish the desire to support episcopal authority, whether the bishop in question chose to condone or to condemn incestuous bonds. For example, when the Neustrian King Chilperic I (561–584) rightfully accused one of his bishops, Praetextatus of Rouen, of having consecrated the incestuous marriage between Chilperic's son Merovech and the latter's aunt Brunhild, the rival queen of Austrasia,

---

59. On (early) medieval conflict resolution in general, see, among others, W. Davies and P. Fouracre, eds., *The Settlement of Disputes in Early Medieval Europe* (Cambridge: 1986); P.J. Geary, 'Living with Conflicts in Stateless France: A Typology of Conflict Management Mechanisms, 1050-1200', *Living with the Dead in the Middle Ages* (Ithaca: 1994), 125-60; S.D. White, *Feuding and Peace-Making in Eleventh-Century France* (Variorum Collected Studies Series 817) (Aldershot: 2005); W.C. Brown and P. Górecki, eds., *Conflict in Medieval Europe: Changing Perspectives on Society and Culture* (Aldershot: 2003); A.-J. Bijsterveld, ed., *Negotiating Secular and Ecclesiastical Power: Western Europe in the Central Middle Ages* (International Medieval Research 6) (Turnhout: 1999); Idem, *Do ut des: Gift giving, Memoria, and Conflict Management in the Medieval Low Countries* (Middeleeuwse studies en bronnen 104) (Hilversum: 2007); as well as some articles on the political ramifications of exclusion, exile and excommunication in: L. Napran and E. Van Houts, eds., *Exile in the Middle Ages. Selected Proceedings from the International Medieval Congress, University of Leeds, 8-11 July 2002* (Turnhout: 2004).
60. D. Shanzer, 'History, Romance, Love, and Sex in Gregory of Tours', *Decem libri historiarum*', *The World of Gregory of Tours*, eds. K. Mitchell and I.N. Wood (Cultures, Beliefs and Traditions: Medieval and Early Modern People 8) (Leiden: 2002), 395-418, here 406-8.

Gregory took the side of Praetextatus.[61] Gregory's opinion is not surprising, considering the fact that he received his bishopric from the hands of Brunhild and her husband Sigebert I (561–575), who was murdered by Chilperic's men.[62] Gregory wanted to support Praetextatus against Chilperic's accusations, notwithstanding the bishop's complicity in a clearly incestuous marriage. He was staggered when Chilperic organized a council in Paris (577), during which the latter tried to usurp the episcopal privilege to excommunicate Praetextatus.[63] After obtaining a forced confession from Praetextatus, who suddenly admitted his desire to murder the king, Chilperic produced a book of law in which it was stated that any bishop who was guilty of murder, adultery or perjury had to be excommunicated, as well as deposed.[64]

The canon in question is thought to have come from the *Collectio Dionysiana,* a collection of canons by Dionysius Exiguus, composed during the first half of the sixth century. The collection was well known and might have contained the text to which Chilperic referred.[65] However, the king seems to have wilfully misinterpreted an important part of the canon, where it is stated that the sinful bishop was to be deposed, but not excommunicated – *non tamen communione privetur*![66] So it would seem that Chilperic either adapted the rule from the collection to turn it to his own political advantage, or that he made up the canon altogether. Indeed, according to Gregory, Chilperic went against various articles of canon law regarding the deposition and excommunication of clerics. But then, Gregory

---

61. *Historiarum libri X,* eds. W. Levison and B. Krusch, MGH Scriptores rer. Merov. 1.1 (Hannover: 1937), V/18, 217-23; VII/16, 337-8. C. Urso, 'Per una storia dei rapporti tra Stato e Chiesa nella Gallia merovingia. Il processo a Pretestato, vescovo di Rouen', *Vetera Christianorum* 30 (1993), 289-306.
62. I.N. Wood, 'The Individuality of Gregory of Tours', *The World of Gregory of Tours,* eds. K. Mitchell and I. Wood (Cultures, Beliefs and Traditions: Medieval and Early Modern People 8) (Leiden: 2002), 29-46.
63. Pontal, *Conciles mérovingiens,* 173-4. Cf. M. de Jong, 'Gregorius, Praetextatus en Chilperik. Over de reputatie van een slechte vorst', *Utrechtse historische cahiers* 22 (2001), 82-96, here 89-91.
64. *Historiarum libri X,* eds. Levison and Krusch, V/18, 223: 'Episcopus in homicidio, adulterio et periurio depraehensus, a sacerdotio divillatur'.
65. *Historiarum libri X,* eds. Levison and Krusch, V/18, 223 (notes 1, 3). Cf. F. Maassen, *Geschichte der Quellen und der Literatur des canonischen Rechts im Abendlande bis zum Ausgange des Mittelalters,* I (Graz: 1870), 421 (note 2), 439.
66. *Canones qui dicuntur apostolorum collectionis Dionysianae,* c. 25, ed. C.H. Turner, Ecclesiae occidentalis monumenta iuris antiquissima et conciliorum Graecorum interpretationes Latinae. Opus posthumum, I/1 (Oxford: 1939), 18: 'Episcopus aut presbiter aut diaconus, qui in fornicatione aut periurio aut furto captus est, deponatur, non tamen communione privetur'.

himself was not adhering to the exact letter of the law either. At no point did he confront Praetextatus with his complicity in this case, nor did he explicitly rebuke Brunhild and Merovech for their incestuous relationship. His main concern was the violation of episcopal authority in general, and the infringement on the *privilegium excommunicandi* in particular.

Gregory did, however, praise Nicetius of Trier when the latter reprimanded king Theudebert I (533–548) for tolerating incest among his courtiers.[67] It would seem that this time, at least, the bishop did intend to enforce the incest laws. However, Gregory was actually more concerned with guaranteeing the effectiveness of the sentence of excommunication. Indeed, King Theudebert allowed his companions to attend the bishop's Mass, despite their excommunication by Nicetius. This evident flouting of the latter's authority was what really troubled Gregory, who for the rest paid little attention to Theudebert's indulgence with regard to incest.[68] A preliminary note to the story, added by Gregory, removes all doubt: the bishop of Tours wanted to offer his readers some words to show his support for a sacerdotal excommunication, be it to instruct the people or to amend the ways of their king (*ad roborandam censuram sacerdotum*).[69] Gregory must have realized to what extent the impact of the incest regulations – and Church law in general – depended on the efficiency of the excommunication.

The loopholes in canon law may have provoked a modest attempt to 'judicialize' excommunication – a term to denote the growing set of rules for the procedure of excommunication. The term has been applied by Sarah Hamilton and Richard Helmholz to explain an emerging tendency to combat careless excommunications, which were issued almost as a curse, without proper trial. Helmholz investigated the origins of this process for twelfth-century England; Hamilton found earlier traces of the phenomenon concerning England as well as the Continent from the tenth century onwards.[70] An analysis of the Merovingian canons of the sixth and seventh centuries pushes these origins even further back in time. With the power to excommunicate also came the risk of abuse. Soon, bishops began to warn

---

67. *Vita Nicetii*, ed. B. Krusch, MGH Scriptores rer. Merov. 1.2, 727-33.
68. Cf. K. Uhalde, 'Proof and Reproof: the Judicial Component of Episcopal Confrontation', *Early Medieval Europe*, 8 (1999), 1-11, here 9-10.
69. *Vita Nicetii*, ed. Krusch, 729: 'Quibus de causis pauca loqui placet ad roborandam sacerdotum censuram vel ad instructionem populi sive etiam ad ipsorum regum praesentium emendationem.'
70. R.H. Helmholz, 'Excommunication and the Angevin Leap Forward', *Haskins Society Journal* 7 (1995), 133-49. S. Hamilton stated her conclusion during a lecture titled *Curse or Procedure? Excommunication in Practice, 900-1050* at the *International Medieval Congress* of 2007.

Canonical Legislation on Incest and Excommunication

each other not to impose the sentence lightly. At the council of Orléans (549) only those crimes prescribed by the Church Fathers were thought deserving of excommunication. Religious exclusions following small and light offences were strongly discouraged.[71] The warning must have had little effect since it had to be repeated at the council of Clichy (626-627): 'A bishop should not excommunicate someone rashly!'.[72] To fight such abuse, the procedure of excommunication was better delineated. The council of Tours (567) was the first to give detailed instructions concerning this matter. The council stipulated that a sentence had to be preceded by three warnings. Only if the third admonition – in writing – failed to elicit the desired effect, should the bishops assemble to fulminate an excommunication. Next, the sentence had to be proclaimed with the full consensus of the bishops, abbots and priests of the province, although it is not clear whether this process was prescribed for full excommunications as well as for mere eucharistic exclusions. Finally, the perpetrator was excommunicated and denied all social contact, but absolution was never to be refused in case of penitence.[73] At several councils it was added that an excommunication could not be canonically absolved without the permission of the bishop who had issued the sentence.[74]

Obviously, a process consisting of three written admonitions which preceded a unanimously proclaimed sentence was meant to prevent thoughtless excommunications. These stipulations must also have served to throw clarity on the sentence's regulations, thus improving its efficiency. Ironically though, it seems plausible that the complex procedure made it easier to postpone a sentence. The process of judicialization may therefore

---

71. Orléans (549), c. 2, *Concilia Galliae*, ed. de Clercq, 149: 'Ut nullus sacerdotum quemquam rectae fidei hominem pro parvis et levibus causis a communione suspendat, praeter eas culpas, pro quibus antiqui patres ab ecclesia arciri iusserunt committentes.' The Church Fathers could rely on 1 Cor. 5.11, in which Paul demanded social exclusion in case of sexual crimes, selfishness, idolatry, intoxication, gossip and robbery: 'si is qui frater nominatur, est fornicator, aut avarus, aut idolis serviens, aut maledicus, aut ebriosus, aut rapax, cum eiusmodi nec cibum sumere'.
72. Clichy (626-627), c.6, *Concilia Galliae*, ed. de Clercq, 292: 'Episcopus non temere quemquam excommunicare debet'.
73. Tours (567), c. 25, *Concilia Galliae*, ed. de Clercq, 192-3. The canon was aimed at those who usurped Church property, but the different steps of the admonition process would become the standard for (full) excommunications. Cf. Reynolds, 'Rites of Separation', 405-33.
74. Paris (556-573), c. 7; Lyon (567-570), c. 4; Auxerre (561-605), c. 39, *Concilia Galliae*, ed. de Clercq, 202, 208, 269: 'Si quis presbyter aut quilibet de clero aut de populo excommunicatum absque voluntate ipsius, qui eum excommunicavit, sciens receperit [...] simile sententia subiacebit.'

have been detrimental to the impact of excommunications in general and to incest laws in particular. Admittedly, the lack of sources makes it difficult to substantiate such a supposition. Nevertheless, two stories in Gregory of Tours's *Historia Francorum* do offer some confirmation.

Eulalius, count of Clermont, avoided his excommunication on the ground that he had not been tried and thus could not be excluded from Communion. Eulalius had been accused of having murdered his mother and had subsequently been excommunicated by Bishop Cautinus of Clermont (†571). However, Eulalius' claim that proper canonical procedure had been disregarded forced Cautinus to give in. He lifted the excommunication and allowed Eulalius to take part in Mass once more. Apparently, the evidence held by Cautinus was insufficient to bring the count before an assembly of bishops. Forced to admit defeat, he warned Eulalius that God would surely know if he took Communion while being stained with the sin of matricide.[75]

Following Merovech's illicit marriage to his aunt Brunhild, King Chilperic I had forced his son to withdraw behind cloister walls. Merovech, however, managed to escape and sought asylum in the church of Saint Martin of Tours. There, he asked Gregory for permission to receive Communion. Even though Gregory had supported Praetextatus of Rouen for celebrating Merovech's marriage to Brunhild, he nevertheless hesitated to grant Merovech's wish. However, Merovech was well-informed about the laws on excommunication procedure (the rules on incest having apparently slipped his mind when he contracted his marriage). Promptly, he reminded Gregory of the same rule to which Eulalius had successfully referred to avoid his penalty. Indeed, Merovech could not be excommunicated without the consent of Gregory's colleagues, given during a proper trial. Strangely enough, Gregory seems to have been less familiar with correct procedure, since he found it necessary to consult the relevant passages of canon law with regard to Merovech's assertion. In the end, however, Merovech got what he wanted. Gregory conceded and administered the Eucharist, and afterwards never again took the trouble to initiate the lengthy process of excommunication, effectively dropping the case altogether.[76] Hence the attempt to judicialize excommunication may have complicated the implementation of incest laws altogether.

At the end of the sixth century, Church and king embarked upon a joint effort to enforce incest law.[77] In 585 King Guntram called for judicial cooperation between the spiritual and secular authorities. To uphold justice and equity, Guntram promised to intervene in those cases where offenders

---

75. *Historiarum libri X*, eds. Levison and Krusch, X/8, 489.
76. Ibidem, V/14, 207-8.
77. Mikat, *Inzestgesetzgebung*, 133-9.

could not be corrected by episcopal penalties.[78] Eleven years later, Childebert II issued a similar decree. Childebert first listed those bonds that were deemed incestuous, and recommended such infractions to the bishop's judgment. The king then added: 'May he who shall not obey his bishop and shall hence be excommunicated, incur God's perennial condemnation and be entirely banned from our palace. May all his possessions be transferred onto his relatives if he does not accept the medicines of his bishop.'[79] The same instruction was repeated at the council of Clichy (626/27), at the request of King Clothar II.[80] At Clichy, Merovingian incest legislation came to completion. The early stages of its history had been marked by a conflict over the Church's demand for secular support for excommunications. Eventually, such an endorsement was indeed offered – at least theoretically.

Conclusion

When reading the œuvre of Gregory of Tours in combination with the legislative texts from sixth-century Merovingian councils, we gain the distinct impression that excommunication could not easily be enforced against members of the lay aristocracy. Ironically, an attempt to improve the efficacy of the sentence by judicializing its procedure probably only added to this difficulty. Presumably, such judicialization eroded the impact of excommunication, since it became harder to enforce without a proper trial. Frequent canonical prohibitions on absolving an excommunication without permission of the responsible bishop attest to the difficult enforcement of excommunications. This might explain why Gregory felt the need to

---

78. *Guntchramni regis edictum*, ed. A. Boretius, MGH Capit. 1 (Hannover: 1883), 12: 'Convenit ergo, ut, iustitiae et aequitatis in omnibus vigore servato, distringat legalis ultio iudicum quos non corrigit canonica praedicatio sacerdotum'.
79. *Childeberti secundi decretio,* ed. A. Boretius, MGH, Capit. 1 (Hannover: 1883), 15: 'De praeteritis vero coniunctionibus, quae incestae esse videntur, per praedicationem episcoporum iussimus emendare. Qui vero episcopo suo noluerit audire et excommunicatus fuerit, perenni condemnatione apud Deum sustineat et de palatio nostro sit omnino extraneus, et omnes res suas parentibus legitimis amittat qui noluit sacerdotis sui medicamenta sustinere' (my translation). Augustine, basing himself on Scripture, defined an excommunication as a medicine for the sinful soul: 'haec prohibitio nondum sit mortalis, sed medicinalis'. Augustine, *Sermo CCCLI, De utilitate agendae poenitentiae,* c. 4, 10, ed. J.-P. Migne, Patrologia Latina 39 (Paris: 1841), 1546. Cf. F. Keygnaert, 'Van medicijn tot wapen in de strijd om het kerkbezit. De canonieke ontwikkeling van excommunicatie in de Merovingische concilies (511–ca. 675)', *Millennium. Tijdschrift voor middeleeuwse studies* 22 (2008), 3-22, here 7-9.
80. Clichy (626-627), c. 10, *Concilia Galliae,* ed. de Clercq, 293.

promote this ecclesiastical censure among the powerful: *ad roborandam censuram sacerdotum*.

Indeed, the successful implementation of Church law may have depended on the efficiency of the main ecclesiastical weapon to punish transgressions against that law. Seen in this light, it might be necessary to reconsider some conflicts which initially seemed merely to concern incest law. A dispute between the Burgundian King Sigismund and his bishops at the beginning of the sixth century illustrates this. The quarrel involved Sigismund's treasurer, Stephanus, who had contracted an incestuous marriage to Palladia, sister of his dead wife. The Burgundian bishops realized the importance of the laity respecting the Church's main weapon. The king, on the other hand, could not afford his treasurer to be excommunicated religiously *and* socially. When Sigismund refused to accept the ecclesiastical sentence, the bishops threatened to disturb daily rites – a forerunner of the local interdict. In reaction, Sigismund took advantage of the loopholes in the incest laws, which were inconclusive about the appropriate penalty for transgressions. As a result, a compromise was reached, through which Stephanus and Palladia probably incurred a eucharistic excommunication, which, however, did not exclude them from all social contact.

At the end of the sixth century, enforcing incest law became less dependent upon the Church's ability to impose an effective excommunication. The Church profited from the kings' desire for stability and unity, receiving royal support to put ecclesiastical penalties into effect. Cooperation between secular and religious jurisdiction improved and would continue to do so in the Carolingian period. Still, throughout the Middle Ages, secular authorities would continue to perform a balancing act, trying to shore up the penalty of excommunication without turning it into too powerful a weapon in the hands of the Church.

PRIVATES ON PARADE: IMPOTENCE CASES AS EVIDENCE FOR MEDIEVAL GENDER

Frederik Pedersen

Introduction

When Tedia Lambhird brought a case before the consistory court in York in 1370 to have her marriage to John Sanderson dissolved because of his impotence, the witness Thomas Stephenson told the court that he had been present three years previously in a barn belonging to John Sanderson, senior, where he saw Tedia Lambhird and John Sanderson, junior, attempting intercourse.[1] He got a good look in, for he tells the court that he saw John's member *'submissam et nullo modo se erigentem'*. 'Bizarrely', a modern commentator exclaims, 'we are then told that John's brother felt his penis'.[2] This remark can be criticised for two things. Firstly, I translate *palpare* as 'stroke', not 'feel'. This is the translation given by most standard Latin Dictionaries.[3] Taken together with its associated adverb ('bizarrely')

---

1. Thomas, filius Stephani (York: Borthwick Institute of Historical Research Cause Papers E-series 105, 1370 (henceforth: CP E 105)
2. P.J.P. Goldberg, 'John Skathelok's Dick: Voyeurism and 'Pornography' in Late Medieval England', in *Medieval Obscenities. Papers presented at a seminar series at the University of York's Centre for Medieval Studies, from January to December 2001*, ed. Nicola McDonald (Woodbridge, UK and Rochester, NY: York Medieval, 2006), 107. Goldberg is referring to the deposition of Thomas Stephenson, who is the only witness to testify about this event: *'vidit fratrem carnalis ipsius Johannis, de quo agitur, palpare ibidem virgam Johannis predictam'*: CP E 105 (1370)
3. To stroke, to touch softly, to pat, caress, coax, wheedle, flatter. Charlton T. Lewis, *A Latin Dictionary Founded on Andrews' Edition of Freund's Latin Dictionary*

this sentence conveys the unsettling picture of an incestuous homo-erotic encounter, a suggestion at which I think John Sanderson's brother would loudly protest. Secondly, the analysis omits the equally 'bizarre' incident on 29 November 1370 when one of the matrons appointed by the court to investigate Sanderson's erectile dysfunction deposited John Sanderson's penis in semen.[4] Taken separately, these events may appear baffling and the omission of the second event invites the reader to interpret the event as a possible homo-erotic encounter.

However, we should consider the possibility that the two events could have been intended to cure John Sanderson, a task we shall see would not have been possible given the state of corrective surgery at the time. In addition, similar events are to be found in other cases: his brother stroked John Sanderson's penis to help him achieve an erection in the same manner Robert Lyncoln did in an impotence case half a century later,[5] and the matron with the bowl of semen was undoubtedly trying to help the impotent John Sanderson in the best way she knew: by joining John Sanderson's non-functional penis to the effluent of one that did work, she expected to see John Sanderson improve in 'virile work'. Her actions are one example of a folk medicine that is no longer practised and is certainly no more incomprehensible than the fact that the sole investigation of a woman found among the York Cause Papers focussed not on whether the woman's hymen had ruptured, but on describing visual aspects of her breasts.

Both these events should be contextualised in their own time, in order to be de-sexualised and moved into a more clinical, and, I think, ultimately more comprehensible, context. Indeed, I shall argue later in this paper that John Sanderson suffered from a recognisable congenital defect, and that the court transcripts in York contains the earliest identifiable clinical description of a second-degree anterior *hypospadias* combined with *cryptorchidism*, or undescended testes.

Impotence in Church Courts: a Question of Male or Female Dysfunction?

I have argued elsewhere that the church courts functioned well and provided sensible solutions to marital disputes.[6] Their main concern was to make sure

---

Revised, Enlarged, and in Great Part Rewritten, in collaboration with Charles Short (Oxford: 1987), s.v. *palpo*.
4. A full transcription of the relevant witness accounts are given in note 22 below.
5. CP F 175, 1430. There are several witnesses, but the one I am particularly referring to is Robert Lyncoln.
6. Frederik Pedersen, *Marriage Disputes in Medieval England* (London: 2000).

that the outcomes of marriage disputes could be said to be equitable. This is especially true in the delicate matter of impotence. In its approach to this problem the law took in at least the part that 'there is neither male nor female' from Paul's letter to the Galatians and applied this principle to marriage disputes.[7] Impotence in the sense employed by canon law does not distinguish between male and female, and neither did the courts. Gender historians have correctly identified the fact that although sexual dysfunction can affect both men and women, all the surviving court cases focus on proving male sexual dysfunction.[8]

I have only come across one case in which a physical examination was made of the woman, the investigation aimed to establish whether she was still a virgin. The court wished to establish the likelihood of her husband's sexual dysfunction, not to establish if *she* was capable of intercourse. In contrast to modern methods the investigation focussed not on whether the woman's hymen had ruptured, but rather described visual aspects of her breasts, in particular the nipples, through which 'it is said and believed among women that virginity can most truly be proven'. Thus the depositions in this case about the woman's virginity seem to have been based on a particular superstition (which the witness implies may be local to York) that the disappearance of *le kirnell* in a woman's breasts indicated her loss of virginity.[9]

---

7. Galatians 3:28.
8. Compare James A. Brundage, *Law, Sex, and Christian Society in Medieval Europe* (Chicago: 1987), 290–92 and two articles by the same author: 'The Problem of Impotence', in *Sexual Practices and the Medieval Church*, ed. Vern L. Bullough and James Brundage (Buffalo, New York: 1982), 135–40 and 'Impotence, Frigidity and Marital Nullity in the Decretists and Early Decretalists', in *Proceedings of the Seventh International Congress of Medieval Canon Law, Cambridge 23–27 July 1984*, ed. Peter Linehan (Citta del Vaticano: 1988), 407–23 See also R. H. Helmholz, *Marriage Litigation in Medieval England*, Cambridge Studies in English Legal History (Cambridge: 1974) and Charles Donahue Jr., *Law, Marriage and Society in the Later Middle Ages: Arguments About Marriage in Five Courts* (Cambridge: 2008). The latter must always be consulted in tandem with Charles Donahue Jr. 'Texts & Commentary', in *Law, Marriage and Society in the Later Middle Ages* (Cambridge: 2008), http://www.cambridge.org/resources/0521877288/5363_9780521877282tc_pc673–976.pdf, which is not included in the printed book and only available on the Internet or as part of the electronic version of the book.
9. CP F 175, *Joan, uxor Roberti Ireby*: 'dicit quod aliud signum in huiusmodi mamillis existens, *le kirnell* vulgariter nuncupatam, per quod signum inter mulieres communiter dicitur et reputatur virginitas potest verissime probari, fuit molle fractum ac in plures percellas seperatum quod si dicta Katherina virgo stetisset durum, firmum et integrum fuisset'. Qtd. from Bronagh Kane, *Impotence and*

Modern historians have interpreted impotence cases as an expression of a gender bias by the courts, but I am convinced that gender has little to do with legal practice in the medieval church courts. Not only were the courts in their legal practice only concerned with the proper functioning of the *conjugal unit* (and for that reason they make little reference to gender), but the litigants and the witnesses showed the same disregard for *gender* as a category. In addition, in its analyses of the impediments to marriage the canon law refers to the *impotentia coeundi* or the *frigiditas* of the parties. This phrase refers equally to men and women, and in theory women were equally likely to find themselves be the defendants in suits for annulment for impotence. However, focusing on the man and his ability to have an erection was the easiest way to argue the likelihood that the marriage was going to be consummated and by implication whether any offspring was legitimate and able to succeed to estates and property. Such an approach also allowed for fewer problems of interpretation: an erection is, after all, an erection.

Turning our attention to the laity and its legal sophistication, the evidence shows that witnesses – lay or clerical – had a sound knowledge of procedure and actively participated in the legal process: male witnesses in one case from 1430 (CP F 175), challenged the conduct of the investigation of the defendant's erectile function. They expressed their concerns about the procedure, in particular over the way in which the investigation had been conducted – the matrons appointed for the task of investigating the man's erectile function had insisted on the man denuding himself in the cold upper room of a public house in the middle of January before roughly handling his genitals with cold hands.

The Legal Procedure in Cases of Impotence According to Canon Law

Canon law distinguished between two kinds of impotence; permanent and temporary. *Permanent impotence* was caused by a congenital incapacity for sex. In order for this to be a reason for annulment of marriage the condition had to have been concealed from the contracting party. In the early period of classical canon law, Pope Alexander III (1159–1181) had also allowed a marriage to be dissolved on the grounds of *temporary impotence* (which was generally supposed to have been caused by sorcery), a practice that was discontinued by Pope Innocent III (1198–1216), possibly as a consequence

---

Virginity in the Late Medieval Ecclesiastical Court of York, No. 114, Borthwick Paper (York: 2008), 37.

of his encounter with this argument in his confrontation with Philip II of France over his consort, Ingeborg of Denmark.[10]

In their discussions of the problem the decretalists insisted on three methods of proof, all three of which were necessary to gain an annulment: a physical examination of the parties, the sworn testimony of witnesses and the evidence of three years of cohabitation.[11] How these procedural rules were implemented in practice seems to have been subject to significant variation in individual courts. In the most comprehensive survey of legal procedure in marriage cases over several jurisdictions, Charles Donahue lists only two cases from Paris.[12] The Parisian courts dealt most effectively with these two cases of male impotence and seem to have followed the canon law more literally than the English courts. In one case the court passed sentence based on the evidence of two doctors, the sworn testimony of the wife, and the oaths of six men who swore that they believed the testimony of the wife and that they had no knowledge of the man having intercourse with another woman. In the other case, both the man and the woman swore to the impotence and their statement was substantiated by a master of medicine, a surgeon and the oaths of five men.[13]

The practice of the English courts called for the participation of more 'experts'. Although there is some slight variation in the material left to us from the York consistory court (which will be commented on below), they generally involved a physical examination of the man's erectile function by different numbers of 'honest women', who attempted to stimulate the impotent man, often, but not always, by baring their breasts and by kissing

---

10. Robert Davidsohn, *Philipp II. August von Frankreich und Ingeborg* (Stuttgart: 1888); Helene Tillmann, *Papst Innocenz III*, Bonner historische Forschungen, vol. 3 (Bonn: 1954); Georges Duby, *Medieval Marriage: Two Models from Twelfth-Century France*, trans. Elborg Forster, foreword by John Baldwin, The Johns Hopkins Symposia in Comparative History, vol. 11 (Baltimore: 978); Jean Gaudemet, 'Le dossier canonique du mariage de Philippe Auguste et d'Ingeburge de Denmark (1193–1213)', *Revue historique de droit français et étranger* 62, no. 1 (1984): 15; John W. Baldwin, 'La vie sexuelle de Philippe Auguste', in *Mariage et sexualité au moyen age: Accord ou crise?* ed. Michel Rouche (Paris: 2000), 217–29; Frederik Pedersen, 'The Danes and the Marriage Break-up of Philip II of France', in *Adventures of the Law*, Proceedings of the Sixteenth British Legal History Conference, Dublin, 2003, ed. Paul Brand, Kevin Costello, and W. N. Osborough (Dublin: 2005), 54–69.
11. Physical examination X 4.15.1; three years and witnesses: X 4.15.7.
12. Donahue, *Law, Marriage and Society*, 145, 277–78 and 295–96.
13. Donahue, *Law, Marriage and Society*, 371. Texts are transcribed in Donahue, 'Texts & Commentary', no. 738–39.

and fondling the man.[14] Despite the reservations one might have about the heavy-handed approach of the English church courts, only in one fifteenth-century case did the man under investigation 'pass' such an examination, a failure (or should that be 'success') rate of one-sixth.[15] This leaves five impotence cases from the court in York in which male defendants unsuccessfully submitted to the court's investigation. In at least three of these remaining cases, the man had an identifiable genital malfunction that would have made it impossible for him to have intercourse. Indeed, in one of these cases I shall present evidence that the person in question suffered under a congenital condition of ambiguous gender. Thus, although there is some slight difference across Europe in the way the physical evidence was gathered, European church courts seem to have applied the required standards of proof. However, the courts encountered the problem only rarely: the dossiers of only six pre-Reformation cases survive from the consistory court in York (making up only three per cent of the total record of marriage cases), two have been identified among the diocesan archives in Canterbury and another two are found in the episcopal court act book in Ely. The rules of canon law – which made it impossible for the impotent partner to remarry[16] and demanded that he or she return to the spouse if the dysfunction should disappear – would create a deterrent from bringing this kind of suit without good cause.[17] It is clear that these cases were few in number and that the accusation of impotence was rarely made frivolously.

---

14. On the practice of the English courts in impotence cases, see Helmholz, *Marriage Litigation*, 87–90; Jacqueline Murray, 'Trial by Congress', *The Lawyers Weekly* 6, no. 44 (20 March 1987): 20–21, 31; Jacqueline Murray, 'On the Origins and Role of "Wise Women" in Causes for Annulment on the Grounds of Male Impotence', *Journal of Medieval History* 16, no. 3 (1990): 235–49; Pedersen, *Marriage Disputes*, 30, 88, 115–20, 136–37, 145–48, 190, 208; Goldberg, 'John Skathelok's Dick: Voyeurism and "Pornography" in Late Medieval England'; Kane, *Impotence and Virginity*; Derek G. Neal, *The Masculine Self in Late Medieval England* (Chicago: 2008).
15. CPF 175 (Barley c. Barton, 1433-34). Donahue does not investigate the witness accounts in CPF 224 (Gilbert c. Marche, 1441). CPF 40 alleges impotence but has no surviving witness accounts: Donahue, 'Texts & Commentary', 718. Canterbury Sede Vacante S.B. III no. 127 (1292) Canterbury Cathedral archives, Y1.1, f. 70r. Cambridge University Library, Ely Diocesan Records, D/2/1, ff. 100-154 (passim). Kane, *Impotence and Virginity*, 8.
16. X 4.15.2.
17. X 4.15.1.

The Courts and Impotence in Practice

The rest of this paper will analyse two fourteenth-century cases from York. These deal with genuine and identifiable genital malformations. In both cases, the wife alleged that her husband was not endowed with adequate genitals for the performance of intercourse, and in both cases the marriage was annulled by the court in York.[18] Though the plea was the same, the method of proof differed in the two cases: one man was exposed to a physical examination, the other resisted such a procedure and the court passed sentence without it. This difference in treatment was most likely a reflection of the difference in social standing and political power of the defendants. One case came from the lower gentry or indeed peasantry, while the other involved a young person who, had their life progressed normally, would have become a major player in English politics. Both cases were heard by the York court in the short period 1368–1370 and though they do tell us something about gender in fourteenth-century Yorkshire they are so unusual that in terms of gender as a category they cannot illuminate anything beyond very broad and platitudinous statements about maleness or masculine self-awareness, and, as we shall see, one of the defendants may not genetically have been a man at all. If similar defects were proven in the other pleas for annulment heard by the medieval courts in England – and all the evidence points to this – it is safe to say that even the somewhat heavy-handed English procedure served its purpose. It is unlikely that a false claim would be brought given the public nature of the legal proceedings.

Impotence Case: CP E 159

We mentioned the case between Tedia Lambhird and John Sanderson above, Tedia Lambhird, the wife of John Sanderson, junior, petitioned the court in York in June 1370, to have their marriage dissolved on the grounds of John's impotence. The couple had previously cohabited for four years, after which time Tedia moved to live apart from John. This informal separation came to the attention of the Dean of Holderness, Thomas of Saint Martin, who summoned the couple and ordered them to resume cohabitation. They did so for an unspecified length of time, but since January 1370 they had lived in separate households.

---

18. CP E 105, 259. I have previously commented on the medical aspects of these cases, but this paper presents a more fully argued case for my diagnoses. Cf. Frederik Pedersen, 'Middelalderens arkiver', *Ugeskrift for læger/Danish Medical Bulletin* 162 (December 2000): 7000–7001.

John Sanderson's impotence was widely known. Not only had it come to the attention of the Dean, but the witness Thomas Stephenson from *Wele* had seen the couple:

> ... in a barn in Wele belonging to John Sanderson, the father of John, the defendant, on a certain day around the feast of the Ascension of our Lord three years ago, before the hour of nones of that day, trying to perform intercourse with due diligence for that work. And he says by his oath that he then saw the member of said John laying low and in no way rising or becoming erect. And at that time he saw the brother of said John stroke the said member of John. And he says that he often saw said John and Tedia, concerned in this case, both before and after that time lying together in one bed, but he did not see them trying to perform intercourse.[19]

When the case was later heard in York, the court decided to have John examined *per aspectum corporis*. The description of John's penis given by the three women who investigated him on 28 November 1370 leaves no doubt that his impotence had a physical explanation:

> And she says that the member of said John is like an empty intestine of mottled skin and it does not have any flesh in it, nor veins in the skin, and the middle of its front is totally black. And said witness stroked it with her hands and put it in semen and having thus been stroked and put in that place it neither expanded nor grew.[20] Asked if he has a scrotum with testicles she

---

19. '... in orreo Johannis Sanderson, patris carnalis Johannis, de quo agitur, apud Wele quodam die circa festum ascensionis domini, tribus annis elapsis, ut credit, ante horam nonam ipsius diei, carnali copule operam adhibentes cum diligentia debita in hac parte. Et dicit in juramento suo quod tunc vidit virgam ipsius Johannis submissam et nullo modo se erigentem vel erectam. Et tunc vidit fratrem carnalem ipsius Johannis, de quo agitur, palpare ibidem virgam Johannis predictam. Et dicit quod sepius tam post quam ante dictum tempus vidit ipsos Johannem et Tediam, de quibus agitur, uno lecto simul nudos jacentes, sed non vidit eos carnali copule operam adhibentes' (CP E 105, 1370).

20. This appears to be the only known instance of this nexus of words being used in English sources. My decision to translate it as 'semen' is based on the following reasoning: Lewis, *A Latin Dictionary*, s.v. *flos* has the translation 'the best part of something' or 'the highest part, the top, crown, head of a thing, froth of wine'; R.E. Latham, exec. ed., *Revised Medieval Latin Word-List from British and Irish Sources*, The British Academy (London: 1965), s.v. *flos* has 'menstruation'. *Flos* thus refers to some sort of distillation or effluent. Its conjuction with the masculine *fratris* makes it impossible for it to refer to an effluent from the female body, such as menstrual blood, and it therefore refers to an effluent from the male body. (I would like to express my gratitude to the neo-Latin discussion group on the

says that he has the skin of a scrotum, but the testicles do not hang in the scrotum but are connected with the skin as is the case among young infants.[21]

The court in York passed sentence within a fortnight, annulling the marriage of Tedia Lambhird and John Sanderson.[22]

The prompt decision of the court and the three matrons' clinical descriptions of John Sanderson make it clear that his condition was not temporary and that he suffered from two conditions well known in the paediatric literature: the first condition is *hypospadias*, a birth defect of the urethra in the male which involves an abnormally placed urinary meatus (opening). Instead of opening at the tip of the glans of the penis, a hypospadic urethra opens anywhere along a line running from the tip along the underside of the *stemma* of the penis to the junction of the penis and scrotum or perineum. The urethral meatus opens on the glans penis in about 50–75 per cent of cases; these are categorised as first degree hypospadias. Second degree (in which the urethra opens on the *stemma*), and third degree (when the urethra opens on the perineum) occur in up to 20 or 30 per cent of cases, respectively. The more severe degrees are more likely to be associated with chordee, in which the penis is incompletely separated from the perineum or is still tethered downwards by connective tissue, or with un-

---

Internet whose comments about the meaning of the phrase are condensed in this note).

21. *Isabella de Wairgrave* deposed: '. . . et dicit quod virga dicti Johannis est quasi quedam intestina vacua de mottica pelli, non habens carnem interius nec venas in cute. Et est medietas anterior eiusdem nigra totaliter. Et ista testis palpavit dictam virgam cum manibus suis et posuit eam in flore fratris. Et sic palpata et deposita nec dilatabat se nec crescebat. Interrogata si habet bursam cum testiculis dicit quod est ibi pellis bursalis sed testiculi non pendent in bursa sed sunt contigui cum carne in unguinibus sicut est in juvenibus infantibus' (CP E 105, 1370). *Johanna de Wyghton* explained that the penis was submerged in semen: '... Et examinata diligenter in causa de qua in presenti processu memoratur requisita de impotentia Johannis Sanderson dicit quod hesterna die fecit parari dicto Johannii in domo istius testis bonum ignem et bona cibaria et potum competente et dictus Johannes collocavit se juxta dictam ignem in quadam cathedra et ista testis palpavit et cepit inter manus suas virgam dicti Johannis quadem virga nullo modo valuit se erigere sed semper permansit in eodem statu quasi finis unius vacue intestine. Et dicit in juramento suo quod reputat se scire quod dictus Johannes non potest prefatam Tediam carnaliter cognoscere nec aliquam aliam mulierem et hoc se dicit dicere in periculo anime sue et sicut voluit scire Deo respondere in die judicii. Preterea dicit quod vidit virgam dicti Johannis deponentam circumquaque in flore fratri et nec se dilatebat nec crescebat.'

22. On 12 December 1370.

descended testes (cryptorchidism).[23] The descriptions of John's penis by the three matrons make it clear that he is suffering a second degree hypospadias (black 'spot' halfway down the front) and undescended testes ('...skin of a scrotum, but the testicles do not hang in the scrotum but are connected with the skin as is the case among young infants').[24]

Another Impotence Case: CP E 259

John Sanderson and his family may have been embarrassed by John's condition, but they were not secretive about it. The family was most likely not rich or influential, and I have been unable to uncover further information about them. They appear to have been lower gentry or even peasants, and despite a thorough search through local sources I have not found any mention of Sandersons or Lambhird/Lamberts. By contrast I am almost snowed under by the information I have found about the Paynels and Cantilupes, who were the protagonists in the almost contemporary case between Katherine Paynel and Nicholas Cantilupe from 1368-69 (CP E 259). An entire volume of *Early Yorkshire Charters* is dedicated to the Paynel Fee[25] and the Cantilupes are well known, not only for St Thomas of Hereford, the last pre-Reformation saint and canon lawyer, but also for Nicholas senior, third baron Cantilupe, who was an important player in the early Hundred Years' War and a close associate of King Edward III. The stakes were thus much higher and, as we shall see the congenital defect was so incapacitating that the defendant defied the court, endured

---

23. The defendant John Skathelok in another case, (CP F 111, 1432), seems to have had either chordee or, like John Sanderson, hypospadias See the translation of extracts from the case, particularly the description of John's penis given by the witness Joan Semer, in P. J. P. Goldberg, ed. and trans., *Women in England c. 1275–1525: Documentary Sources*, Manchester Medieval Sources (Manchester: 1995), 219-222.
24. Cryptorchidism is the absence of one or both testes from the scrotum. This usually represents failure of the testes to move, or 'descend'. About 3% of full-term and 30% of premature infant boys are born with at least one undescended testicle, making cryptorchidism the most common birth defect of male genitalia. However, most testes descend by the first year of life (the majority within three months), making the true incidence of cryptorchidism around 1% overall.
25. Charles Travis Clay, ed., *The Paynell Fee*, vol. 6 of *Early Yorkshire Charters*, Based on the manuscripts of the late William Farrer, Yorkshire Archaeological Society Record Series, Extra Series, vol. 3 (1939).

excommunication and reacted with violence to the possibility of a court case.²⁶

The case was recently featured in a review of a book on masculine identity, but the analysis of the case in the book itself is so riddled with factual and transcription errors and linguistic misunderstandings that it is necessary to restate the facts.²⁷

The Cantilupe family was one of the richest and most influential baronial families in England. Nicholas Cantilupe, junior (c.1342–1370) was the grandson of Baron Nicholas Cantilupe (c. 1301–1355), a nephew of St Thomas of Hereford. Nicholas Cantilupe, senior, had become third baron Cantilupe around 1321 and he served in the Flemish and Scottish wars of Edward III and received numerous summonses to parliament between 1336 and 1354. During December and January 1340-41 Edward II twice sent him to Canterbury to summon Archbishop Stratford to London and commissioned him to try corruption and other crimes throughout the north-east Midlands. He was granted a papal dispensation to continue his marriage

---

26. This case ultimately led to the murder of Nicholas' brother, who died in 1375. Most likely this spectacular murder had been planned for more than four years and involved the complicity of at least eighteen people. I am currently engaged in a major project to establish the social, personal and political contexts and motives behind this murder.
27. Neal, *The Masculine Self in Late Medieval England*, 142–50 (review by Robert Mills, 'The Masculine Self in Late Medieval England, review of *The Masculine Self in Late Medieval England* by Derek G. Neal', *Times Higher Education*, 8 January 2009, http://www.timeshighereducation.co.uk/story.asp?sectioncode=26&storycode=404901). In addition to getting the names of the litigants wrong, Neal's reading of the case, in particular his analysis of the use of the word *frigiditas* and the many literary allusions seem to be based on a twentieth-century understanding of phrases and contexts, rather than informed by an understanding of the procedures employed by the canon law and the courts. His treatment of the libel of the case as a piece of literature which imbues it with highly unlikely rhetorical devices (p. 143) and the clever, but entirely unconvincing interpretation of Nicholas' abduction of Katherine as 'a parody of the biblical annunciation scene' (p.146-146) reads like a bad piece of post-modern literary criticism. His statement that Nicholas had been married before is simply wrong: had Neal read carefully he would have realised that the Joan mentioned in Nicholas' *inquisitio post mortem* of 12 March 1370 is Joan Kymas, who married Nicholas' grandfather, baron Nicholas Cantilupe, in 1341 (*Edward III*, vol. 13 of *Calendar of Inquisitions Post Mortem and Other Analogous Documents Preserved in the Public Record Office Prepared Under the Superintendence of the Deputy Keeper of the Records* [London: HMSO, 1954], 106) and who was granted a papal dispensation to remain in that state despite being related to Nicholas Cantilupe within forbidden degrees two years later. William Henry Bliss, ed., *Calendar of Entries in the Papal Registers Relating to Great Britain and Ireland, Papal Letters*, vol. 2 (London: H.M.S.O., 1893), 14,

to Joan de Kyma, the daughter of Sir Humphrey de Littlebury, in 1343.[28] In October 1349, when Nicholas, junior was seven years of age, he hosted the translation of the relics of St Thomas of Hereford (Thomas de Cantilupe) at Hereford. Between 1339 and 1354 he received a series of licences to endow the Carthusian priory of Beauvale, which he founded within his park at Greasley in December 1343. He also founded Cantilupe College in Lincoln Cathedral close, whose priests celebrated at the altar of St Nicholas within the cathedral.[29] In 1354, as one of the barons of the realm, he signed a petition to the Pope asking him to determine the English right to the French crown, giving his name as Nicholas de Cantilupo, *dominus de Grisley*.[30] When he died in 1355 he was seised of the manor of Eselburgh (Buckingham), Ilkeston (Derby), the castle of Greasley (Nottingham), and Livington and other lands in Lincolnshire. Having previously excluded his son and heir, William, from his succession he was succeeded by William's son Nicholas (junior), then aged thirteen.[31] Nicholas junior could thus draw on the social and political networks of several chancellors, bishops and even a saint, St Thomas of Hereford. He was also to become the last generation of the Cantilupe family to be in possession of the lands assembled by the family over the previous century and he and his brother William, who served with John of Gaunt in Aquitaine 1370–1373, were to be the last potential barons Cantilupe.

Both plaintiff and defendant lived within the jurisdiction of the archdiocese of Canterbury and initial steps in the case were taken in Lincoln. The case was heard before the York consistory court, however, possibly because of the turmoil of the brief episcopal reign of Simon Langham who, having resigned as chancellor of Edward III, was in the process of joining the college of cardinals in Avignon in 1368. The first surviving document in the case is a letter dated 23 March 1368 constituting Master Robert Hakthorp as the proctor of Katherine Paynel, daughter of

---

28. Bliss, *Calendar of Entries in the Papal Registers Relating to Great Britain and Ireland. Papal Letters*, 14.
29. Richard Partington, 'Cantilupe, Nicholas, Third Lord Cantilupe (c.1301–1355)', in *Oxford Dictionary of National Biography*, ed. H. C. G. Matthew and Brian Harrison (Oxford: 2004), http://www.oxforddnb.com/view/article/4567, accessed 19 April 2009.
30. Thomas Rymer, *Foedera, conventiones, littera et ejusconque generis acta publica, inter reges anglae et alios quosvis imperatores, reges, pontifices, principes, vel communitates; ab ingressu Guillelmi I in anglicam, A.D. 1066 ad nostra usque tempora habita aut tractata*, vol. 1 (London: 1827), 284.
31. Partington, 'Cantilupe, Nicholas, Third Lord Cantilupe (c.1301–1355)'. I have been unable to ascertain the reason why Nicholas senior disinherited his son, but it may have been related to William's possible indictment before the King's Bench in 1355.

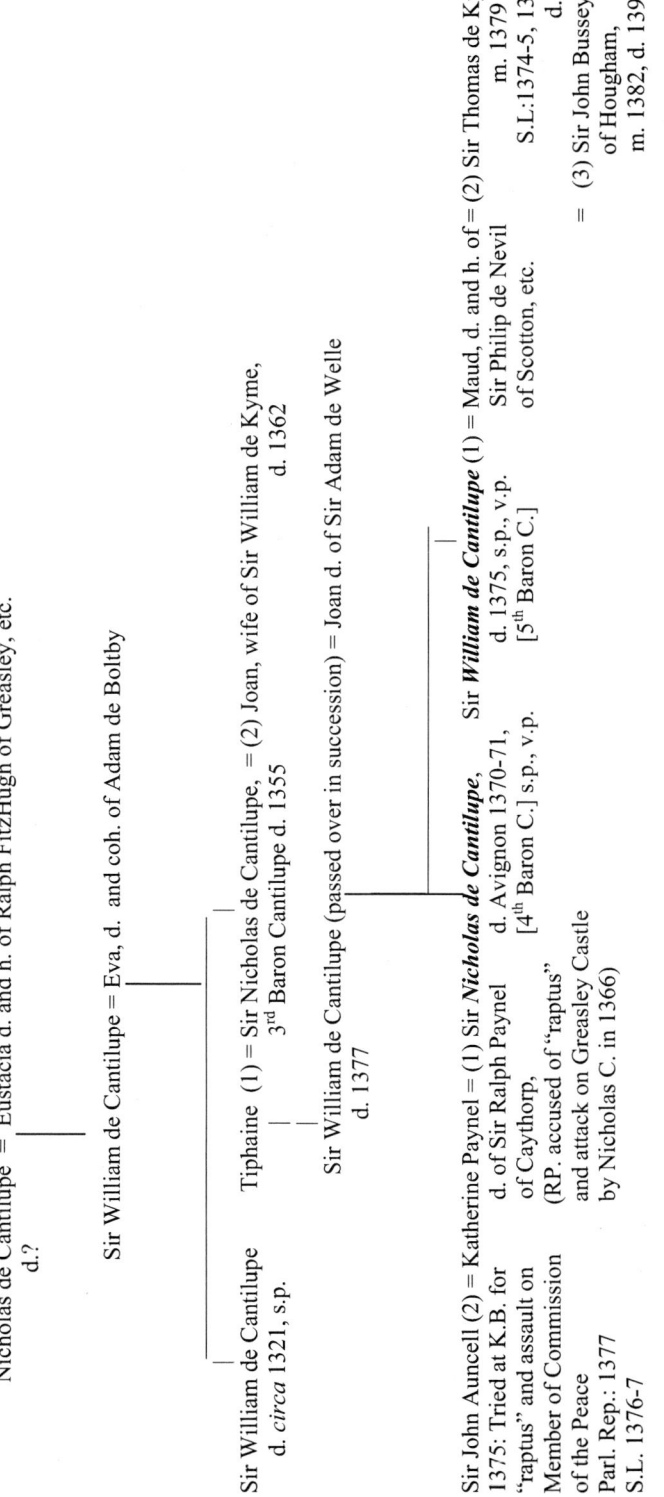

Ralph Paynel, knight. She applied for court protection on 22 April 1368 and within a week she was not only given the court's permission to move away from Nicholas while the case lasted, but from 1 May 1368 she stayed in the care of Lady Margaret, wife of Sir Edmund Hastings, of the fortified Roxby castle (near Pickering) in Yorkshire.[32]

In her libel, Katherine told the court that she had married Nicholas Cantilupe four years earlier, when she was aged sixteen and he was aged twenty-two, and that he had not yet had intercourse with her. Seven witnesses were heard for Katherine between 7 and 27 June 1368. Three of them were recalled by the court, and, on 15 July they gave slightly a different version of events. Though they tell the same basic story, they present 'newly-remembered' facts that seem to have been part of a conscious strategy to ratchet up pressure on Nicholas and to strengthen the Paynel version of an ongoing dispute at the King's Bench concerning an attack on the Cantilupe stronghold, Greasley castle.[33]

The two sets of accounts agree on the basic facts. The couple had married four years earlier and moved to Nicholas' manor/castle in Greasley in Nottinghamshire, but it soon became clear that all was not well. After only a few weeks of cohabitation, Katherine returned to her parents. Initially she refused to explain what was the matter, but in private she told her confidante, Margaret Halton, that Nicholas did not have any genitals. When

---

32. Probably a nephew of Sir Ralph Hastings, Sir Edmund Hastings of Roxby, Yorkshire. Cf. Simon Walker, 'Hastings Family (per. c.1300–c.1450)', in *Oxford Dictionary of National Biography*, ed. H. C. G. Matthew and Brian Harrison (Oxford: 2004), http://www.oxforddnb.com/view/article/54526, accessed 22 April 2009.

33. Rosamund Sillem who first published the case in 1936 was unable to find interrogations that followed up this commission. This led her to conclude that the commission of *oyer et terminer* granted to Nicholas Cantilupe was not acted on (Rosamund Sillem, ed., *Records of Some Sessions of the Peace in Lincolnshire, 1360–1375*, Publications of the Lincoln Record Society, vol. 30. [Hereford: 1936], lxviii). Both Bellamy and Platts use only the documents published by Sillem. John Bellamy, *Crime and Public Order in England in the Later Middle Ages*, gen. ed. Harold Perkin, Studies in Social History (London & Toronto: 1973); Graham Platts, *Land and People in Medieval Lincolnshire*, History of Lincolnshire (Lincoln: 1985). However, a transcript of the deposition of Robert Raufchaumberlayn Paynel (i.e. Ralph Paynel's chamberlain) contained in KB 27/434, m. 60 has since been published in Morris S. Arnold, ed. and trans., *Select Cases of Trespass from the King's Courts, 1307–1399. Vol.1*, Selden Society. Publications, vol. 100 (London: Selden Society, 1985), 83–84. Unfortunately, there is still not a full transcript of the King's Bench proceedings which contain the additional evidence of John de Hevore and Katherine's confidante, Margaret Halton.

her parents learned about this they were incredulous. Her father said Katherine 'was stupid and she knew not what to do',[34] but she must have persisted in her story, for a few weeks later Master Thomas Waus, who was the official of the archdeacon of Stow and the rector of the church at Berghton near the Paynell estate, was present when she explained that Nicholas was impotent and 'unable to emit semen'.[35] Thomas advised that Katherine would have to return to Nicholas to see if 'the said Nicholas could improve somewhat in the necessary male work'.[36] This second cohabitation lasted for about two years. At the end of that period Katherine returned to her parents and said that 'in the forum of conscience', i.e. in confession, it had been announced to her that her case could proceed to an annulment by a court.[37]

Katherine produced seven witnesses in the York consistory court, who all swore to having heard about the impotence, either directly from Katherine or from neighbourhood rumour. Master Thomas Waus related to the court that Katherine had sworn:

> That she often tried to find the place of the said Nicholas' genitals with her hands when she lay in bed with said Nicholas and he was asleep, and that she could not stroke nor find anything there and that the place in which Nicholas' genitals ought be is as flat as the hand of a man.[38]

Margaret Halton, Katherine's confidante and *socia in lecto* since childhood, explained that Katherine had told her about Nicholas' impotence only three days after the marriage was celebrated. The other five witnesses confirmed the existence of neighbourhood rumour but could not confirm Katherine's report.

---

34. '...quod fuit fatua et quod non intellexit quid fecit'.
35. 'Et tunc recessit dicta Katherina a consortio dicti Nicholai et rediit ad patrem suum apud Caysthorp et in presentia istius jurati (i.e. master Thomas Waus) conquesta fuit dicto patri sui et matri sui quod non cohabitaret cum dicto Nicholo eo quod non potuit cognoscere eam carnaliter sicut deceret marito cognoscere uxorem et quod non habuit genitalia nec potuit emittere semen' (CP E 259, 1368-9).
36. '...si dictus Nicholaus posset in opere virili necessario in hec parte convalescere...' (CP E 259, 1368-9).
37. '...in foro conscientie fuit nuncupatum sibi quod prosequeretur ad divorcium celebrandum inter eos.' (CP E 259, 1368-9). In CP E 18 the *forum conscientie* refers specifically to the confessional.
38. 'Et dicit quod audivit Katarinam referre quod sepius temptavit manibus suis cum jacuit in lecto cum dicto Nicholo et ipse dormiebat locum genitalium dicti Nicholi et quod nulla palpare nec invenire potuit ibidem et quod locus in quo genitalia sua deberent esse est ita planus sicut manus hominis' (CP E 259, 1368-9).

Both the physical deformity alleged by Katherine and the history of Nicholas' short life indicates a particular birth defect, a *congenital adrenal hyperplasia*. Congenital adrenal hyperplasia (CAH) affects both boys and girls. Those with the condition lack an enzyme needed by the adrenal gland to make two hormones, cortisol and aldosterone.[39] Without these hormones, the body produces excessive amounts of androgen, a type of male sex hormone. This causes male characteristics to appear early or inappropriately.[40] Estimates of the prevalence of the condition vary, but the most recent meta-study suggests that one in 18,000 children is born with congenital adrenal hyperplasia.[41] There are two variations of this syndrome: 67 per cent of babies with CAH have the salt-losing variant of the syndrome and will die within a year if untreated.[42] Sufferers from the salt-losing form of CAH will die in infancy, because they cannot produce enough salt-retaining hormones to maintain a sustainable electrolytic balance in their fluids. Among the remaining 20 per cent of babies born with CAH, non-salt-losing girls are usually healthy. Today CAH is treated with hormone replacement, replacing one or both of the missing hormones.

However, medicine was of course much different in the Middle Ages and the condition may ultimately have caused Nicholas' premature death in Avignon in January 1370. The fact that Nicholas survived to take the inheritance from his grandfather in 1355, and from his step-grandmother in 1362, makes clear that s/he was one of the 20 per cent of children with the less severe form of CAH – non-salt losing CAH – in which their salt balance is largely normal. In stressful situations, however, some people with non-salt losing CAH may become salt losers and therefore current advice on living with CAH recommends extra attention being paid to common illnesses and stress-inducing situations, such as injury and exercise.[43]

---

39. Perrin C. White, 'Congenital Adrenal Hyperplasia and Related Disorders', in *Nelson Textbook of Pediatrics*, ed. R.M. Kliegman, R.E. Behrman, and B.F. Stanton (Philadelphia, PA: 2007).
40. Deborah P. Merke and Stefan R. Bornstein, 'Congenital Adrenal Hyperplasia', *The Lancet* 365, no. 9477 (18–24 June 2005): 2125–36.
41. Songya Pang and Anastasia Clark, 'Congenital Adrenal Hyperplasia Due to 2:L - Hydroxylase Deficiency: Newborn Screening and Its Relationship to the Diagnosis and Treatment of the Disorder', *Screening* 2 (1993): 105–39.
42. Cf. http://www.patient.co.uk/showdoc/40002792/ (accessed 26 April 2009).
43. http://www.magicfoundation.org/www/docs/100/congenital-adrenal-hyperplasia. In this connection it is interesting to note that whereas Nicholas' brother William had a career as a soldier and was immediately put on a retainer in the retinue of John of Gaunt on the death of his brother in 1370, there are no traces of this for Nicholas. That Nicholas was unable to perform strenuous physical work is also suggested by the fact that he did not ride with his men to abduct Katherine in Lincolnshire but met them at the gate of Greasley Castle.

Though no-one ever raised any questions about Nicholas' gender in the course of the case in York, Nicholas had much to defend. At their first hearing Katherine's witnesses did not mention the threats that Nicholas Cantilupe had made in order prevent his condition becoming known. Her return to Nicholas' castle in Greasley was presented as the result of the mediation of Thomas Waus.[44] However, soon after Nicholas had initiated proceedings against Ralph Paynel at the King's Bench *and* had entered replications to Katherine's witnesses in which he which he claimed that she had sworn that Nicholas had known her carnally, a more violent version of events was presented. Three witnesses – Master Thomas Waus, Margaret Halton and Master Robert Bekeby, her father's chaplain – were re-examined on 15 July 1368. As stated above, Margaret Halton now told the court that Katherine had returned to her parents only three days after the marriage was celebrated and that she had confided to Margaret about Nicholas' impotence soon after. Thomas Waus now confirmed to the court that discord had arisen within a month of the marriage, and that far from being the result of mediation, the reunion of Katherine and Nicholas had taken place when Nicholas had his men abduct her 'weeping and wailing' to Greasley castle on the Wednesday after the Assumption of the Virgin (i.e. 15 August) 1366.

At the castle gate, Nicholas met Katherine and her companions and:

> ...he said with a grim face: 'Woman, you are cursed among all women'. And he led her and this witness and the other aforementioned fellow witnesses into a certain chapel situated within that castle, and there said Katherine was spoken to in these words: 'You know well that I am sufficiently potent to copulate with you having genitals that are good enough'. And she answered: 'Yes'. Said Nicholas added: 'I wish that you swear that I am able to have intercourse, having sufficient natural instruments, as has been said, and that you henceforth do not leave my company without my special permission and that you do not reveal this counsel in any way'. To which Katherine answered: 'I will swear to whatever was said by you'.[45]

---

44. Thomas Waus described the events like this: 'Et hanc querelam dicte Katerine audivit iste juratus, ut dicit, vicisies et postea, mediante isto jurato, de consensu patris et matris dicte Katherine ipsa fuit reducta in comitiva istius jurati apud Crislay ad dictum Nicholum. Et ibidem iste juratus fecit eosdem Nicholum et Katherinam concordes. Et sic ipsa Katerina de consilio parentum suorum et istius jurati ad probandum si dictus Nicholas posset in opere virili necessarie in hac parte convalescere. Cohabitavit cum eodem in thoro et mensa fere per duos annos extunc sequentes'. (CP E 259, 1368-9).
45. CP E 259, 1368-9, deposition of Robert de Bekeby, a chaplain to Katherine's father: '...[loquebatur] torvo vultu: maledicta es mulier inter omnes mulieres. Ipsamque statim una cum iste jurato et aliis contestibus proximis prenotatis in quodam oratorio situato in eodem castro introduxit, ubique dicta Katerina alloquita

The witness, Richard Bekeby, the Paynels' chaplain seems not want to press the point of Nicholas' violent abduction of two members of the church, one of whom was the official of the archdeacon of Stow. But he gives the impression of having been abducted with Katherine and his two fellow witnesses. Nicholas had put further pressure on Katherine by showing her a room he had made as a prison for her where he intended to keep her if she did not comply with his wishes[46] and by having the stocks readied for Katherine in case she refused to take the desired oath.[47] This story is in sharp contrast to the complaint that Nicholas made to the king, that Sir Ralph Paynel and others had broken into his castle at Greasley, ravished his wife, Katherine, and carried her away, together with goods and chattels of his. A commission of *oyer and terminer* was appointed to investigate the case.[48] The abduction story was contained in the second set of depositions on 25 July, and the York court moved quickly. It sent Robert Bekeby a mandate to cite and compel Nicholas to appear for a physical examination on the Monday before the feast of St Michael (26 September 1368). The

---

fuerat sub his verbis: tu scis bene quod ego sum sufficienter potens tecum carnaliter comiscere, habens instrumenta ad coheundum satis apta. Que respondit, sic. Dicit insuper Nicholas: volo quod te jures quod ego sum potens ad coheundum, habens instrumenta naturalia, ut premittitur, et quod tu de cetero non recedas a comitiva mea sine licentia mea speciali, et quod consilium meum nullatenus reveles. Ad que dicta Katerina respondit: volo jurare quecumque vobis fuerunt prolata'.

46. 'Interrogatus qualiter compulsa fuerat ad jurandum dicit quod dictus Nicholas dixit isti jurato quod nuncquam cum eo moretur nisi tunc prestaret hunc juramentum. Et nicholominus iste juratus vidit locum ad modum carceris ordinatum quem dictus Nicholas sibi ostendit pro mora et inclusione dicte Katherine nisi juramentum hunc prestitisset. Et postquam dicta Katherina dictum prestitit juramentum, audivit iste juratus ipsam dicere dicto Nicholo: Quidquid vos dicetis ego volo facere vobiscum et in omnibus concordare. Et per premissa scit iste juratus, ut dicit, quod si quamdam confessionem extunc fecit vel emisit dicta Katherina de potentia coeundi prefati Nicholi vel quod ipse fuit potens in opere copule carnalis, illam confessionem fecit metu ducta, ut premittitur, compulsa, quia a tempore quo dicta Katerina venit ad castrum predictum, ut prefertur, semper fuit sub metu et districtu dicti Nicholi non habens suam ipsius liberam potestatem' (CP E 259, 1368-9).

47. (*Margaret Halton* agreed with the other witnesses) 'hoc addito quod habuit compedes paratos in quibus poneret eandem Katerinam nisi sibi in omnibus acquiesceret et prestaret hunc juramentum' (CP E 259, 1368-9).

48. Rosamund Sillem believed that this commission was never followed through (Rosamund Sillem, ed., *Records of Some Sessions of the Peace in Lincolnshire, 1360–1375*, Publications of the Lincoln Record Society, vol. 30. [Hereford: 1936], Lxviii). However, Morris Arnold published parts of the proceedings contained in KB 27/434 in 1985: Arnold, *Select Cases of Trespass from the King's Courts, 1307–1399. Vol.1*, 83–84. The remaining documents in the case are still awaiting investigation.

summons was read out to Nicholas on 6 August, but he clearly avoided being exposed to a physical examination though he presented himself before the consistory court in Lincoln during the previous week. On 21 April 1369[49] the consistory court of York passed a sentence which deviates from the norm in that it specifically said that the court's decision was reached through *allegata, proposita, confessata et alia probationum generalia*, in other words through circumstantial evidence.[50] The court had passed its sentence but Nicholas' non-appearance for a physical examination provided procedural grounds for the court in York to grant Nicholas permission to appeal to the Apostolic See. Having taken out letters of attorney to ensure the smooth running of his estates in 1369, Nicholas travelled to Avignon but died there in mid-February 1370.[51]

It is not surprising that Nicholas Cantilupe's actions did not prejudice the court against him: the court was concerned with proper procedure and Nicholas used this to force the legal process to a standstill. The court provided every possibility for delay and it was not until nine months after the reading of his summons, when Nicholas had exhausted all his dilatory tactics, that the court passed sentence against him.

At the time of his death Nicholas must have been between twenty-seven and twenty-eight years of age. Inquisitions post mortem were taken in May and July. They showed him to be seised of Little Claydon and Eselbergh (Buckingham), Ilkeston (Derby), Greasley Castle and Kynmerley and Helmsill (of the honour of Peverel).[52] Greasley was the largest manorial holding, at over 5500 acres, incorporating towns, villages and hamlets from Selston to Nuthall and Eastwood. The adjoining manor of Ilkeston in

---

49. This date is surprising. Nothing seems to have happened in the case between July 1368 and April 1369, but the date is clearly *not* a scribal error: the scribe copied out the last part of the year in full as 'm ccc lx *nono*'.

50. '... factis est interrogatoriam ex officio venerabile Nichiholo et Katerine, partibus antedictis, coram nobis personaliter comparentis sequentibusque responsionibus ad interrogatoriam supradictum. ... quia per allegata proposita, confessata et alia probationum generalia inveniens...'

51. On Friday before St Petrus in Cathedra, 45 Ed III. One inquisition gives the *obit* as Friday before Valentine's Day *44–47 Edward III*, vol. 13 of *Calendar of inquisitions post mortem and other analogous documents preserved in the Public Record Office prepared under the superintendence of the Deputy Keeper of the Records* (London: HMSO, 1954), 76–78.

52. A second inquisition about Greasley and Ilkeston was taken on 12 July 1370. The manors of Wythcall, Kynthorp and Lavyngton caused some concern as well: three inquisitions were taken: 8 May, the Saturday after St Barnabas (feast day 11 June) and 28 June. The first two had fourteen jurors, while the published record does not inform us how many swore to the last inquisition. *Inquisitions Post Mortem, 44–47 Edward III*, 76–78.

Derbyshire increased that holding to a huge swathe straddling the River Erewash. Nicholas also died in possession of Wythcall, Kynthorp and Lavyngton, three manors in Lincolnshire. The inquisition says these were now held by *Katherine, his wife*, which indicates that the secular courts regarded the marriage case as pending. The manor of Lavyngton was held by knight's service from the archbishop of York.[53] From the Close Rolls we learn of an order by the king dated 25 September 1371 to deliver the manor of Ilkeston and the castle of Greasley to William Cantilupe, Nicholas' brother, and we also learn that William was abroad in Aquitaine at the time of Nicholas' death.[54] From a later Patent Roll we learn that Katherine wasted no time in getting married again: on 3 December 1371 she contested the rights to the manors of Wythcall, Kynthorp and Lavyngton with her new husband, John Auncell, knight.[55] John Aunfell (*sic*) and Katherine's brother, John, appear as witnesses to the citation to appear for a physical examination which was read out to Nicholas on 6 August 1368.

Statistics and Secular Development

The Cantilupe case is an astonishing case, and will be the subject of more studies in the future. We must take the case seriously and approach it with sensitivity and we must strive not to apply anachronistic terms or concerns on the medieval material. Without a sound knowledge of medieval procedure we are bound to go wrong in our analysis. An example of how a lack of knowledge can lead us astray is one modern observer's surprise at the length of cohabitation of Nicholas and Katherine, which is based on a lack of understanding of the canon law and its requirement for three years' cohabitation. Ignoring the requirements of X 4.15.7, which *requires* that the couple live together for three years, he characterises Nicholas' and Katherine's cohabitation as '...a suspiciously long time for any woman to have put up with this situation'.[56] I have been unable to identify the 'frustration of a gentry family seeing a perhaps long-negotiated marriage falling apart', which the same author finds in that part of Margaret Halton's deposition when she described Katherine Paynel's parents' reaction when they learned the nature of Katherine's complaint. Though her father was certainly blunt, their initial thought that she did not know how to have

---

53. *Inquisitions Post Mortem*, 76–78.
54. *Calendar of Close Rolls. Edward III, 1327–1377*, vol. 1360–64 (London: 1896), 252.
55. John Burke, *Peerages, Extinct, Dormant and in Abeyance*, vol. 1–3 (London: 1840), 108.
56. Neal, *The Masculine Self in Late Medieval England*, 144.

intercourse when she returned to them, presumably still being a virgin, should not surprise anyone. On the contrary, the parents can be said to have behaved reasonably once their shock and surprise over what she told them had subsided: they let her stay with them for six months, they took the advice of Master Thomas Waus, the official of the archdeacon of Stow, and they arranged for a very orderly transfer of Katherine, who returned to Nicholas in the large company of Waus, Master Robert Bekeby, the rector of Berghton, one of the churches in the Paynell fee, Margaret Halton and 'many others'.

However, these events must have shocked Katherine and she had been rightly reticent and uncertain about how to reveal the startling truth behind the breakdown of her marriage. The family soon decided to support Katherine: her parents did not force her to return to her husband. Thomas Waus took her complaint seriously and induced her to bring her suit before the bishop of Lincoln, which she did accompanied by her mother, Thomas Waus, Margaret Halton and others.[57]

Finally, we must also marvel at the aftermath of this case. The annulment of the marriage clearly created bad blood between the two families.[58] William Cantilupe, his brother, succeeded Nicholas on the latter's death, but it was only four years later, in 1375, that Ralph Paynell came to be involved in William's murder.

Conclusions

It is always risky to draw conclusions on the basis of such complex and sparse evidence, but the York material makes it is possible to *very tentatively* suggest a development over time. The first preserved impotence case from York, the Cantilupe case, does not include a physical examination of the man. There are undoubtedly good reasons why Nicholas Cantilupe should have been able to avoid the examination. His status as the nephew of

---

57. Though Thomas Waus and unspecified others were present in Thomas Waus' room, Margaret Halton also testifies that the matter of Nicholas' impotence was discussed in private between the bishop, Margaret, and the two Paynel women.
58. Given events in 1355 and 1360, it is likely that the bad feeling between the families already existed when the marriage of Katherine and Nicholas was contracted between 1360 and 1362. For this date see Robert Raufchamberlayn's statement that Katherine contracted marriage while under-age. Morris S. Arnold, ed. and trans., *Select Cases of Trespass from the King's Courts, 1307–1399. Vol.1*, Selden Society. Publications, vol. 100 (London: 1985), 84. My guess is that when Nicholas, third baron Cantilupe, died in 1355, the Paynels laid claim to lands seized by the Cantilupes and that the marraige between the heirs of the two houses was arranged to settle the dispute.

a saint (and teacher of canon law), his social standing as major landowner (if not quite a baron) and his incontestable familiarity with canon law would have given him the knowledge to evade the court for a long time. The fact that he issued a letter of attorney in 1369 and died in Avignon in January 1370, only nine months after receiving permission by the court in York to pursue an appeal at the papal court, shows that he was able to put the legal system of the church to efficient use if he wished to do so, as does the fact that the case appears to have lain dormant in York for almost a year due to his dilatory tactics. John Sanderson was less fortunate and did not avoid the court's examination, but in his case there were only three 'good and honest' women present when the examination took place. The examination of John Skathelok (CP F 111, referred to above) involved a more motley group of female witnesses. I think that a case can be made that they included prostitutes: one of them came from a neighbourhood in York that was associated with prostitution and none of them were described as married, but this seems to have been an aberration. In the last case, William Barton's two examinations in CP F 174 involved no less than thirteen witnesses, four of whom were men. We thus see a pattern of increasing complexity in the composition of the tribunals but also an increasing willingness to challenge the validity of their findings. Perhaps we might suggest that by 1450 the English way of doing things had outlived its usefulness.

Modern scholars have surveyed surviving court records of medieval England to describe the parameters of medieval masculinity. One modern commentator has suggested that the courts were involved in producing pornography for individual consumption, another suggests that Nicholas Cantilupe had chosen to construct an unsuitable masculine identity, and others suggest that the impotence we see in these medieval cases may have been caused by the court-room scenario itself. Some of these modern approaches may yield important insights, but the interpretation of these unusual cases is a task that must be approached with an open mind, a willingness to accept the prejudices and superstitions of the past as real motivators instead of indicating the existence of a thick smoke-screen which obscures the 'real' (and decidedly twentieth-century) fears and phobias, and a sound knowledge of the contemporary culture and the legal framework that produced the sources that survive today. Only if the historian can avoid imposing his or her own prejudices on the sources and base his or her analysis on a reading of the cases in their entirety can we hope to uncover what thoughts and assumptions lie behind the processes of medieval ecclesiastical courts. Modern historians have been willing to see expressions heavily laden with meaning in actions that they either do not understand or find repulsive.

In this paper I have argued against such an ahistorical approach and invited the reader to take a more holistic approach involving legal, social and biographical factors. Such an approach yields even more startling results than one would expect when simply mining the archives for evidence confirming that medieval sexual fears and medieval gender formation is fundamentally similar to our own.

SCHOOL OF LIFE: LEARNED LAW AND THE SCHOLASTIC HABITUS

Helge Dedek

Learned Law – Bookish Law

In his article 'Learned Law, *Droit Savant*, *Gelehrtes Recht*: The Tyranny of a Concept', Professor Kenneth Pennington gave a vivid description of a situation that, as he put it, 'evoked a stylized ritual speaker and audience' – a presentation to an audience of historians, focusing on doctrines of the learned law:

> Hard-headed historians squirmed and wiggled in their seats until the last syllable of doctrine had passed the lips of the speaker. As soon as the chair of the session permitted questions, their hands shot up to ask the inevitable, pragmatic, down-to-earth question: 'Yes, yes. All that you have told us is quite interesting and perhaps even correct. But what does the theory of the learned law have to do with the practice of the courts, lawyers, litigants?'[1]

From the perspective of the 'hard-headed historian' thus depicted, the doctrinal disputes of the learned law were to be dismissed as lifeless theoretical acrobatics. Professor Pennington, writing in 1994, described how this intellectual gap had begun to close with the appearance of scholarship that showed the practical relevance of the learned law in everyday legal

---

1. K. Pennington, 'Learned Law, *Droit Savant*, *Gelehrtes Recht*: The Tyranny of a Concept', *Syracuse Journal of International Law and Commerce* 20 (1994), 205.

life.[2] With the monitum that more work needed to be done, that particularly among legal historians the traditional 'disciplinary' divide between Romanists and Canonists had to be overcome to understand how the *ius commune* operated in practice, Pennington concluded:

> The Ius commune was not bookish law, was not the law of the greats, to be read, savored, and returned to the shelf, was not learned law in contrast to real law. It was the cauldron from which much of the precious metal of all European legal systems emerged.[3]

Let us take a closer look at this passage. The second sentence of this conclusion deserves unconditional endorsement. The importance of the *ius commune* for the legal realities of modern Europe is widely acknowledged, perhaps now even more than in 1994; a growing awareness tied to the process of the 'Europeanization' of law has triggered a heightened sensitivity and interest for the common legal past and identity. Many a time the *ius commune* has been invoked as a lodestar for the harmonization of European private law, for the new '*Ius commune Europaeum*'.[4] Also commendable, without a doubt, is the ambition to explore in more detail the practical operation of the learned law. However, the statement that the *ius commune* was 'not bookish law' seems to me in need of further explanation: the *ius commune*, I would like to add, and this shall be the starting point of this modest vignette, was of course *not only* bookish law; but bookish it was.

'Bookishness' appears to be a(n) (even) less attractive characteristic in laws than it is in people (tastes differ, one hopes): the 'law in the books' bears the stigma of irrelevance, as opposed to the (as Pennington puts it) 'real law', or, to use another popular expression, the 'law in action'.[5] The bookish jurist is the one who, in an act of misguided worship of his beloved

---

2. Giving particular credit to the works of Richard Helmholz and Charles Donahue: see, e.g., R. H. Helmholz, *Roman Canon Law in Reformation England* (Cambridge: 1990); See also, most recently, C. Donahue Jr., *Law, Marriage, and Society in the Later Middle Ages* (Cambridge: 2007).
3. Pennington, 'Learned Law', 215.
4. See *e.g.* J. Smits, *The Making of European Private Law, Towards a Ius Commune Europaeum as a Mixed Legal System* (Antwerp: 2002), 5, 6 *et passim*.
5. On the terminology frequently used in sociolegal and 'realist' scholarship, see, e.g., D. Nelken, 'Law in Action or Living Law? Back to the beginning in sociology of law', *Legal Studies* 4 (1984) 157, 158ff.; see also on the historical significance of this dichotomy in the American realist discourse, S. Macaulay, 'The New Versus the Old Legal Realism: "Things Ain't What They Used To Be"', *Wisconsin Law Review* (2005), 365, 367ff. On recent theoretical scholarship that criticizes the 'in action / on the books' distinction as artificial, see M. Constable, *Just Silences* (Princeton NJ: 2005), 46ff.

texts has, in his state of academic exaltation, lost touch with the secular and mundane realities of the craft: 'Let us not become legal monks', as Roscoe Pound famously warned.[6] Against this backdrop, it is understandable that if one attempts to highlight the *relevance* of the *ius commune*, one would try to emphasize its *practical* impact. It has been an important and no doubt meritorious focus of *ius commune* research to attest to this impact. This ambition to further a more holistic understanding of the learned law, however, should not come at the cost of understating its 'bookishness'. The roots of the learned law in academia, the fact that it is intellectually so closely connected to the emerging culture of European university is obviously the origin of many of the civilian tradition's most distinctive traits.

These peculiarities are the product of the particular condition of the discourse that drove the development of the *ius commune*, which was academic and scholarly in nature, and which bore the marks of what Pierre Bourdieu has called the 'scholastic point of view'.[7] This particular perspective, Bourdieu has argued, is related to the specific and completely unique quality of thinking that takes place in academic space:

> The scholastic view is a very peculiar point of view on the social world [...], on any possible object of thought that is made possible by the situation of *skholè,* of leisure, of which the school – a word that also derives form *skholè* – is a particular part, as an institutionalized situation of studious leisure.[8]

This particular situation creates a space where the intellect is allowed to 'play seriously' in the Platonic sense: to confront intellectual problems for the sake of confronting them, outside the 'urgency of the practical situation'.[9] This detachment from practice is a luxury that presupposes a certain 'retirement from the world.'[10]

The origins of the learned law are inextricably interwoven with the origins of that peculiar space of 'studious leisure', the Western university. In that sense, the learned law was, from the moment of its conception, 'bookish' and – resonating with Bourdieu's 'retirement from the world' – even 'monkish'. One might object that it would be misleading to describe the early legal academics as locked away in the ivory tower: legal historians have underlined the role of legal academics as (over time, more and more)

---

6. R. Pound, 'Law in Books and Law in Action', *American Law Review* 44 (1910), 12, 36.
7. P. Bourdieu, 'The Scholastic Point of View', in Bourdieu, *Practical Reason. On the Theory of Action* (Stanford CA: 1998), 127.
8. Bourdieu, 'The Scholastic Point of View', 127-8.
9. Bourdieu, 'The Scholastic Point of View', 128-9.
10. Bourdieu, 'The Scholastic Point of View', 129.

involved in legal practice,[11] and historians have described the medieval scholar as being well integrated into the newly flourishing urban space, the environment to which, as traditional scholarship has it, this new type of intellectual owes its emergence.[12] This is all true, but it does not call into question the fact that legal texts produced by 'learned' authors also grew out of their specific scholastic condition. We are about to depict just 'one view of the cathedral', an aspect that merits further exploration. In this paper, I want to draw attention to some hitherto unexplored aspects of the 'scholasticism' of the learned law, starting from Bourdieu's theoretical conceptualization of the 'scholastic' condition and moving to reflection on actual medieval Scholasticism as a structure that shaped the views of medieval jurists and therefore the character of medieval learned law. Continental legal history is also the history of European higher education, of the scholar, the 'legal monk' in his peculiar scholastic condition.

A Bookish Life: The School, a 'World Apart'

My focus is therefore on the peculiar life-world of the medieval scholar and teacher of Roman canon law and how it left its trace in legal discourse – it is in this sense that I have interpreted the motto of our meeting, which implies a connection between 'law' and 'private life'. On a panel on learned law, one could have easily imagined under this heading a contribution that pursues this connection in the opposite direction, which asks – following the predilection for the law 'in action' we have outlined above – the impact of doctrine on 'private life'.

What do we mean when we talk of 'private' life in the Middle Ages? One of the most prominent tendencies in conceptualizing the 'private sphere' appears to be to equate the 'private' with the 'personal'.[13] We are all aware, however, of the problems that come with the anachronistic application of words such as 'private' or 'privacy' and the connotations that almost automatically spring to our 'modern' mind. It seems, nevertheless, intuitively right to subsume under 'private life' those moments in life that one usually shares exclusively with those one is the closest to. Yet only the enlightened bourgeois of the eighteenth century began to claim a 'private

---

11. See *e.g.* F. Wieacker, *A History of Private Law in Europe*, trans. T. Weir (Oxford: 1995), 55 on the Glossators and the Commentators practicing and rendering expert opinions.
12. See, e.g., J. Le Goff, *Intellectuals in the Middle Ages*, trans. T.L. Fagan (Oxford: 1993), 63ff.
13. J. A. Weintraub, 'The Theory and Politics of the Public/Private Distinction', *Public and Private in Thought and Practice. Perspectives on a Grand Dichotomy*, eds. J. A. Weintraub and K. Kumar (Chicago: 1997), 1, 5ff.

sphere' and a 'private life' in the modern sense of the word.[14] What does 'private' signify beyond utter intimacy in a world where solitude was rare, and where even matters of conscience and belief would not have been seen as one's own 'private' matter in the modern sense?

Scholars like Georges Duby have tried to answer the question 'what was private in the Middle Ages?' by carefully approaching the subject through language.[15] Duby unearths different meanings that *'privatus'* can assume: besides designating private property, he points to the rule of St Benedict, where 'private' is used to describe the non-festive, the non-holy days. In that sense, 'private' describes 'daily life', normal life rather than only its most intimate moments. Duby also points out the usage of 'private life' as signifying life in a separated, closed community.[16] This usage refers to monastic communities. Mind you, our Scholastics did not live in monastic reclusion but in the midst of the sometimes rowdy life in the cities[17], at times being quite unruly themselves. They were, however, part of a specific, even separated, community. Mia Münster-Swendsen has referred to this condition as 'exile – a common, even quotidian, experience among these intellectuals and schoolmen [that] could be reconfigured to form part of the ascetic practice aiming at perfection'.[18] Unlike actual monastic reclusion, this deliberate exile was aimed, according to Münster-Swendsen, not at liberation from the world (and the total *mors civilis*) but at liberation from what is mundane – in Weberian terms, *'Weltablehnung'* rather than *'Weltflucht'*.[19] In that sense, the academic community indeed constituted a 'world apart'.[20] This world, this life-world in which the medieval scholars were deeply immersed, defined their life, status, and corporate (in the truest

---

14. See most notably, J. Habermas, 'The Public Sphere: An Encyclopedia Article', *New German Critique* 3 (1974), 49, 50ff.; J. Habermas, *The Structural Transformation of the Public Sphere. An Inquiry into a Category of Bourgeois Society*, trans. T. Burger and F. Lawrence (Cambridge MA: 1991), 11ff.
15. G. Duby, 'Introduction. Private Power, Public Power', *A History of Private Life II. Revelations of the Medieval World*, ed. G. Duby and trans. A. Goldhammer (Cambridge: 1988), 3ff.
16. Duby, 'Private Power, Public Power', 5.
17. Le Goff, *Intellectuals in the Middle Ages*, 63ff.
18. M. Münster-Swendsen, 'Medieval "Virtuosity": Classroom Practice and the Transfer of Charismatic Power in Medieval Scholarly Culture c. 1000–1230', *Negotiating Heritage [:] Memories of the Middle Ages*, Mette B. Bruun and Stephanie Glaser eds. (Turnhout: 2008), 43, 47.
19. Ibid.
20. J. W. Baldwin, *The Scholastic Culture of the Middle Ages, 1000–1300* (Lexington, MA: 1971), 99; see also M. Münster-Swendsen, 'The Model of Scholastic Mastery in Northern Europe c. 970–1200,' *Teaching and Learning in Northern Europe 1000–1200*, S. N. Vaughn and J. Rubenstein eds. (Turnhout: 2006), 305, 307: 'Scholastic world.'

sense of the word) identity to an extent that we would perceive as *personal* and penetrating deeply into the realm of the 'private'.[21] How much our approach to what is 'private' has changed – and how problematic it is to use this language so fraught with meaning to our modern ears, particularly in our academic context – is illustrated by the fact that 'private' carries, for us, the connotation of a privileged space, to be enjoyed by the individual under exclusion of 'the public'[22]; while in the medieval academic context, we also encounter *'privatus'* in the sense of *being deprived*, of being stripped of the privilege of belonging. *'Qui privatus est ab Universitate, intelligatur esse privatus comodo singulorum'*, for example, the statutes of the University of Padua tell us, describing the sanction for a scholar offending the statutes: social excommunication.[23] This all-defining and all-encompassing life-world, naturally, also conditioned the thinking of the medieval university jurist and imprinted its marks, irrevocably, on the legal discourse in continental Europe in its formative, its childhood years.

The Scholastic Habitus

The life-world that shaped this discourse and thought patterns of its participants is the life-world of the school: 'School' as used by Bourdieu as derived from *skholè,* as the epitome of the institutionalization of a 'scholastic' sphere beyond the 'urgency of the practical situation'. The beginnings of legal education mark the institutional beginnings of the university – the particular shape this institutionalization has taken in

---

21. See, e.g., regarding the ethical dimension of what it means to be a scholar – displaying a 'virtuous habitus', see Münster-Swendsen, 'Medieval "Virtuosity", 44ff. *et passim*; on the 'model of mastery' (pertaining in particular to the period from 970 to 1200) as involving interaction with the student based on affinity and love, see Münster-Swendsen, 'Scholastic Mastery', 305, 307 *et passim*. A historically less accurate, yet entertaining depiction of how being a member of a medieval university penetrates deeply into what we would perceive as 'private' is rendered by A. L. Gabriel, 'The Ideal of the Medieval Master', *The Catholic Historical Review* 60 (1974), 1ff. According to W. Frijhoff, the character of the university as a 'greedy institution' that was 'all-embracing' and that 'took upon itself to regulate its members' whole lives [*sic!*]' changes only with the ascendancy of a new paradigm of specialized higher education as epitomized in the French *hautes écoles* (W. Frijhoff, 'Chapter 2: Patterns', *A History of the University in Europe, vol. 2. Universities in Early Modern Europe 1500–1800*, ed. H. de Ridder-Symoens (Cambridge: 1996), 43, 46).
22. See, e.g., E. Goffman, *The Presentation of Self in Everyday Life* (Garden City, NY: 1959), 115.
23. Cited in H. Rashdall, *The Universities of the Middle Ages, vol. 1* (Oxford: 1895), 17, note 1.

Europe. It was, of course, the life-world of the school not only in the symbolic sense, but also as the expression of the specific 'school' culture that characterized medieval education; namely, Scholasticism as a historical phenomenon. What is it that we mean when we talk about 'Scholasticism' in this concrete sense? It is standard textbook fare to refer to the works of the canonists and legists as Scholastic. In many instances, this label is attached without much reflection on its implications. What does it mean to be a 'Scholastic', to produce work that is 'Scholastic'?

'Scholastic' will often have a pejorative ring to it. Such connotations are, as we all know, the result of a concerted attack on the achievements of medieval authorities by the Renaissance Humanists.[24] Although by no means historically tenable, a tradition was born of marginalizing 'scholasticism' and ridiculing its achievements, a tradition that turned Scholasticism into a swearword. This tradition was carried on by scholars such as Jacob Burckhardt and is one instance of what Lee Patterson once called the 'ubiquity of the master narrative' of the Middle Ages as an age of intellectual standstill before the re-beginning of the Renaissance.[25] However, even if we want to transcend and think we have transcended this simplistic (and simply factually inaccurate) narrative, we still sometimes stand clueless before the writings of the medieval jurists, their formalism, their predilections for exhaustive enumerations and symmetrical distinctions and sub-distinctions. In particular, we moderns are troubled by how medieval thinkers attempted to reconcile their goal of applying a rational method with seemingly unreasonable assumptions, in short, to reconcile reason and faith; as legal historian Franz Wieacker put it, 'we cannot understand the medieval jurist's belief that in the *Corpus Iuris* reason itself has become verbalized, that the word is *ratio scripta*'.[26]

It is through the lens of another sociological concept developed by Bourdieu that we gain additional insight into the role Scholasticism had to play in the formation of the seemingly irrational components of medieval legal discourse: his concept of *habitus*. This well-known concept explains human agency as influenced by dispositions that human beings are socialized into, and that operate beneath the level of consciousness and

---

24. D. R. Kelley, 'Civil Science in the Renaissance. Jurisprudence Italian Style', *Historical Journal* 22 (1979), 777, 778; C. G. Nauert, 'Humanism as Method. Roots of Conflict with the Scholastics', *Sixteenth Century Journal* 29 (1998), 427; C. G. Nauert, 'The Clash of Humanists and Scholastics. An Approach to Pre-Reformation Controversies', *Sixteenth Century Journal* 4 (1973), 1.
25. L. Patterson, 'On the Margin. Postmodernism, Ironic History, and Medieval Studies', *Speculum* 65 (1990), 87, 92.
26. Wieacker, *History of Private Law in Europe*, 35.

discourse.[27] As a collaborator of Bourdieu's, Professor Wacquant explains:[28]

> [H]abitus is a mediating notion that helps us revoke the common-sense duality between the individual and the social by capturing 'the internalization of externality and the externalization of internality,' that is, the way society becomes deposited in persons in the form of lasting dispositions, or trained capacities and structured propensities to think, feel, and act in determinate ways, which then guide their creative responses to the constraints and solicitations of their extant milieu.

I want to posit that approaching Scholasticism as such a habitus helps us understand medieval legal discourse that is not only, as we have heard so many times,[29] a function of the economic upswing of the twelfth century, but also the product of the interaction between its protagonists, the jurists, and their particular milieu of the school, which shaped them and was in turn shaped by them at the same time.

This, of course, requires a willingness to deviate from or at least supplement the 'definitions' of Scholasticism that we are used to. Scholasticism is commonly defined either through form or substance. The Neo-Thomist school of thought of the early twentieth century, most notably connected with names such as Jacques Maritain or Jacques de Wulf, insisted on a substantive definition of Scholasticism as a philosophy (while displaying a certain neglect of the strains of thought that were competing with Thomas' Aristotelianism).[30] Writing at the beginning of the twentieth century as well, Martin Grabmann stands for the attempt to conceptualize Scholasticism as a method and a methodology rather than a substantive philosophy:[31] he describes it as a way of reasoning and thinking born out of

---

27. P. Bourdieu, 'Intellectual Field and Creative Project', *Social Science Information* 8 (1969), 89; P. Bourdieu, *Outline of a Theory of Practice*, trans. R. Nice (Cambridge: 1977), 72.
28. L. Wacquant, 'Habitus', *International Encyclopedia of Economic Sociology*, eds. J. Beckert and M. Zafirovski (London: 2006), 315, 318.
29. See e.g., on the *studium civile* in Bologna, N. Schachner, *The Medieval Universities* (New York: 1962), 148.
30. M. L. Colish, 'XVIII [.] Remapping Scholasticism', in M. L. Colish, *Studies in Scholasticism* (Burlington: 2006) 5-6.
31. M. Grabmann, *Die Geschichte der scholastischen Methode nach den gedruckten und ungedruckten Quellen*, (Basel: 1909). A more recent version of this approach is presented by Le Goff, *Intellectuals in the Middle Ages*, 86ff.

the traits of the *trivium* and, at the same time, an adaptation of science to the needs of pedagogy.[32]

Medieval legal discourse surely cannot generally be called Scholastic in the former sense, in the sense of a philosophy: in his analysis of references to Aristotle in the works of the Glossators, German legal historian Gerhard Otte has warned against attaching the label 'scholastic' to these works simply because their time of origin coincides with the ascent of High (philosophical) Scholasticism, a fact that says nothing about the actual philosophical background of the jurists.[33] If we understand 'Scholasticism' as the methodology of the school, the 'Scholastic' quality of canonist and legist scholarship has been the focus of many works that show how jurists applied the methods of the *artes liberales*: Otte's work about dialectic modes of reasoning in the writings of the Glossators come to mind,[34] or, as to canonist scholarship, C.H.F. Meyer's work on the technique of the *distinctio*.[35] Conceptualizing Scholasticism as habitus builds on this formal understanding, but emphasizes that a *méthodos*, a way of doing something, is not necessarily the expression of a conscious application of rational principles (as in the modern understanding of 'scientific method'), but can also be guided by structures that operate sub- or preconsciously. Scholasticism can be understood as such a 'structuring structure'[36] that informs social action: as a way of thinking, a mindset growing out of a 'scholastic culture'[37] that was engulfing the school-men, barely making a distinction between the 'public' and the 'private'.

The first scholar to describe Scholasticism as a 'mental habit' was art historian Erwin Panofsky in his famous lecture on *Gothic Architecture and*

---

32. See M. de Wulf, *An Introduction to Scholastic Philosophy. Medieval and Modern*, trans. P. Coffey (New York: 1956), 35, who criticizes the formal 'definition'.
33. G. Otte, 'Die Aristoteleszitate in der Glosse, Beobachtungen zur philosophischen Vorbildung der Glossatoren', *Zeitschrift der Savigny-Stiftung für Rechtsgeschichte Rom. Abt.* 85 (1968), 368, 391.
34. For a prominent example, see G. Otte, *Dialektik und Jurisprudenz, Untersuchungen zur Methode der Glossatoren* (Frankfurt a.M.: 1971). Regarding the reception and exposure to the art of dialectics, he claims that the Glossators went beyond the standard of the trivial curriculum and the "schoolbooks" in use at the time: *ibid.* at 21.
35. For an exhaustive treatment of the subject, including the roots in the Greek *diairesis*, see C. H. F. Meyer, *Die Distinktionstechnik in der Kanonistik des 12. Jahrhunderts* (Leuven: 2000), 63ff. See also Wieacker, *A History of Private Law in Europe*, 36.
36. See, e.g., Bourdieu, *Outline of a Theory of Practice*, trans. R. Nice (Cambridge: 1977) 72.
37. See, e.g. Baldwin, *Scholastic Culture, passim;* Münster-Swendsen, 'Scholastic Mastery', 308 *et passim*.

Scholasticism.[38] According to Panofsky, Gothic architecture is, put in simple terms, 'Scholasticism set in stone'. The architects and master builders could not help but be influenced by Scholasticism since 'the school' held a 'monopoly in education',[39] being the crucial 'habit-forming force'.[40] When Bourdieu developed his concept of habitus, he actually drew on this work, fine-tuning the concept as used by Panofsky. This is no mere coincidence: Bourdieu emphasized time and again the paramount importance of institutionalized education. The significance, the 'habit-forming force', of institutionalized education is paradigmatically displayed in the dominance of 'the school', of scholastic school-education:

> [I]n a society where the transmission of culture is the monopoly of a school, the underlying affinities uniting works of learned culture (and at the same time behavior and thought) are governed by the principle emanating from the educational institution, which is entrusted with the function of transmitting consciously (and also in part unconsciously) the unconscious, or more precisely, of producing individuals who possess this system of unconscious (or extremely obscure) schemes which constitute their culture. Obviously it would be naive to stop looking for an explanation at this point, as if the school was an empire within an empire, and as if culture had its absolute beginnings there. But it would also be naive to take no account of the fact that the school, by the very logic of its functioning, modifies the content and spirit of the culture it transmits, or to forget that its express function is to transform the collective heritage into an individual and common unconscious.[41]

Panofsky, constructing his argument on architecture, focused on 'the school' as an educational monopoly that had a cultural impact even on those who were 'outsiders', namely, architects and builders. For the 'insiders', the schoolmen, the school was not only an educational institution, it was, at the same time, their 'milieu,' in short: a form of life.

The Gravitational Force of the Academic Field

1. What Remains (and Remained) Unsaid in Legal Discourse

Bourdieu himself has applied his theory to 'the law': in his analysis of 'the legal field', he describes the importance of the 'legal habitus' as shaping legal discourse, its actual predictability owing more to the shared 'habitus'

---

38. E. Panofsky, *Gothic Architecture and Scholasticism* (Latrobe, PA: 2005), 21
39. Panofsky, *Gothic Architecture*, 22.
40. Panofsky, *Gothic Architecture*, 21.
41. Bourdieu, 'Intellectual Field', 89, 118.

of legal actors than to the axiom of the 'formal rationality'[42] of the law.[43] In this analysis, Bourdieu also takes into account the role of academics in this 'legal field'. However, Bourdieu focuses mainly on the 'law in action', the administration of conflicts. Yet legal academics are as well positioned in the 'academic field' and therefore subject to its particular gravitational force. If we can assume that there is a specific scholastic/Scholastic habitus at work here, growing out of the specific milieu of the school, we can understand as well that habitual, subconscious mechanisms are at work in the production of legal texts that have nothing to do with the immediate application of law in the courts, with the resolution of conflicts or with the social dimension of law as part of the 'field of force'. When inquiring into the 'bookishness' of the learned law, accepting Scholasticism as habitus adds the significance of the 'subconscious' as another layer to the analysis.

How would factors that operate on an unconscious level influence the production of legal texts, which appears to be the paradigm of applied rationality, the exercise of reason? To answer this question, we have to undertake a little excursus, venturing from our medieval schoolmen to modern legal theorists. Of course, the Western scholarly tradition of legal thought, a tradition of 'scientific rationality' in itself,[44] has traditionally been reluctant to admit the significance of what cannot be rationally explained. Mainstream theory scholarship is still mostly centred on rules and questions of normativity.[45] However, a different type of theory scholarship, which has been called 'apocryphal jurisprudence',[46] has in the last decades directed its attention towards what remains unsaid in legal discourse and which Pierre Schlag has called 'legal aesthetics': 'A legal aesthetic is something that a legal professional both undergoes and enacts, most often automatically, without thinking'.[47] Such an understanding does not idealize law as a hypostasis of pure reason, but accepts it as what it is, a *man-made artifact*. It is people who shape legal discourse by writing about law, people conditioned by their environment with all its fashions, styles, tastes. These are best understood not as conscious preferences, but as factors that inform action habitually.

---

42. M. Weber, *Economy and Society*, eds. G. Roth and C. Wittich (Berkeley CA: 1978), 654.
43. P. Bourdieu, 'Force of Law. Toward a Sociology of the Juridical Field', *Hastings Law Journal* 38 (1986-87), 814, 833.
44. H. P. Glenn, *Legal Traditions of the World*, 3rd ed. (Oxford: 2007), 19.
45. See D. Manderson, 'Apocryphal Jurisprudence', *Studies in Law, Politics and Society* 23 (2001), 81; D. Manderson, *Songs without Music: Aesthetic Dimensions of Law and Justice* (Berkeley CA: 2000).
46. Manderson, 'Aprocryphal Jurisprudence', 84.
47. P. Schlag, 'The Aesthetics of American Law', *Harvard Law Review* 115 (2001-2002), 1047, 1053.

2. Pedagogy as Functional Factor

Let us now, equipped with these theoretical tools, return to our schoolmen. Functional accounts of the peculiarities of scholastic legal writing can be rendered, stemming from both the realm of 'the legal' and from the academy: harmonizing, creating *concordantia* between seemingly disparate, but at the same time authoritative, legal texts is necessary for the application of the law as well as for its pedagogical transmission. The pedagogical function of Scholastic thinking that expresses itself even in scholarly writings is particularly important for understanding the academic conditioning of the 'learned law' – Scholasticism was '*Wissenschaft in der Gestalt der Schule*',[48] scholarship in the form of 'school'.

The connections between scholastic writings and scholastic pedagogy are, first of all, displayed by the use of typical forms such as the gloss and the *quaestio*. The gloss has been called 'clearly a by-product of teaching' by *lectio*.[49] The form of the *quaestio* also signifies the strong link to education, not only being a literary genre, but also a ritualized form of learned dispute. Pedagogy, however, also helps to explain at least partially the method itself. Panofsky names the ambition to establish '*concordantia*' (achieved through the method of *distinctio*: proving that authorities are *diversa, sed non adversa*) as one of the two main aspirations of Scholasticism.[50] The well known proverb: 'Bene judicat qui bene distinguit' – he who distinguishes well, judges well – had its pedagogical counterpart: 'Bene docet, qui bene distinguit' – he who distinguishes well, teaches well.[51] It is easy to see how the attempt to reconcile contradicting authorities (through distinction) can have a pedagogical motivation: legal materials which are accepted as normative and authoritative are simply not expected to contradict each other. Along the same lines, the second main tenet of Scholasticism Panofsky pinpoints, *manifestatio*,'[52] can be interpreted in educational terms. *Manifestatio* calls for the elucidation of the process of reasoning itself and thus accounts for the much derided Scholastic 'formalism' of exposition and for the typical style of tedious enumerations. According to Panofsky, *manifestatio* demands '1) totality (sufficient enumeration), 2) arrangement according to a system of homologous parts and subparts (sufficient articulation) and 3) distinctness and deductive cogency (sufficient interrelation)'.[53] The intellectual paradigm underlying the ideal of *manifestatio*, however, is once more that of the scholar as school-teacher,

---

48. Schlag, 'Aesthetics of American Law', 1047, 1053.
49. Wieacker, *A History of Private Law in Europe*, 44.
50. Panofsky, *Gothic Architecture*, 64.
51. See, *e.g.*, Meyer, *Distinktionstechnik*, 65.
52. Panofsky, *Gothic Architecture*, 31.
53. Panofsky, *Gothic Architecture*, 31.

teaching through his writings, trying to achieve a height of clarity in his explications.

3. Scholasticism as 'Style' and Scholastic 'Aesthetics'

Be this as it may, this functional account does not explain the (at times) obsessive pursuit of the Scholastic ambitions of order and harmony that also expresses itself in legal texts. The Scholastic jurists developed their sophistic style of reasoning into a fine art of utmost subtlety, beyond what is justifiable in merely functional or utilitarian terms. An example is the utterly hypertrophic doctrine of '*interesse*', a theory of damages that was based on the scattered and often contradictory use of '*quod interest*' in the Digest and the Codex. The entangled and intricate debate haunted the civil law up to the age of the codifications; seventeenth-century jurist Scaccia gave the famous warning that the doctrine of *interesse* is a vast sea that few navigate without peril.[54] In the sixteenth century, Petrus Rebuffus would devise an 'arbor super interesse' from which 48 varieties of the *interesse*[55] grew – an excess that was a continuation of the Scholastic debate that invented and re-invented subcategories of the *interesse* and new versions of their relationship to each other; an excess that cannot be explained by its usefulness either for the application or the teaching of law.

Let us, therefore, try another explanation and return to the idea of 'legal aesthetics' as a pattern legal actors adhere to 'most often automatically, without thinking'.[56] The jurists themselves, as we know, referred to the phenomenon of 'style' to describe the difference between the 'new' Humanist *mos gallicus* as opposed to the 'scholastic' *mos italicus*. The usage of the word 'mos', which does not only mean 'custom' but also 'manner' and 'style', implies that more was at stake than one scientific methodology being replaced by another one. To distinguish themselves from the medieval Scholastics, the Humanists underlined their more sophisticated style[57] – a particular style being, *vice versa*, a crucial element of what it meant to be 'Scholastic'. Beyond this circumstantial evidence, how are we supposed to re-construct the medieval aesthetics of law? If there is (unsurprisingly) no body of medieval literature on *legal* aesthetics, are there '*non-legal*' medieval statements on aesthetics? I cannot engage here in the rich debate among art historians on the intricacies of medieval aesthetics and the possible risks of using this – anachronistic – term. In short, if we speak of medieval aesthetics, we have to be aware of the fact that since the

---

54. S. Scaccia, *Tractatus de commerciis et cambio*, Genevae, 1664, § VII Gl. II n. 18, S. 443f.: '*mare amplissimum, in quo pauci sine periculo navigarunt*'.
55. Cited according to an edition of the Codex: Codicis DN. Iustiniani (...) libri IX priores, Tomus Quartus, Venedig, Apud Iuntas, 1592, col. 2129-30 recto.
56. Schlag, 'Aesthetics of American Law', 1053.
57. See e.g. Kelley, 'Civil Science in the Renaissance', 778.

inception of the 'discipline' of aesthetics in the eighteenth century, the term has been limited to what has been defined as 'Fine Arts'.[58] Medieval 'aesthetics', as a philosophy of beauty, was not limited to the Fine Arts, but rather related to 'art' in the broad sense the term was given at the time. 'Art' meant simply 'knowing how to make'.[59] 'Art' in the sense of *ars* included the crafts, but also the 'Liberal Arts'. As we know, the academic community in the newly bustling urban space, despite constituting its own social field, modelled its self-perception and its form of organization on the self-confident craftsmen and their guilds.[60] De Bruyne, one of the 'classics' on medieval 'aesthetics', points out that such theories were, given the all-encompassing scope of 'art', 'as valid for the doctor, laborer, shoemaker as it is for the painter and sculptor'.[61]

Let us now return to Erwin Panofsky and his lecture on *Gothic Architecture and Scholasticism*. As noted above, Panofsky claims that Gothic architecture is Scholasticism set in stone, Scholasticism, again, understood not as a set of philosophical or theological insights, but as a 'mental habit'. We remember that this idea inspired Bourdieu in his development of the concept of habitus. For us, Panofsky's work is relevant in yet another dimension: he presents the Scholastic 'mental habit' as extending to the realm of the aesthetic. If Panofsky has demonstrated how understanding Scholastic rationality helps to clarify the 'visual logic' of Gothic architecture, drawing this connection helps us, *vice versa*, to understand the 'aesthetic' dimension of the Scholastic style. In other words, when we read that a Gothic rose window 'was created to the rhythm of yeses and noes of the *Sic et Non* of Abelard or a thirteenth-century disputation',[62] not only do we learn about the omnipresence of the scholastic mindset even in the Gothic workshop, but also about the fact that there was a certain 'rhythm' to the organization of pieces of Scholastic scholarship.

If we take a closer look at actual Scholastic writings on 'aesthetics', we get the impression that the substance of Scholastic philosophy preaches what the Scholastic method practices. Scholastic 'aesthetics' are centred on order, harmony, proportion, symmetry, congruence, consonance, *concordia*,

---

58. P. O. Kristeller, 'The Modern System of the Arts: A Study in the History of Aesthetics Part I,' 12 (1951) *Journal of the History of Ideas,* 496ff. *et passim*
59. U. Eco, *The Aesthetics of Thomas Aquinas,* Hugh Bredin trans. (Cambridge MA: 1988) 164.
60. See also Münster-Swendsen, 'Medieval "Virtuosity", 50: '[T]he *magister* is a craftsman – an *artifex* – who transforms the crude and unformed student material into a work of art'.
61. E. De Bruyne, *The Esthetics of the Middle Ages*, trans. E. B. Hennessy (New York: 1969), 180ff.
62. Baldwin, *Scholastic Culture,* 114.

concordantia. Umberto Eco[63] has called this the 'quantitative' approach to beauty, inherited from ancient Greek thought. These are the threads that run through all Scholastic theories of the beautiful (coming from writers as diverse as Grosseteste, Bonaventure, Albertus Magnus, Aquinas and even Ockham).[64] It is important, once again, to underscore that these aesthetic ideals do not apply exclusively to physical appearance, or, particularly in the case of *consonantia*, to music. Beauty, as a truly universal quality, equated with 'the good' in philosophical writings,[65] is an ideal to be aspired to by everyone involved in any form of creation. As the inclusion of the *artes liberales* shows, this aesthetic paradigm also pertains to scholarly activities. It also applies to the exercise of reason, to a 'well-proportioned' thought, and to the 'purely rational concordance between things'.[66] Consonance had transcended its technical origins in musical harmony and implied, in a general sense, a fitting together, compatibility and 'natural cohesion' between two or more elements, which also implied an 'ordering' of one thing to another and to the whole. 'Pure harmony' is, as de Bruyne described it 'the agreement and unification of dissimilar things'.[67]

As mentioned earlier, an interesting and, in my opinion, instructional example is furnished by the doctrine of *interesse*, an example of a discourse that, at least partly, has become *l'art pour l'art*. In this context, the medieval jurist was facing from the outset a particularly complex challenge: the Roman sources in this field are particularly cryptic, unwieldy and contradictory. To establish a coherent theory of damages that still could be said to be rooted in these sources, their 'dissonance' had to be overcome, and '*concordantia*' had to be established. The Scholastic technique

---

63. Umberto Eco, *Art and Beauty in the Middle Ages*, trans. H. Bredin (New Haven CT: 1986), 28.
64. See Eco, *Art and Beauty*, 29ff. W. Tatarkiewicz, *History of Aesthetics. vol. 2. Medieval Aesthetics*, ed. C. Barrett (The Hague: 1970), 213ff.
65. On 'moral aesthetics' see, *e.g.,* De Bruyne, *The Esthetics of the Middle Ages*, 89; Eco, *Art and Beauty* 21. This co-extensiveness is important for Münster-Swendsen, 'Medieval "Virtuosity"', 49f., when – in the context of what she calls the 'virtuous habitus', elaborating on '*ars*' as encompassing an aesthetic and ethical dimension: 'the transmutation [sc.: of the scholar towards a 'more perfect sense of selfhood'] is achieved through the application of meticulous practices and disciplines, which are connected with the notion of ars. Like the seven artes liberales themselves, it involves a method and is consciously regulated that combine ethics with aesthetics. In the art of rhetoric, for example, the ability ot express oneself in correct and beautiful language (recte scribendi or docendi) is directly connected with the art of living righteously (recte vivendi) – there can be no order without beauty and no beauty without order, and in this world all the arts aspire to and guarantee the existence of both.'
66. K. E. O'Reilly, *Aesthetic Perception, A Thomistic Perspective* (Dublin: 2007) 20.
67. De Bruyne, *Esthetics*, 63.

employed to reconcile these contradictions would, as Harold J. Berman put it, have to draw generalizations from disparate phenomena and use the whole as a basis for the interpretation of the parts, without destroying their integrity as parts. In the light of this technique, Berman concluded: 'Thus, scholasticism was more than a method; it involved also a philosophy'.[68] We might add: this 'philosophy' could (also) have been an aesthetic; and as unlikely as this might seem at first glance, if we go beyond the definitions of Scholasticism as 'method' or 'philosophy' and perceive it as mindset, as 'habitus', we understand how such 'legal aesthetics' could have operated below the level of legal consciousness and official discourse. This shall suffice – unlike in my oral presentation during our meeting, I shall not further elaborate on the doctrine of *interesse* and how it might exemplify the role of such aesthetics – I have discussed my views in more detail in a different venue.[69] Such a discussion involves a certain degree of doctrinal technicality, which I want to spare this circle of – less doctrinally inclined – readers.

Some Concluding Observations

This brings us back to where we started, to Professor Pennington's neat description of the impatience experienced by historians of law who are made to sit through a lecture on doctrine, delivered by a legal historian. This particular *traditional* way of conceptualizing historical scholarship as a history of doctrine (as opposed to a 'social' history reconstructed by the scrutiny of the 'law in action') is flowing out of a scholarly tradition that is itself learned, self-referential, academic, *bookish*. It is another example of the 'scholastic point of view' we diagnosed at the very outset of our inquiry as such a distinctive trait of the continental legal tradition – a mentality that was first engendered by the Scholastic writings that constituted the renaissance of Roman law in Western Europe. I have tried (though not in the vein of *doctrinal* legal scholarship) to highlight this 'bookishness' as another frontier of the research on the production of legal texts that is deeply rooted in academic culture. Scholasticism is the focal point of this academic culture: a culture that elevates the school to a way of life. This far-

---

68. H. J. Berman, 'Religious Foundations of Law in the West: An Historical Perspective', 1 (1983) *Journal of Law & Religion* 3, 8.
69. H. Dedek, 'Die Schönheit der Vernunft. (Ir-)Rationalität von Rechtswissenschaft in Mittelalter und Moderne', *Rechtswissenschaft* 1 (2010), 58, 76ff. See also H.J. Wieling, *Interesse und Privatstrafe vom Mittelalter zum Bürgerlichen Gesetzbuch* (Cologne: 1970) 81ff.; *H. Lange*, 'Bartolus' Einfluss auf die Entwicklung des Schadensersatzrechts', in *Bartolo da Sassoferrato, Studi e documenti per il VI centenario,* vol. 2, (Milan: 1962), 281ff.

reaching impact can be understood by approaching it through the lens of the concept of habitus, a concept that served us as a heuristic tool to explain better the structures that inform the interaction of social agents with their environment within a 'given field'. Conceptualizing Scholasticism as a habitus guides us towards factors that usually are not taken into account in the analysis of legal discourse: the irrational, the subconscious. This pursuit has given us the opportunity to take a fresh look at the production of legal texts, to see them as artifacts that abide by a certain aesthetic.

The anecdote Professor Pennington relates gives rise to another, final observation. The encounter he describes is not only the display of oblivion towards the social impact of the law on the part of the hopeless doctrinalist. It is also the description of a clash of cultures *within* an academic 'discipline'. The heuristic interest of the historian of law in history departments outside the legal academy has been different from that of the legal historian. The historian of law has traditionally not been primarily interested in the 'internal' development of the law; 'the law' rather provides historians with a means (that is, surviving sources in writing, particularly in respect to periods before common literacy)[70] to describe social reality[71] – hence the predilection for the law applied to facts, the 'law in action'. In contrast, 'legal history' as studied in the law faculties has *traditionally* been instrumental to the study of 'law': legal historians have tried to contribute to the legal debates of the day by introducing a historical argument to the discourse. The French humanists who constituted what Donald R. Kelley has called the 'first historical school of law'[72] were all *lawyers*; and, as Kelley reminds us, 'conservative professionals' at that, who sought to improve jurisprudence while being intensely loyal to their profession.[73] These were the beginnings of what became a tradition of 'legal history' that henceforth – from Cujas's 'first' via Savigny's 'second' historical school to today's European experts on the *ius commune* who aim to contribute to the debate around a European Private Law – was preoccupied with the internal (doctrinal) mechanisms of the law, and even voluntarily assumed an instrumental, ancillary role towards the law 'in force'.

Only in the last few decades, with the increasing degree of specialization of historical scholarship and the liberation of legal

---

70. See, *e.g.*, C. Verhoeven, 'Court Files', *Reading Primary Sources,* M. Dobson and B. Ziemann eds. (Oxford: 2009) 91.
71. One of the few historians who has reflected explicitly on the interest of historians in 'the law' remains E.P. Thompson – see, e.g. E.P. Thompson, *The Poverty of Theory* (New York: 1978) 96; 'The Rule of Law', *The Essential E.P. Thompson*, D. Thompson ed. (New York, New Press: 2001) 432, 438ff.
72. D. R. Kelley, 'The Rise of Legal History in the Renaissance' 9 (1970) *History and Theory* 174, 178.
73. Kelley, 'Rise of Legal History', 181.

scholarship from its internal, 'legal' perspectives, has this chasm between the different perspectives shrunk. However, the respective academic fields inexorably exert their gravitational forces, forces that are at work when we formulate the questions we are asking. My inquiry into the 'bookishness' of the learned law was ultimately driven by an interest in the theoretical structure of legal discourse itself and its non-conscious, non-rational components – a perennial problem that even the theorists of modern law have only recently begun to tackle. While attempting to transcend the boundaries of doctrinal legal history scholarship as traditionally practised, my reflections remain a pursuit that (besides making the historians in the audience squirm and wiggle in their seats!) ultimately is an expression of the 'scholastic' condition of a *legal* academic: not a depiction of (private) life through law, but an attempt to add some brushstrokes to the portrayal of law by highlighting its context – the life-world of the school. We began our inquiry with the quotation: 'The Ius commune was not bookish law, […], was not learned law in contrast to real law'.[74] We might now conclude that as bookish as it was, the learned law was indeed real law since its bookishness, its learned-ness, was an expression of its very reality.

---

74. Pennington, 'Learned Law', 215.

Prosecuting and Proving Sexual Infidelity at the Court of King Arthur: The Case of Guinevere v. Lanval

Stephen D. White

Introduction: Lanval's Trial

Here are the facts of the case of *Guinevere v. Lanval*, as reported in Marie de France's 'Lai de Lanval' (c.1170).[1]
An anonymous queen easily identifiable as Guinevere secretly offers her love to Lanval, whom King Arthur had previously failed to reward for his loyal service but who later received a better reward when a beautiful fairy

---

1. In the text and notes, numbers in parentheses refer to line numbers in 'Lanval', in *Lais de Marie de France*, ed. Karl Warnke and trans. Laurence Harf-Lancner, Lettres Gothiques, ed. Michel Zink (Paris, 1990), 135-67. Other editions consulted include: 'Lanval' in Marie de France, *Lais*, ed. Alfred Ewert (Oxford, 1944), 58-74; Marie de France, *Le lai de Lanval*, ed. Jean Rychner (Geneva, 1958), 22-77, which prints four different manuscript versions of the poem; and 'Lanval', in *Les lais de Marie de France*, ed. Jean Rychner (Paris, 1966), 72-92. Direct translations from the poem are from 'Lanval', in *The Lais of Marie de France*, trans. Glyn S. Burgess and Keith Busby (Harmondsworth, 1986), at 73-81. I have also consulted 'Lanval', in *The Lais of Marie de France*, trans. Robert Hanning and Joan Ferrante (Durham, NC, 1978), 105-23. The entire paper owes much to Paul Hyams for his helpful comments and criticisms of earlier versions of this paper, one of which was published as Stephen D. White, 'Tshest', sexual'nye prityazaniya i perevoratshivanie ierarhiy v "Lai de Lanval" Marii Francuzskoy'. Russian trans. of 'Honor, Sexual Harassment, and the Reversal of Hierarchies in Marie de France's "Lai de Lanval"' in *Homo historicus: Sbornik pamyati Yuriya L'vovitsha Bessmertnogo; Essays in Memory of Yuri Bessmertny on the 80th Anniversary of His Birth*, ed. Alexandre O. Tshubarian (Moscow: 2003), 130-51.

princess gave him infinite wealth, love, and seisin of her body, but all on condition that he never speak of her. Lanval rejects Guinevere's offer, saying that he does not wish to betray his lord Arthur. But he thereby insults the queen, who insults Lanval in return by saying that he obviously prefers young boys to women. Next, Lanval pays back the queen by insulting her, declaring that in every respect, she is inferior to his own love's lowliest serving-maid. However, by mentioning his love, Lanval believes, he has broken the condition on which she had given herself to him.

Guinevere tries to avenge Lanval's insults by seeking justice from King Arthur, to whom she mendaciously complains, first, that Lanval had shamed her by seeking her love and, second, that when she rejected him, he insulted her in the way already mentioned. After summoning Lanval, the king modifies Guinevere's first complaint against Lanval by charging that he had betrayed him by seeking his wife's love. In addition, Arthur accuses Lanval of insulting the queen. Lanval flatly denies the first accusation and meets the second by expressing regret for what he had said to the queen, but only because he had lost his own love by speaking of her. The king seeks counsel about how to proceed in the case from the men of his household, who recommend that the case be heard in the king's great council, once Gawain and his companions agree to be pledges for Lanval's appearance in this larger court, where Arthur's magnates and other men will judge Lanval's case. At the great council, the judges hear the king's charges and Lanval's responses. After they debate the case privately, their spokesman, the count of Cornwall, then reports that the king's first charge that Lanval had sought the queen's love should be dismissed on the grounds that only one person – namely the queen – had accused him. As for the second charge, about insulting Guinevere, the count declares that Lanval will be acquitted if he can provide proof that he spoke truthfully about the superiority of his lover's serving-maids to the queen. In that case, according to the judges, he should not be judged as having spoken spitefully to her. Lanval worries that by speaking of his love, he has lost her but, at the last minute, she and her serving-maids appear before the court. Since they prove their superiority to the queen, and his love offers her own defence of Lanval, they secure Lanval's acquittal. He and the girl then abandon Arthur's court and ride off to the Isle of Avalon.

Literary Studies of Law in Lanval's Trial

In analysing this well-known trial scene, literary scholars have often argued that Marie de France constructed it as critique of both the judicial procedures that Arthur's court uses in this literary law case and those of her own day, on which she modelled them.[2] Don A. Monson observes, 'La scène du procès nous montre dans les détails une procédure lourde et encombrante qui ne fonctionne pas, même lorsqu'elle est suivie scrupuleusement et à la lettre. Car malgré toutes les précautions prises . . . il est clair que cette procédure serait totalement incapable d'aboutir toute seule à un résultat juste, que seule l'intervention de l'Autre Monde empêche une injustice éclatante.'[3] Even though Arthur's court follows 'scrupuleusement la procédure féodale' according to Edgard Sienaert, there are unmistakable signs of institutional breakdown throughout Lanval's trial.[4] 'Dès la plainte portée par la reine,' he writes, 'toute la pompeuse et compliquée machine judiciaire arthurienne se met en branle. De l'accusation à l'acquittement, le procès occupe tout près de la moitié du lai . . . . Le monde chevaleresque d'empêtre dans ses propres rites, se sclérose dans ses innombrables questions de procédure vétilleuse où on respecte la lettre de la loi, mais non l'esprit.'[5] Jacques Ribard made a similar diagnosis of the workings of feudal justice in Lanval's trial when he wrote: '[C]'est tout un univers sclérosé dont les usages féodaux et juridiques vont se trouver comme ridiculisés. Qu'on pense seulement à cet interminable ballet des "jugeüers" empêtres dans leur juridisme étroit: il suffira d'une apparition féminine, éclatante dans sa quasi nudité, pour le faire apparaître étonnament vide et dérisoire.'[6]

---

2. On the trial, see, in addition to the works cited below, E. A. Francis, 'The Trial in Lanval', in *Studies in French Language and Mediaeval Literature Presented to Professor Mildred K. Pope* (1939; reprinted Freeport, NY: 1969), 115-24; *The Lais of Marie de France*, trans. Robert Hanning and Joan Ferrante (Durham, NC: 1978), 123-5; Paul R. Hyams, 'Henry II and Ganelon', *Syracuse Scholar* 4 (1983), 22-35 at 31-5; and W. Rothwell, 'The Trial Scene in *Lanval* and the Development of the Legal Register in Anglo-Norman', *Neuphilologische Mitteilungen* 101 (2000), 17-36 with a useful appendix of 'legal' terms at 31-3. See also Paula Clifford, *Marie de France: Lais* (London, 1982), 56-60; Ernest Hoepffner, *Les lais de Marie de France* (Paris : 1935), 56-71; Y. Otaka, 'Le vocabulaire de la justice chez Marie de France', *Studies in Language and Culture*, 6 (1980), 103-233; Glyn S. Burgess, *The Lais of Marie de France: Text and Context* (Athens, GA : 1987), esp. 19-20, 122-5, 104-6.
3. Don A. Monson, 'L'idéologie du lai de Lanval', *Le moyen âge* 92 [5th ser. 1] (1987): 349-72 at 367. According to Hanning and Ferrante, *Lais of Marie de France*, 125, the 'legal system works only because the lady appears. . . . If she had not come, injustice would have prevailed.' See also Burgess, *The Lais of Marie de France*, 20.
4. Edgard Sienaert, *Les lais de Marie de France: du conte merveilleux à la nouvelle psychologique* (Paris: 1978), 100.
5. Sienaert, *Les lais*, 104.
6. Jacques Ribard, 'Le lai de Lanval: essai d'interpretation polysemique', in *Mélanges de philologie et de littérature romanes offerts à Jeanne Wathelet-Willem* (Liège: 1978), 529-44 at 531. John M. Bowers, 'Ordeals, Privacy, and the *Lais* of Marie de

The effect of these exercises in the not-so-new-historicist study of law in medieval literature is to incorporate Lanval's trial into a much broader thesis about the trial scenes included in many Old French and Anglo-Norman literary works of the late twelfth and earlier thirteenth centuries. More than thirty years ago, 'the relationship between Old French literature and the judicial transformation of the twelfth and thirteenth century' was the subject of R. Howard Bloch's influential study of *Medieval French Literature and Law*, which set the tone for subsequent work on the same subject.[7] Treating epics and romances as 'aristocratic' genres that were 'deeply rooted in the evolving legal ethos of their time,' Bloch argued that both kinds of narratives simultaneously reflected and contributed to 'a common legal crisis' in 'values and institutions, as texts seeking to reproduce the [judicial] practices of [Marc Bloch's] "first feudal age" offer a persistent critique of their inadequacy'.[8] As other writers on law in medieval French literature followed Bloch, it became conventional to assume that the creators of these literary law cases or, at least, most of them represented so-called 'feudal' judicial procedures just as unfavourably as Marie de France supposedly did in Lanval's trial.[9]

However, in their eagerness to enlist Marie de France into the late twelfth-century movement toward a legal revolution that would rationalize judicial procedures and abolish the judicial duel, commentators on the poem failed to note two important points about the trial. The first is that, procedurally, the only real flaw in Lanval's trial is the receptivity of King Arthur, as lord of the court hearing the case, to the false accusation of treason made by the queen against an honourable man whom the king had never favoured. In fact, the close reading of the trial presented below will show that Arthur's court deserves much of the credit for Lanval's acquittal.

France', *Journal of Medieval and Renaissance Studies* [later *Journal of Medieval and Early Modern Studies*], 24 (1994), 1-31 at 21 reads Lanval's trial as a critique of 'the dark side of the jury trial under direct royal supervision'. Jacqueline Eccles, 'Marie de France and the Law', in *Les lieux interdits: Transgression and French Literature*, ed. Larry Duffy and Adrian Tudor (Hull: 1998), 15-30 at 16, 17, sees the jury of presentment, not the trial jury, as the object of Marie de France's critique, which 'deals with the moral dilemma of criminal trials' conducted under the new system of justice that Henry II introduced in the Assize of Clarendon (1166).

7. R. Howard Bloch, *Medieval French Literature and Law* (Berkeley: 1977), 1.
8. Bloch, *Medieval French Literature*, 10, 11.
9. Ross G. Arthur, 'The Judicium Dei in the *Yvain* of Chrétien de Troyes', *Romance Notes* 28 (1987), 3-12; Nicole Cazauran, 'Duels judicaires dans deux "Proses": Le triomphe des parjures dans *Ogier le Danois* et *Meurvin*', *Romania*, 108 (1987) 79-96; John W. Baldwin, 'The Crisis of the Ordeal', *Journal of Medieval and Renaissance Studies* 24 (1994), 327-53; Sarah Kay, *The Chansons de Geste in the Age of Romance: Political Fictions* (Oxford: 1995), 52.

Its scrupulous observance of traditional judicial procedures in cases of treason gives the barons who judge the case an opportunity to evaluate the charges against Lanval, find legal grounds for dismissing the more serious charge of treason against the king, construe the truth of insulting words as proof that they were not spoken out of spite, tacitly take account of their presumption that the queen's accusation was made out of malice, and allow the girl and her serving-maids to appear in court to defend Lanval in court against the charge of having shamed the queen. Indeed, Lanval's trial even brings out the probative value of trial by battle since the poem's concluding scene can be read as gender-bended judicial duel, in which the serving-maids of Lanval's love and ultimately the girl herself prove by their bodies against the body of the queen that they are more beautiful and thus nobler than she is.[10] At the same time, the girl demonstrates that the queen had falsely accused Lanval of preferring boys to women.

Overall, the poem depicts this form of trial as a fully effective vehicle for acquitting a blameless defendant and thus protecting him against precisely the kind of treason that Beaumanoir, the late thirteenth-century author of the *Coutumes de Beauvaisis*, defines as 'giving false witness in order that someone will be put to death, or disinherited, or .. banished or . . . hated by his liege lord'. This passage should be understood in the light of the statement preceding it that 'treason is when one gives no impression of hatred and hates mortally'.[11] If so, then far from exposing the inadequacy of traditional judicial procedures, Marie de France's 'Lai de Lanval' simultaneously dramatizes both the dangers of a false accusation of illicit sex against an honorable defendant when made to a bad king who listens to evil counsel and the capacity of a court of lay nobles to adjudicate it, acquit the falsely accused defendant, and expose his accuser as a traitor.

Sexual Treason Trials: Four Types of Cases

In these respects, moreover, Lanval's trial closely resembles other trials in twelfth- and thirteenth-century French literary works where a court adjudicates an accusation of what might be called sexual treason or infidelity against a man or a woman of the great nobility. Before looking more closely at the proceedings of Arthur's court in the trial of Lanval, the

---

10. On the conventionalized undertaking by an appellant to prove 'by his body' and that of the defendant to defend by 'his body', see, e.g., *Britton: The French Text Carefully Revised*, ed. Francis Morgan Nichols, 2 vols. (Oxford: 1865), Book I, chap. 33 (100-1); online http://www.anglo-norman.net/cgi-bin/and-getloc. Accessed 16 April, 2010.
11. Philippe de Beaumanoir, *Coutumes de Beauvaisis*, ed. A. Salmon, 3 vols. (1899; Paris: 1970), vol. 1, chap. 30, nos. 826-7.

paper will consider four kinds of trials of this general type in order to explain how such literary law cases served as vehicles for criticizing, or at least humorously satirizing, the political and legal culture of twelfth and thirteenth-century courts and not what they represented as traditional judicial procedures, including the judicial duel (or trial by battle). These procedures, when properly followed, were represented as fully adequate to the task of preventing honourable defendants such as Lanval from false or at least ill-intentioned accusations of treason by treacherous appellants, such as the queen, and the royal lords of courts, such as Arthur, who listened to their evil counsels.

(1) The literary trials that resemble Lanval's trial closely in most respects, since they concern appeals of treason that are flagrantly false, can be illustrated by an extended trial scene in *Les sept sages de Rome*, where the emperor Vespasian's second wife falsely accuses his son by his first wife of rape. The queen is smitten by the youth and tries to seduce him; but when he rejects her advances, she tears her clothing, bloodies her own face, raises the hue and cry, and charges that he tried to ravish her. However, the young man's trial in the emperor's court ends with the young man's acquittal and the empress's condemnation as a traitor.[12] In *Le roman de Waldef*, an Anglo-Norman text dated to c.1200–1210, the wife of King Ode of Poitou rejects the advances of a wicked seneschal, who then falsely accuses her of sexual infidelity. Initially, the king condemns Ode to death by burning without a proper trial; but he later realizes his mistake, accuses the seneschal of treason, defeats him in battle, and has him burned on the pyre prepared for the queen's execution.[13] The same story-line is played out in a thirteenth-century romance called *Joufroi de Poitiers*, where a wicked seneschal at the court of the king of England asks the king's wife Alice for her love. When she rejects him, he tells the king that he had found a kitchen boy having sex with her. The king immediately has her arrested and, without convening his court to hear the case, swears to have her burned or hanged. But when the eponymous hero of the story hears of the queen's plight, he asks the king to knight him and tells him that he and queen have been betrayed by the seneschal. In response to Jouffroi's accusation, the

---

12. Mary B. Spear, ed., '*Le roman des Sept Sages de Rome*': *A Critical Edition of the Two Verse Redactions of a Twelfth-Century Romance*, Edward C. Armstrong Monograph on Medieval Literature, vol. 4 (Lexington, KY: 1989). For a similar trial, see Herbert, *Le roman de Dolopathos*, ed. Jean-Luc Leclanche, Les Classiques Français du Moyen Âge, 3 vols. (Paris : 1997).
13. *Le roman de Waldef*, ed. A.J. Holden, Bibliotheca Bodmeriana (Cologny-Geneva : 1984), lines 7,602–8,110.

seneschal makes his denial; but in the ensuing judicial duel, he is defeated and killed by the champion of the falsely accused queen.[14]

A more intricately constructed trial of the same basic type takes place in *Le roman de Silence*, a late thirteenth-century poem about a girl called Silence, who is brought up as a boy because her father wants a male heir and who is sent to the court of King Evan of England. There, King Evan's wife, Queen Eufeme, is smitten by Silence and when he/she rejects her advances, she accuses him/her of trying to rape her. The king tries to protect Silence from the queen by sending him/her, with a letter of friendly introduction, to the King of France. But the queen of England replaces this letter with a forged letter that informs the French king to execute Silence for having brought a kind of shame on the King of England that is too horrible to mention. When Silence reaches the French king's court, however, he/she is pardoned because, before reading the letter, the King gives him/her a kiss of peace. At the end of the story, of course, Silence's false accuser, the queen of England, is condemned as a traitor and executed.[15]

(2) Whereas trials of the first type are usually presented ironically and humorously, those falling into a second category are played out as legal melodramas. In several *chansons de geste* and in a number of thirteenth-century romances, a treacherous nobleman at the king's court tries to seduce the king's wife, telling her that if she accepts his proposition, he will kill the king and marry her so that together they will rule her dead husband's kingdom. When the virtuous queen rejects him, he fabricates grounds for accusing her of adultery and persuades the king to put her on trial in his court. Initially, flagrant procedural irregularities prevent the falsely accused queen from proving her innocence. But after going into exile and enduring terrible hardships, she is exonerated at a later trial, while the false accuser is condemned to a traitor's death.[16] If there can really be a good example of this kind of two-part literary trial, it is probably the one in a story called *Macaire*, where the eponymous traitor seeks the love of Blanchefleur, wife of Charlemagne. When she rejects him, he tells the emperor that he suspects her of having sex with another man and, with Charlemagne's approval, undertakes to entrap her with her lover. Meanwhile, Macaire's henchmen have smuggled a dwarf into Blanchefleur's bed, while she is drunk on spiced wine. After finding the queen and the dwarf in bed together,

---

14. *Joufroi de Poitiers: Roman d'aventures du xiiie siècle*, ed. Percival B. Bay and John L. Grigsby (Geneva: 1972), lines 186-632; and *Joufroi de Poitiers: Traduction critique*, trans. Roger Nöel, Studies in the Humanities: Literature, Politics, Society (New York: 1987), 29-46.
15. *Silence: A Thirteenth-Century French Romance*, ed. and trans. Sarah Roche-Mahdi, revised ed. (East Lansing, MI: 1999), lines 37110-5144.
16. For brilliant analyses of stories that include such trial scenes, see Kay, *Chanson de Geste*.

Charlemagne kills the dwarf and puts his wife on trial in his court. Because Blanchefleur is denied the opportunity she should have had to clear herself, she initially fails to win an acquittal in her husband's court, goes into exile, and endures terrible hardships. But at a later trial, the faithful dog of the queen's most faithful knight fights and wins a judicial duel against Macaire and forces him to confess to his odious treason.[17]

(3) A third kind of trial of a defendant falsely accused of illicit sex provides the framework for a small group of early thirteenth-century poems, which is known as 'the wager cycle' because the plots always turn on a bet between two men about a woman's chastity. At the royal court, one nobleman bets another nobleman that he can seduce the latter's wife or mistress on the understanding that the winner of the bet will take the loser's land. The first nobleman fails to seduce the woman, but by presenting to the court what all the men there – including the second nobleman – take to be evidence that he succeeded, the first man wins the bet and takes the land of the second, who promptly exiles his wife or mistress. Only after the woman endures further hardships and humiliation is she reconciled with her dimwitted husband or lover, who finally sees through his rival's plot and comes back to the king's court with proof of his rival's treason. At a second trial, which is essentially a continuation of the first, the second nobleman, in effect, defends her against a false accusation of illicit sex by truthfully accusing his rival of falsely accusing her and convinces the court to execute the first nobleman as a traitor. Through the same process, the same man not only re-establishes the woman's honour; he also regains his own honour in both senses of the word since he recovers his own land.[18]

Viewed from one perspective, these literary trials reveal much about the misogynistic sexual anxieties of male nobles about the sexual fidelity of wives, including queens, and the chastity of marriageable young women. However, these literary *placita* also bring out with equal or even greater clarity the political, even legal, anxieties of aristocratic members of Anglo-French court societies about the kind of treason I have already mentioned. That is, they express the fear of those who give false witness about illicit sexual conduct for the purpose of making the accused hated by his or her lord and suffer dishonour in one or both senses of the word and possibly banishment or death. In discussing sexual infidelity, legal historians have understandably focused on the problem of proving it in the absence of

---

17. *Macaire*, ed. François Guessard, Anciens Poètes de France (Paris : 1866), 32-63, 75-107.
18. *Le conte de Poitiers*, ed. V.-Frédéric Koenig (Paris : 1937); Jean Renart, *Le roman de la rose or of Guillaume de Dole (Roman de la Rose ou de Guillaume de Dole)*, ed. and trans. Regina Paski (New York : 1995), lines 4602-5655; Gerbert de Montreuil, *Le roman de la violette*, ed. Douglas Labaree Buffum, SATF (Paris: 1927), lines 3947-4117, 5070-5332.

witnesses and the use of ordeals to do so. But just as important was the problem of disproving accusations of illicit sex or, at least, contesting rumours about it and the problem of defending and restoring the honour of nobles, particularly women, said to have engaged in it. The most direct historical evidence for the importance of this issue is necessarily anecdotal since it comes from texts that re-cycle rumours about the sexual liaisons of well-known figures, notably Eleanor of Aquitaine.[19] However, in cases where one can gauge the potential political and even legal consequences of this kind of rumour-mongering or gossip, one can see it as part of the never-ending competition for place and patronage in court societies, where dishonouring rival competitors was as much a part of the game as was flattering the ruler.[20] If we extend the simple notion of flattering a ruler as simply currying favour with him to encompass playing on his fears, identifying the real or imaginary enemies who threatened him, and providing a means to eliminate them, it is easy to see how closely the flattery that court critics such as John of Salisbury satirized could be associated with the treason of bearing false witness about illicit sexual conduct in order to make someone hated by his or her lord and even with the truthful tale-bearing associated with the men called *lozengiers* in twelfth-century Occitan and French poetry. Even when *lozengiers* tell the lord of a court the truth about the adulterous relationship between his wife and one of his men, they are still depicted as 'traitors' and 'felons' because their purpose is to advance at court by simultaneously ingratiating themselves with the lord and destroying the reputations of the lovers, one or both of whom they envy and hate with the kind of secret 'hatred' that Beaumanoir identified in the passage cited above as the essence of 'treason'.[21]

(4) This way of understanding treason and traitors helps to explain how literary authors represented a fourth type of trial in which a court faces the problem of adjudicating an accusation of sexual treason that is 'true' in the sense of being factually accurate and consistent with what the audience knows about it, but also 'false' in the sense of being motivated, not by a desire to do right, but rather by hatred and a desire to do harm to the accused by making his lord hate him. To the extent that Lanval's trial

---

19. See, in particular, Peggy McCracken, *The Romance of Adultery: Queenship and Sexual Transgression in Old French* (Philadelphia: 1998).
20. See, above all, Robert Bartlett, *England under the Norman and Angevin Kings, 1075–1225* (Oxford: 2000), 28-35.
21. See above note 11. On 'treason', as represented in French and Anglo-Norman lawbooks and in literary trial scenes, see, generally, Stephen D. White, 'Alternative Constructions of Treason in the Angevin Political World: *Traïson* in the *History of William Marshal*', *e-Spania*, 4 December 2007, 1-47. URL: http://e-pania.revues.org/document2233.html . Consulted 12 April 2010.

concerns a complaint that Lanval spoke words to the queen that insulted her for the purpose of insulting her, it resembles trials of the fourth type, including the trial of Yseut Béroul's *Roman de Tristan*[22] and the trial of Guinevere in *La mort le roi Artu*.[23] These cases have sometimes troubled modern readers because the female defendants – Yseut in the first case and Guinevere in the second – are presented more favourably than either their accusers or their royal husbands. Worse yet, the adulterous queens are not punished, whereas their accusers and royal husbands, who are the lords of the courts that judge them, are denounced as traitors and felons. However, trials of this fourth type are easier to understand if one thinks of them as variants of the second type of trial, in which traitors try to avenge their shame and advance themselves by falsely accusing their enemies, their rivals, or their enemies' or rivals' wives or lovers of sexual betrayal. In presenting the trials of Yseut in Béroul's *Roman de Tristan* and of Guinevere in *La mort le roi Artu*, the author invariably characterizes the adulterous queen's accusers as acting out of hatred against the queen and her lover but as concealing this hatred and deceitfully representing themselves as acting out of loyalty to the adulterous queen's royal husband. Like the accusers in the third type of trial, they hate the defendant with secret hatred, which drives them to give witness that is 'true' in the sense of factually accurate but 'false' in the sense of being motivated by secret hatred and thus by treason so that according to Beaumanoir, as we have seen, the accused 'will be put to death, or disinherited, or ... banished or ... hated by his liege lord' – or, in this case, her lord and husband the king.[24]

In *La mort le roi Artu*, the author clearly states, before describing Agravain's discovery of the 'fol amour' between Lancelot and Guinevere, that he did not love Lancelot, which, in this context, means that he hated him. Knowing of Agravain's hatred of Lancelot, the audience recognizes that he misrepresents his own motives when he later says to Arthur that he is telling him about the love between Lancelot and Guinevere so that the king

---

22. For Yseut's trial, see Béroul, *Tristan*, in *Les Tristan en vers*, ed. and trans. Jean Charles Payen (Paris: 1974), 1-141. For the view that Yseut's trial presents the judicial procedure used in it unfavourably, see, e.g., John W. Baldwin, 'The Crisis of the Ordeal: Literature, Law, and Religion around 1200', *Journal of Medieval and Renaissance Studies* 24 (1994), 327-53 at 330-1, 336-9. For valuable comments on the trial, see McCracken, *Romance of Adultery*, pp. 72-83 and passim; the most deeply researched study remains that of Pierre Jonin, *Les personnages féminins dans les romans français de Tristan au xiie siècle: études des influences contemporaines* (Aix-en-Provence: 1958), pp. 59-108.
23. For the immediate background to the trial and the trial itself, see *La mort le roi Artu: roman du xiiie siècle*, ed Jean Frappier (Geneva: 1964), cc. 87-93 (110-23).
24. Beaumanoir, *Coutumes de Beauvaisis*, vol. 1, chap. 30, no. 827 (430).

can avenge his dishonour.²⁵ Since Gawain, Agravain's brother, later sees clearly that Agravain acts out of hatred for Lancelot when he seeks to entrap the lovers and secure their condemnation as traitors by Arthur's court, he, Gawain, later refuses to participate in the entrapment; after it succeeds and results in the court condemning Guinevere to death, Gawain condemns King Arthur, in turn, for countenancing the act of 'disloyalty' that led to the court judging that Guinevere should die for her 'disloyalty' in lying with Lancelot instead of Arthur.²⁶ Here, traditional judicial procedures are subverted by the king, who bullies the judges of his court into condemning Guinevere for treason and judging that she should die. However, the queen is exonerated and her accusers duly condemned for their treason by the people of Camelot. When they learn of the court's judgment on the queen, they construe it as a 'false' judgment, acquit the queen, denounce Arthur for his 'disloyalty' (while adding that he can still repent of it), and curse the 'traitors' who engineered the queen's condemnation, declaring that they should die in shame.²⁷ This judgment is then executed, in effect, by Lancelot and his men, who save Guinevere from burning and kill, among others, three of the men who had entrapped the queen, namely Agravain and his two brothers, Guerrehet and Gaheriet. In the end, traditional judicial procedures do the trick, albeit with terrible consequences for Arthur's kingdom.

The trial of Yseut in Béroul's *Tristan* resembles Guinevere's trial in *La mort le roi Artu*. Here, the fact that the three barons and the dwarf who accuse Tristan and Yseut of loving each other shamefully are consistently denounced as 'felons' makes it clear that although their accusation is, in one sense, true, it is also 'treason', as King Mark's people declare it to be, after Tristan is entrapped and condemned to death without trial – a procedure that Mark's seneschal Dinas condemns.²⁸ In this case, where King Mark's court acquits Yseut of loving shamefully, while Mark and Yseut's accusers are totally humiliated, traditional procedures do work, though they have to be manipulated by Yseut, who swears her famous equivocal oath, with the connivance of King Arthur, who supplants King Mark as lord of the court.²⁹

In these ways, the creators of the fourth type of trial for sexual treason show that even 'true' accusations of illicit sex could be 'false' in the sense of treacherous and that the accusers were the real traitors, not the adulterous queen or her lover, even if he was the queen's husband's man. They also

---

25. *La mort le roi Artu*, c.4.10-18 (3-4), c.6.1-10 (3-4).
26. *La mort le roi Artu*, cc. 87-9 (110-13), cc. 93.1-30 (121)
27. *La mort le roi Artu*, c. 93.54-7 (122).
28. For denunciations of the accusers as felons, see, e.g., Béroul, *Tristan*, lines 402, 587, 658, 976, 1030; for the protest by Dinas about condemning Tristan to death 'sanz jugement', line 1070.
29. For Yseut's oath and acquittal, see Béroul, *Tristan*, lines 4165-4234.

show, contrary to what some critics have argued, that even in these unusual cases, traditional judicial procedures, if managed properly, work. They are adequate to the task of achieving just outcomes.

Lanval's Trial Re-visited

To see how the procedures work in Lanval's case, we must first present an overview of the entire case and then consider how it proceeds, step by step.

As Marie de France's 'Lai de Lanval' opens, the hero and future defendant in the case of *Guinevere v. Lanval* is living at the court of King Arthur, who forgets him when giving wives and lands to the counts and barons of his Round Table in return for their service against the Picts (17-19). None of Arthur's men supports him. Most envy his valour, largesse, beauty, and prowess; and even those who appear to love him would not complain if something bad happened to him (20-6). Even though Lanval is a king's son of high birth, he is far from his own heritage and has spent all his money (27-30). The king has given him nothing and he has not asked him for anything (31-2). Lanval is 'very sad, very worried' (34) and does not know where to seek help (38). However, his fortunes improve greatly when he leaves Arthur's court. Two richly dressed young women summon him to the court of a beautiful, fabulously wealthy young maiden ('*pucele*': see, e.g., 93, 108, 601), whose retinue includes beautiful female servants and no men at all. She grants 'her love and her body' ('S'amur e sun cors li otreie': 133), along with unlimited wealth, on the condition that 'if this love were to become known' (148) he would never see her again or have 'seisin' – that is, rightful possession – of her body ('Ne de mun cors seisine aveir': 150).[30] After agreeing to the girl's stipulation that he not boast about her (151-2), Lanval enjoys her company and is so richly clothed by her serving-maids that 'there was no more handsome youth in the whole world' (176). Returning to Arthur's court, he has all the wealth necessary to become a generous lord, while he secretly sees the girl as often as he wishes (217-18). By offering hospitality to every knight at Camelot who needs it (201-8), distributing gifts to strangers and friends, freeing prisoners, and patronizing jongleurs (209-14), Lanval experiences joy and pleasure (215).[31] Moreover, the knights of the Round Table show favour to Lanval, whom they now see as 'generous and courtly' (233). Gawain and Yvain invite him to join them

---

30. On terminology, see Rothwell, 'Trial Scene'. The girl's conditional grant of her body to Lanval has implications for the rest of the story.
31. 'Lanval donout les riches duns,/ Lanval aquitout les prisuns,/ Lanval vesteit les jugleürs,/ Lanval feseit les granz honurs!/ N'i ot estrange ne privé/ A ki Lanval n'eüst doné' (209-14).

and other knights in enjoying themselves in a garden by the tower where the queen was (221-38).[32]

However, when Arthur's unnamed queen, who, though never named, is easily identifiable as Guinevere, offers Lanval her love, his new-found joy turns to grief (332). After he rejects the queen's offer on the grounds that he does not wish to betray his lord Arthur, she angrily accuses him of preferring boys to women. He retaliates by declaring her inferior to his own love's poorest serving maid (299). As a result, he not only incurs the queen's anger ('La reïne s'en curuça;/ Iriee fu': 275-6); he also loses his lover by breaking the condition under which she granted herself to him. Worse yet, after the queen mendaciously complains to Arthur that Lanval had sought her love and also makes a better-founded, though still false, charge that he had insulted her after she had rejected him, Arthur angrily threatens to have Lanval hanged or burned (325-8).[33] However, he later decides to seek counsel with his household knights about how to proceed in the case (381-4). They, in turn, refer Lanval's case to a larger court (391), after Gawain, Yvain and other knights agree to be pledges for his appearance before it. There, a group of judges including magnates and other men from outside the king's immediate household are to decide whether the case should proceed and, if so, how (415-26). They dismiss the charge that Lanval had wronged Arthur but require him to produce the girl in order to prove the truth of what he had said to the queen about her inferiority to the girl's meanest serving-maid. Although Lanval fears that the girl has abandoned him forever, she and her serving maids arrive at the last possible moment to defend him in the king's court. Persuaded by the visible evidence that she and her maids provide and by her defence of Lanval (623-8), the judges make a final award that sets Lanval free ('Delivrez est par lur esgart': 629) so that he can leave Arthur's court with the girl, who takes him away to Avalon (633-46).

How is Lanval's acquittal achieved? Though essential to achieving it, the girl's court appearance is only the final stage in a lengthy, step-by-step, politicized, and yet convention-bound, legal process through which the hostile encounter between Guinevere and Lanval is repeatedly reinterpreted by different members of the court – including the two protagonists, Arthur, Arthur's household knights, and members of the king's great court – until the dispute is finally reduced to a matter of right and honour that the court resolves by seeing and hearing the girl and her female retinue. If the court does not, by itself, do right to Lanval, it proceeds in such a way as to provide an occasion for right to be done in the case and for honour and

---

32. Gawain says of Lanval, 'tant est larges et curteis/ E sis peres est riches reis' (231-2).
33. On the queen's complaint against Lanval (316-24) and the king's accusation against him (363-70), see below.

shame to be allocated in the right and honourable way. In doing so, the court does not simply act as an adjudicatory agency; it also constitutes a political arena for continuing the game of honour through conflict and re-negotiation. Initiated by the queen's complaint that she has been shamed, the *plait* ends with the queen herself being shamed. Whether Marie treats the process favourably or ironically, she shows that Lanval owes his chance of acquittal to a judicial process which, though cumbersome, leaves room for political manœuvring that eventually works in his favour, satisfies certain members of Arthur's court, and has the effect of shaming the queen.[34] The manœuvres are sometimes difficult to decode partly because Marie assumes familiarity with the conventions of court procedure and with multiple traditions of romance and epic literature and partly because she treats hypocrisy and self-interest as such ingrained features of court life that one can never assume that anyone at court speaks truthfully.

The judicial process that culminates in Lanval's acquittal goes through six phases, each of which involves an encounter among two or more people:

(1) Lanval's altercation with Guinevere.

(2) Guinevere makes a complaint to Arthur.

(3) Arthur summons Lanval and makes two complaints against him; Lanval answers.

(4) Arthur and his household knights consider the case of Lanval, who secures pledges.

(5) The great court convenes, hears the case, and the judges make their award.

(6) The great court sees what they need to see in order to acquit Lanval.

Most of these encounters, which involve more and more people as the trial proceeds, are structured by conventionalized judicial practices and discourse that conjointly serve simultaneously to constrain speech and to create resources or weapons to be used by participants in competing for honour. The procedural conventions, which everyone (except possibly the queen) acknowledges, constrain and limit what can be done or said; but they almost always leave room for the participants to make better or worse choices. Only certain things are sayable at a court hearing, just as they are in the public society of the court, but participants still have some leeway to impose their own interpretations on what they or others say and do and to hint at more than they themselves say or do.

---

34. According to Monson, 'L'idéologie', 369, Marie's account of the trial is 'plus nuancé' than is her earlier treatment of Arthur's court 'puisqu'il comporte, à côté de vives critiques, quelques traits positifs qui préparent le dénouement heureux'.

1. Lanval and the Queen

Lanval's relations with Guinevere are sharply contrasted with his relations with his lover. She gives Lanval her love when he is totally isolated at Arthur's court, whereas Guinevere does so only after his new-found wealth has enabled him to gain the friendship of many knights, including Gawain and Yvain. The girl's encounter with Lanval involves, among other things, an exchange of amorous words and sexual love between people who treat each other as equals; the queen's encounter with Lanval is a disputatious exchange of insults between an older woman who denies a younger man's masculinity and a young, honourable man who literally reviles the queen by denying her beauty and even her nobility. Because the queen mendaciously claims to have previously honoured, cherished, and loved Lanval (263-4), her gift of illicit love to him ('Ma drüerie vus otrei' [267]) differs from the girl's gift of love ('S'amur e sun cors li otrei' [134]) not only because the girl's love is honourable and the queen's dishonourable, but also for other reasons. Represented as a means of extorting sexual service from Lanval in return for gifts the queen has never actually made to him, the queen's offer is, in Pierre Bourdieu's terms, an act of 'gentle violence' by means of which the queen claims sex from Lanval by representing it as an obligatory counter-gift for a gift that she had never actually made to him.[35] The encounter starts with a lie and continues in the same key of hypocrisy, mendacity, and hostility. Whereas Lanval previously gave up everyone else for the girl (128), he rejects the queen's gift (270). When he justifies his refusal to accept the queen's offer of a bad gift and thereby insults the queen, he says nothing about the girl or about the queen's lack of sexual appeal and cites as his reason for rejecting her offer that he does not wish to break faith with the king by committing a misdeed (*mesfait*) against him (274). Lanval's response is appropriate but also aggressive, since he insults the queen partly by rejecting her gift of love and partly by implicitly accusing her of breaking faith with her husband by offering love to one of the king's followers. Angrily avenging the multi-dimensional response through which Lanval has just insulted her, the queen raises the stakes in her honour game with Lanval by retaliating against him with a more serious insult of her own. Treating Lanval's rejection of her gift as evidence that he has no interest in women and has sex with boys, she attacks his manliness, his class status, and his standing at court, by calling him 'a base coward and evil recreant' (283) who is unfit to follow Arthur (284-6). In response, Lanval retaliates in kind by denying her beauty, moral worth, femininity, and noble status. He does so by making an angry retort that further angers the queen and that simultaneously violates the terms of his agreement with the girl. Instead of simply rejecting the queen's accusation that he enjoys

---

35. Pierre Bourdieu, *Outline of a Theory of Practice*, trans. Richard Nice (Cambridge: 1977), 191-7.

sex with boys rather than sex with women, Lanval insults Guinevere by declaring that she is inferior in every way (301-2) to his own lover's poorest *meschine*. This insult differs from the insults Guinevere has just hurled at Lanval, because, as everyone at Camelot later learns, it is also the truth. But truth is not the only issue. Lanval's assertion is still an insult, which denies the queen's beauty and nobility and which leaves her distressed, angry, and humiliated (304-6). The force of the insult becomes clearer and clearer as we notice that the queen, who is praised in other poems as the most beautiful woman in the world, is never praised, described, or even named in the poem.

2. Guinevere and Arthur

Having been shamed by Lanval, the queen is desperate to take vengeance on him. But how? Since she has already come out the loser in her verbal exchange with Lanval and since it is apparently unthinkable for her, as a woman, to take direct vengeance against him herself, she can get revenge only through the mediation of others. Goading the king into action with a display of passive aggression, she says that she will never rise from her sickbed until the king has done right to her with respect to the complaint she would make (307-10). This strategy, however, is problematic. In order to secure help from her husband in avenging her shame, she must widen the scope of her conflict with Lanval in order to secure support from the king, to whom she misrepresents her shame so that she can appear blameless. Describing this encounter truthfully to the king would only cause her further shame, prevent her from getting the king's support, and possibly make her the target of the king's revenge. The queen therefore opts for a blend of truth, half-truth, and total mendacity when she complains to Arthur and asks for his mercy (Quant el le vit, si se clamma;/As piez li chiet, merci li crie: 314-15). She says that: (1) Lanval shamed her (Et dit que Lanval l'ad hunie: 316); (2) he asked for her love (De druërie la requist: 317); (3) because she refused him, he insulted and reviled her (Pur ceo qu'ele l'en escundist,/Mut la laidi e avila: 319-20); (4) he boasted of a love who was so well-bred, noble, and proud that the poorest servant she had was worthier than the queen (314-24). By complaining that Lanval asked for her love when the reverse was true and by misrepresenting his reason for insulting her, Guinevere lies about her encounter with him. Still, several parts of her plaint are true. Lanval did, indeed, shame and revile the queen (nos. 1 and 2) when he boasted about his love (no. 4); he also shamed her by rejecting her offer of illicit love (*druërie*). In the short run, Guinevere's ploy works: she gets her husband's support in her dispute with Lanval. But in the long run, the strategy that the king, egged on by his wife, follows in seeking revenge against Lanval is also risky for him and for her. By associating himself with the queen and seeking an extreme form of vengeance, the king has to put his own honour on the line in several different ways – by revealing the queen's shame and his own to others, by widening the scope of the dispute to include his entire court, and by assuming the obligation to put the queen's case and his own into legal discourse appropriate to a treason trial. Once again, both the queen's strategy and the king's succeed in the short run. By securing her husband's support in her dispute with Lanval, the queen gets an opportunity to avenge her shame; and by transforming a dispute of which he knows nothing into a treason trial, the king gains an opportunity to avenge his wife's shame and his own, as he puts Lanval on trial for treason. In the long run, however, the two strategies are risky for both king and queen. In transforming the queen's complaint about Lanval to her husband into an appeal of felony made to the men of Arthur's household, the queen and king invite public scrutiny of her conduct and her honour, as well as the conduct and honour of Lanval; they also provide the court with an opportunity to examine a marriage in which the queen bullies her husband. Moreover, the truth of the king's word as well as the queen's is publicly assessed in a *plait*, where the conduct of all the participants is constrained by the need to observe conventions about what is and is not sayable in court. Some of these conventions work to the king and queen's advantage, others do not.

3. Arthur and Lanval

The hero came out ahead in his encounter with the queen; but his next encounter is a standoff. The king is determined to take vengeance against Lanval; but the latter acknowledges no wrong. When he responds to the queen's cry for mercy by unleashing his anger and ill will at Lanval (Li reis s'en curuça forment: 325; Li reis li dit par maltalant: 362), Arthur ensures that the case will be adjudicated by at least some of his followers; he also transforms his wife's accusation against Lanval by giving greater weight to his own dishonour than he does to hers (316). After angrily swearing, in the conventional way, to have Lanval 'burned or hanged' if he 'could not defend himself in court' (325-7) and then summoning him (329-31, 352-6), the king says: (1) that Lanval greatly wronged him; and (2) that he acted villainously in shaming and reviling him and insulting the queen.[36] The accusation is ironic in several respects. First, Arthur accuses Lanval of making a villainous 'plea' as he himself initiates a 'plea' that is itself villainous. Second, the king accuses Lanval of an offence that Lanval has actually refused to commit and focuses more attention on this offence than he does on the offence that Lanval did, indeed, commit. Third, the king, unlike Lanval and the audience, does not know – or, at least, not for certain – that although Lanval did not wrong him by asking for the queen's love, Lanval had already betrayed him by acquiring another lord, namely the girl.

---

36. 'Vassal, vus m'avez mut mesfait;/Trop commençastes vilein plait/De mei hunir e avillier/E la reïne ledengier!': 363-6.

Nevertheless, the king and queen are unwittingly trying to avenge Lanval's disloyalty and to shame the girl by refusing to acknowledge that what he said about her and her servants might be true. By making himself a party to the queen's dispute with Lanval and by initiating what amounts to an appeal of felony that must be publicized and adjudicated in a large forum, the king – who has already shamed Lanval by withholding gifts that Lanval clearly merited while giving them to courtiers inferior to him – now shames Lanval grievously in ways that demand repayment on a grand scale. The king, along with the queen, is now an appropriate target for Lanval's revenge, which must bring Arthur at least as much shame as he caused Lanval and possibly more. Moreover, the king initiates a judicial process that neither he nor the queen can fully control as he decides, out of fear that he will otherwise suffer criticism for his handling of his dispute with Lanval, to summon his men to tell him how to do right (dreit: 383) in the case. The judicial process that Arthur initiates ultimately leads to the release of Lanval and to the humiliation of both king and queen.

In the short run, it is Lanval, not the king, who is constrained by judicial conventions, since he can do no more than contest the king's charges against him. Because the accusation that he had wronged the king is totally false, he can meet it by denying, word for word, that he caused dishonour or shame to his lord by asking for the queen's love (371-4). His response to the other accusation is necessarily more complex because the charge is not totally false. Instead of mendaciously denying that he has spoken the words that insulted the queen, he, like other defendants in imaginary treason cases, makes what amounts to an exception to the king's accusations made against him. While acknowledging that he did, indeed, speak the words that the queen and then the king attributed to him, Lanval maintains 'the truth' of what he said to her about his love and expresses regret for his words, not because they affronted the queen, but rather because by saying them he lost his love (375-8). By undertaking to provide whatever proof the court may require of him, Lanval increases the likelihood that the king's appeal against him will be heard in a larger forum, where the king and queen will exercise less power over proceedings in the case and where he may get a more favourable hearing. In a forum of this kind, the queen's honour and the king's, as well as his own, will become objects of scrutiny.[37]

4. Arthur, his Household Knights, and Lanval

When Arthur displays great anger at Lanval's responses, which shame the king and queen alike, he manifests his determination to continue the dispute, which he turns into a public test of his own honour, Lanval's and the

---

37. See Hyams, 'Henry II and Ganelon', 32.

queen's. He moves the case forward in a conventional way by summoning his men and asking them to tell him what he should do about the case so that no one can speak ill of him about it (381-4). By publicly implicating himself in the queen's complaint against Lanval in a larger forum, the king raises the stakes in the case, which now proceeds in a way that may bring him either honour or more shame but that ultimately results, one can assume, in many people faulting him for his decision (384). On the one hand, the king now has an opportunity to take public vengeance on Lanval for committing what he represents as legal offences against him (not the queen), namely a felony and a misdeed. On the other hand, any failure on the king's part to take public vengeance for those offences will bring him and the queen greater shame than they would have incurred if they had abandoned the idea of speaking publicly about the queen's shame. What will happen next now depends on the decision of Arthur's household knights, who have several options about how to proceed. They may convict Lanval on the king's word, in which case, since felony is punishable by execution, the king would be entitled to burn or hang Lanval. They may also acquit Lanval of all charges, or else ask the king to show him mercy. However, instead of choosing any of these courses, Arthur's household knights render a more complicated and ambiguous judgment.

Although the knights do not openly side with Lanval, their intervention in the case marks the beginning of the process through which Lanval finally gets right, honour and revenge, while the king and queen suffer multiple forms of shame. The knights – who seem to occupy a lower social position than at least some of those who later participate in the case – judge that, provided that he can give pledges for his appearance, Lanval should have his case heard in a great court that includes royal followers from outside Arthur's household (389, 393). On substantive, evidentiary and procedural grounds, this award is both legally equivocal and politically noncommittal. Although the knights do not support the king's charges against Lanval, as Arthur must have wanted and expected, they do not and perhaps cannot assess the charges as critically as do the count of Cornwall and other judges at a later stage of the trial.[38] On the question of what form of proof should be used to determine the outcome of the case, the knights take no position at all. Instead, they make procedural judgments that might favour Lanval or Arthur, depending on what happens next and how members of the great court later assess the case. On the one hand, by requiring Lanval to give pledges for his appearance in court, the knights show deference to the king by acknowledging the seriousness of his charges against Lanval; they also impose on Lanval an obligation that may prove difficult or even impossible for him to fulfil, since, as a foreign knight, he has no kinsmen at Camelot to

---

38. According to Hyams, 'Henry II and Ganelon', 32, 'Possibly Arthur had hoped to end the case by exiling or imprisoning Lanval without the need for any trial'.

act as his pledges and may well find no one willing to act in this capacity, particularly since he has no friends at the court or, at least, had none at the start of the story. On the other hand, by providing that if Lanval can find pledges, he will have his day in the king's great court, which includes knights and barons who do not belong to the king's household, Arthur's knights give Lanval some hope of defending himself before judges who are less subject to Arthur's power than they themselves are. Maybe he has friends to pledge for him or people who would like to see the case continue. At the same time, the household knights relieve themselves of the burden of resolving the case definitively and help to transform it into an even more complex and politicized process, whose outcome will be more difficult for the king to control. Arthur's household knights, in other words, do not simply act either as Lanval's friends or as mere instruments of royal vengeance against Lanval. As it turns out, their award, which is also a delaying tactic, works in Lanval's favour.

At this point in the case the decision of Gawain and all his companions to act as Lanval's pledges (400-1) ensures that Lanval will have his day in court, where he will have supporters with a strong practical political interest in his acquittal. Having previously said nothing about the case, Gawain, who has only recently befriended Lanval, supports his new-found companion. Why? This manœuvre cannot be interpreted simply as an expression of Gawain's deep friendship for Lanval, since Gawain is surely one of those courtiers who 'feigned the appearance of love' for Lanval but 'who would not have uttered a single regret if misfortune had befallen him' (24-6). Instead, Gawain's decision to support Lanval is best seen as a form of muted resistance to the king and queen and as a sign that their charges against Lanval have no credibility with members of the king's court. At this point in the case, members of Arthur's court have taken no position on the merits of the case against Lanval; but by making several significant decisions about how the case will proceed, Gawain and the king's household knights exercise influence on what will happen next and what the final outcome of the case will be.

5. The Great Court (i)

By the time the great court assembles, support for Lanval and disapproval of the case against him are evident. His pledges, who bring him to court, openly show their support for him by displaying the sadness they supposedly feel on his behalf (419) and also, one assumes, their own, since a judgment against Lanval is bound to bring some kind of dishonour to those who supported him. Moreover, the court now includes 'a hundred [barons] who would have done all in their power to have [Lanval] released without a trial because he had been wrongly accused' (423-4). Instead of explaining why they believe the appeal against him is false, the poem implies that they must have grounds for doubting the word of the king and queen. Do they doubt that Lanval could possibly have requested the queen's love? If so, why? Is the queen known for falsely complaining that her husband's men have insulted her and/or requested her love? Is she known for offering her *druërie* to some of them or even all of them? Is it assumed that even if her accusation was accurate, it was false in the sense of being made maliciously? In any event, although Lanval's supporters do not succeed in liberating him, they still manage to improve his position in the case. After the king asks for judgment in accordance with the claim and the response (424-5), the judges split into two factions. On one side are those who, without necessarily believing that Arthur and the queen have 'right', want 'to condemn [Lanval] in order to satisfy their lord' (431-2). On the other side are those who are, or profess to be, worried for Lanval (428-9). Neither faction prevails. Instead of either condemning Lanval or freeing him, the judges reach a compromise judgment, which the count of Cornwall reports to the king in a way that conceals these issues.

Noting that Arthur has accused Lanval of both felony (felunie: 439) for seeking the queen's love and a misdeed (mesfait: 440) consisting of insulting the queen, the count first treats the accusation of felony so perfunctorily as to signal its lack of merit.[39] Because only the king had appealed Lanval of 'felony' (443), the count says, there should have been no need for him to make a defence to this appeal, except that 'one should honor one's lord in all things' (446-8). Lanval, therefore, should simply be bound by his oath of denial and the matter of dealing with the charge should be left to the judges, who, the count implies, will simply dismiss it. Turning to the accusation that Lanval wronged the queen by angering her with a boast about his love, the count gives another judgment. On the one hand, if, by producing the girl as his 'warrantor' (sun guarant: 451), he can show that the words that angered the queen were 'true' (veir: 453), he will then be entitled to the court's mercy because he will have shown that he did not speak the words in order to revile the queen (pur vilté: 456). On the other hand, if the girl does not appear as Lanval's warrantor (garant: 457), then he must lose his service to the king and leave him (457-60). As it turns out, Arthur definitively loses the service of Lanval, who had already been recruited by another lord and will eventually leave Arthur for good.

The count's judgment is ambiguous. Although he says that Lanval will have to be punished unless he provides a kind of evidence that he has already said he cannot produce (378), he also gives him a chance to rebut the charge that he has wronged the queen; and in the event that Lanval cannot rebut the charge, the judgment provides a penalty for the wrong, namely banishment from the court, which is considerably lighter than the

---

39. For a plausible alternative to this way of interpreting the accusations against Lanval, see Hyams, 'Henry II and Ganelon', 33.

punishment of burning or hanging that the king and queen initially hoped to impose on him. Moreover, the judgment construes Lanval's alleged offence against the queen in a way that simplifies the task of rebutting it and, as it turns out, provides him with an another opportunity to shame the queen, this time publicly. Instead of deciding that the case should turn on whether Lanval shamed and reviled Guinevere (as he did) or on whether he intended to do so (as he did), the count's judgment makes the question of Lanval's guilt turn on whether his intentionally shaming boast was true. In this way, the judges' award, as articulated by the count, leaves open the possibility that the process of judging Lanval will turn into a process of judging the queen.

Should we assume that the count made an empty gesture in providing Lanval with an opportunity to prove that his boast about his love was true? Or should we impute to the count and some of the other judges an interest in securing an opportunity to compare the queen with Lanval's love and her serving girls? The answer depends on what assumptions we make about the judges' knowledge of the case and of the court and how they assessed both Lanval's ability to produce the girl and the likelihood that he told the truth about Guinevere's inferiority to her and to her serving maids. Because the judges could hardly have known about the fantastic circumstances that almost prevented Lanval from producing the girl, their judgment looks like a deliberate attempt to set up a test of his boast. To what end? Since many of the judges evidently believed that Lanval had been accused very wrongly (rettez a mut grant tort: 434) and since the count of Cornwall maintained that he could not have reviled Guinevere if his boast about the superiority of his love and her girls to the queen were true (456), then the judges' decision to test the truth of his boast must be tantamount to a decision to facilitate the humiliation of a queen whose inferiority even to serving maids would be easy to prove. Because the judges' award makes them the judges of the proof to be offered about the relative merits of Lanval's lover and her maidens as compared with the queen, they are providing themselves with an occasion for shaming their own king and queen. Once again, the court's decision on a procedural issue incorporates both an implicit judgment on a substantive one and a strategic move with multiple meanings in the game of honour.

5. The Great Court (ii)
Up to this point, the poem has described successive stages of a judicial process in which qualified support for Lanval and qualified resistance to the king and queen gradually develop among the king's followers and in which the king and queen fail to use the court as a means of restoring honour by avenging their shame. Now the poem shows how, in the trial's final phase, the court becomes an arena not just for adjudicating the queen's complaint

against Lanval, but for judging women by viewing and evaluating their bodies and for redistributing honour and shame among the men and women of the court. Almost a quarter of the poem is devoted to describing the three-part proof that the girl and her serving maids present on Lanval's behalf and the court's ongoing evaluation of it. Because Lanval has previously told the queen that she is inferior to his lover's poorest serving girl 'in body, face and beauty, wisdom and goodness' (298-302), praise of these specific qualities in the girl and her servants shames the queen by implicitly calling attention to her inferiority to other women, including those who are far beneath her in status. Moreover, because the girl acts as Lanval's lord as well as his lover, she demonstrates her superiority to the king as well as to the queen. As the poem's descriptions of the beauty and nobility of the girl and her serving girls become progressively longer and more lavish, so does the joy and sense of honour of Lanval's supporters. At the same time, one may assume, the rage and shame of the king and queen become more and more obvious but less and less effective. But the king salvages something.

At the last minute, the proof the judges have called for is presented to the court in stages. First, as two beautiful girls, dressed 'only in purple taffeta, next to their bare skin' (471-6), ride into the court on palfreys, the judges look at them with pleasure (472-7); Gawain then happily points them out to Lanval (478-83). When the two girls tell the king to prepare for their lady's arrival (490-4), the king complies with their request (495-8); but he angrily demands an immediate judgment from the barons of the court, who reply that because of the ladies they saw, they have made no judgment and wish to continue the trial (504-6). When two other girls arrive, nobly dressed (510) and riding on Spanish mules, the sight of them leads Gawain to believe that one of them must be Lanval's lover (523) and it brings 'joy' to all the men, who think Lanval is saved (516). 'Many praised them highly for their bodies, faces, and complexions. They were both more worthy than the queen had ever been' (529-32). When they request hospitality for their lady and an audience with Arthur, the king complies with both requests, but still presses his men for an immediate judgment on Lanval's case (535-46).

Finally, when the barons are again on the point of rendering a judgment in the case, Lanval's girl appears, riding a palfrey with the richest of trappings (551-8). She dismounts before the king and allows a viewing of her body; 'in the sight of all, [she] let her cloak fall so that they could see her better' (605-6). The girl's superiority to Guinevere, who is never described, is obvious (559-68). As she passes by in a dark purple robe, with a sparrow hawk on her wrist, followed by a greyhound (571-4), she is viewed by everyone, including the judges, who marvel at her (575-84). Lanval's friends, now very numerous, judge her to be 'the most beautiful woman in the world' (592). Having shown the judges everything they needed to see and more, the girl supports her man Lanval by providing more evidence than the court's judgment had required. She declares, first, that she has loved the king's man Lanval; second, that the queen was in the wrong; third, that Lanval never sought the queen's love; and, finally, that if she herself can acquit him, he should be set free. After Arthur grants that the barons' lawful judgment will prevail, they unanimously decide that Lanval has defended himself against the charge against him.

Of these four statements, only the first and last are strictly relevant to the question of whether the words of Lanval that upset the queen were true. The second and third statements simply corroborate Lanval's denial of the treason charge that the judges had, in effect, dismissed at an earlier stage of the *plait*. When combined with the proof of her femaleness that the girl has already presented to the court by dropping her robe, her initial statement that she has loved Lanval implicitly shows that she had previously given him 'seisin' of her body – a female body – and rebuts the queen's private insult that he preferred boys to women. The girl thus warrants her man in two different senses; by proving that he had seisin of her (female) body against the queen's insult that he did not even desire a female body and by avenging the shame the queen's insult had caused to her – that is, the girl's – own man Lanval. She does this not just by sending her serving maids to show that even they were more beautiful and better in every way than the queen, but by appearing in court herself, disrobing, and showing that she and not the queen is the most beautiful woman in the world. Therefore, she not only performs but embodies the roles of king and queen that Arthur and Guinevere, respectively, should perform and embody but do not. That is why, when she rides off to Avalon with Lanval at the end of the poem, she is riding in front and he behind, and not the other way around.

Conclusions

If we look back over the entire course of Lanval's trial, as Marie de France represents it with remarkable attention to points of law and judicial procedure, we can readily see that the girl's appearance at the end was necessary only to secure vengeance for him, as his warrantor, against the queen for insulting him, even though the vengeance is evident only to Lanval, the girl, the queen, and the audience. Moreover, the previous appearance of the girl's serving maids was necessary only to provide what the judges of Arthur's court were willing to accept as proof that what Lanval had admittedly said to the queen about the queen was true and, even more importantly, would be taken as proof that he had not said out of spite what he had actually said out of spite. Of course, members of the poem's audience, at least, know that Lanval had been justified in saying what he had said out of spite, in retaliation for what the queen had said to him out of spite, in retaliation for his refusal to accept her offer of illicit love so that he would not betray his lord Arthur, whom Lanval had already abandoned, in a sense, for becoming the man of another lord, namely the girl, who had provided Lanval with everything – and more – that he should have received from Arthur, who had betrayed Lanval by failing to reward him for his service when he rewarded the other knights at his court by giving them wives and lands.

However, if the appearance of the girl and her serving maids in Arthur's court is necessary to achieve vengeance for Lanval against the queen and the king as well, it is the members of Arthur's court who do right to him. They do this partly by dismissing, on legal grounds, the accusation that Lanval had shamed and betrayed the king by seeking the queen's love and by providing him with what they must consider to be a foolproof way of proving that what he said about the queen was true and, as already mentioned, that they would take the truth of what he said, as they would determine it, as proof of his motives in saying what he admittedly said to the queen. However, the judges of Arthur's great court would have been in no position to make their two awards – one dismissing the first charge and the other proposing a procedure for disproving the second – had it not been for the fact that previously traditional judicial procedures had been followed in the case. The great court had proceeded in the traditional way, with King Arthur presenting the appeal against Lanval, Lanval making his answer, and the king then turning over the case to the judges, who retire, in the usual way, to discuss it and reach the judgment that the count of Cornwall reports. However, the case would not even have been heard in this court if it had not been referred there by the small court of Arthur's household knights, which follows traditional procedures in handling the case as well. It hears the king's complaints against Lanval and Lanval's response and then decides that Lanval should have his day in court, provided that he can provide pledges for his appearance there. Since Gawain and other knights stand pledge for Lanval, his case will be heard in the king's great court, just as the household knights provided for. But how did the case reach the household knights? Because King Arthur referred it to them, after he, too, had followed what Marie represented as traditional judicial procedures for hearing the complaint against Lanval. He summoned Lanval to appear before him. He made the two complaints against him and then heard the responses, which Lanval made in due form, denying the first complaint word for word and then making a kind of exception to the second.

So what went wrong? Only this. The queen was a felon and, acting out of hatred for Lanval, tried to secure vengeance for an insult by making a complaint to the king, who heard it rather than dismissing it. However, once the king decided that the complaint should be adjudicated by using traditional judicial procedures and consulting his men, Lanval's case proceeded just as it should have done, because, for whatever reason, the men of Arthur's court did right to the defendant, as they could do by following traditional judicial procedures.

PRIVATE LIFE IN CANON LAW COLLECTIONS ATTRIBUTED TO BISHOP IVO OF CHARTRES

Bruce C. Brasington

Introduction

By 1100 there was no lack of ecclesiastical regulation concerning the laity. Their 'private lives', above all in sexual matters, had been the subject of canon law for centuries.[1] The canonical collections attributed to Bishop Ivo of Chartres (†1115) are typical in this regard, for they contain an abundance of Biblical, conciliar, patristic, and papal decrees on how laymen should behave.[2] This essay considers some of these texts found in abbreviated versions of the Ivonian *Decretum* and the Pseudo-Ivonian *Tripartita*. Some already ancient by the late eleventh century, others new, they treat topics

---

1. Jean Gaudemet, 'Les laics dans les premiers siècles de l'église', *Communio* 12.1 (1987), 61-75, rp. with same pagination in *Droit de l'église et vie sociale au moyen age* (Northampton: 1989). That the laity were not unaware of the canons and sometimes challenged or interpreted them is discussed by Wilfried Hartmann, 'Rechtskenntnis und Rechtsverständnis bei den Laien des frühen Mittelalters', *Aus Archiven und Bibliotheken. Festschrift für Raymond Kottje zum 65. Geburtstag*, ed. Humbert Mordek (Frankfurt: 1992), 1-20. On sex, see James Brundage, *Law, Sex and Christian Society in Medieval Europe* (Chicago: 1987). An interesting study of the 'private' world of dreams is provided by Isabel Moreira, 'Dreams and Divination in Early Medieval Canonical Sources: The Question of Clerical Control', *The Catholic Historical Review* 89.4 (2003), 621-642, especially at 642.
2. For bibliography, manuscript information, and provisional editions of these collections (as well as information on Ivo's letters and the likely Pseudo-Ivonian *Panormia*), http://project.knowledgeforge.net/ivo/, accessed on 28 June 2009.

such as married women inspired by an excess of religious zeal, controversy over the churchyard and its inhabitants, and parental authority in arranging marriage.

De Causis Laicorum

One of the more paradoxical features of early medieval canon law is that, while canons treating the laity are everywhere, they are nowhere in particular. As Martin Brett has noted, only with the Ivonian *Decretum*, book 16, do we encounter a discrete section *De causis laicorum*. Here bishops are exhorted to defend the poor against secular power; ecclesiastical synods are reminded that laymen should not speak unless asked. Canon after canon warns laymen not to defy bishops, steal ecclesiastical property, or interfere in monasteries. From serfs to kings, the canons cover the entire social and political order. *De causis laicorum* is a comprehensive jumble.

Such sprawling contents were typical for a canonical collection around 1100. The purpose of the *Decretum*, as had been the case with canonical collections for centuries, was to preserve and organize tradition. What light it might shed on how 'private life' was understood by Ivo and his contemporaries, however, is faint, for the canons compiled here were already centuries old, the most recent from Carolingian councils. Additionally, the book lacks internal subdivisions that might reveal discrete themes perceived by the compiler.

We are fortunate, however, that two abbreviated versions of the Ivonian *Decretum* also contain an appendix following book 16; Rome, Accademia dei Lincei ms. 41 E 1 (F) and London, BL Harley ms. 3090 (H).[3] Palaeographical analysis argues for both manuscripts being Anglo-Norman, with H being considerably older than F, perhaps by two generations.[4] By the second half of the twelfth century, F had arrived in Italy, where texts were added.[5]

---

3. See two studies by Martin Brett, 'Canon Law and Litigation: The Century Before Gratian', *Medieval Ecclesiastical Studies in Honour of Dorothy M. Owen*, eds. M.J. Franklin and Christopher Harper-Bill (Rochester: 1995), 21-40. especially at 39-40 and 'Editions, Manuscripts, and Readers in Some Pre-Gratian Collections', *Ritual, Text and Law. Studies in Medieval Canon Law and Liturgy Presented to Roger E. Reynolds*, eds, Kathleen G. Cushing and Richard F. Gyung (London: 2004), 205-219, also Bruce C. Brasington, 'Collections of Bishops' Letters as Legal *Florilegia*', *Law Before Gratian. Law in Western Europe c. 500–1100*, eds. Per Andersen, Mia Munster-Swendsen, Helle Vogt (Copenhagen: 2007), 73-122.
4. Personal communication from Dr Martin Brett, 19 March 2009.
5. The following is added towards the end of the appendix: HU. sanctę Pisanę ęcclesię Dei gratia archiepiscopus Venerabili et karissimo fratri R. eadem gratia

Both manuscripts share seven canons (Appendix I), most of which deal with the family. Condemnation of adultery was hardly unusual, but it is striking that several of the patristic texts chosen for the appendix concern women who, inspired by religious zeal, had taken an initiative against wayward husbands. While we can never be absolutely certain to what extent such ancient canons spoke to contemporary concerns, their addition does not seem accidental. Giles Constable has noted that women's 'prominence in religious life, and society generally, at this time are still not clear and may have been demographic and socio-economic as well as religious in nature'.[6] Perhaps some particularly enthusiastic women prompted our scribe to add these patristic texts.

Like marriage and adultery, heresy was not an unusual topic for a canonical collection. By the time our appendix was composed, heretical movements were active throughout the West.[7] Some of their adherents embraced a personal, rigorous following of the apostolic life. Perhaps such evangelical zeal prompted some women, as their sisters had in the patristic period, to cast adulterous husbands out of the marriage bed and hand over money and land to support monks.[8]

Populoniensi episcopo, salutem et omne bonum. Sicut tua bene novit prudentia te quoque et me presente dominus papa ęcclesiam tuam Pisane supposuit ęcclesię, et mihi ut metropolitano tuo tibi deceteero precepit obedire. Nosti quidem non obedire et nolle adquiescere ut scelus deputatur ydolat<r>ię. Super his etiam iam bis per sapientes et industrios viros monitus ut venires distulisti, et obedientiam ex <ore> domini pape tibi iniunctam neglexisti. Nunc igitur tertio te fraterna in Domino caritate monemus et ut ad nos ulterius venire non differas, per iniunctam tibi obedientiam obtestamur. Paratus enim sum te ut fratrem karissimum recipere, diligere, et honorare. Alioquin valida est manus Domini, et beati Petri contemptorem tangere, et in directum reducere, printed by Paul F. Kehr, 'Papsturkunden in Rom', *Nachrichten von der Gesellschaft der Wissenschaften zu Göttingen. Philologisch-Historische Klasse* (1903), 1-161, 505-591 at 161.

6. Giles Constable, *The Reformation of the Twelfth Century* (Cambridge: 1998), 65. On the numerous female patrons of the new religious orders, for example the Cistercians, see Constance Hoffman Berman, *The Cistercian Evolution. The Invention of a Religious Order in Twelfth-Century Europe* (Philadelphia: 1999), 162-163, with charter evidence from France.
7. In general, Malcolm Lambert, *Medieval Heresy: From the Gregorian Reform to the Reformation*, 3rd ed. (Oxford: 2002). That canonists and theologians were not always certain what these new movements believed or intended – an indication that this part of the laity's 'private life' was particularly opaque – has been the subject of considerable debate, on which see Peter Biller, 'Through a Glass Darkly: Seeing Medieval Heresy', eds. Peter Linehan and Janet L. Nelson, *The Medieval World* (London: 2001), 308-326, and Peter D. Diehl, *The Papacy and the Supression of Heresy in Italy, 1150–1254*, (Dissertation, UCLA: 1991). I thank Dr Diehl for these references.
8. Constable, *Reformation*, 158-159.

The appendix also includes older conciliar texts supporting posthumous anathematization. In 1100, canonical tradition was by no means unified on whether or not the dead could be damned.[9] Pope Vigilius had declared: 'It is a serious matter to insult the dead, even if they were laymen, and certainly those who as bishops left this life'. It was best to leave such judgments in God's hands.[10] On the other hand, there was the infamous 'Cadaver Synod', where the body of Pope Formosus, by order of his successor, Stephen VI, was exhumed, placed on trial, mutilated, and cast into the Tiber, only to be subsequently hauled out and his decrees reinstated.[11]

There is also scattered evidence concerning the exhumation of the dead by those who felt the deceased had been inappropriately executed or buried. At least one twelfth-century bishop ordered men to reclaim a dead man from an alien cemetery.[12] Thietmar of Merseburg mentions unnamed individuals who, convinced an unjust execution had taken place, had reburied the deceased.[13] Legislation contemporary with our appendix also warns against

---

9. There was also the prohibition inherited from classical law of violating the grave, on which see Arnold Angenendt, 'Der 'ganze' und 'unverweste' Leib-eine Leitidee der Reliquienverehrung bei Gregor von Tours und Beda Venerabilis', *Aus Archiven und Bibliotheken*, 33-50 at 34, citing a letter of Gregory the Great prohibiting the touching of corpses.

10. Concerning the deceased Theodore of Mopeuestia: Grave est insultare defunctis, vel si laici fuerint, nedum illis qui in episcopatu hanc vitam deposuerunt. Iustissimum enim apparet prudentibus viris cedere prescienti uniuscuiusque voluntatem, et cognoscenti qualis unusquisque futurus sit (JE 935, from 553 on the dispute of the 'Three Chapters').

11. His contemporary, Auxilius, who had defended the status of clerics ordained by him, later attracted the attention of writers in the Investiture Contest, notably Peter Damiani and Humbert of Silva Candida. See Uta-Renate Blumenthal, *The Investiture Contest. Church and Monarchy from the Ninth to the Twelfth Century* (Philadelphia: 1988), 75-76.

12. In 1108, the bishop of Hereford sent men to Gloucester to retrieve the body of a man so that he could be reburied, on which see Julia Barrow, 'Urban Cemetary Location in the High Middle Ages', *Death in Towns. Urban Responses to the Dying and the Dead, 100–1600*, ed. Steven Bassett (London and New York: 1992), 78-100, at 81.

13. Thietmar of Merseburg (*Chronicon*, III, 9,10), accessed at http://www.mgh-bibliothek.de/digilib/thietmar.html, on 29 June 2009. In 979 Count Gero of Alsleben had been compelled to fight an accuser, Waldo, in order to defend himself from a charge of disloyalty. Gero lost. By the judgment of Otto II and the princes, he was beheaded. There is evidence that some disagreed with the sentence. Gero's innocence was confirmed after three years. His body was exhumed and both it and its clothing were undecayed, sure signs of sainthood. On Gero, see also http://www.genealogie-mittelalter.de/gero_sippe/gero_graf_von_alsleben_979/gero_graf_von_alsleben_+

the violation of cemeteries – though exhuming the dead is not mentioned – and prohibits the burial of excommunicates.[14]

A text from earlier in the century may also shed some light on these included canons. The treatise *De sepultura eorum qui falso excommunicati dicuntur non turbanda* reports that 'zealots' conducted their own 'cadaver synod':[15]

> The light of orthodoxy, so many years obscured in our parts, began once again to shine and ... the Wigbertian or Henrician heresy is condemned and anathematized. With heretics abdicating in flight, Catholics are being appointed to cathedral sees ... But then, such a zeal for the divine law was stirred up that also the corpses of the pseudo-bishops were being cast out from the churches, and all those ordained by them were suspended from their duties until the convening of a general audience.

The author goes on to note that the bones (at least, the skull) of the antipope Clement III had met a similar fate at Ravenna. After being interred in the cathedral for six years they had been thrown out. He then lists a number of authorities, including both Vigilius and the case of Formosus and his rehabilitation, to declare such desecration of the tombs of bishops and abbots a presumption against divine authority. There had been no 'canonical accusation' levelled against the bishops while they lived. Nevertheless, some believed the deceased either had been, or deserved to be, excommunicated. They were willing to pass judgment and did not hesitate to violate what, to us, would seem the most private of spaces, the grave.

Perhaps a similar situation was the reason for the appended texts in our manuscript. If so, then they provide a glimpse into how a community viewed the residents of its churchyard.[16] We see the tension between what the canons of the Church proclaimed – and maintained through priests and

---

979.html, accessed on 28 June 2009. On the undecayed body signifying sanctity, see Angenendt, 'Der 'ganze' und 'unverweste' Leib'.

14. *Councils and Synods with Other Documents Relating to the English Church*, vol. 1 in 2 parts, eds. D. Whitelock, M. Brett, C.N. Brooke (Oxford: 1981), 2.801, Legatine Council of London, 1143, c. 6, and 2.799, from Roger of Wendover.

15. *De sepultura eorum qui falso excommunicati dictuntur non turbanda*, ed. Ernst Dümmler, MGH Ldl. 3.697: Sic nimirum sic per tot iam annos obnubilata lux oriri copeit nostris in partibus orthodoxa....contempnatur et anathematizatur heresis Wigbertina vel Heinriciana; abdicatis sive fugatis heresis catholici kathedris pontificalibus destinantur...Deinque in tantum divinae legis subito zelus efferbuit, ut etiam ipsa cadavera pseudoepiscoporum ab aecclesiis eliminarentur, quotquot autem ab ipsis erant ordinati, usque ad generalem audientiam ab officiis suspenderentur. On the text, see the *Geschichtsquellen des deutschen Mittelalters* accessed at http://www.repfont.badw.de/D.pdf on 1 July 2009.

16. Barrow, 'Urban Cemetary Location', 78-79.

bishops – and parishioners' feelings about who really deserved Christian burial.[17] Concerning a much later case, where neighbours exhumed an excommunicated woman and clandestinely reburied her remains within the church, David Cressy notes that, 'Local sentiment held that no neighbour should be denied this prospect because of the inconvenience or ill-fortune of excommunication ... we see a determination to do what was best, by means official or unofficial, to resolve controversial problems, and to achieve community cohesion'.[18] The converse, no less concerned with 'community cohesion', may be at work in both the appended texts and the *De sepultura*. The unwanted and undeserving dead were not neighbours: they deserved expulsion.

Tensions between the living and the dead surface in another appendix of texts, this time appended to the 'B' version of the Pseudo-Ivonian *Tripartita* preserved in a Berlin manuscript originally from Maria Laach. (Its medieval provenance is unknown.) Among various texts treating concerns relevant to a monastic audience, one is particularly interesting – a letter from Pope Sylvester II to Arnulf, Archbishop of Rheims (Appendix II). If, as seems likely, the manuscript was written somewhere in the region, including a decretal to Rheims would not be unusual. It has attracted my attention, however, not only because it is found nowhere else among the collections attributed to Ivo but also because I believe that, like other texts in this appendix, it addressed a contemporary concern: rights pertaining to a parish cemetery.[19]

Even when the dead were not being exhumed or their remains cast about, the medieval churchyard was anything but quiet. While hallowed as

---

17. Jean-Claude Schmitt, *Ghosts in the Middle Ages. The Living and the Dead in Medieval Society*, tr. Teresa Lavender Fagan (Chicago: 1998), 142-144, on Yorkshiremen in the fourteenth century witnessing apparitions of excommunicants and interpreting them as confirmation of the Church's sentence. On the 'limits of written sources', above all the elite view of clerics in light of anthropological insight and archaeological evidence, the latter giving insight into popular belief and practice, see Patrick Geary, *Living With the Dead in the Middle Ages* (Cornell: 1994), chapter 2.
18. David Cressy, *Agnes Bowker's Cat. Travesties and Transgressions in Tudor and Stuart England* (Oxford: 2000), chapter 8: 'Who Buried Mrs. Horseman? Excommunication, Accommodation, and Silence', 136-137. The case comes from the seventeenth century.
19. Maria Laach in the twelfth century had two cemeteries. One was for the monks, servants and friends of the cloister, another was within the church itself, where abbots and patrons were buried. See Bertram Resmini, *Das Erzbistum Trier. Die Benediktinerabtei Laach* (Berlin and New York: 1993), 37-38. As yet, however, I have not uncovered any disputes over *sepulturae* involving Maria Laach or neighbouring cloisters.

immune from external jurisdictions – above all secular – and violence,[20] such sanctions were frequently ignored, to judge by their frequent repetition in canonical collections.[21] Cemeteries were arenas where families competed, conscious both of the merits of being buried as close to the saints as possible and how their resting place stood in comparison with those occupied by their friends and rivals.[22] They were also among the most visible symbols of parish identity. This may have been the reason that prompted Arnulf to write to his predecessor at Rheims. The cemetery in question was surely outside the city walls at the monastery of Saint-Rémi. Along with surrounding churches and houses, it had been enclosed with a wall in the early tenth century.[23] Archbishop Seulf had intended this complex of sacred

---

20. Cécile Treffort, *L'Église carolingienne et la mort. Christianisme, rites funéraires et pratiques commémoratives* (Lyon: 1996), 119-153, also Barrow, 'Urban Cemetary Location', 80-81, 93, noting how cemeteries in urban settings could be connected with markets and thus serve as spaces protected, physically and legally, for business and even the issuing of charters. On the choice of burial site, see Élisabeth Zadora-Rio, 'Lieux d'inhumation et espaces consacrés. Le voyage du pape Urbain II en France (août 1095-août 1096)', *Lieux sacrés, Lieux de culte sanctuaires. Approches terminologiques, méthodologiques, historiques et monographiques*, ed. André Vauchez (Paris: 2000), 197-213 at 198, locating the period after 1000 as a 'third stage', where a rite of consecration became the norm, thus ensuring, at least in theory, the hallowed and immune space, also p. 200 on twelfth-century discussions on whether burial in consecrated ground conferred any spiritual benefit.
21. Barbara H. Rosenwein, *Negotiatng Space. Power, Restraint and Privileges of Immunity in Early Modern Europe* (Cornell: 1999), 178-179. For various violations and 'encroachments' recorded by English sources, see Christopher Daniel, *Death and Burial in Medieval England 1066–1550* (London and New York: 1997), 87-115, especially 110-115.
22. Marie-Thérèse Lorcin, 'Choisir un lieu de sépulture', *A Réveiller les morts. La mort au quotidien dans l'Occident médiéval*, eds. Danièle Alexandre-Bidon and Cécile Treffort (Lyons: 1993), 245-252 at 246, 252. That ethnic, historical, and social elements are not easily reduced to comprehension through methodology, is emphasized by E. Crubézy, 'Le "recrutement" et l'organisation des cimetières pariossiaux: perspectives pour une ethnohistoire', *L'environnement des églises et la topographie religieuse des campagnes médiévales. Actes du iiie congrès international d'archéologie médiévale*, eds. M. Fixot and E. Zadora-Rio (Paris: 1994), 132-138 at 133,
23. Françoise Poirier-Coutansas, *Les Abbayes Bénédictines du Diocèse de Reims* (Paris: 1974), 4, 23-24. Remigius' body itself had been absent from the cathedral since 900. Flodoard's account of the saint's translation from the cathedral to the monastery, in the presence of a large number of secular lords, hints that Archbishop Hervé had been under some duress, not the least reason being that his predecessor, Fulk, had been assassinated that year, on which see Peter P. O'Keefe, *A History of the Metropolitan Office at Rheims from Hincmar (845–882), to the 'Romana*

and secular buildings as a *castellum* for defensive purposes. Over time, the monastery had gained the castle, now called both a burg and *suburbium*, and adjacent properties.[24]

To a twelfth-century reader, this letter would bring to mind *sepulturae*, rights to burial dues. Priests had long expected such payments.[25] Parishes and monasteries alike guarded them jealously.[26] By the time of Arnulf's letter, papal privileges granting *sepulturae* were increasingly common.[27] When claims between bishops and monasteries clashed, litigation could be complicated and protracted.[28]

Perhaps our letter chronicled a similar dispute in the late tenth century, one that still spoke to a later audience. The choice between cemeteries reflected divisions between families and parishes.[29] Such conflicts between urban and suburban factions, often represented by rivalling churches or monastic houses, were common, as suburbs grew in size and competition over valuable properties and rights increased.[30] Some wished to be buried in the 'ancient cemetery', a choice taken as a slight by some of those living in Rheims itself. Such conflicts would be freighted with ancient disputes over

---

Ecclesia' of Innocent IV (1243–1254), (Dissertation, Fordham University: 1971), 105-106.

24. Poirier-Countansas, *Les abbayes*, 24, and 28, noting that in the tenth century the monastery possessed at least nine parish churches. The *castellum* also gained royal immunity. See also pp. 8-9 on the monastery's growing independence from archiepiscopal control.
25. For example, the Anglo-Saxon 'soul-scot', on which see Richard H. Helmholz, *The Oxford History of the Laws of England. The Canon Law and Ecclesiastical Jurisdiction from 597 to the 1640s* (Oxford: 2004), 43. For papal letters treating disputes over burials as part of priests' incomes from tithes, see Jayne E. Sayers, *Papal Judges Delegate in the Province of Canterbury 1198–1254* (Cambridge: 1971), 188-189 and n. 4.
26. Treffort, *L'Église carolingienne*, 165-167, 172-179. For Italian examples from the twelfth century, see Christopher Wickham, *Courts and Conflict in Medieval Tuscany* (Oxford: 2004), 73.
27. Treffort, *L'Église Carolingienne* 178 n. 63, a bull of Gregory V from 999 to an abbey in Avignon.
28. Wickham, *Courts and Conflict*, 251. That somewhere between 10 and 20% of gifts to Cluny in the tenth and eleventh centuries were for the privilege of being buried in its grounds is noted by Constable, *The Reformation of the Twelfth Century*, 83.
29. On intra- and extramural churches and their burial rights (here the case of Gloucester), see Barrow, 'Urban Cemetary Location', 84-85.
30. Dietrich Lohrmann, 'Papstprivileg und päpstliche Delegationsgerichtbarkeit im nördlichen Frankreich zur Zeit der Kirchenreform', *Proceedings of the Sixth International Congress of Medieval Canon Law*, eds. Stephan Kuttner and Kenneth Pennington (Vatican City: 1985), 535-550 at 541-542, concerning Rheims.

parish boundaries and family allegiances to particular monastic churches.[31] The conflicting claims of lay patrons figured as well.[32] These disputes could even penetrate the family itself – broadly defined – —whose servants, retainers, vassals, and guests who died on location might be buried elsewhere.[33] Such disputes were no less common in the twelfth century.

Granted, a single text is slender evidence indeed, but I see no reason why this papal letter might not concern the maintenance of *sepulturae*. Monastic burial rights were no less important, for the new orders, for example the Cistercians, made sure their patrons were buried at their foundations.[34] Our letter reminded those who consulted *de causis laicorum* in this manuscript that rivalries between parishes, those within and without the walls, did not extend to the cemetery. Community was to be preserved, so that the living might have hope and the dead, peace.

Finally, we return to the appendix of canons to F, the abbreviated Ivonian *Decretum* preserved in the manuscript from Rome, Academia dei Lincea. The appendix adds 62 canons to those it shares with H, the Harleian abbreviated *Decretum*. These range across a wide variety of subjects. A number of recent papal decisions are included, for example, canons from Urban II's Council at Clermont in 1095 and decretals from Pope Calixtus II. This concern to include more contemporary – and presumably useful and relevant – texts is reflected by an item I have included as Appendix III. It concerns valid marriage.

In his monumental study of canon law and sexuality, James Brundage observes that 'The sexual agenda of the reformers also included a strong commitment, not only to deny marriage to the clergy, but to reorganize marriage among the laity as well'.[35] While Gratian and his commentators, aided by civil law, set the conditions and terms for this project, the laity were not equally enthusiastic about being 'reorganized', especially in such a tradition-bound and vital area of 'private life'. An *interrogatio* added by a second hand in the F appendix reflects tensions between the Church's legal and moral agenda and family practice.

Throughout the twelfth century, canonists debated what made a valid marriage. The chief point of contention was whether coitus was necessary, or merely consent.[36] A related question was the age at which valid marriage

---

31. Wickham, *Courts and Conflict*, 267, on a particularly dramatic late twelfth-century dispute dividing two sides of the same street.
32. Ibid., 269.
33. Ibid., 268.
34. On the burial of female patrons, see Hoffman Berman, *The Cistercian Evolution*, 20, 70-71.
35. Brundage, *Law, Sex, and Christian Society*, 183.
36. Ibid., 236-238. The papal decretals of the second half the twelfth century frequently engage such issues. See, for example, *Die Collectio Francofurtana: eine*

could occur. Gratian located that age as seven,[37] following the teaching of the School of Laon, which was known to our scribe.[38] The 'interrogatio' treats parental vows contracting marriage for their underage or unknowing children alongside agreements 'de futuro'. Both of these were forbidden. This added text was practical, and could serve as a guide in actual legal process. It also demonstrates the everyday realities confronting canon law. For the laity resisted such efforts to restrict their freedom to contract the marriage alliances that were so essential to the maintenance, and extension, of lineage and patronage.

Canon Law, Private Life, and Proceduralist Society

Commenting on twelfth-century canon law, Dominque Bauer notes:

> From a historical perspective it can be stated that the stronger and the more present proceduralism gets, the stronger social control and organization becomes. Historically seen, the refinement of law and legal formulae emerges side by side with proceduralism. The genesis of legal validity has to be situated within an institutional framework.[39]

The texts examined above shed light on this increasing interest in procedure. That the Church wanted to define and control the private lives of the laity was nothing new in the early twelfth century; what was unprecedented was how procedures to accomplish this ecclesiastical regulation were developing under the influence of scholastic hermeneutic, civil law, and sacramental theology. Moreover, it no longer sufficed to compile, preserve and organize older tradition concerning the laity; newer texts were necessary in order to address a growing volume of litigation about the affairs of adults, children,

---

französische Decretalensammlung. Analyse berührend auf Vorarbeiten von Walter Holtzmann (+), eds. Peter Landau and Giesela Drossbach (Vatican City: 2007), titles 1-2.

37. Brundage, *Law, Sex, and Christian Society*, 238.
38. Heinrich J.F. Reinhardt, *Die Ehelehre der Schule des Anselm von Laon. Eine theologie- und kirchenrechtsgeschichtliche Untersuchung zu den Ehetexten der frühen Pariser Schule des 12. Jahrhunderts* (Münster: 1974), 75-78 at 77, also n. 12. See the *Sententiae Atrebatenses*, ed. O. Lottin, 'Les 'Sententiae atrebatenses', *Réchérches de théologie ancienne et médiévale* 10 (1938), 205-224, 344-355 at 355: Item queritur de patribus qui iurant inter se filiis nescientibus uel infra annos positis an sit coniugium? Non: quia non fuit par consensus utriusque.
39. Dominique Bauer, 'The Twelfth Century and the Emergence of the Juridical Subject – some Reflections', *Zeitschrift der Savigny-Stiftüng für Rechtsgeschichte. Kanonistische Abteilung* 121 (2004), 207-227, at 212.

even the dead. In the appended texts to the Ivonian *Decretum* and the *Tripartita*, we find how anonymous compilers were attempting, in Bauer's words, to 'refine' the canon law, both old and new, to strengthen the claims of the Church – whether secular or religious – against the laity.[40]

Almost a century ago, Rudolf Sohm advanced the controversial thesis that it was not until the late twelfth century – shortly after our appendices were composed – that canon law actually appeared for the first time in the history of the Church. Until Alexander III, the canons had carried a sacramental, not juridical, conception of the Church. This is not the place to dwell at length on his much-disputed work;[41] nevertheless it is striking how, in the sphere of the canon law's treatment of 'private life', we do see a transformation at work somewhat reminiscent of what Sohm argued.

At the beginning of the eleventh century, Burchard's *Decretum* had not differed essentially from its predecessors when it came to the laity and private life. It was merely richer in texts. After that, however, from strings of canons only occasionally adorned with rubrics we find, with the Ivonian *Decretum*, a discrete section on the laity. In appendices, old and new texts were added to 'refine' (echoing Bauer) so that the Church might better regulate marriages and burials. The inserted '*interrogatio*', probably originating in the *Sententiae Atrebatenses*, points the way towards both the *summae* – with their increasing sophistication in formulae – and the *ordines iudiciorum* – no less sophisticated in their procedure.[42] It was no longer enough to condemn lay transgression in moral or – and here I echo Sohm – theological language.[43]

Unlike Sohm, I do not wish to argue that there had been no canon law on private life or any other subject prior to the twelfth century. There had been plenty of that. What had begun to change, and I hope this is at least suggested by the texts considered in this paper, is how 'private life' was coming under a system of institutional, legal control. This was shaping an

---

40. On the clerical effort to establish 'hegemony' over the laity, with some lay cooperation, for example by the Patarines, see André Vauchez, *The Laity in the Middle Ages. Religious Beliefs and Devotional Practices*, ed. Daniel E. Bornstein, transl. Margery J. Schneider (Notre Dame and London: 1993), 43.
41. For an eloquent critique, see Stephan Kuttner, 'Reflections on Law and Gospel in the History of the Church', *Liber amicorum monsieur Onclin*, eds. Jean Lindemans and H. Demeester (Louvain: 1976), 199-209. For a more recent review of the debate, Bruce C. Brasington, 'Avoiding the "Tyranny of a Concept": Structural Considerations Concerning Twelfth Century Canon Law', *Das Eigene und das Ganze. Zum individuellen im mittelalterlichen Religiosentum*, eds. G. Melville and M. Schürer (Münster, Hamburg and London: 2002), 419-438.
42. Linda Fowler-Magerl, *Ordines iudiciorum and Libelli de ordine iudiciorum: From the Middle of the Twelfth to the End of the Fifteenth Century* (Turnhout: 1994).
43. Bauer, 'The Twelfth Century', 213.

'objective order' of the laity.[44] The additions to pre-Gratian collections such as the Ivonian *Decretum*, while local and likely idiosyncratic in nature, mark points of friction between the Church's interest in imposing order and lay deviance from this agenda. Some wives wished to dispose of their husbands and property as they saw fit. Not every parishioner was happy with who had been buried in his churchyard. Fathers and mothers were determined to have their children marry in the most advantageous way. From bedrooms to cemeteries, some lay men and women resisted the strictures of the canon law, proof that the 'private' was, at it remains, the most unpredictable and difficult sphere of human action for any legal system, to define and control.

---

44. Ibid., 227, discussing 'objective order'.

APPENDICES

I. Shared Appendix of Canons to ID 16 (FH)

Ieron' ad Amandum presbiterum. Ista soror que ut dicit vim – voluerit non potest. (A woman who had put aside a notoriously adulterous husband must do penance before being admitted to communion.)

Item ad Eustochium. Quamquam apostolus orare nos semper – referatur gloria creatori. (Concerning the canonical hours.)

Augustinus in libro de cura pro mortuis gerenda. Orantes de membris corporis sui faciunt – humilius atque frequentius. (On the practice of true religion.)

Ex sermone eius ad coniugatos. Fratres mei, audiunt me viri, audiunt – Pretium suum attendat, tabulas legat. (Neither adulterous men nor women are to be tolerated.)

Ex epistola eiusdem ad Egdigiam. Factum est ut vinculum continentie quo se – refectio, vobis autem angustia. (Addressed to a religious woman who had angered her husband by giving most of what she had to two monks. She had ceased to sleep with him and assumed that he had no control over her property. Augustine rebukes her, reminding her of the conjugal bond.)

Sane profertur a quibusdam qui dicunt – memorie episcopis Constantinopolitanis.
(In favour of posthumous anathematization of heretics.)

Actio iiii. Sancta synodus dicit, Augustini religiosi memorie – nos gesta significant.
(From the Fifth Ecumenical Council, asserting that even if they had not been accused of heresy while living, heretics could be anathematized *post mortem*.)

II. Appendix to a Second Version of the Tripartita, B. 29

De illis quos unus aut ambo parentes sancte religioni tradiderunt. Ex concil. Tolet. X cap. vii. Quoniam huc usque dissolutionis effectus interdum – religioni semper inhereat.[45]

Ex priuilegiis et epistolis Siluestri pape.[46]
Siluester episcopus seruus seruorum Dei Arnulfo Remorum archiepiscopo salutem et apostolicam benedictionem. Nuper nobis ad notitiam perlatum est – optato in pace quiescant. Ex privilegiis et epistolis Silvestris pape. Silvester episcopus servus servorum Dei Arnulfo Remorum archiepiscopo salutem et apostolicam benedictionem. Nuper nobis ad noticiam perlatum est, quod inter cives vestros de sepulture loco dissidentia sit, cum alii in urbe, alii extra in cimiterio antiquo sancti Remigii sepiliri desiderent atque ideo ab his, quibus intra urbem locus placet sepulture, eucharistia negatur illis, qui morientes in cimiterio predicto extra urbem sepeliri deposcunt. Sed canones asseverant, nulli in extremis eucharistiam negandam, nisi solummodo excommunicatis et satisfacere nolentibus. Perniciosum etiam atque sceleratum recte intuentibus videtur, cum quilibet salutaria atque vivifica auferendo, fratrem in morte impie relinquit. Apostolica ergo auctoritate precipimus, ut nulli morientium preiudicium fiat, nulli eucharistia negetur, qui in extremo penitentiam profitetur. Omnibus qui volunt liceat, in cimiterio antiquo sancti Remigii absque refragatione tumulari, quatinus et vivi certam tumulandi spem habeant, et defuncti in loco optato in pace quiescant.

Ex concilio Triburiensi. Nulli sacerdoti esse licitum una die in uno altari plusquam tres missas celebrare. Statuimus et iudicamus nulli sacerdoti – conveniat altari precipimus.

Ex concilio Caballionis. Vt pro fideli<bus> defunctis singulis diebus missas celebrare liceat. Visum [preterea *canc.*] nobis est ut in omnibus – pia matre communi.

---

45 De loco sepulture *in mg.*
46 (JL 3932), on which see Paul Ewald, 'Mittheilungen', *Neues Archiv* 8 (1883), 354-365 at 364.

III. Continuation of the (F) Appendix

app. 35 [change of hand] Interrogatio de coniugiis
De patribus qui iurant inter se, filiis nescientibus, vel infra annos positis an sit coniugium. R. Non. Quia [ ] fuit par consensus utriusque, et stulte iurant, nec coguntur infantes propter hoc.
Item. Si quis iurat se accepturum aliquam tali conditione si pater suus dederit ei x marcas vel huiusmodi simile, quere si sit coniugium. R. Non. Et si interim habet rem cum alia non est adulterium quia non fuit consensus de presenti, sed de futuro, et si ille non dederit in termino constituto pecuniam, fides eius salva remanet, nec cogetur ut recipiat.
Item. Si quis dat fidem absque condictione se accepturum aliquam usque ad tempus definitum, et interim aliam receperit, periurio tenebitur sed non separab[untu]r. Non enim fuit coniugium.
Item. Si quis <puer *in mg.*> infra annos positus det fidem alicui item infra annos, quando uo' ad annos quocumque eorum nolente, non erit coniugium. Et si tunc fieri velint, legalis consensus est faciendus.
Item. Si quis habens annos det fidem alicui infra annos, et illa postquam ad annos venerit voluerit, utrum ille possit eam non accipere, ad quod est dicendum secundum quosdam quod non debet cogi, cum non esset coniugium cum illa esset infra annos. Magister autem Anselmus dicebat quod in una persona erat coniugium, in alia non.

CIVIL CUSTODY AS COERCIVE MEASURE IN MEDIEVAL LAW

Harry Dondorp

Introduction

One of the coercive remedies available to enforce legal and contractual duties in Dutch law is called *lijfsdwang*. Dutch courts can order imprisonment in order to compel a judgment debtor to perform what is due. This contrasts both with French law, which abolished all *contrainte par corps* together with imprisonment for debt in 1867, and with German law, which restricts *Beugehaft* to performances of a personal nature that cannot be carried out by someone else, such as the disclosure of information or the presentation of documents.[1] Since 1933, the Dutch Code of Civil Procedure has generally allowed civil imprisonment, albeit as a remedy of last resort, for all legal duties and contractual obligations.[2]

In the nineteenth century – more precisely from 1811, when the French *Code de procédure civil* (1806) was promulgated in the Netherlands under Napoleon, until 1933 – the Dutch adopted the French system. The draftsmen of the French codes considered it uncivil to use imprisonment as a coercive measure to enforce contractual obligations to do something. In their view, a breach of contract was insufficient reason to infringe upon one's liberty. Hence, Article 1142 *Code civil* (1804) provides that 'any obligation to do or not to do [something] resolves into damages in case of non-performance on the part of the debtor'. Civil imprisonment as a coercive measure was not unknown, however. The *Code de procédure civil* allowed it in a limited number of situations,

---

1. Cf. *Zivilprozessordnung* § 888.
2. Cf. *Wetboek van Burgerlijke Rechtsvordering* artt. 585-600.

similar to those already summed up in an ordinance of 1667.³ Apart from merchant law, imprisonment was used to enforce the legal duty of guardians, curators, and sequestrators to render account and return the goods entrusted to them.⁴

In 1815, immediately after the Napoleonic period, a proposal was made to reinstate the modes of execution of Roman-Dutch law.⁵ A decade later, the 1828 draft of the Dutch Code of Civil Procedure proposed to apply civil imprisonment to enforce duties of a personal nature – comparable to the German *Beugehaft* – but in 1838 the Dutch legislature preferred to retain the French system, which remained in place until 1933.

Coercive Measures in the Dutch Republic

Roman-Dutch law distinguished between civil custody (*gijzeling*) and imprisonment for monetary debts. The former was a mode of execution unknown in other countries. William de Groot (the younger brother of Hugo Grotius for whom Grotius wrote his *Inleidinge tot de Hollandsche rechts-geleerdheid*) remarked in 1655: 'In our country there is a system unknown to other nations by which judgments condemning a person to render account or to perform an act are executed [...] called gyseling'.⁶ During the period of the Republic, the strong arm of the law helped to enforce court orders to restore an object to its owner. Obligations, however, were enforced through *gijzeling* – that is, all obligations other than to pay a certain sum of money, irrespective of whether the performance due consisted in delivering an object, doing something or refraining from doing something.⁷ By contrast, if a defendant was

---

3. Cf. *Ordonnance de Louis XIV du mois d'avril 1667 rélatives aux usages des cours de parlement,* title 34. *De la décharge du contraintes par corps,* art. 1-7.
4. With regard to civil imprisonment in 19th-century Dutch law, see J.H. Dondorp and H. de Jong, 'Coercive measures to enforce obligations under Dutch law (1838–1933)', *The Right to Specific Performance, The Historical Development*, ed. J. Hallebeek and J.H. Dondorp (Antwerp: 2010), 135.
5. *Ontwerp van wet betrekkelijk de manier van procedeeren in civiele zaken* (The Hague: 1815), art. 370, 400.
6. Cf. Willem de Groot, *Inleyding tot de practijk van den Hove van Holland* (The Hague: 1656), I.7 no. 24. This is a translation of his *Isagoge ad praxin fori Batavici* (Amsterdam: 1655).
7. The fact that court orders to do something were executed by means of *gijzeling* does not necessarily imply that the courts ordered performance in kind of contractual obligations. Grotius (1583–1645), for instance, stated that the debtor could discharge his obligation through a payment of damages. See below, note

condemned to pay a certain sum of money, his goods were seized and sold. If he had no property, the debtor was incarcerated.

The 1580 ordinance on the procedure in the lower courts in the province of Holland described the *gijzeling* mode of execution as follows:

> All judgments by which a person is condemned to render an account or to perform any other act, shall thus be executed after ten days have elapsed and after summons has been issued as follows: the judgment debtor shall be ordered to place himself in *gijzeling* in a certain inn under penalty of ten guilders. And if he does not place himself in *gijzeling* on the day fixed for that purpose, and if the process-server fails to find him at the inn, he shall be attached and led to the nearest town, where he shall be lodged in the gaol at a cost of three pennies a day. If he places himself in the inn, and having been there for fourteen days is not as prudent to perform the act to the satisfaction of the court, he shall be apprehended and lodged in the gaol at a cost of three pennies per day. If, after having been lodged in the gaol for a month, the judgment debtor still does not satisfy the judgment, the judgment holder shall be entitled to request the court to tax the act and convert it into a money judgment.[8]

In his 1939 Leyden dissertation Steyn emphasized that one should not confuse civil custody and imprisonment for debt.[9] In the province of Holland, for example, if the court had condemned someone to pay a certain sum of money, the process-server (*deurwaerder*) levied execution

---

51. Groenewegen (1613–1652) and Van Leeuwen (1627–1652), denied this, however. See: R. Zimmermann, 'Das römisch-holländische Recht und seine Bedeutung für Europa', *Juristenzeitung* 45 (1990), 831; K. Nehlsen-Stryk, 'Grenzen des Rechtszwangs: Zur Geschichte der Naturalvollstreckung', *Archiv für die civilistische Praxis* 193 (1993), 546; J.H. Dondorp, 'Specific performance: a historical perspective', *Specific Performance in Contract Law: National and other Perspectives*, ed. J. Smits, G. Hesen, and D. Haas (Antwerp: 2008), 278.

8. Cf. *Ordonnantie van de Iustitie in den steden en ten platte lande van Holland*, 1 April 1580, art. 31 (Groot Placaet-boek, vol. 2 (The Hague: 1664), 702) as translated by Steyn. Cf. I.C. Steyn, *Gijzeling, The Historical Development of the Mode of Proceeding in 'Gijzeling' in the Provincial Court of Holland from 1531* (Leiden: 1939), 96. A similar rule applied in the province of Utrecht, when the court had ordered 'rekeninge te doen ofte eenig ander feyt ofte werk te praesteren'. Cf. *Nieuwe ordonnantie [...] over het platte land en de provincie Utrecht*, 21 March 1594, art. 86 and 88 (Groot Placaet-boek van Utrecht, vol. 2 (Utrecht: 1729), 1183). In Utrecht the debtor was transferred from the inn to the Utrecht gaol after eight days.

9. Cf. Steyn, *Gijzeling* (n 8), 4-10.

upon the judgment debtor's goods. Only if he did not possess sufficient property he was apprehended and lodged in jail. He was to remain there at the cost of three pennies a day, until the judgment creditor had received satisfaction in full[10] – either in fact or (if an insolvent debtor ceded all his goods) in fiction. If the court had condemned someone to do something and he failed to comply, after ten days the judgment creditor could proceed *in cas van gijzeling*. First, he gave notice to the judgment debtor to carry out the court's sentence within 24 hours. Subsequently, he gave a second notice combined with an order to appear in *gijzeling* at a particular inn some days later,[11] if the sentence had not been carried out to his satisfaction. Subsequently, if the judgment debtor was not found in the inn at the day specified, the judgment holder could request an order to apprehend and imprison the debtor – but in some cities, like Haarlem, only after a second notice to appear in *gijzeling* failed to produce him. The 1579 and 1581 ordinances of the appellate courts in The Hague (*Hoge Raad* and *Hof van Holland, Zeeland en West Friesland*) contained similar provisions.[12]

Confinement or Imprisonment?

Gijzeling began as confinement in an inn. Apprehension and incarceration were ordered only if the debtor failed to appear at the inn, or if – having taken residence there – after fourteen days he still did not satisfy the court order. The 1594 ordinance of the neighbouring province of Utrecht indicates the circumstances of such confinement. Judgment debtors were lodged at the cost of ten pennies per day, a sum the judgment holder had to pre-arrange on security. In the execution of sentences of the Utrecht appellate court, the costs of *gijzeling* were ten

---

10. Cf. *Ordonnantie* 1580 (n 8), art 28. In Utrecht, however, the appellate court applied *gijzeling* in order to compel the judgment debtor to point out property which could be taken in arrest and sold. Cf. *Ordonnantie ende instructie op de stijl van procederen voor den Hove van Utrecht*, 3 April 1583, rubr. 17, art. 1.
11. Fourteen days in the execution of sentences of the Hof van Holland. Cf. *Ampliatie van de instructie van den Hove van Holland*, 21 December 1579, art. 14 (Groot-Placaetboek, vol 2 (The Hague: 1664), 770). On the execution of judgments of the Hof van Holland, see Steyn, *Gijzeling* (n 8), 52-94; M.Ch. le Bailly, *Procesgids Hof van Holland, Zeeland en West-Friesland* (Hilversum: 2008), 53-54 and 66-72.
12. The order to apprehend and imprison a judgment debtor from the province of Zeeland was (because of the distance) issued after two notices to appear in *gijzeling* in an inn in The Hague, as was the case in the execution of judgments of the *Hoge Raad*.

pennies in the first week, seven in the second. This was a charge for accommodation and two meals – in winter the inn-keeper could charge two pennies extra for fire.[13] In the seventeenth century, the charges of the The Hague *Casteleny* (from the French *chateau*), where judgment debtors of the appellate courts had to appear in *gijzeling* from 1659 on, were two guilders for a meal at the common table where diplomats, officers, burghers and merchants wined and dined. Their servants were served for 15 pennies. Meals of other debtors cost 25 pennies, beer included. These charges did not cover the price of accommodation of 12 pennies. For the lodging of impecunious debtors in *gijzeling*, who provided their own food but were supplied with sleeping accommodation, eight pennies were charged in summer and twelve in winter, provided they were supplied with blankets and fire. Debtors who desired something out of the ordinary were bound to pay for it themselves.[14]

The period during which the judgment debtor confined himself to the inn was used to discuss what precisely must be done to satisfy the court. In order to oppose the *gijzeling*, the judgment debtor had to appear at the inn on the specified day; otherwise, the judge would not hear him. If he put himself in *gijzeling* and presented a written tender containing a specified statement of the manner in which he was prepared to satisfy the judgment immediately, after a summary hearing the judge usually released him provisionally,[15] on the understanding that he would once more appear in *gijzeling* if he failed to perform his obligations. This could be because the court decided that the manner specified in the tender did not satisfy, or because the performance specified in the tender was not carried out. In that case the judgment debtor was given notice to reappear at the inn – unless the date by which the act must be carried out had already been fixed in the summary procedure.

As discussed, the 1580 ordinance on the procedure in the lower courts in the province of Holland provided that the judgment debtor, if he appeared at the inn appointed for his confinement and remained there for fourteen days, but neither opposed the *gijzeling* nor satisfied the

---

13. Cf. *Ordonnantie* 1583 (n 10), art. 1 and 2; there is no such provision in the 1594 ordinance on procedure in the lower courts of Utrecht.
14. Cf. *Ordonnantie van den Hove op 't stuck van salaris van de advocaten ende procureurs, deurwaerders etc.* 16 January 1659, art. 40-50 (Groot Placaet-boek, vol 3 (The Hague: 1664), 651).
15. The case was concluded summarily by filing the claim of *gijzeling*, an answer stating the manner in which the judgment debtor alleged to perform his obligations, a replication and rejoinder. See Simon van Leeuwen, *Manier van procederen in civile en criminele saaken* (Amsterdam: 1677), 108 note 9; Steyn, *Gijzeling* (n 8), 97.

judgment, would be apprehended and lodged in the gaol of the nearest city at the cost of three pennies a day.[16] In Utrecht, he was transferred to the gaol after eight days, where he was held at his own expense for two and a half pennies. For those few pennies the warden was not obliged to serve more than thin beer and bread. A 1585 instruction for the warden of the *Voorpoort*, the gaol of the appellate court in The Hague, indicates that the charges varied. The gaoler could charge up to twelve pennies per day for everything a prisoner consumed – a sum that the judgment holder must pre-arrange. Those who had been imprisoned at a cost of six pennies or less per day, it said, were to be supplied with thin beer, bread and a little butter or cheese.[17] This sum was more than the charge of three pennies for debtors who had placed themselves in *gijzeling* in an inn, but were transferred to the *Voorpoort* after two weeks.

The 1580 ordinance on the procedure in the lower courts in Holland on the default of a debtor who had not placed himself in *gijzeling* at the fixed day also provided for imprisonment at a daily charge of three pennies. Such a low charge meant that the prisoner was served no more than thin beer and bread, just enough to keep him alive. Whether this also applied in the execution of sentences of the appellate courts is not certain, because the ordinances are silent on the issue. Article 14 of the *Ampliatie van de instructie van den Hove van Holland* ruled that a debtor who did not appear at the inn was to be apprehended and imprisoned in the *Voorpoort*, but did not state at what cost. The 1585 instruction for the gaoler indicates that up to twelve pennies could be charged. Simon van Leeuwen explained that the creditor could petition for imprisonment at a lower charge after fourteen days – apparently analogous to the situation where the judgment debtor had placed himself in *gijzeling* in an inn – if he still did not satisfy the court's sentence.[18]

---

16. Cf. *Ordonnantie* 1580 (n 8), art. 31.
17. Cf. *Ordonnantie voor den Cipier van den Voorpoort,* 15 November 1585 (ed. G.G. Calkoen, 'De gevangenpoort of Voorpoort van den Hove', *Die Haghe* 6 (1906), 90), art. 21: 'Die op 6 st(uyvers) te tracteren met klein bier, broot mit weynig boter of kaes, tot nootelyk onderhout'.
18. Cf. Simon van Leeuwen, *Manier* (n 15), 22.3.5. See also art. 21 of the *Ordonnantie op de manier van procedeeren te Haarlem van 1 September 1751*, which adopted more or less the practice in the appellate court. In the eighteenth century the creditor could put in his request after a month. Cf. Steyn, *Gijzeling* (n 8), 60 n 4 and 66 n 4.

Gijzeling as a Medieval Coercive Measure

The seventeenth-century procedure of confinement in an inn as a mode of execution in Holland and Utrecht is an adaptation of the medieval *otage* in French customary law, and of the medieval *leisten, einlegen* or *einreiten* in the indigenous law of the German-speaking countries, called *obstagium* in Latin sources. In origin it was not a mode of execution, but an extra-judicial coercive measure – usually applied before any judgment was given. *Gijzeling* has its roots in the obligations of noblemen.[19] Noblemen confirmed contracts they concluded, as well as promises and oaths they gave, by a further promise that members of their household would place themselves under house-arrest in an inn in case of default. The coercive function of this promise was twofold. On the one hand, debtors had to pay the costs of their confinement, which would be high since they wined and dined according to their status. On the other hand, a debtor could not make use of those members of his entourage who were under house-arrest staying with their horses and servants at the inn. Thus, although these noblemen wined and dined at the inn, they promised not to leave until the performance due was carried out.[20] Those who promised to place themselves in confinement for another were called *fideiussores* in the medieval Latin sources, but they had nothing in common with sureties in Roman law, who promised, if necessary, to pay another person's debt.[21]

The few thirteenth-century examples from the Low Countries concern noblemen – as in the rest of Europe. In 1257, for instance, Alard of Brecht, who sold land to a Cistercian abbey, promised that four of his men would place themselves in *gijzeling* in Valkenburg in case of nonperformance.[22] In 1263, Gerard Clenke and Hacko van Hardenberg lent 200 pounds to the bishop of Utrecht and obtained Coeverden castle as collateral. To secure restitution of the castle when the bishop repaid his

---

19. See W. Ogris, 'Die persönlichen Sicherheiten im Spätmittelalter, Versuch eines Überblicks', *ZRG Germ. Abt.* 82 (1985) 168; S. Bressler, *Schuldknechtschaft und Schuldturm, Zur Personalexekution im sächsischen Recht des 13. – 16. Jahrhunderts*, Freiburger Rechtsgeschichtliche Abhandlungen 42 (Berlin: 2004), 313-315
20. Cf. M. Rintelen, *Schuldhaft und Einlager im Vollstreckungsverfahren des altniederländische und sächsischen Rechtes* (Leipzig: 1908), 115ff.
21. Cf. R. Caillemer, 'Les idées coutumières et la renaissance du droit romain dans le sud est de la France', *Essays in Legal History Read before the International Congress of Historical Studies* ed. P. Vinogradoff (Oxford: 1913), 178; Ogris, *Sicherheiten* (n 19), 165-176.
22. Cf. B.H.D. Hermesdorf, *De herberg in de Nederlanden, een blik in de beschavingsgeschiedenis* (Arnhem: 1977), 180-181.

debt, they promised that eight knights would place themselves in *gijzeling* in Deventer, if they (Clenke and van Hardenberg) breached their contract.[23] In several fourteenth-century documents, the debtor himself is among those who must confine themselves in an inn, for instance in Utrecht, Kampen, and Groningen.[24] Hence, the coercive function of *gijzeling* changed, because from then on *gijzeling* meant an infringement of the debtor's own liberty. Over time, the role of *gijzeling* as a variant type of personal surety for another's debt dwindled. In the sixteenth century such contracts were almost non-existent. A late example occurred in 1599 when Count Edzard of Oostvriesland gave notice that 36 abbots, prelates and courtiers had to appear in *gijzeling* in Emden on the day of Pentecost, because a loan of 8000 guilders was not repaid. In Germany such contracts were forbidden in 1577. From then on not only German sureties, but also debtors could no longer bind themselves to appear in *gijzeling*, while such contracts were null.[25] This could be the reason why William de Groot wrote in 1655 that *gijzeling* was not known in other countries.

As a prelude to the aforementioned general ordinances in the Low Countries, many towns in the fifteenth and sixteenth centuries applied *gijzeling* as a mode of execution. Some differentiated between house-arrest for the town's burghers and confinement in an inn for foreigners.[26] Many also applied *gijzeling* to monetary debts.[27] In a number of situations, *gijzeling* was used as an extra-judicial mode of coercion to compel magistrates: for example, a *keur* of 1484 decreed that aldermen in

---

23. Cf. J.A. Feith, 'Het leisten', *Groningsche Volksalmanak* 1892, 18.
24. Cf. Hermesdorf, *Herberg* (n 22), 183, 186; Feith, *Leisten* (n 23), 19-20.
25. *Reichspolizeiordnung* 1577, title 17 § 10: 'So wollen wir hiemit die Leistung in künftigen Schuld oder Gültverschreibungen einzuverleiden gäntslich verboten haben. Da auch einige Verschreibung gleichwohl hinfürters darauf gestellt wurde, soll dieselbe Leistung nunmehr iure publico verbotten, an ihr selbst nichtig, und danach kein Bürg noch Schuldner zu leisten, noch auch den Wirten [...] etwas zu zahlen verschuldigt sein.'
26. Cf. Hermesdorf, *Herberg* (n 22), 186 (referring to Elburg, Zutphen, and Gorkum),
27. In Schoonhoven and Vlissingen, for instance, *gijzeling* was one of the modes of execution. Cf. *Costumen Vlissingen* (Vlissingen: 1757) III, art. 8; *Keuren, Ordonnantien en Statuten van Schoonhoven* 1557, executie, art. 51. See also *Aanteekeningen hoofdzakelijk betreffende den stijl van procedeeren voor het Hof van Holland*, rubr. 23 art. 6: 'Administratores civitatis, pagi, collegii sive societatis hoc goudent privilegio, ne statim executionem patiantur, maer werden gegyselt tot dien einde.' Edition: *Uit de practijk van het Hof van Holland in de tweede helft van de zestiende eeuw, een handschrift*, ed. L.J. van Apeldoorn (Utrecht: 1938), 132.

Zeeland who failed to render judgment in six weeks had to place themselves in *gijzeling* at an inn.[28] Many towns decreed that magistrates who were obliged to render account at the end of their office had to place themselves in *gijzeling* if they had not done so within a month.[29] Their sanction for not appearing was a fine, not imprisonment.

Until 1579, as a collection of notes written between 1550 and 1570 on the procedure of the *Hof van Holland* indicates, courts were reluctant to order a judgment debtor's arrest and imprisonment, *viz.* only if the judgment was sufficiently specific to preclude discussion on how it should be carried out, and then only after three subsequent orders to appear in *gijzeling*.[30] The ordinance of 1579 specified that the debtor would be apprehended and imprisoned if a single notice to appear in *gijzeling* was ineffectual.[31]

Gijzeling and the Learned Law

The decretal *Ex rescripto* (X 2.24.9), a letter of Pope Alexander III (1159–1181) to the bishops of Saintes and Chalons in France, concerns a case of *gijzeling*. As security for a payment of 8000 *solidi* by their abbot, several monks had sworn that they themselves, or other monks in their place, would appear in *gijzeling* (*obstagium*).[32] A certain W. and his wife had agreed to act as sureties, and had sworn to indemnify the creditor themselves, in the event the monks breached their promise. The pope decided that the abbot, monks and sureties must be compelled to bring about fulfilment of the agreement as they had sworn.[33]

The ordinary gloss to the *Liber Extra*, composed and revised by Bernard of Parma until 1266, noted that canon law apparently acknowledges

---

28. Keur 1484 *De keuren van Zeeland,* ed. R. Fruin, (The Hague: 1920), 200-201.
29. Cf. Rintelen, *Schuldhaft* (n 20), 218.
30. Cf. *Aanteekeningen* (n 27), rubr. 23 art. 5.
31. Cf. *Praxis et ordo iudiciorum curiae hollandiae: de stijl van het Hof van Holland met verwijzingen naar het Ius Commune* Verslagen en Mededelingen Stichting tot Uitgaaf der bronnen van het Oud-vaderlandse Recht 10, ed. J. Hallebeek and C.H. van Ree (Maastricht: 1998) 14.5: 'Hodie uyt cracht van 't eerste default wort verleent een tweede gyselinge met apprehensie, instructionis [= *Ampliatie* (n 11)] articulus 14'.
32. X. 2.24.9: ... 'Super haec predictus abbas quosdam ex monachis obsides dedit, qui de obseruanda conuentione iurauerunt, ut si ipsi deficerent alii monachi loco eorum in obstagio ponerentur.' ...
33. X. 2.24.9: ... 'Ideoque mandamus, quatenus tam abbatem, quam monachus, quam V. et uxorem ipsius studiose monere curetis, ut sicut iuraverunt, eandem conventionem faciant adimpleri'. ...

gijzeling, although the *Corpus iuris* prohibits a creditor from accepting the debtor's son as a 'pledge'. To resolve this contradiction, Bernard pointed out that the creditor is not allowed to alienate a bailsman, but only to detain him until the agreement is fulfilled. As another possible solution, Bernard distinguished between bailsmen to secure money debts and those to secure other performances, for instance, to comply with the arbiter's decision.[34] Bernard did not elaborate on the manner in which *gijzeling* was to be enforced.

Around 1275, referring to this gloss, William Durant, a pupil of Bernard of Parma, noted in his *Speculum iudiciale* that an agreement of bailsmen to confine themselves in a certain place would be valid, and that, according to Uberto da Bobbio, general custom legitimizes laying foot irons. The same holds true, Durant reported, for scribes who have agreed to write or stay at a certain place.[35]

With regard to scribes, Accursius's son Cervotto explained in a gloss that entered into the *Glossa Ordinaria* to the Digest (as gloss *Sive* ad D. 39.1.21.4), that foot irons could be used to force scribes to fulfil their contracts, because book production is vital to the University.[36] For instance, in 1262 the University of Padua decreed that upon a student's request its judges must order the apprehension and detention of both the scribe and his bailsmen until the agreed performance is fully carried out. The University of Lerída in Spain decreed in 1300 that scribes can be apprehended after the rector's permission has been obtained, and subsequently can be detained 'on water and bread' until they have fulfilled their contracts. For this purpose, clerks were to be transferred to

---

34. Bernardus Parmensis, gloss *Obsides dedit* ad X 2.24.9: 'Voluntate illorum alias detineri non possunt. Sed qualiter liberos homines obsides erunt contra illa iura ... Respondeo: non tenet obligatio in libero homine ut ius constituatur in eo tamquam in pignore, nec tenet alienatio ..., sed detinetur liber homo qualitercumque ut fiat quod conuenit, ut hic factum narrat. Vel non potest obligari pro pecunia, sed pro pacto ineundae pacis uel consimili. supra de arb. c. Exposita. (X 1.43.11)'.
35. William Duranti, *Speculum iudiciale* (ed. Basel 1574 repr Aalen 1975, 760): ... 'In scriptoribus autem ualere potest si conueniant ut debeant in certo loco stare uel scribere, quo casu etiam in compedibus poterunt retineri. Et idem in obsidibus. ut extra de iureiur. Ex rescripto (X 2.24.9), propter consuetudinem generalem secundum Uber. (= Uberto da Bobio)'.
36. Cf. the gloss *Sive* ad D. 39.1.21.4: 'Ex hac littera collige arg. quod scriptor potest cogi precise ad scribendum et poni in compedibus ... et est ratio ne turbetur publica utilitas, idest Studium, sicut et hic ne contempnatur edictum pretoris'. On the authorship of the gloss, see F.P.W. Soetermeer, 'La carcerazione del copista', *Rivista Internazionale di Diritto Commune* 6 (1995), 172-175.

their bishops, while laymen could be detained in the student's house.[37] The practice of laying foot irons to enforce the copying of books is, however, much older. Early manuscripts contain instances where the scribe had not completed his work voluntarily, as shown by the following remark in a tenth-century work: 'I have copied a part of this book not out of free will, but enforced by the laying of foot irons'.[38]

Was this practice in accordance with Roman law, as taught at the universities? The first glossator known to refer to this mode of coercion is Odofredus. In several of his lectures, Odofredus posed the question whether a scribe can be forced to copy law-books '*adeo ut ponatur in compedibus*'.[39] He discussed the preliminary question, *viz.* whether a scribe is bound to perform in kind. If the creditor must content himself with damages, as some texts in the *Corpus iuris* suggest, it would be wrong to enforce performance in kind. Odofredus took civil custody for granted as a mode of coercion – though he restricted detention of bailsmen to the debtor's sons and only for non-monetary debts[40] – for he neither compiled Roman law texts that spoke of foot irons nor discussed whether such a strenuous mode of coercion was justified.

Odofredus reported that the glossators (*antiqui doctores*) had once unanimously decided at an examination in the Church of St. Peter in Bologna that a student can choose between a claim for specific performance and a claim for damages. According to Odofredus, these glossators

---

37. Cf. Soetermeer, *Carcerazione* (n 36), 156-157.
38. W. Wattenbach, *Das Schriftwesen im Mittelalter* (Leipzig: 1886 repr. Graz: 1948), 440: 'Quandam partem huius libri non spontanea uoluntate sed coactus compedibus constrictis scripsi, sicut oportet uagum atque fugitiuum uincire'; see, for other examples, H.E. Braun, 'Von der Handschrift zum gedruckten Buch', *Buchkultur im Mittelalter, Buch – Bild – Kommunikation*, ed. M. Stolz and A. Mettauer (Berlin and New York: 2005), 223.
39. Cf. Odofredus, ad D. 39.1.21.4, ad D. 42.1.13.1 and C. 4.65.22, discussed by T. Repgen, *Vertragstreue und Erfüllungszwang in der mittelalterlichen Rechtswissenschaft* Rechts- und Staatswissenschaftliche Veröffentlichungen der Görres-Gesellschaft NF 73, (Paderborn: 1994) 104-105; Soetermeer, *Carcerazione* (n 36), 169-170; J.H. Dondorp, '*Precise cogi*, enforcing specific performance in medieval legal scholarship', *The Right to Specific Performance, The Historical Development*, ed. J. Hallebeek and J.H. Dondorp (Antwerp: 2010), 45-47.
40. Cf. Odofredus, ad C. 4.10.12 (ed. Lyons 1552, repr Bologna 1968, fo. 202va): 'Nos dicimus quod liberi homines non possunt pro obsidibus dari. Quando dabo filium meum pro obside hoc esse non potest, quia ob aes alienum etc. (C. 4.10.12). Licet tamen de iure ita sit, in contrarium fit tota die. Non tamen nego quin pater filium in obsidem dari potest quo casu potest uendere et pignorare. ut infra de pa. qui filios di. l. i. (C. 4.43.1), quia cui quod plus est licet, multo fortius quod minus est'.

also maintained that, if the student sought performance in kind, the scribe would forced to fulfil his agreement – and foot irons would be laid. In their view, unless the *Corpus iuris* explicitly states otherwise (as, for instance, D. 3.3.43, concerning a promise to the defendant to represent him in court) no one can discharge his obligation to do something through a payment of damages.

Odofredus apparently referred to the view of Azo and Hugolinus, who had taught that obligations to do are enforced *precise* – meaning that the debtor cannot pay damages instead.[41] In their view, it derived from D. 39.1.21.4 that it was up to the plaintiff to decide whether the defendant must perform the contract as yet, or pay damages.[42] Accursius adopted this line of thought in his gloss *Obligatonibus* ad D. 42.1.13.1. These jurists did not elaborate, however, on the manner in which performance in kind was to be enforced. Odofredus's assumption that the *antiqui doctores* allowed the use of shackles as a coercive measure may therefore be inaccurate.

Odofredus himself considered it wrong to derive a general rule (*regula*) from D. 39.1.21.4.[43] In his view, the general principle is formulated in D. 42.1.13.1.[44] Azo and Hugolinus had derived from this text the principle that damages can be claimed in case of nonperformance, even though they were not promised. In Odofredus's

---

41. Cf. Azo, Summa C. 7.47; Hugolinus, gloss *Servari* ad C. 4.65.22 in Ms. Praha NM XVII A 10, fo. 98rb. 'Et precise cogentur ad factum. arg. ff. de operis no. nu. Stipulatio § Siue (D. 39.1.21.4) ... iudex causa cognita operarum locatarum iubebit obseruari conuentionem, quia nolit seruare, fiat condempnatio quanti iurabitur in litem ut ff. e. Si cui locauerim (D. 19.2.48) etc. ad legam istam supra titulo precedente Quoniam (C. 4.64.5) infra de ingenuis Si uestram (C. 7.14.11). h(ugolinus)'. Azo had also reported that all the Bolognese doctors agreed that in case of contracts for work or labour one could be forced to work for some time. See Azo, summa C. 4.65.
42. D. 39.1.21.4 concerns an *operis novis nunciatio*: a builder guarantees to demolish what he builds in case the court decides it is built illegally. If the court so decides, he must do as he promised or compensate with damages, whatever the plaintiff chooses.
43. Cf. Odofredus, ad D. 39.1.21.4 no. 13 (ed. fo. 11va): ... 'Quia duas leges inuenio et plures que dicunt quod prestando interesse qui tenetur ad factum liberatur quam leges que dicunt quod prestando interesse non liberetur. Unde ex pluribus legibus constituo regulam'.
44. See the end of D. 42.1.13.1, which reads: 'when he does less (than promised), because of his nonperformance he will be condemned to pay a certain sum of money, as is usual for all obligations to do'. The context concerns a promise to prevent that anything would harm the creditor of a *stipulatio*. Odofredus's principle is phrased in this text, but does not derive therefrom.

opinion, D. 42.1.13.1 rules that judgement must be in damages. In other words, as a rule, the debtor discharges his obligation to do something by paying damages. Odofredus acknowledged five exceptions, of which four derive directly from the *Corpus iuris*. The fifth is the scribe: '*item fallit cum quis promisit suis manibus scribere, ut dixi per* C. 6.51.9b *et* D. 46.3.31'.[45] In the view of Odofredus, the reason why a scribe could be forced to perform in kind is that performance by substitution is disallowed. As a consequence, only a highly personal obligation would be enforced by civil custody.[46]

In Orléans, Jacques de Révigny rejected this line of thought – possibly imported by Odofredus's pupil Pietro Peregrossi. He objected that it does not follow from the fact that a debtor may choose who carries out the act, that he may also discharge his duty by payment of damages. De Révigny sided with Azo, Hugolinus and Accursius, concluding that as a rule obligations to do something bind *precise*. A creditor can thus demand performance in kind. Revigny also discussed the coercive measures. Pledges can be taken, fines (payable to the claimant if the debtor does not comply with a court order) can be imposed, and the debtor can be apprehended and detained: '*et ego intelligo quod compelletur precise ad factum corporis retentione, quia capietur et ponetur in compedibus*'.[47] Hence, he considered the custom to enforce the work of scribes by laying foot irons to be in consonance with the law.

Dino de Mugello, who taught in Bologna from 1284, maintained that as a rule debtors discharge their obligation to do something by paying damages, and acknowledged the exceptions found in the *Corpus iuris*. In this respect, he sided with Odofredus. He rejected, however, Odofredus's fifth exception (the scribe), as can be seen from his addition to the abovementioned gloss *Sive* written by Accursius's son Cervotto. The gloss argued that foot irons may be used to enforce performance in kind, because public interest demands the copying of law-books.[48] Dino objected that detaining someone (*in carcerem includi*) until he has done what he promised amounts to enslavement for debts, prohibited in Roman

---

45. Odofredus, ad D. 39.1.21.4 no. 14 (ed. Lyons 1552, repr Bologna 1968, fo. 11va).
46. Repgen, *Vertragstreue* (n 39), 104, ascribes this view erroneously to Accursius. The gloss *Obligationibus* ad D. 42.1.13.1 refers to an opinion of other glossators (*tertii*), who maintain that debtors who may perform by substitute may also discharge their obligation through a payment of damages.
47. Jacques de Revigny, ad D. 39.1.21.4 (ed. Soetermeer 1995, p. 178); see also Jacques de Révigny, ad D. 45.1.2.5 (ed. Soetermeer 1995, p. 178), ad D. 19.1.1.1 (ed. Schrage 1985, p. 62) and ad C. 4.65.22.
48. See above, note 36.

law. Three texts from the *Corpus iuris* offered support for Dino's view. C. 4.10.12 prohibits the enslavement of (money) debtors, D. 43.29.2 compares someone who cannot go where he pleases with a slave, and D. 35.1.71.2 rules that a judge cannot compel a legatee to guarantee that he will fulfil a condition in a last will, *viz.* not to abandon the testator's monument, because keeping such a promise would infringe his right of liberty.[49]

The preliminary question, *viz.* in what situations the court must award damages instead, remained disputed in the fourteenth century. None of the various distinctions made in Italy and France were generally acknowledged.[50] Bartolus de Saxoferrato was the first to bring them together successfully in one coherent system, which became the new starting point for the *ius commune*. Bartolus's distinction between acts prescribed by law or testament, on the one hand, and contractual obligations to do something on the other, became fundamental. The former can be enforced in kind, but a debtor may discharge the latter through a payment of damages. The rule Odofredus had found in D. 42.1.13.1, *viz.* that the court awards damages in case of nonperformance, became a fundamental principle of the law of contract in early modern times. Hugo Grotius, for instance, wrote in his *Inleidinge tot de Hollandsche rechts-geleerdheid* (first edition published in 1631, but written during his captivity at Loevestein), that according to natural law a debtor, whenever he can, must do what he promised; however, it suffices according to positive law to pay the creditor's damages, or the contractual fine, if one has been stipulated for the case of nonperformance.[51]

---

49. Cf. Dino de Mugello, *Apostille* in D. 39.1.21.4 (ed. Lyon 1531 repr. Bologna 1971 sine fo.): 'Et hoc probo tali arg. primo, quia si hoc esset uerum quod glosa (Sive ad D. 39.1.21.4) dicit uideretur esse imposita quedam species seruitutis propter aes alienum, quod iste (lege esse) non debet. ut in l. Ob es C. de act. et ob. (C. 4.10.12), nam includi in carcerem est quedam species seruitutis. ut. infra de libero ho. exhi. l.ii. (D. 43.29.2) et pro hoc est arg. ff. supra de cond. et demon. l. Titio § Titio (D. 35.1.71.2)'.

50. With regard to scribes, see Soetermeer, *Carcerazione* (n 36), 182-184. The many references to Roman law texts compiled by the Milanese lawyer Signorolus de Homodeis († 1371) to back up Cervotto's simple justification *et est ratio ne turbetur publica utilitas, id est studium*, did not convince Albericus de Rosate. He followed the opinion of Dynus, though he considered all copyists villains and promise-breakers. The Toulouse professor Guillaume de Cuhn adopted De Révigny's view, so did Pierre de Belleperche.

51. Hugo de Groot, *Inleidinge tot de Hollandsche rechts-geleerdheid* III.3.41 (ed. Dovring, Fischer & Meijers 1965, 214): 'Doch hoe wel nae 't aengebooren recht iemand die iet toegezeit heeft te doen, gehouden is zulcks te doen, ingevalle het hem doenlick is, zoo mag hy nochtans nae 't burger-recht volstaen, mids

Bartolus's pupil, Baldus d'Ubaldis (1327–1400) considered Bartolus's teaching on contractual obligations too strict. In the view of Baldus, parties decide themselves whether the debtor can discharge his obligation by a payment of damages.[52] Performance in kind should not, however, be enforced by vexation and torments, but through taking pledges and imposing fines.[53]

---

        voldoende den bedingher ofte aenneemer de waerde van 't gunt hem daer aen was gelegen, ofte de straffe zoo daer eenige is bedonghen by gebreck van de daed te voldoen'. See also note 6.

52. Cf. Baldus d'Ubaldis, ad D. 3.3.54.4.
53. Cf. Baldus d'Ubaldis, ad C. 4.65.22 (ed. Venice 1577, fo. 143): 'Queritur ergo an praecise potest cogi ad operandum. Et dic quod aut intelligitur praecise, id est per supplicia et tormenta, et non cogitur. ... aut intelligas praecise, id est captis pignoribus [uel] mulcta indicta, et tunc aut aequitas dictat precise cogi, quia alius nesciret uel non posset tales operas facere, ut quia erat solemnis scriptor et tunc cogitur praecise'.

CANON LAW AND CELIBACY: THE SEXUAL URGES OF THE SECULAR CLERGY IN FIFTEENTH-CENTURY BRUGES

Hendrik Callewier

Introduction

'Sunt omnes libidinosi, scortatores et adulteri?' ('Are all of them lechers, whore-hoppers and adulterers?'). These are the words of Romboudt de Doppere, a priest and chaplain connected to the church of Saint Donatian in Bruges at the end of the fifteenth century.[1] His rhetorical question refers to his colleagues, members of the secular clergy, and at the very least it suggests that the celibacy imposed by canon law upon all clerics in major orders, was not strictly observed by all members of the Bruges clergy.

---

1. Romboudt de Doppere, *Fragments inédits de Romboudt De Doppere découverts dans un manuscrit de Jacques De Meyere*, ed. H. Dussart, Recueil de chroniques, chartes et autres documents concernant l'histoire et les antiquités de la Flandre, Série 3 (Bruges: 1892), 63. About Romboudt de Doppere, see A. Gebruers, *Leven en werk van Romboudt de Doppere (+ 1501): een bijdrage tot de geschiedschrijving van het Graafschap Vlaanderen*, Master's thesis, Katholieke Universiteit Leuven (Louvain: 1988); J. De Mey, 'Doppere, Rombout de, magister artibus en notarius publicus te Brugge', *Nieuw biografisch woordenboek*, 16 (2002), 301-305.

Celibacy in Canon Law: The Synodal Statutes of the Diocese of Tournai

The definitive introduction of celibacy in the Roman Catholic Church is usually situated during the Second Lateran Council (1139). After centuries of discussion, it was stipulated that priesthood and marriage were mutually exclusive. At the Fourth Lateran Council (1215), it was determined how priests violating celibacy were to be punished: they might lose their income or even their benefice.[2] These stipulations of canon law were implemented in the synodal statutes.

None of the thirteenth-century statutes of the diocese of Tournai, to which Bruges belonged, explicitly refers to concubinage, but parish priests were forbidden to invite male parishioners and their wives for a meal, or to have dinner with them at their homes. If such an invitation had nevertheless been accepted, the priest had to limit his visit to the actual meal. There was to be no conversation with the lady of the house, with a daughter, or with a maid. Women under the age of sixty were not allowed to collect alms or to spend the night in the house of a priest.[3] The *synodalia antiqua*, probably composed at the beginning of the fourteenth century, not only mention such preventive measures, but also discuss suitable punishments. No woman under the age of forty was to live under the same roof as a priest, with the exception of his mother or a sister. Offenders had to pay a fine to the dean. If the dean neglected to collect these fines, he would have to pay double the amount to the officiality out of his own pocket.[4] In the statutes of 1366, it is said that all members of the clergy concerned had to give up their concubines within a month after these statutes had been published; non-

---

2. M. Vleeschouwers-Van Melkebeek, 'Mandatory Celibacy and Priestly Ministry in the Diocese of Tournai at the End of the Middle Ages', *Peasants & Townsmen in Medieval Europe. Studia in honorem Adriaan Verhulst*, eds. J.-M. Duvosquel and E. Thoen (Ghent: 1995), 681-684; D. Vergauwen, *Over de schreef. Middeleeuwse priesters voor de rechter* (Louvain: 2004), 34-35. About the demand for celibacy in the early Church, see S. Heid, *Zölibat in der frühen Kirche. Die Anfänge einer Enthaltsamkeitspflicht für Kleriker in Ost und West* (Paderborn: 1997). For an interesting case-study about the implementation of celibacy through provincial and episcopal statutes: B. Nilsson, 'A Fight against an Intractable Reality: The Efforts at Implementing Celibacy among the Swedish Clergy during the Middle Ages', *Sacri canones servandi sunt. Ius canonicum et status ecclesiae saeculis XIII-XV*, ed. P. Kraft (Prague: 2008), 596-617.
3. J. Avril, *Les statuts synodaux français du XIIIe siècle. Tome IV. Les statuts synodaux de l'ancienne province de Reims (Cambrai, Arras, Noyon, Soissons et Tournai)* (Paris: 1995), 340.
4. Bruges, Archief Grootseminarie, Handschriften, nr. 401.

compliance would be punishable by excommunication and loss of benefice.⁵ Also the 1417 statutes threatened offenders with excommunication and a fine. Moreover, it was explicitly stated that the deans had to report the names of offenders to the officiality.⁶ According to the synodal statutes of 1462 – a stipulation which was repeated in 1481 – all clerics involved were to renounce their concubines immediately and the deans had to submit the names of offenders to the officiality. However, no concrete punishments were mentioned.⁷

The Fifteenth-Century Councils

Another normative source concerning celibacy in the fifteenth century is the conclusions of the various councils from that period. These clearly suggest that during the fifteenth century there was an attempt to enforce celibacy more strictly. Still, at the Council of Basel in 1435 it had been suggested, by Enea Silvio Piccolomini and Panormitanus among others, that celibacy should be abolished completely, but this suggestion had been ignored. A decree with regard to concubinage was included in the session of 22 January 1435. In it, all clerics were ordered to give up their concubines within the next two months, on penalty of loss of benefice and a prohibition to exercise their office.⁸ It took several intermediary stages, but in the end these measures also took effect in the diocese of Tournai. Indeed, the conclusions of the Council of Basel were rather well adhered to in the French dioceses thanks to the Pragmatic Sanction of Bourges issued in 1438.⁹ There also, the French Church adopted the decree entitled *De concubinariis*. According to

---

5. J.E. A Loewenstein and J. Le Groux, *Summa statutorum synodalium cum praevia synopsi vitae episcoporum Tornacensium, ubi rerum memorabilium notitia, patronorum jura, &c. indicantur a tempore sancti piati dioecesis apostoli & patroni* (Lille: 1726), 57.
6. Bruges, Archief Grootseminarie, Handschriften, nr. 401.
7. V. Tabbagh, 'Les statuts synodaux de Tournai au XVe siècle: les limites d'une volonté de réforme', *De Pise à Trente: la réforme de l'Eglise en gestation. Regards croisés entre Escaut et Meuse*, eds. M. Maillard-Luypaert and J. Cauchies, Centre de recherches en histoire du droit et des institutions. Cahiers 21-22 (Brussels: 2005), 40-42.
8. J. Helmrath, *Das Basler Konzil 1431-1449. Forschungsstand und Probleme* (Cologne and Vienna: 1987), 336.
9. In May 1438 the French clergy assembled at the invitation of King Charles VII to discuss the reform decrees of the Council of Basel. The result of this meeting was called the Pragmatic Sanction, which adopted some of the reform decrees of that Council: J. Helmrath, *Das Basler Konzil*, 303-304, 343; H. Müller, *Die Franzosen, Frankreich und das Basler Konzil (1431-1449)* (Paderborn: 1990), II, 823-828.

this decree, every *concubinarius* who failed to abandon this practice within two months after the publication of the decree would forfeit the revenues of his benefices for a period of three months. If, after that period, he still refused to give up his concubine, all his benefices would be taken from him and he would not be allowed to receive new ones until the moment he renounced his concubine. Children born from such concubinage were not allowed to live with their father. At the provincial council of the archdiocese of Rheims in Soissons in 1455, the battle against concubinage was one of the main subjects, following the decisions taken in Basel and Bourges.[10]

Violations of Celibacy by the Bruges Clergy

So how did these canonical stipulations relate to the sexual practice of the clergy in fifteenth-century Bruges? The passage quoted from the chronicle by De Doppere already indicated that many failed to observe celibacy. Their illicit and unchaste activities were referred to by the general term 'incontinentia'. The most common practice was concubinage, which presupposes a more or less stable relationship of a cleric and a woman. Celibacy could also be violated by more casual sexual contacts. The humanist and priest Jan van der Veren, who maintained close relations with several Bruges clerics, expressed his ideas on this matter in a letter, in which he strongly advised a friend against marriage, since, according to him, marriage equalled torture. He himself, so he wrote, had been so prudent in his youth as to never engage in marriage, and he had been so wise as to become a priest, so that he might devote himself better to free love, without attachments.[11]

Rape, sodomy and visiting brothels were rather extreme forms of violation of celibacy, which would also have been considered unacceptable among laypersons. For instance, with the help of a chaplain, Guillelmus Belledame, a canon of the church of Saint Donatian abducted and raped a sixteen-year-old girl, and she reputedly died of the consequences.[12] Numerous similar incidents can be found in the archival sources, more specifically the *Acta Capituli* of the church of Saint Donatian. Unfortunately, the accounts of the officiality were only partially

---

10. Loewenstein and Gousset, *Summa statutorum*, II, 726-739.
11. G.G. Meersseman, 'L'épistolaire de Jean van der Veren et le début de l'humanisme en Flandre', *Humanistica Lovaniensia* 19 (1970), 130.
12. Bruges, Bisschoppelijk Archief, A. 51, f. 118r.

preserved.[13] As a result, it is not possible to calculate the precise numbers or the percentage of clerics who did not observe celibacy one way or another.[14] Similar research for other regions in the Low Countries, however, reveals that 45 to 60 per cent of all priests failed to do so.[15] This would appear to be a realistic percentage also for Bruges, since we know that of the fourteen canons residing in the church of Saint Donatian in 1467, ten lived in concubinage or had done so in the past.[16] In any case, the incontinent clerics were more than a 'significant minority'.[17]

---

13. *Compotus sigilliferi curie Tornacensis 1429-1481*, ed. M. Vleeschouwers-Van Melkebeek, Koninklijke commissie voor geschiedenis, publications in -4, 3 vol., (Brussels: 1995); Bruges, Bisschoppelijk Archief, A. 49-57.
14. M. Vleeschouwers-Van Melkebeek, 'Mandatory Celibacy and Priestly Ministry', 695.
15. E.J.G. Lips, 'De Brabantse geestelijkheid en de andere sekse. Een onderzoek naar celibaatschendingen bij de Brabantse parochiegeestelijken in de vijftiende en de zestiende eeuw', *Tijdschrift voor Geschiedenis* 102 (1989), 19; A.J. Bijsterveld, *Laverend tussen Kerk en wereld. De pastoors in Noord-Brabant 1400-1570* (Amsterdam: 1993), 344-345. Concerning celibacy in the Swiss diocese of Geneva, see: L. Binz, *Vie religieuse et réforme ecclésiastique dans le diocèse de Genéve pendant le grand Schisme et la crise conciliaire (1378-1450)*, Mémoires et documents publiés par la Société d'histoire et d'archéologie de Genève 46 (Geneva: 1973), 357-364.
16. On 15 December 1466 and 9 February 1467, Martinus de Mol, Carolus van Overtvelt, Jacobus van Overtvelt, Burchardus Keddekin, Petrus de Mil and Henricus le Muet were punished by the chapter: Bruges, Bisschoppelijk Archief, A. A. 53, f. 215v, 221v; R. De Keyser, *Het Sint-Donaaskapittel te Brugge (1350-1450). Bijdrage tot de studie van de hogere geestelijkheid tijdens de late Middeleeuwen*, doctoral thesis, Katholieke Universiteit Leuven, Faculteit Letteren (Louvain: 1972), 323. The other canons who did not respect celibacy during their ecclesiastical career were Johannes Meurin, Johannes Coolbrant, Balduinus Spoet and Victor de Zwavenarde: Bruges, Bisschoppelijk Archief, A. 55, f. 152v, A. 56, f. 80v; Bruges, Stadsarchief, Oud Archief, nr. 208; W. Van Hille, *Inventaire des lettres de légitimation enregistrées aux Chambres des Comptes de Lille et de Brabant, au Conseil de Brabant et aux Conseils privés espagnol et autrichien des Pays-Bas de Franche-Comté* (Kortemark-Handzame: 1979), 130.
17. K.A. Taglia, '"On Account of Scandal ...": Priests, Their Children, and the Ecclesiastical Demand for Celibacy', *Florilegium* 14 (1995-1996), 60. Some authors even suggest that 80 to 90 per cent of the clergy was continent in practice: J. Bossy, *Christianity in the West 1400–1700* (Oxford: 1985), 65.

Attitude of the Ecclesiastical Authorities

How did the local ecclesiastical authorities react with regard to these violations of celibacy, which were punishable by very severe penalties according to canon law? No efficient remedy could be expected from the officiality, certainly not for clerics living in concubinage. The fines levied by the officiality had no disciplinary effect, but should rather be regarded as a kind of tax on concubinage.[18] At the beginning of the sixteenth century, Erasmus still denounced the practice.[19] Moreover, we get the distinct impression that members of the clergy, who were not subject to secular jurisdiction because of the *privilegium fori*, were treated more leniently for sexual offences than were laypersons. For instance, Nicolaus Beils, a cleric of the church of Saint Donatian, was pronounced guilty of sodomy, and yet he was re-admitted to the choir after he had served a time in prison.[20] A secular court in Burgundian Bruges usually sentenced offenders guilty of that same crime to death.[21]

An often underestimated aspect in the assessment of the functioning of the officiality is its limited authority. The clergy of the Bruges collegiate churches – usually consisting of some 100 to 150 persons – came under the exclusive jurisdiction of their chapters. The canons hardly ever took firm action against clerics who failed to observe celibacy, unless they damaged the reputation of the church in doing so.

Let us have a look, for instance, at their attitude towards Jacobus Honin, a chaplain of the church of Saint Donatian who frequented a brothel. The man in question was a regular visitor of a certain Johanna in the red-light district. During one of his visits, he and a layman, both inebriated, attacked and injured two persons, and for this, he was arrested by officers of the law. The incident caused quite a stir and the chaplain was sentenced by the chapter to a disciplinary pilgrimage to Cologne. In this case, the

---

18. Lips, 'De Brabantse geestelijkheid', 26; Bijsterveld, *Laverend tussen Kerk en wereld*, 348.
19. L.E. Halkin, 'Erasme et le célibat sacerdotal', *Revue d'histoire et de philosophie religieuses* 57 (1977), 499.
20. Bruges, Bisschoppelijk Archief, A. 53, f. 291r, 351v; *Compotus sigilliferi curie Tornacensis*, ed. Vleeschouwers-Van Melkebeek, 318.
21. M. Boone, 'Le très fort, vilain et detestable criesme et pechié de zodomie': homosexualité et répression à Bruges pendant la période bourguignonne (fin 14e – début 16e siècle)', *Beleid en bestuur in de Oude Nederlanden. Liber amicorum Prof. Dr. M. Baelde*, eds. H. Soly and R. Vermeir (Ghent: 1993), 1-17; M. Boone, 'State Power and Illicit Sexuality: The Persecution of Sodomy in Late Medieval Bruges', *Journal of Medieval History* 22 (1996), 135-153.

offender did not get into trouble because he had visited a brothel – which he did quite often – but because of his intoxication and the resulting brawl.[22]

Other mentions of punishments of persons visiting brothels in Bruges also contain aggravating circumstances, such as alcohol abuse or fights. Anyone making a discreet visit to a brothel was probably left alone, in keeping with the attitude of the urban government, which tolerated prostitution as long as public order was not disturbed.[23]

One explanation for the lax observance of the canonical decrees in Bruges was the collegiate character of the chapters. Indeed, it was not easy for a canon to fight concubinage, when most of his colleagues were guilty of it. This is illustrated by the vain attempts of a certain Johannes Wijts to enforce celibacy. This canon had represented the chapter of Saint Donatian at the provincial council of Soissons in 1455. Upon his return to Bruges, during the chapter meeting he strongly urged his colleagues to impose the strict conciliary stipulations concerning celibacy. The opinions of the other canons were divided on the subject, because some of them were themselves at fault. After repeated insistence, finally an ultimatum was presented: all priests connected to the church of Saint Donatian were to send away their concubines or other women of questionable character with whom they were living within the following six weeks. However, almost two months after that term had expired, canon Wijts had to conclude that the situation remained more or less the same. He once more urged the chapter to take measures. The chapter now agreed to have the names of those living in concubinage recorded in a notarial deed. That same day, Wijts presented a list of names, but it was not accepted as evidence because it was not accompanied by witness statements. After this, the dean of the chapter ordered Wijts not to disclose the names on his list; instead, he was to invite the priests who were involved to have a discreet word on the matter with the dean. It is highly doubtful that these talks with the dean were very effective. Still, an example was made of a lower cleric, the singer Johannes Boubert, whom the chapter would only allow to become a priest if he gave up his concubine. The man accepted the condition and was ordained a priest. A few months later, however, he was given a rap on the knuckles for once more having a suspect relationship with his maid.[24]

The attempts of canon Wijts indicates how long it took for canonical stipulations to gain acceptance on a local level. Nevertheless, there would be new attempts to increase the observance of celibacy. The bishop of

---

22. Bruges, Bisschoppelijk Archief, A. 53, f. 69v.
23. G. Dupont, *Maagdenverleidsters, hoeren en speculanten. Prostitutie in Brugge tijdens de Bourgondische periode (1385-1515)*, Vlaamse Historische Studies 10 (Bruges: 1996), 121-122, 160-161.
24. Bruges, Bisschoppelijk Archief, A. 52, f. 53r, 54r, 55r, 59r, 62r, 68v, 82r.

Tournai, Guillaume Fillastre, was annoyed by the lax attitude of the chapter of Saint Donatian concerning sexual offences. As part of his visitation of the church in 1466, he demanded that everybody living in concubinage should be punished within the next two weeks. Despite protestations from the chapter, which disputed the bishop's authority in these matters, in the end charges were brought against six canons and they were convicted, as well as an unspecified number of lower clerics.[25]

In 1483, Petrus Bogart, the dean of the chapter of Saint Donatian, complained about priests with concubines. He said that the faithful took offence to it and that the practice brought shame upon the Church.[26] However, it was not until 1486 that the chapter, by a majority vote, put an end to the scandals caused by some of the priests of the church of Saint Donatian, who – so it was said – 'lived shamelessly and visibly to all with concubines, thus offending against common decency and disrespecting the sacraments'. Two canons, Franciscus de Meulebeke and Johannes de Hoya, were commissioned to persuade the suspect clerics to give up their concubines. Moreover, inquiries had to be made regarding the chapter's authority to take judicial steps against them.[27]

Apart from these general measures against concubinage, the *Acta Capituli* also mention punishments of individual clerics. In three instances, an appointment was withheld or a cleric was threatened with the loss of the income from his benefice if he kept his concubine.[28] In other cases, the priest was not so much punished because he lived in concubinage, but rather because the repudiation of his concubine had caused a major scandal. Indeed, when canon Petrus Basin refused his concubine access to his house, the spurned lover stood yelling and swearing in front of his door, for two or three hours, and this event greatly embarrassed the clergy of Saint Donatian. The canon admitted the facts, but in his defence he claimed that the woman had tried to force her way into the house against his will, even though he had ended his relationship with her three months earlier, before his pilgrimage to Rome.[29] Another cleric, chaplain Balduinus de Busco, in 1482 had obeyed the order of the chapter to repudiate his mistress and deny her access to his house. The woman, however, did not agree and protested against this measure, together with some other girls desirous of living with

---

25. M. Prietzel, *Guillaume Fillastre der Jüngere (1400/07-1473). Kirchenfürst und herzoglich-burgundischer Rat,* Beihefte der Francia 51 (Stuttgart: 2001), 336-342; Bruges, Bisschoppelijk Archief, A. 53, f. 115v, 222v.
26. Bruges, Bisschoppelijk Archief, A. 56, f. 12r.
27. Bruges, Bisschoppelijk Archief, A. 56, f. 116r.
28. Egidius Joye in 1454, Balduinus Spoet in 1455 and Arnoldus Ratgheer in 1459: Bruges, Bisschoppelijk Archief, A. 51, f. 357v; A. 52, f. 12v, 106r.
29. Bruges, Bisschoppelijk Archief, A. 56, f. 114r-v.

Balduinus. It ended in a brawl during which Balduinus seriously injured one of the women by scratching her in the face, which caused quite a scandal[30].

Reactions of the Lay Population

The violations of celibacy also complicated relations with the lay population. In 1483, for instance, Balduinus van Deusen, a chaplain of the church of Saint Giles, was murdered by a cuckolded husband.[31] Four years earlier, an innkeeper had forcibly entered the church of Saint James and had bashed in the skull of the priest who was seeing his wife.[32] This does not mean that violence was unavoidable in such situations, however: when Bruges citizens lodged a complaint against clerics who had bothered their wives or daughters, they usually hoped to be awarded some compensation. In 1451, Rolandus Scriptoris, the dean of Saint Donatian, was sued, not for raping and impregnating a woman, but because the compensation he had paid to mother and child had been insufficient.[33] A Bruges carpenter accused Johannes Plouvier, a singer in the church of Saint Donatian, of abducting and deflowering his daughter. He demanded restitution of his daughter, who was indispensable in his household because she was responsible for the laundry. Johannes admitted that he had a relationship with the daughter, but he swore that this only happened with her consent.[34] Even so, more and more lay persons became vexed with the debauchery of certain clerics. The chapter more than once quoted precisely this as an argument for taking firm action against clerics living in concubinage.[35]

Increasing Intolerance

Recent research suggests that a woman and a priest living together were, to all intents and purposes, accepted as common law husband and wife by their

---

30. Bruges, Bisschoppelijk Archief, A. 55, f. 190r, 196v.
31. Nicolaes Despars, *Cronijcke van den lande ende graefscepe van Vlaenderen, van de jaeren 405 tot 1492*, ed. J. De Jonghe (Bruges: 1839-1840), IV, 236; *Het boeck van al 't gene datter geschiedt is binnen Brugghe, sichtent jaer 1477, 14 februarii, tot 1491*, ed. C. Carton, Maatschappij der Vlaemsche Bibliophilen, 3e série, nr. 2 (Ghent: 1859), 59.
32. C. De Haan and J. Oosterman, *Is Brugge groot?* (Amsterdam: 1996), 75.
33. Bruges, Bisschoppelijk Archief, A. 51, f. 279v.
34. Bruges, Bisschoppelijk Archief, A. 51, f. 160r-v.
35. Bruges, Bisschoppelijk Archief, A. 56, f. 12r, 116r.

medieval contemporaries.[36] The concubine partook of the status and the wealth of the priest, as a result of which her position was more secure than that of an unmarried woman, and so historiography assumes that concubinage was widely tolerated. Indeed, the parishioners of a medieval parish might even have exerted some social pressure on their spiritual shepherd to take a concubine. If the parish priest was in a stable relationship, the village wives and daughters ran less risk of being harassed. Moreover, the sons of priests were fully accepted in late medieval society. This image, which is probably mainly applicable to rural communities, does not quite tally with the reality of a fifteenth-century metropolis such as Bruges. There, the position of the concubine was far less attractive: she might be sent away at a moment's notice. In the case of Bruges, also the supposed tolerance towards sons of priests should be somewhat reconsidered. Indeed, there are several examples of a priest's son being refused a position in the church of his father.

Moreover, tolerance for concubinage clearly dwindled in the second half of the fifteenth century: it may have remained difficult to have all members of the clergy strictly obey the stipulations of canon law regarding celibacy, but there is no doubt that the Bruges clergy was increasingly pressured to do so. The reform spirit of the fifteenth-century councils slowly but irrefutably seeped through to the local level. The stricter implementation of the observance promoted in conciliary decrees went hand in hand with an increasing repression and intolerance with regard to priests ignoring those precepts, and yet the percentage of clerics violating celibacy remained quite high. This would only change after the Council of Trent and the beginning of the Counter Reformation.[37]

---

36. Bijsterveld, *Laverend tussen Kerk en wereld*, 362-363; M.A. Kelleher, '"Like Man and Wife": Clerics' Concubines in the Diocese of Barcelona', *Journal of Medieval History* 28 (2002), 351; B. Schimmelpfennig, 'Ex fornicatione nati: Studies on the position of priests' sons from the twelfth to the fourteenth century', *Studies in Medieval and Renaissance History* 2 (1980), 32; R.N. Swanson, 'Angels Incarnate: Clergy and Masculinity from Gregorian Reform to Reformation', *Masculinity in Medieval Europe*, ed. D.M. Hadley (London: 1999), 174. Some examples that support this thesis: J. Gaudemet, *Eglise et cité. Histoire du droit canonique* (Paris: 1994), 493.
37. R. Mols, 'De seculiere clerus in de 17de eeuw', *Algemene Geschiedenis der Nederlanden*, 8 (Haarlem: 1979), 380.

SEXUALITY IN EARLY CHURCH LAWS IN NORWAY AND ICELAND

Bjørn Bandlien

Introduction

The Christianisation of Norway and Iceland was a long and complex process, involving many religious, political and cultural aspects. Sexuality, here defined as an identity constituted by sexual acts, is one intriguing aspect of Christianisation, since the sexual power of the aristocracy over women and dependants has been argued to be very important in Viking Age and medieval society. However, the scholarly consensus seems to be that this 'pre-Christian' sexuality continued well into the thirteenth century, more or less untouched by the Church's attempts to regulate sexual acts. Moreover, the Church seems to have had little power to persecute violations on sexual matters until the thirteenth century at least. Chieftains continued to have concubines and children born outside wedlock flourished. Early ecclesiastical legislation on sexual transgressions has thus been seen as a failure.

As a consequence, historians seem to think that the early Church laws in law books from the period from the formal Christianisation around the year 1000 until the establishment of the Norwegian Archbishopric of Nidaros in the middle of the twelfth century included sexual transgressions just because they were imported from foreign law collections, not because these laws were supposed to have any impact on society.[1] It is this presumption that I will challenge here. My thesis is that the regulation of sexual acts in the early Christian laws, rather than being just empty rules,

---

1. Jenny Jochens, 'The Church and Sexuality in Medieval Iceland', *Journal of Medieval History* 6 (1980), 377-392.

was important in certain contexts and constituted a Christian sexuality, but not necessarily a sexual identity in contrast with the 'pre-Christian' one.

As elsewhere in Europe, there were secular laws existing side by side with the Church laws. Church laws usually were integrated as a section in the law books, usually at the beginning. In Norway, there were four regional law codes up to the last quarter of the thirteenth century, when they were replaced by a law code for the whole country. In Iceland, the law book *Grágás* also had a Church law section, written down first in the beginning of the twelfth century, but with revisions up to the thirteenth century.[2] In both Norway and Iceland, the earliest preserved manuscripts of these Church law codes are from the late twelfth century and in most cases later, which makes it difficult to determine when individual modifications and additions were made. Still, there are several related paragraphs which both the Icelandic and Norwegian Christian law sections have in common and which probably date from the eleventh or early twelfth centuries, the period before the Norwegian reform movement in the late twelfth century. This will be proper to understand how – and to what extent – the Church tried to regulate sexual behaviour and what part it had in constructing Christian social and sexual identities.[3]

In one respect, Christianisation was a legal transformation – in the sense that Christian law codes were introduced from the early eleventh century. In fact, some Icelanders interpreted the conversion as a legal dispute. In the earliest preserved history of Iceland, *Íslendingabók*, written c. 1122–33, the Icelandic historian Ari Þorgilsson showed great concern about the perseverance of the Icelanders' legal unity after the conversion. After the mischief between the missionary Bishop Þangbrandr and some of the heathens, the issue of religious difference came to be heatedly discussed at the *Alþing* in 1000 (or possibly 999).[4]

---

2. According to the Christian law section in *Grágás*, this section was written down shortly after 1122 by the Bishops Þorlákr Runólfsson of Skálholt and Ketill Þorsteinnson of Hólar after the advice of Archbishop Asser of Lund, cf. *Grágás*, ed. Vilhjálmur Finsen, 3 vols. (Reykjavík: 1852-1883), vol. Ia, p. 36.
3. This problem was partly inspired by the study by Allen J. Frantzen on the sociology of sex in Anglo-Saxon laws and penitentials in *Before the Closet. Same-Sex Love from Beowulf to Angels in America* (Chicago: 1998), 138-183.
4. Cf. *Íslendingabók*, ch. 7: 'sogðusk hvárir ýr logum við aðra', in *Íslendingabók.Landnámabók*, ed. Jakob Benediktsson, Islenzk fornrit 1 (Reykjavík: 1968); *The Book of Icelanders. The Saga of Conversion*, transl. Siân Grønlie, Viking Society for Northern Research, Text Series 18 (London: 2006), 9. Recent discussions on the Christianization of Iceland include Dag Strömbäck, *The Conversion of Iceland. A Survey*, Viking Society for Northern Research, Text Series 6 (London: 1975); Jenny Jochens, 'Late and Peaceful: Iceland's Conversion through Arbitration in 1000', *Speculum* 74 (1999), 621-655; Jón Hnefill

According to Ari, the great danger was that Christians and heathens would renounce their legal community with one another, as the Christians wanted the chieftain Síðu-Hallr to announce a law for the Christians at the assembly. Síðu-Hallr was wise enough to put his own interest aside, and instead he asked the lawspeaker Þorgeirr for his advice. Although he was a pagan, Þorgeirr strongly recommended the Icelanders should confirm their practice of having one law. If not, he feared great peril would strike the island. Þorgeirr then made the famous compromise that every Icelander should be baptised, but the practices of exposure of infants and eating horsemeat should be regulated according to traditional laws. Even sacrifices to heathen gods were allowed if done in secrecy. What Þorgeirr achieved, according to Ari, was that all Icelanders still had 'one law and one religion' (*ein log ok einn sið*). However, there is no mention of clerical organisation, building churches, or attending masses. The important step was to baptise all Icelanders and to respect Christian laws.

This almost mythological story of Christianisation through legal arbitration is unique in medieval Europe. Nothing of the sort is found in the case of Norway, where historians have emphasised the relation between the rise of royal power and Christianisation.[5] In Norway, Christian law codes were formally introduced at an assembly at Moster in western Norway in 1024, led by King Óláfr Haraldsson and his English bishop, Grimkell. Although it is possible that this first Christian law code was not written down at Moster, a section on Christian law became incorporated in the four district laws of Norway probably later in the eleventh century. The Icelandic Christian law code was written down as part of the law collection titled *Grágás*, written down early in the twelfth century. By this time, both Norway and Iceland had a Christian section in their respective law codes.

Secular laws continued to regulate sexual behaviour, especially in connection with two areas.[6] First, there were the cases of the transgressions

---

Aðalsteinsson, *Under the Cloak. A Pagan Ritual Turning Point in the Conversion of Iceland*, 2nd edn. (Reykjavík: 1999); Orri Vésteinsson, *The Christianization of Iceland: Priests, Power, and Social Change 1000–1300* (Oxford: 2000); Hjalti Hugason, 'The Acceptance of Christianity in Iceland: An Attempt at a New Interpretation', *Church and People in Britain and Scandinavia*, ed. I. Brohed (Lund: 1996), 45-57; idem, *Upphaf kristni og kirkju til 1150*, Kristni a Íslandi 1 (Reykjavík: 2000).

5. For a recent overview, see Sverre Bagge and Sæbjørg Walaker Nordeide, 'The Kingdom of Norway', *Christianization and the Rise of Christian Monarchy. Scandinavia, Central Europe and Rus'c. 900–1200*, ed. N. Berend (Cambridge: 2007), 121-166.

6. On the following, see especially Preben Meulengracht Sørensen, *The Unmanly Man: Concepts of Sexual Defamation in Northern Society*, Viking Collection 1

of women who belonged to a free householder, whether as wife, daughter or slave. Second, the laws sought to punish sexual libels against free men. In both cases, the secular laws constructed a sexuality that was immersed in a discourse of household and honour. On one hand, sexual transgressions were to be punished if they transgressed the rights of a householder. This clearly also concerned the free householder's honour, as did the paragraphs on libels alluding to being a passive participant in a sexual relationship or accusing men of bearing children.

Such accusations were often called *ýki* (exaggerations) or *nið* (shameful libel). No one could legitimately punish the accuser besides the one who was accused, and to do so was important to protect the latter's social position. The man accused of sexual perversity might, if he was reluctant to face his opponent, lose the legal rights free men normally had, such as being part of an oath-group or being a witness. If the accuser failed to prove his words, he was himself to be excluded from the community. Defamation in the secular laws thus challenged a free man's social and sexual identity, presumably because of the very real threat such accusations could pose to one's position in society.

The secular laws also regulated marriage and adultery, but made the woman far less the legally responsible party compared with, for example, the Anglo-Saxon and Burgundian laws. The head of the household was responsible for defending the women of his (or sometimes her) household, and executing punishment on the transgressors. The regulation of unmarried daughters was less regulated than that of married women, and the highest compensation was to be paid for offences against high status women. This general picture is confirmed by sagas, in which women are seldom punished for adultery, but the husband projects his anger at the male transgressor. In one of the few known legal cases, an unmarried woman is said to be personally responsible for her sexual acts. Thus if a free woman has slept with a slave then she is said to be socially degraded in the same way.

This points to a notion of sexuality that was closely linked to social status, and where the men's right to defend their honour is connected first to the legal right of free men to defend their masculine sexuality from verbal libels, and second the ability to do so in real action. Furthermore, the legal implication of sexuality is that (accusation of) perversity is something that can be used as a punishment, rather than it being the case that any sexual act that could be interpreted as perverse or marginalising the subject can be regarded as legally forbidden in itself.

(Odense: 1983); Bjørn Bandlien, *Man or Monster. Negotiations of Masculinity in Old Norse Society* (Oslo: 2005), 115-134.

The Early Law Codes

To understand the link between the Scandinavian version of the Christian world-view and the place of sexuality within it, we move from responses of *nið* and scorn to the early Christian law codes. The acceptance of Christianity was of course a necessary step for the development of ecclesiastical organisation in Scandinavia, but forming Christian law codes was certainly a huge leap. I will here in particular focus on what might be the oldest preserved Christian law code in Scandinavia, that of the district of Borgarþing in eastern Norway. The regulation of taxes demanded by the bishop for performing his services (abolished after the introduction of tithes during the early twelfth century) and the regulation of private churches indicate a dating before the large-scale revisions in the middle of the twelfth century. Here it is sufficient to affirm that the law was shaped before the Norwegian reform movement in the late twelfth century, although there are paragraphs that might be later additions.

My prime concern here is not to look at single paragraphs in the Christian law sections that can reflect society, but how the laws represent a Christian frame and how sexuality was confined within them. The overall spatial orientation moved from the household and the *þing* assemblies to the centres of Christian faith: 'This is the foundation of our laws; that we shall bow to the east and give due respect to Christ, the Church, and clerics'.[7] With this opening, the Christian law of Borgarþing states that the whole meaning of Christian law is based on the orientation and humility towards the 'east', to proper Christianity. Already in this passage, the Christian identity is founded in the appropriation of the geographical orientation of European Christianity. The Christian legal community is situated in the 'west' (indicated by the phrase to 'bow to the east') rather than the barbarian realms of the north; barbarian identity is replaced by identification with papal Christianity. In its most concrete form, this must have been expressed through the celebration of mass in church. The altar became the compass of religious geography. This bestowed authority on the church's servants as they were positioned at the altar. Bowing for Christ should imply showing esteem for the local church and clerics.

---

7. 'Þet er uphaf lagha uarra. at austr skulum luta oc gevaz kristi rækia kirkiur oc kenne menn', *Borgartings kristenrett*, in *De eldste norske kristenrettene*, eds. E.F. Halvorsen and M. Rindal, Norrøne tekster 7 (Oslo: 2008), I.1. A similar opening is also found in the Christian law section of Gulaþing in western Norway, cf. *Den eldre Gulatingslova*, eds. B. Eithun, T. Ulset and M. Rindal, Norrøne tekster 6 (Oslo: 1994), 32. This opening was seen as a clear evidence of English influence by Absalon Taranger, *Den angelsaksiske kirkes indflydelse paa den norske* (Kristiania: 1890), 417-418.

The Christian law of Borgarþing proceeds to construct the Christian subject, from birth, via baptism and marriage, to death. Everyone born in the legal district was to be baptised and brought up as a Christian. However, a significant section is devoted to the exposure of infants born with *ørkumbl* ('bodily disabilities'). The law gives considerable attention to these exceptions, listing babies without a mouth, with heels where the toes are supposed to be, neck on the chest, eyes in the neck, and even children with the flippers of a seal or a dog's head.[8]

Thus the next part of the Christian law concerns the definition of what a human, or Christian, can be. All infants who were found 'not monstrous' should be baptised, and by this the parents 'lift them up from heathendom' (*hevia ór heiðrnum dome*). Failing to or postponing baptism would, on the other hand, eventually make the parents 'heathens by their child'.[9] They were then no longer acting as Christians, and became by definition heathens.

Next follows the regulation of time and the consumption of meat. Eating meat should be abstained from on certain days and in certain periods. This regulation of time is also the principle for the organisation of intercourse in marriage; the heading of this section in the law can be translated as: 'Now everything is the same in meat and marriage'. This introduces the forbidden times of the year, of the week, and of the day for intercourse. For example, intercourse is forbidden during Lent, but allowed in the evenings of Sunday, Monday, Wednesday and Friday. However, the forbidden times were not absolute, a priest could allow intercourse on most of these days, including during nights before Mass and nights during Lent.

The other principle regulating sex is kinship. More grave than to have sex before mass or on fast days was to have incestuous sexual relations. A man who has sex with a woman within the third degree, or marries a woman within the fifth degree and refuses to separate, receives the harshest punishment; they forfeit their property and should leave the land for heathen lands, 'because they are not willing to be Christians'. This statement concerns not only a religious demarcation, but also resembles closely the sentence of outlawry in secular laws. In this context, outlawry means 'never [to] return to where Christians are'. This punishment is imposed on mothers

---

8. *Borgartings kristenrett*, I.4. This is also found in the Christian law sections in Eidsivaþing and Gulaþing, in the latter case said to have been removed in the revision of Archbishop Eysteinn, cf. *Den eldre Gulatingslova*, ch. 21, p. 44. This treatment of such monstrous infants may be influenced by Augustine's discussion in *De Civitate Dei*, Book XVI.8, although the heads of seals is unique.
9. *Borgartings kristenrett*, I.4; cf. *Den eldre Gulatingslova*, 44: where all children should be baptised, disabled children were to be 'lifted from heathendom and laid down in the church to die'.

who kill their infant children,[10] on people who eat dogs, cats or horses[11], on men having incestuous intercourse[12], and those who initiate divorce and are not willing to return to their spouse.[13] Despite being baptised, these people have shown their disrespect for Christian laws and are confined to the same spatial margins as the monstrous children; to the non-Christian realms.

In other paragraphs, the unmarried woman's sexuality is more directly in focus. This is not a question of the woman being 'heathen' or sinful; it is rather an interest in the women's relatives – whether the penalty should be paid to her husband, brother or son, for instance. If she is unmarried, it is most crucial to determine who the father of the child is. This is partly to do with the question of the child's place in the line of inheritance, but also – and this seems to be the reason for including it in the 'Christian Law' – to see if the child was born of an incestuous relationship. When raped, a woman has the right of full compensation from the violator. Only once, in an addition to the law from the twelfth century, is the unmarried woman who is secretly having sex with a man condemned as a 'fornicating whore'. But still there is no straightforward condemnation of her behaviour – it is just pointed out that her relatives might be somewhat unhappy with her sexual acts.

The main theme of the Christian law of Borgarþing is how individuals should attain and preserve their identity as Christians. Christian identity is constructed on spatial categories, with the Church and the clerics at the centre and those not baptised on the periphery. Even Christians could be marginalised if they did not observe the Christian rituals. It is significant that this terminology of exclusion is quite similar in the early Christian law and the secular laws; the main difference is the central place from which these were expelled and the acts that caused this to happen. Seen in context with the language of outlawry in the secular laws, the early Christian laws mainly appropriated Norse categories, but relocated the outlaws of the household society as excommunicated from the Christian community.[14]

---

10. *Borgartings kristenrett*, III.3.
11. *Borgartings kristenrett*, V.13.
12. *Borgartings kristenrett*, XV.2.
13. *Borgartings kristenrett*, XVII.1.
14. There is no agreement as to whether the eastern Christian law sections were influenced by English Church laws, by the German canonist tradition, or most of all by regional emendations, especially Burchard of Worms, see the recent contributions of Olav Tveito, 'Erkebiskop Wulfstan av York og de eldste norske kristenrettene', *Norsk teologisk tidsskrift* 108 (2007), 170-186; Torgeir Landro, 'Dei eldste norske kristenrettane. Innhald og opphav', unpublished Master's thesis (University of Bergen: 2005); Jan Brendalsmo, *Kirkebygg og kirkebyggere. Byggherrer i Trøndelag ca 1000-1600* (Oslo: 2006).

Sexual transgressions in this older Christian law of Borgarþing were not related primarily to a presumption of lustful desire. Instead, the early Christian laws leave the matters of, for instance, adultery and proper marriage to the secular laws, albeit including regulations of kinship and time. In the secular laws the discourse of social denigration or elevation through sexual relations is prominent. The emergence of a Christian identity in the early legislation of the Church was closely connected to the possession of the central place, relegating heathen practices to the margins. Sexual transgressions connected to time (holy days) and social space (kinship related to incest) were part of the acts that could jeopardise a man's identity as a Christian, but baptism and the consumption of meat had at least as much prominence as sexual relations.

The absence of a more thorough treatment of sex in the early Christian laws indicates that the early Church did not replace the secular discourse. In respect of marriage, it supplemented rather than did anything to change the institution of marriage and the discourse of honour connected to the control of the sexual life of the subjects of the household. An identity based on inner lust or desire thus cannot be deduced from the early Christian codes, neither can incest and fornication be seen as subjects more dire for their loss of Christianity – this was primarily to do with the respect of regulation of time and kinship. The concept of sin was connected more to lack of respect for the Church's rituals and calendar than any inner sexual urge of the individuals – the sex acts are listed matter-of-factly rather than as being grounded in 'human nature' of some kind.

This should make us change the way we understand the 'failure' of the Church to change the sexual conduct of the laity in the period after Christianisation. The Church laws did not challenge the 'household/honour discourse' of sexuality, but made sexual transgressions concern members of kin and feast days.[15] The main distinction is that of the 'Christian vs. heathen' in relation to practices connected to the year.[16] Thus, there is no

---

15. This is confirmed by the fact that many regulations in the Norwegian Christian law sections concerning marriage, are placed in the secular law sections in the Icelandic *Grágás*, cf. Gunhild Kværness, *Blote kan ein gjere om det berre skjer i løynd. Kristenrettane i Gulatingslova og Grágás og forholdet mellom dei*, Kults skriftserie 65 (Oslo: 1996).

16. This seems to be in line with Patrick Wormald's argument that the legal programme of Wulfstan of York was to create a 'holy society' that acted in accordance with the will of God, cf. Patrick Wormald, 'Archbishop Wulfstan and the Holiness of Society', *Anglo-Saxon History. Basic Readings*, ed. D.A.E. Pelteret (New York: 2000), 191-244. On the importance of 'heathen' in the writings of Wulfstan, see Audrey L. Meaney, 'And we forbeodað eornostlice ælcne hæðenscipe: Wulfstan and Late Anglo-Saxon and Norse "Heathenism"', *Wulfstan, Archbishop of York*, ed. M. Townend, Studies in the Early Middle Ages 10

interest in, for example, a homosexual relationship and only indirect mention of concubines (as 'fornication') since these have no special place in this discourse. To the laity, these regulations were linked to their respect for certain holy days and to the regulations on sexual relations with kin, more than being identified on the basis of the sexual acts themselves or having concubines.

Changing the Legal Discourse

This legal discourse of sexual transgressions changed fundamentally during the twelfth century. The most evident example of this is the penitential issued in the 1180s by the Icelandic Bishop Þorlákr Þórhallsson of Skálholt.[17] The immediate background of this penitential was probably that the Icelandic Church had to make decisions for its dioceses on its own while the Norwegian archbishop was in exile for several years at this time. It consists of 25 paragraphs, structured specifically on male sexual transgressions. §§ 2-17 deal with penances that priests could impose for transgressions by the laity, moving from graver to lesser sins. §§20-24 list transgressions for which only the bishop could decide the penance, focusing especially on penances for priests who did not perform their clerical duties well.

The penitential of Þorlákr is remarkable, not only because of its late date – this was after all some 130 years after Peter Damian showed scepticism towards such lists of sins – but also because it is one of the strictest in its genre, although based on foreign sources.[18]

Þorlákr's purpose was, according to his introduction, to impose penance for 'capital sins' (*hofuðsyndir*) (§1). In his interpretation, capital

---

(Turnhout: 2004), 461-500; see also Tveito, 'Erkebiskop Wulfstan av York'. This differs slightly from Burchard of Worms' *Decretum*, where references to Jews, heretics and pagans in his sources are occasionally replaced with other categories. Still, Burchard stated that if a person refused to listen to the warnings of the Church, he should be seen as a gentile or pagan. They were to be excommunicated and Burchard stated that their presence would infect the Christian society, see Greta Austin, *Shaping Church Law around the Year 1000. The Decretum of Burchard of Worms* (Aldershot: 2009), 42, 182-186.

17. On this penitential, see Sveinbjörn Rafnsson, 'The Penitential of St. Þorlákur in its Icelandic context', *Bulletin of Medieval Canon Law*, n.s. 15 (1985), 19-30.
18. Sveinbjörn Rafnsson suggested that this penitential was influenced by the penitential of Bartholomew of Exeter, cf. Adrian Morey, *Bartholomew of Exeter, Bishop and Canonist. A Study in the Twelfth Century* (Cambridge: 1937); David N. Bell, 'Introduction', *Bartholomaei Exoniensis Contra fatalitatis errorem*, ed. D.N. Bell, Corpus christianorum, cont. med. 157 (Turnhout: 1996), v-xxii.

sins were almost all connected to sexual acts. The first and gravest sin is sexual relations that a man would have with another man or with any four-footed animal (§2). Then follows the sin of double adultery (§3), then single adultery, intercourse on the most observed feast days and with a woman in childbed, eating meat during fast, major perjury and abortion (§4). Then come regulations on incestuous relations (§§5-11). §§12-13 deals with intercourse without impediments (*meinalaust kallað*), that is between unmarried but unrelated partners. The penance for this was comparatively low. It takes no regard to whether this kind of intercourse may have involved some kind of disgrace for the women's family, or of the social status of the involved partners.

Þorlákr instead introduced another kind of social stratification. He divided the male sexual transgressors in dichotomised pairs; the rich should do more penance than the poor, the holy more than the unholy; the learned more than the unlearned; the highly ordained more than lesser ordained, the blessed more than the wretched, the elderly more than younger ones (§ 17a). Additionally he graded the penance, and thus the degree of pollution a man could incur, by the object with which he satisfied his carnal desire: 'For that shall be least punished which is done in lustfulness as an awake man, if he is polluted by friendliness with a woman. More if a man is polluted by his own hands. More if a man is polluted by drilled wood. Most if a man is polluted by another man's hands.'[19]

This is not a distinction between men of different sexual orientations or preferences, rather a growing degree of pollution connected to the devices a man used to satisfy his carnal desire in non-penetrating sexual acts, moving from the quite acceptable contribution of a woman, via masturbation and wood, to the pollution of other men's hands. Any identity based on sexual acts that is similar to a 'sodomite' is not found. The main issue is to identify acts that pollute men with increasing gravity. In this respect, Þorlákr's penitential was well founded within the early medieval tradition.

These sexual transgressions were different from the traditional discourse of sex in several respects. First, Þorlákr was interested in sexual acts that were never considered before, especially such acts as masturbation and relations to drilled wood. This had had no social significance before, but for Þorlákr they were signs of pollution. Likewise, the social status of the

---

19. *Diplomatarium Islandicum*, 16 vols (Copenhagen: 1857-1952), vol. 1, no. 43, p. 243: 'Firir þad skal minzst bioda. þess er j lostaseme er misgert ath uakanda mannj. ef hann saurgaz af blijdlæti uith kono. Meira ef madr saurgaz af hondum sijnum sialfs. Meira ef madr saurgaz af trie borodo. Mest ef madr saurgaz af annars karlmanz hondum'. Cf. Sveinbjörn Rafnsson, 'Skriftaboð Þorláks biskups', *Gripla* 5 (1982), 107-108 (§17b).

sexual object is irrelevant to Þorlákr (as long as they are, in the case of female partners, unrelated to the man). It is always the 'active' partner who is condemned. Þorlákr is interested in the lustful desire of the man, not the motivation of social degradation of the object of that desire. In opposition to the traditional way of thinking, taking the *active* part in all sexual relations outside marriage disgraced powerful men. On the other hand, the marginalisation connected to *nið* has no place in the vocabulary of Þorlákr.

However, in one respect the penitential is similar to the secular laws. The gravity of the sin was graded according to social position, as in the secular laws, in that men were most heavily punished. By emphasising the special responsibility of the clergy and the aristocracy, Þorlákr probably intended to link social distinction to sexual sins and the mastering of lust. Through a focus on male sexual transgressions, despite any violations of honour, the intention could hence also be to increase the chastity of the clergy. The penitential of Bishop Þorlákr was meant for the correction of the Icelandic laity as well as clerics, but the most immediate audience was most likely the clerics who were supposed to impose the penances on men. When the sexually active layman could be punished by this new 'sexual élite', an élite defined not by dominating women or other men sexually, but by controlling and punishing laymen's sexual behaviour, this made a forceful alternative to the traditional social meaning of sex.

We are fortunate enough to know more about the context of Þorlákr's concern about men's sexual behaviour through several letters sent by the Norwegian Archbishop Eysteinn to the Icelandic aristocracy. Eysteinn had never been to Iceland, but his letters chastising the Icelanders were probably instigated by reports from Þorlákr. In 1173 Eysteinn was worried about the rumours that some chieftains 'both learned and lay' led 'evil and unclean lives', like cattle, which induced all Christians to sinfulness. As a contemporary homily puts it, carnal lust was the national sin of the Icelanders. The prime reason for this 'unclean life' was that they had put aside their wives and taken mistresses in their place, or even had both wives and concubines in their households at the same time, thus disregarding holy matrimony.[20]

---

20. *Diplomatarium Islandicum*, vol. 1, no. 38, pp. 221-222 (1173): 'svmer hafa konvr sinar latit. ok horkonur under þær tekit. svmer hafa hvarartveggiu. jnan hus [med] sier og lifa so ogæzskv life. er alla kristna menn dregur til synda [...] Nu verdure fyri þui sia Ogipta so lengi 9 landi ydrv. at þeir bera hofdingia nofn hier er slikv fylgia. svmer lærder en svmer olærder. Nv kann eg marga at nefna. þa er j storglæpvm standa. En ek vil en eigi hropa þa at sinne fyri alþydv. En þo vil eg vandal ydvarn eigi lengur bera. þviat mer er nu glæpur manna kunnr. og so nofn þeirr kvnnig er giortt haffa'. ('Some have left their wives and taken adulterous women in their place. Some have both [a wife and an adulterous woman] in their

In 1173 Eysteinn did not wish to mention the names of those who committed these grave sins, but around 1180 he sent a new letter in which he addressed more specifically the powerful and highly respected chieftains Jón Loptsson and Gizurr Hallsson. These are depicted in the contemporary sagas as wise and powerful arbiters in many feuds. They were also ordained as deacons. Eysteinn probably knew the two men personally; Jón had stayed in Norway in 1163-1164, while Gizurr had been a *stallari* at the court of King Sigurðr munnr in the 1150s, when Eysteinn was a priest in the retinue of the co-regent King Ingi. Eysteinn complained that these two men disregarded holy matrimony. The charge was justified as we know from contemporary sagas, especially in Jón's case; he lived with and had children with Ragnheiðr, the sister of Bishop Þorlákr, even though he was already married. In this letter Eysteinn emphasised the unclean life of the Icelanders, with special reference to sexual relations outside marriage. The letter especially charged the male aristocracy with this, and it is clear that the archbishop wanted them to be an example for the rest of the laity. But when they knowingly broke the commandments of God, they dishonoured themselves. This argument is clearly a break with the practice of building alliances through concubines.[21]

---

houses with them. They are conducting an evil life that draws all Christian men into sin [...] Now this disgrace prevails so long in your country because those who adhere to it have the title of lords, some learned, some of the laity. Now I can name many of those who are committing grave crimes. But I do not want to mention them aloud in front of people. Still I cannot bear your difficulties any longer since I know the crimes of some men and also the names of those who have committed them').

21. *Diplomatarium Islandicum*, vol. I, no. 54, pp. 262-263 (c. 1180): 'En of engan hlut synest oss meira 9 fatt. helldur en vm ohreinlife manna hier. og kvenna far. er eigi þarf fyri yckur at skyra vm. hversv stadfest bodord. er. af gvdz sjalfs mvnne bodit. En þier hafit þat med suivirding firrzt ener agæstustu menn. lifit bufiar life. rekit eigi hiuskap. ne þat helga samband er iegi ma slitna. nema kona manz hore under hann. og þo med þeim einvm hætte. at hvortvegia halldi sier fra savrlife medan þav lifa bæda. eda saman byggiazt. En med þvi at hofdinngiar hafa slika ohæfv j sinne samviskv. og af þvi treystazt þeir eigi hirtingar ord at hafa fyri alþydv. þa er þar komit at allra rad hallast j einn stad. ens meira. og hins minna' ('But no matter concerns us more than the unclean lives of men, and their relationships with women, which is not necessary to explain for you, since it is a firm commandment given by God himself. But you have with greatest dishonour shunned it; the best men live the lives of cattle, not respecting marriage, that holy bond that must not break, – unless the wife may be adulterous under him and then only when both promise to stay away from polluting life while they both are alive or live together. But because chieftains have such bad lives on their consciences, then we cannot expect that chiding words will have effect on the common people. Then all will be the same, neither more nor less.')

The main distinction based on sexual behaviour in his letter was that between 'clean' and 'unclean'. By this logic, living in adultery was not much better than committing bestial acts.[22] On the wrong side of 'clean' there was a sliding scale, from 'minor' transgressions down to such crimes. In the rhetoric of Eysteinn, then, by neglecting pure life the aristocracy were not in a position to be leaders for the common people. This should then be a matter for those on the right side of 'pure'. At the same time as they tried to regulate the marital and sexual behaviour of chieftains, Bishop Þorlákr and Archbishop Eysteinn tried to introduce clerical celibacy. The clergy was to defend Christianity against chieftains who were 'spilling Christianity' (*kristne spell*), as Archbishop Eysteinn put it – a crime that in the Christian law sections of Norwegian law collections was connected to expulsion to heathen lands.[23]

We should hesitate to interpret the cohabitation of Icelandic aristocrats with concubines simply as motivated by 'lust' more than as a political strategy, but when Archbishop Eysteinn did so, he questioned the abilities and power of chieftains. Instead, the laymen in general were to look to the reformed clergy as their authority.

Still, this example shows that in medieval Norway and Iceland it was only by the end of the twelfth century that a tension between discourses of sexuality began – when sexuality without any apparent social impact against another man's honour came to be condemned rather as a result of sinful lust. Compared with this later legislation, the sexuality in the early Christian laws may have been perceived as much more adaptable for the Christians of Scandinavia. The construction of this sexual identity was perhaps less successful, even though the doctrine of consensual marriage became

---

22. It is possible that Eysteinn made a pun on the phrase *blandast við búfé* as found in the Norwegian laws on bestiality. Of the very few references to bestiality in Iceland during the Commonwealth Era are Þorlákr's phrase *eigo vith ferfætt kuikendi* and a reference to relation *við cyqvende* in the Icelandic Book of Homilies, see *Homiliubok, isländska homilier efter en håndskrift från tolfte århundradet*, ed. T. Wisén (Lund: 1872), 211. When they had such total disregard for God's commandments and the laws of the Church, the Icelandic chieftains could be suspected of 'mixing' with cattle as well. According to the Norwegian laws, men who mixed with animals should be castrated, expelled from the Christian community and the cattle should be driven out on the ocean. Such logic may lay behind the words of Eysteinn. A similar tone is found in a letter of Archbishop Eiríkr to the Icelanders written in 1190, *Diplomatarium Islandicum*, vol. I, no 72, on rape as a cause of excommunication.
23. It was probably Archbishop Eysteinn who introduced the paragraph on sodomy in the 1170s. See Kari Ellen Gade, 'Homosexuality and Rape of Males in Old Norse Law and Literature', *Scandinavian Studies* 58 (1986), 124-141; with slightly different interpretation in Bandlien, *Man or Monster*, 186-190.

accepted together with the abandonment of concubinage among the laity in the thirteenth century. However, this development had a close connection to the adaptability of the sexuality to an aristocratic identity in change as it became more closely connected to the royal authority and less to the household discourse.[24] The revisions of the Christian laws in the 1260s and 1270s extended the paragraphs on sexuality and marriage more, especially in order to determine whether a child was legitimate.[25] Still, the Church law of Borgarþing may have been more successful than the reforming sexual identities shaped by Þorlákr and Eysteinn.

---

24. See e.g. Auður Magnúsdottir, *Frillor och fruar. Politik och samlevnad på Island 1120-1400* (Göteborg: 2001); Bjørn Bandlien, *Strategies of Passion. Love and Marriage in Medieval Iceland and Norway* (Turnhout: 2005); Henric Bagerius, *Mandom och mödom Sexualitet, homosocialitet och aristokratisk identitet i det senmedeltida Island* (Göteborg: 2009).

25. On the new Christian laws from the 1260s and 1270s in Norway, see most recently Bjørg Dale Spørck, *Kong Magnus lagabøters kristenretter. Innhold, språk og overlevering* (Oslo: 2006), and her translations and commentaries in *Nyere norske kristenretter (ca. 1260-1273)* (Oslo: 2009). Another important Christian law was issued by the Icelandic bishop of Hólar, Árni Þorláksson, in 1275, see *Járnsíða og kristinréttur Árna Þorlákssonar*, eds. Haraldur Bernharðsson, Magnús Lyngdal Magnússon and Már Jónsson (Reykjavík: 2005).

VOREMUNDE HEBBEN: CHILDREN, ELDERLY AND IMPAIRED PEOPLE IN EIKE VON REPGOW'S *SACHSENSPIEGEL*

Chiara Benati

Introduction: Eike von Repgow's *Sachsenspiegel*

The *Sachsenspiegel* is one of the oldest private *Rechtsbücher* in the German language area and, certainly, the most popular in the German Middle Ages. According to the *Praefatio rhythmica* to the text, its author was *Eike van Repchow* who seems to have belonged to a free noble family whose name came from the village of Reppichau, near Dessau. He can probably be identified with the *Eike von Reppichowe* or *Heico von Repechowe* who appears among the witnesses named in six Saxon documents from the period between 1209 and 1233.[1]

We do not know much about Eike, since the main source for him is the *Sachsenspiegel* itself. From textual evidence, it is possible to assume that its author was not only quite well educated for a layman, but also familiar with the legal practice of the time. In order to write the lawbook as it has come down to us, he must have known Latin, the Scriptures and canon law, as well as Latin literature and German vernacular poetry. Eike may have gained this knowledge in Halberstadt or Magdeburg.[2]

---

1. See also A. Ignor, *Über das allgemeine Rechtsdenken Eikes von Repgow* (Paderborn: 1984), 325 and following.
2. See also Ignor, *Allgemeine Rechtsdenken*, 325 and following.

As mentioned before, Eike's name appears for the first time in a legal document of 1209, where a person with this name is mentioned together with other witnesses. In order to give testimony, he must have been of full age at the time, that is to say, he must have been born in about 1180. In the same way, his disappearance from the sources later than 1233 suggests that he could have died shortly after that year. This assumption about Eike's death and its possible date seems to be confirmed by the fact that, in the text, no reference is made to the imperial statute of peace of Mainz (*Mainzer Reichslandfriede*) imposed by Friedrich II in 1235, nor to the institution of the duchy of Braunschweig-Lüneburg in the same year.[3]

The *Sachsenspiegel* was written by Eike between 1221 and 1224, first in Latin and then translated into German, to please his overlord, Count Hoyer of Falkenstein. The first German version, composed between 1224 and 1225, was followed by three other vernacular versions, in which the text was modified through the insertion of new material.

The *Sachsenspiegel* was extraordinarily popular during the Middle Ages, as testified by its rich manuscript tradition (more than 450 manuscripts, the large part of which are in Middle German) and by its translations and adaptations in other languages.[4]

This study, aimed at identifying all the terms and the expressions used by Eike to define and describe guardianship in medieval Saxony, is conducted on the basis of the main Low German witness transmitting the lawbook: the Oldenburg manuscript (Landesbibliothek Oldenburg, *Codex Picturatus Oldenburgensis*, CIM I 410), edited in facsimile by Schmidt-Wiegand.[5]

Guardianship: Concept and Addressees – Minors

It is a general principle of jurisprudence that people incapable of acting as adults and caring for their own interests because of infancy, (temporary) incapability or disability must undergo guardianship. This is also true for thirteenth-century Northern Germany, as witnessed by Eike von Repgow's

---

3. See also R. Schmidt-Wiegand, 'Eike von Repgow', *Die deutsche Literatur des Mittelalters. Verfasserlexikon,* ed. K. Ruh (Berlin: 1980), 2, col. 400-409, and C. Händl, 'Il diritto nel Sachsenspiegel di Eike von Repgow', *Atti del XVII Convegno dell'Associazione Italiana di Filologia Germanica, Università di Potenza*, ed. L. Lazzari (Potenza: 1991), 111-126.
4. See also U. D. Oppitz, *Deutsche Rechtsbücher des Mittelalters I. Beschreibung der Rechtsbücher* (Köln: 1990), 22.
5. *Der Oldenburger Sachsenspiegel*, ed. R. Schmidt-Wiegand (Graz: 1995).

Sachsenspiegel, which gives a quite precise description of this legal institution.

Children while they are under-age normally undergo paternal guardianship:

> Halt oc de vader sine kindere in voremuntschap na ir moder dode, swan se sic van eme schedet, he sale me weder gheven unde laten al ir moder god, it ne si eme van unghelucke unde ane sine schult gheloset. Dit sulve schal dat wif des vader kinderen don, oft ir vader sterft unde iewelich man, de kindere voremunt is.[6]

The father continues to have guardianship (*voremuntschap*) over his children even after their mother has died. He has to care for their mother's inheritance and, once they are grown up and ready to leave his house, he will return it entirely to them, unless it has been lost accidentally without him being responsible for that. The same applies to mothers whose husband dies and to all guardians (*voremunt*).

In other words, this passage states that, when both parents are alive, the father has guardianship over the children, while mothers play a subordinate role in contemporary family law. Women act as guardians of their own children only if they are widowed, while 'external guardians', that is, persons not necessarily belonging to the familiar nucleus, must be men (*man*). In addition to that, the passage quoted above also contains two central terms for the definition of 'guardianship' in Middle Low German: the weak masculine noun *vormunt, vormunde, vormunder* (compare OHG *foramundo*, MHG *vormunde, vormünde* < OHG, MHG feminine noun *munt* 'protection, force';[7] OFris. *formond, foremund, foremunda*, MDutch *voremonde*)[8] 'guardian, someone who protects another person, especially squanderers, women and minors'[9] and its abstract feminine derivate *voremuntschap, voremunde(r)scop* 'protection, care, guardianship'.[10]

In medieval Saxony, males reached the age of majority at twenty-one, as witnessed by this passage:

---

6. *Oldenburger Sachsenspiegel*, ed. Schmidt-Wiegand, 87.
7. The term has not survived in Modern German, where its root is preserved in the derivates *mündig, Mündel* and in the prefixed form *Vormund*. See also J. and W. Grimm, *Deutsches Wörterbuch* (Leipzig: 1854-1960), 12, col. 2683.
8. See also Grimm, *Deutsches Wörterbuch,* 26, col. 1322 and following.
9. See also A. Lübben and C. Walther, *Mittelniederdeutsches Handwörterbuch* (Leipzig: 1888, reprint Darmstadt: 1995), 513.
10. Lübben and Walther, *Mittelniederdeutsches Handwörterbuch*, 513.

> Over en unde twintigh iar so is de man to sinen daghen comen.[11]

If a man's age is unknown, his beard and axillary hair must be observed in order to ascertain whether he can be considered of age or not:

> Swelikes mannes alder men nicht ne wet, hevet he dar an barde unde dar nedene unde under iewer arme, so sal men weten, dat he to sinen daghen ghecomen is.[12]

The expressions used to indicate minors are *er enes daghen* (lit. 'before one's days') or *binnen enes iaren* (lit. 'within one's years'), which correspond to the verbal phraseme *to enes daghen/iaren comen* 'to come of age'.[13]

It is the guardian's duty to act in the best interests of the ward and to be accountable to them and their heirs for his behaviour. For this reason, a child's heir should not normally become his or her guardian, since if both figures coincide, the guardian will not have to answer for his actions:

> Swe aver des kindes erve is, den sal des kindes voremunde bereden van iare to iare des kindes godes, unde ene des wis maken, dat hes in unplicht nicht ne vordo, sint dat kint to sinen iaren comen is, wente it is dicke en der kindere voremunde und en andere er erve. Swar aver de voremunde ok erve is, dar ne darf he nemanne rekenen des kindes godes noch borghen setten.[14]

In one particular passage, Eike seems to draw a distinction between full age for common legal actions and for feudal purposes:

> Alsi en kint to lenrechte to sinen iaren comen, sin rechte voremunde sal it doch in sinen gode vorstan to sinen bederve, unde sinen heren in des kindes stede na des kindes rechte denen, de wile it sic sulven nicht bedenken ne can van kintheyt eder van dorheyt eder van uncraft sines lives.[15]

Even after a child has come of age, as far as feudal law (German *Lehnrecht*) is concerned, the guardian can continue to represent his former ward in front of the lord as long as the ward is not able to do it himself because of juvenile inexperience, stupidity (*dorheyt*) or physical weakness (*uncraft sines lives*). While both mental and physical impairment are generally

---

11. *Oldenburger Sachsenspiegel*, ed. Schmidt-Wiegand, 110.
12. *Oldenburger Sachsenspiegel*, ed. Schmidt-Wiegand, 111.
13. See also Grimm, *Deutsches Wörterbuch*, 10, col. 2235 and following.
14. *Oldenburger Sachsenspiegel*, ed. Schmidt-Wiegand, 100.
15. *Oldenburger Sachsenspiegel*, ed. Schmidt-Wiegand, 99 and following.

recognized as conditions determining incapability and, as such, the need for guardianship, inexperience or young age (*kintheyt*) is not usually considered relevant after one has come of age. The reference to a possible further intervention of the guardian to help represent his former ward in front of his feudal lord suggests, therefore, this particular sphere of law had – probably because of its social importance – special rules for coming of age.

These special rules for feudal law are explicitly quoted further in the text:

> Kindere iartale is drutteyn iare unde ses weken van erer bort. Doch dorven se des dar na, of se ieman bedeghedinghen will umme ere len, de wile se to eren daghen nicht comen ne sin, dat is en iar unde twintich, so moten se nehmen voremunden enen eres herren man, de se vorsta to lenrechte, deme solen se de were mit vingheren unde mit tunghen loven to behaldene unde to vorlesene.[16]

The minimum age for children to receive feudal privileges is thirteen years and six months. However, until their twenty-first birthday, they are allowed to take one of their lord's men as their representative in front of the feudal court. In this case they will have to swear solemnly (*mit vingheren und emit tunghen*) their loyalty to this guardian both *to behaldene* and *to vorlesene* ('through thick and thin'). In case of a third party's claim over a underage boy's fief, the lord himself is responsible for the privilege he has granted.[17]

Guardianship: Concept and Addressees – Women

If males, even with the abovementioned restrictions, reach majority at twenty-one, females are never considered legally capable, since they must always be submitted to guardianship, either paternal or marital.

> Swen en man wif nimpt, so nimpt he an sine were al ir god to rechter voremuntscap. Dor dat ne mach nin wif eren mannen gheven nine gave an eren eghenen noch an varender have, dat se dat eren rechten erven mede untfere na eren dode, wante de man ne can an sines wives gode nine andere were winnen, wen also he ton ersten mit er in voremuntscap entfenc.[18]

---

16. *Oldenburger Sachsenspiegel*, ed. Schmidt-Wiegand, 270 and following.
17. *Oldenburger Sachsenspiegel*, ed. Schmidt-Wiegand, 271: 'De here is ymmer des kindes voremunde in deme gode, dat dat kint van eme hevet.'
18. *Oldenburger Sachsenspiegel*, ed. Schmidt-Wiegand, 104 and following.

When a man marries a woman, he becomes her guardian and the administrator of her goods, so that she cannot legitimately give him any of her property, in order not to damage her heirs' interests. For the duration of the marriage, the husband cannot, in fact, acquire more authority over the wife's goods than he acquired on the day of the wedding, when he became his wife's guardian.

The husband is always the wife's guardian, irrespective of his social condition. With the marriage, the bride acquires the social status (*recht*) of the bridegroom, even if she originally belonged to a different social class (*nicht evenbordich*):

> Alne si en man sinen wive nicht evenbordich, he is doch ere voremunde unde
> se is sin ghenotinne unde tred in sin recht, alse se an sin bedde gat.[19]

The need for guardianship continues to exist even when a woman becomes a widow. Unless she remarries, she is submitted to the guardianship of a male relative, usually her own children's guardian:

> He is ok der wedewen voremunde, bet se man nimpt, ofte he evenbordich is.[20]

If the two spouses originally belonged to different social classes, once the husband has died, the widow returns to her original status and undergoes the guardianship of a male relative equal of hers, not of her husband.[21] The term employed to indicate the widow's designated guardian is the compound *swertmach* < *swert* 'sword', here as symbol of a man in armour,[22] + *mach, mage* '(blood) relative'[23] (compare also MHG *swertmâc, swertmâge*) 'male relative'.[24]

A girl or a widow may complain about her guardian's conduct: her guardian will be summoned to court three times and, if he does not appear, he will be declared a bad guardian and dismissed. The judge himself will then undertake the plaintiff's guardianship:'

---

19. *Oldenburger Sachsenspiegel*, ed. Schmidt-Wiegand, 112.
20. *Oldenburger Sachsenspiegel*, ed. Schmidt-Wiegand, 100.
21. See *Oldenburger Sachsenspiegel*, ed. Schmidt-Wiegand, 112: 'Swen aver he sterft, so is se ledich van sinen rechte und behalt recht na erer bort. Dor dat mot ir voremunde sin ere neste evenbordighe swertmach, unde nicht eres mannes.'
22. See also Grimm, *Deutsches Wörterbuch*, 15, coll. 2576 and following.
23. See also Lübben and Walther, *Mittelniederdeutsches Handwörterbuch*, 215 and DWB, 12, col. 1435
24. See also Lübben and Walther, *Mittelniederdeutsches Handwörterbuch*, 396 and DWB, 15, col. 2590.

> Claghet maghet eder wedewe to lantrechte over eren voremunde, dat he se untweldeghe egenes eder lenes eder liftucht unde wirt he dor dat vore ladet to dren dinghen unde ne cumpt he nicht vore des dritten daghen rechtes to pleghende, men sal en balemunden, dat is, men sale ne verdelen alle voremuntschap. Sint si de richtere der vrowen voremunt unde weldeghe se van richtes halven eres godes, des se entweldighet was.[25]

Particularly interesting in this passage is the weak verb *balemunden* 'to declare someone a deceitful guardian', denominative from masculine *balemunt* 'deceitful, unfaithful guardian' (compare MHG *palemunt, balgemund*, MDutch *baelmond*, OFris. *balmond*).[26] The very fact that Eike considers it necessary to explain this verb with the gloss *dat is, men sale ne verdelen alle voremuntschap* ('that is he will be deprived by sentence of all guardianships') suggests this is a highly specific legal term, which might not be immediately understandable to his contemporaries.

Without their husband or guardian's permission, married women cannot alienate their property (land or animals). Unmarried women, on the other hand, can sell their land without their guardian's permission, unless he is their heir:

> En wif ne mach oc ane eres mannes ghelof nicht eres godes verghe ven noch eghen vercopen noch liftucht uplaten, dor dat he mit ir in der were sit. Meghede aver unde unghemannede wif vercopet er eghen ane eres voremundes ghelof, he ne si dar erve to.[27]

In court, women must always be represented by a guardian, when they cannot be incriminated for their witness (*vertughen*).[28] If an oath is required (*to eden comen*), it is the woman who has to swear, not her guardian.[29] Describing judicial procedure, Eike distinguishes two forms of guardianship over women: the one exerted by their *rechte voremunde* ('legitimate guardian') and the one committed by the court to a reliable man, who is,

---

25. *Oldenburger Sachsenspiegel*, ed. Schmidt-Wiegand, 110.
26. See also Lübben and Walther, *Mittelniederdeutsches Handwörterbuch*, 25; W. L. van Helten, *Zur lexicologie des altostfriesischen* (Amsterdam: 1907), 25 and *Deutsches Rechtswörterbuch* Online, available at http://www.rzuser.uni-heidelberg.de/~cd2/drw/e/ba/lmun/balmunden.htm
27. *Oldenburger Sachsenspiegel*, ed. Schmidt-Wiegand, 112.
28. *Oldenburger Sachsenspiegel*, ed. Schmidt-Wiegand, 112 and following: 'Maghet unde wif moten voremunden hebben an iewelker claghe, wenten men se nicht vertughen mach, des se vor richte spreket eder dot'.
29. *Oldenburger Sachsenspiegel*, ed. Schmidt-Wiegand, 113: 'Swar it den vrowen to eden cumpt, de solen se sulven don unde nicht er voremunde'.

therefore, *voremunde van richtes halven* (lit. 'guardian because of the court').

> De voremunde van richtes halven sal de ghewere vor se loven unde untfan unde seder nine not dar umme liden, men dat he der warheyt bekenne, alse hes van richtes halven ghevraghet wirt. Men sin voremuntscap ne waret nicht lenghere, wante alse dat richte waret. To ieweliken dinghe mot de richtere wol sunderliken voremunden gheven.[30]

This *ad hoc*-appointed guardian has to swear and receive the *ghewere*[31] for her goods and does not have any disadvantage from this assignment, provided he tells the truth when asked by the court. His guardianship lasts no longer than the trial itself and the judge can appoint one particular guardian for every court session.

The distinction between these two kinds of guardian probably reflects that between the *tutor legitimus* and the *tutor dativus* (or *Atilianus*, since it was introduced in 185 BC in the *Lex Atilia de tutore dando*) present in Roman law.

Guardianship: Concept and Addressees – Elderly People

An *ad hoc* form of guardianship is also mentioned with regard to elderly people, who are defined as 'after their days' (*na sinen daghen*):

> Er sinen daghen unde na sinen daghen mot de man wol voremunden hebben, of hes bedarf, unde wol unberen, of he wil. Swe sines voremunden to hant nicht ne hevet, de sal ene bringhen to den nesten daghe, de ut gheleghet wirt van gherichtes halve umme sine claghe.[32]

---

30. *Oldenburger Sachsenspiegel*, ed. Schmidt-Wiegand, 113.
31. This legal term has a wide spectrum of meanings in German, the largest part of which is calqued on the Latin feminine noun *vestitura,-ae*. The semantic development of the Latin term is, in fact, reflected in its vernacular counterpart which, at the beginning, refers to the formal taking possession of a good – a procedure becoming more and more important as the transfers of ownership of estates did not take place on the land itself anymore – and progressively acquires a new meaning, expressing the legal consequences of this formal act. In this meaning it is employed here to indicate the 'legally protected property' as opposed to the 'mere possession'. See also Grimm, *Deutsches Wörterbuch*, 6, coll. 4784 and following and Lübben and Walther, *Mittelniederdeutsches Handwörterbuch*, 123.
32. *Oldenburger Sachsenspiegel*, ed. Schmidt-Wiegand, 110.

Both under-age and elderly people are free to accept the help of a guardian or to refuse it, according to their wish. Those who do not have a guardian at their disposal will have to bring to the following court session the guardian appointed by the court for that specific case. If, as mentioned above, being under-age means being younger than twenty-one, people over sixty are considered 'after their days':

> Over sestich iar so is he boven sine daghe comen, alse he voremunden hebben sal, of the vil, unde ne krenket darmede sine bote nicht noch sin weregelt.[33]

A man over sixty can be represented by a guardian, if he wants to, without this diminishing the value of both the compensation he would have to pay if he caused damages and injuries to another person (*bote*)[34] and the one he or his family would receive if he were wounded or killed by a third party (*weregelt*).[35]

Guardianship: Concept and Addressees – Impaired People

The *Sachsenspiegel* introduces a fourth category of people who were considered unable to act as legal persons and therefore needed the assistance of a guardian: those who are physically or mentally impaired.[36] This does not mean that all forms of impairment were perceived as equally disabling from a legal point of view. From textual evidence, we can draw a rough distinction between congenital and accidental impairing pathologies: while the former seem completely to preclude any possibility of legal action, the latter usually imply only some limitation to legal capability. So, for example, cripples (*cropelskint*), dwarfs (*dwerghe*) and demented people (*altfile*)[37] have no hereditary right, nor can receive a fief. Given this impossibility, their closest relatives and heirs will take care of them:

---

33. *Oldenburger Sachsenspiegel*, ed. Schmidt-Wiegand, 110 and following.
34. See also Grimm, *Deutsches Wörterbuch*, 2, col. 570.
35. See also Grimm, *Deutsches Wörterbuch*, 29, coll. 320 and following.
36. Consistently with the distinction drawn by disability studies scholars, according to which 'impairment' is the 'medically classified condition' and 'disability' is 'the social disadvantage experienced by people with an accredited impairment' (C. Barnes, G. Mercer and T. Shakespeare, *Exploring Disability: A Sociological Introduction* (Cambridge: 1999), 7), I use the term 'impairment' rather than 'disability' when referring to the physical condition.
37. The interpretation of this term – attested only in Eike's *Sachsenspiegel* and in three other legal texts: *Richtsteig Lehnrecht*, *Goslarischen Statuten* and *Berliner Stadtbuch* – was the object of discussion among both linguists and legal historians.

> Uppe altfile unde dwerghe ne irsterft noch len noch erve noch uppe cropelskint. Swe dan de erven sint und ir neste maghe, de solen se halden mit plaghe.[38]

The term employed here to indicate tutelage is *plaghe* 'care' (compare OHG *phlega*, MHG *phlege, pflege*), both in the general and in the legal sense.[39]

Other forms of impairment are listed in another passage of the *Sachsenspiegel*:

> Wirt och en kint stum gheborn oder handelos oder votlos oder blint, dat is wol erve to lantrechte unde nicht to lenrechte. Hevet aver he len untfanghen, er he wurde aldus, dat ne verluset he nicht dar mede.[40]

If children are born dumb, blind or without hands or feet, they will have their hereditary rights according to the territorial legislation (*Landrecht*), but will not be able to receive or inherit fiefs. If, on the other hand, their impairment is not inborn, but post-traumatic, they will not lose those feudal privileges they had acquired before this trauma occurred. The principle according to which a previously acquired social condition cannot be modified because of some intervening impairment or mutilation also applies to lepers, even though, in their case, no guardian is mentioned. Once a person is a full-blown leper, he or she is excluded from both hereditary and feudal right, but they do not lose those inheritances or fiefs they already have:

> Uppe den menselsuchten man ne irsterft noch len noch erve. Hevet het aver er der suke untfanchen unde wirt he seder siec, he ne verluset it dar mede nicht.[41]

In particular in the second half of the nineteenth century, some scholars thought it was used to indicate hermaphrodites, see for example A. Hoefler, *Altvile im Sachsenspiegel. Ein Erklärungsversuch* (Halle: 1870), IV: 'Dass der Sachsenspiegel eine Bestimmung über Erbunfähigkeit der Zwitter enthalte, ist heutzutage die feststehende, landläufige Annahme aller Juristen.' This conception seems to have been completely rejected by later critics, as witnessed by Lübben and Walther, *Mittelniederdeutsches Handwörterbuch*, 13, explicitly excluding this noun means 'hermaphrodite' and by the parallel Modern German translation in Lübben and Walther, *Mittelniederdeutsches Handwörterbuch*, 80, where it is rendered as *Schwachsinnige* 'demented, stupid'.

38. Lübben and Walther, *Mittelniederdeutsches Handwörterbuch*, 80 and following.
39. See also Lübben and Walther, *Mittelniederdeutsches Handwörterbuch*, 278, and Grimm, *Deutsches Wörterbuch*, 13, coll. 1733 and following.
40. *Oldenburger Sachsenspiegel*, ed. Schmidt-Wiegand, 81.
41. *Oldenburger Sachsenspiegel*, ed. Schmidt-Wiegand, 81.

When describing judicial procedure, Eike again mentions impaired people:

> Lame lude solen antworden, it ne si, dat de claghe to campe ga. Dar is ere voremunde er evenbordighe swertmagh, swe he si, det don wille. Ne magh de lame man, ofte men ene to campe grot, sines rechten voremunden nicht hebben, unde sin recht dar to do, he wint to voremunden, so wet vor eme don wil, eder swen mit penninghen ghemeden magh, al moghe men sinen rechten voremunden biwisen. Weret aver he sic mit kempen, ghene magh ene wol bereden mit kempen to erst nicht ghegrot, unde ne schadet eme to sinen rechte nicht.[42]

Physically impaired (*lame*)[43] people have to answer for their actions in front of the court, unless they are required to engage in a duel. If this is the case, it will be their legitimate guardian's task to fight for them, provided he wants to do that. If this legitimate guardian is not available, when the impaired person is challenged to duel, any volunteer or any mercenary they can pay will represent them. If this mercenary is a professional fighter, it is the plaintiff's right to have recourse to a professional fighter as well, without losing his honour for that.

If a man is only temporarily impaired because of a wound and summons to court the person responsible for his injury, no guardian or professional fighter is necessary, since the duel will be postponed until the plaintiff himself is healed and able to duel.[44]

Concluding Remarks

In this study I have tried to define, on the basis of a lexical, textual and contextual analysis of Eike von Repgow's *Sachsenspiegel*, the role and function of guardians in medieval German jurisprudence. A study of this kind, aimed at sketching a picture of guardianship as legal institution, must necessarily take into consideration those categories of people who, because of their age, sex or health condition, required the assistance of a person

---

42. *Oldenburger Sachsenspiegel*, ed. Schmidt-Wiegand, 113 and following.
43. The adjective *lame* is not used here in the specific meaning of 'paralysed', but in the wider meaning of 'affected by some kind of impairment' or 'mutilated'. See also Grimm, *Deutsches Wörterbuch*, 12, coll. 72 and following.
44. *Oldenburger Sachsenspiegel*, ed. Schmidt-Wiegand, 115: 'Sprekt en ghewundet man de to kampe an, de ene ghewundet hevet, unde ne mach he van unchract des lives den den camp nicht vulbringhen, unde ne hevet he ninen voremunt, de it vor eme don wille, men sal eme deghedinghen bet an de tid, dat he sulven camp vulbringhen moghe.'

caring for them and for their economic interests, representing them in front of court or in a judicial duel.

Eike von Repgow's legal text introduces four major typologies of possible wards (minors, women, elderly and impaired people), undergoing *voremundscap*. Each of these typologies of wards requires a special form of assistance. For this reason, the MLG nouns *voremunde* and *voremundscap* and the verbal phraseme *voremunde hebben* from time to time identify a different figure.

While minors and women enjoy complete hereditary right, but are not considered capable to act according to it and need, therefore, both a guardian and an administrator for their goods, elderly people do not lose their legal capacity with age, and they can require the assistance of a *voremunde* to represent them in court or in a judicial duel.

As far as impaired people are concerned, the precise function of their guardian depends fundamentally on the pathology affecting them. In some cases, not only guardianship is necessary, but also physical care and assistance, as witnessed by the use of the term *phlage*, whose Modern German cognate *Pflege* still preserves this meaning. This happens with inborn, particularly serious, impairing pathologies such as deformity, dwarfism and mental illness, pathologies precluding the possibility of both inheriting and receiving feudal privileges. Other inborn impairing pathologies, such as dumbness, blindness or missing limbs, simply prevent people from becoming feudal vassals and from swearing fealty to a lord, but not from inheriting. No loss of rights is foreseen for people whose disability is the result of some trauma or disease that intervened after they were born. They are, therefore, fully capable of answering for their actions before a court and only need someone else's assistance if physical strength is required, e.g., in a judicial duel. In this case that representative is a professional, mercenary fighter, rather than a true legal guardian.

This large spectrum of different roles and functions, which Eike summarizes under the term *voremunde*, is usually held by one of the ward's closest male relatives. In the majority of cases, minors and women undergo, respectively, their fathers' and husbands' guardianship. These 'natural' guardians are described as *rechte voremunden*, as opposed to *voremunden van richtes halven*, who are appointed *ad hoc* by a judge to represent an incapable person in one specific procedure.

One particular sphere of law, feudal law (*Lehnrecht*), seems to be governed by a specific set of rules, involving, for example, the possibility for a male minor over thirteen and a half to receive feudal privileges. During the time span between this investiture and the coming of age, the boy is supported by both his lord – who becomes his guardian, as far as the feudal goods are concerned – and his men.

On the basis of these concrete situations, Eike von Repgow's *Sachsenspiegel* clearly shows – as I have tried to demonstrate – the complexity and multidimensionality of the legal institution of guardianship in medieval Saxony, a complexity which goes far beyond the apparent simplicity of the terminology employed.

FAMILY FROM A PERSPECTIVE OF DYING – EVALUATING THE POWER OF TESTAMENTS

Jakub Wysmułek

Introduction

In this research I am mainly dealing with the analysis of the late medieval and Early Modern testaments originating from Cracow, the sometime capital of Poland. The origins of the city date back to the ninth century, when it was the capital of the Vistulan tribe as well as an important trade centre.[1] The natural development of Cracow was interrupted, though, due to the Mongol invasions in 1241 and 1259, when the city was conquered and completely destroyed.[2] Grounds for rebuilding the city occurred only after the introduction of the German municipal law in 1257.[3] Because of its profitable trade location and its position as the capital of the Kingdom of Poland, by the end of the fifteenth century Cracow's inhabitants numbered more than ten thousand.[4]

---

1. J. Rajman, Kraków zespół osadniczy, proces lokacji, mieszczanie do roku 1333 (Kraków: 2004) 43, 48; K. Polek, 'Kraków w IX i X wieku', Kraków. Studia z dziejów miasta, ed. J. Rajman (Kraków: 2007), 10-11.
2. Rajman, Kraków zespół osadniczy, 190-191.
3. Probably there was already a small community of German craftsmen on the territory of Cracow, even before 1257: Rajman, Kraków zespół osadniczy, 176-177.
4. M. Bogucka and H. Samsonowicz, Dzieje miast i mieszczaństwa w Polsce przedrozbiorowej (Wrocław, Warsaw and Kraków: 1986), 119.

The testaments, the earliest of which dates from 1303,[5] were gathered from many Cracow municipal books and loose documents. Most of them, however, come from the Cracow Council book of 1427, titled 'Liber testamentorum'.[6] In the first part of the chapter I will discuss briefly the history of testaments in Polish lands, together with the changes of the documentary form. In my view, these testaments express the coming changes in the field of the social life, culture, and mentality of the bourgeoisie. On the one hand, the right of a testator to alienate and bequeath property is progressively expanded, contrary to the Polish customary law of that time and, on the other hand, the content of the testamentary document is subject to a gradual laicisation. In the second part of the paper, I will present a number of interesting examples demonstrating the interrelationships dominating in the medieval municipal family. These records, which refer to the disposition of estates, are the source for an investigation of the new model of the small urban family, struggling with a series of estate problems as well as existential ones.

The History of Testaments in Poland

Until the late thirteenth century, the idea of bequeathing estates was not known in the lands that in the late Middle Ages belonged to the Kingdom of Poland. Written down in the thirteenth century, the so-called Oldest Polish Law, which is the record of the hitherto existing customary law, provides the possibility of inheritance solely by the operation of law. According to this type of succession, the inheritance belongs to the agnate sons. A daughter's only right is to the dowry provided by her father or brother. A widow, however, can use the family property in the event that she does not remarry. In the absence of sons, the family estate becomes the property of the duke. In the event that the decedent's daughter marries, it is the duke who should procure her dowry.[7] However, from the beginning of the thirteenth century we meet in numbers of documents[8] traces of the praxis of law, which could be also marked as a new epoch, showing the influence of the Roman law on the local customary law.[9] Awareness of Roman law was

---

5. Kodeks dyplomatyczny miasta Krakowa. 1253 - 1505, cz. 3, ed. F. Piekosiński, (Kraków: 1882), 368.
6. Liber testamentorum, Archiwum Państwowe w Krakowie, manuscript 772 (hereafter LT).
7. Najstarszy zwód prawa polskiego, ed. J. Matuszewski (Łódź: 1995), 85-87.
8. Statute of Bishop Philip from Buda, 1279. Kodeks Dyplomatyczny Wielkopolski, ed. Towarzystwo przyjaciół nauk poznańskiego (Poznań: 1877), 1, 487.
9. P. Dąbrowski, Polskie prawo prywatne (Lwów: 1911), 67-68.

introduced by the Catholic Church, as in many other countries. It was the Church that accepted and promoted changes in the interpretation of property rights, as well as in the equality of women in the succession to the family property. Consequently, in the thirteenth century women gained the right to inherit property (sooner or later, depending on the actual district)[10], likewise the testament is put into judicial practice as the natural way of disposing of the property. Moreover, the Royal Legal Acts, starting from the Piotrkowski Statute (1356–1362) of Casimir the Great, tried to limit the possibility of bequeathing movable property, supporting the traditional model of inheritance based on the principle of separation of spousal property (separate estates in matrimony).[11] The endeavour to keep the ancestral character of inheriting property would be present also in the noble legislation during the next two centuries.

The same situation, to some extent, also appeared in the cities of the Kingdom of Poland. The development of municipality was a long-term process, which has its origins in prelocation times[12], yet the real stimulus that created conditions for the burgher's estate to emerge was the adoption of the German town law. This system was introduced starting in the second half of the thirteenth century in many cities of Silesia, followed by Lesser Poland, Greater Poland and Red Ruthenia (Lviv). It was based mainly on two sources; the *Weichbild* (*ius municipale*) of Magdeburg and the *Sachsenspiegel* (literally, the Saxon mirror). Its rules of succession did not differ much from Polish customary law. German town law was based on a system of separate estates in matrimony and on the statutory succession of patrimony (immovables) by relatives according to a prescribed legal order. 'In consequence of this type of succession, a wife was not involved in the heritage of her husband, while he, in case the couple was childless, had to give only half of the estate to his wife's heirs'.[13] The movables were divided into *hergewet* – the heritage of a man, and *gerade* – the heritage of a woman.[14] In the territory of the Teutonic State and the cities of Masovia Magdeburg law was applied, with elements of Flemish law, or Kulm law (*ius Culmnese*), in which at times of succession a spouse received half of

---

10. A. Winiarz, Polskie prawo dziedziczenia kobiet w wiekach średnich (Lwów: 1897), 776-777; Dąbrowski, Polskie prawo, 71-72.
11. U. Sowina, 'Testamenty mieszczan krakowskich o przekazywaniu majątku w późnym średniowieczu i we wczesnej nowożytności', Sociální svět středověkého města, ed. M. Nodl (Prague: 2006), 175-176; Winiarz, Polskie prawo, 799.
12. Prelocation times is refered to the period before German town law was introduced
13. Sowina, 'Testamenty mieszczan krakowskich', 176.
14. Bartłomiej Groicki, Tytuły prawa magdeburskiego, ed. K. Koranyi (Warsaw: 1954), 5-6, 15-16.

the estate, while the second part was taken by children or grandchildren. Women and men had equal rights to inheritance.[15]

In Polish customary law common law, both urban law and the law concerning the nobility, the last will was a strange element, which destroyed the established order of succession by particular relatives. The owner of an estate had the right to pass over some heirs until the death of his spouse (i.e., the heirs had the right to the estate only after the death of a spouse). According to the Magdeburg law, it was impossible to leave immovables by will; only movables were to be bequeathed (in comparison with the original rights of succession, this was a concession).[16] Under the strong influence of testamentary practices and of the Church, courts started to grant the right to make a bequest in favour of religious institutions from the so-called unrestricted parts of an estate of the testator (from a quarter to half of the estate). However, the extant wills are good evidence that those rights were often violated, although they remained valid and important. The thorough tracing of the process of gradual liberalisation of the inheritance law for the testator's right of alienation of the property needs the precise analysis of the few testaments preserved from the fourteenth century. However, it could be stated at the outset that because of the coming changes in the municipal law, it slowly rescues the testator from the power of the family. A spousal reciprocal bequest of both estates (*reformatio*) is a particular and very common example of this practice; in such a case, the relatives were excluded from succession. In view of changes in the interpretation of the notion of private property, municipal resolutions (German: *Willekür*) from the sixteenth century allowed married childless couples to do so, although already in the fifteenth century, in testaments from Crakow we can find examples of excluding even one's own children from succession (including as yet unborn children).[17]

It seems that the legal theory and its principles (as seen in this and other examples) are always one step behind the practice of law. The law and its upcoming changes is a distinctive record of alterations in the field of the social relations, culture and mentality of the society.

Changes in Testaments as Indicator of Social Changes

Generally, medieval testaments were written according to a form that was popular all over Europe. I must confess that it is quite astounding to read Czech, German or English testaments, whether written in Latin or in

---

15. Wilkierze miasta Torunia, ed. T. Maciejowski (Poznań: 1997), 68.
16. Sowina, 'Testamenty mieszczan krakowskich', 177.
17. Sowina, 'Testamenty mieszczan krakowskich', 180; LT, 13.

national languages, which in their form as well as in the expressions used are strikingly similar to those written by Cracow citizens. In my view, this is, without a doubt, one more contribution that leads us to an understanding of the unique universalism of medieval culture. Nevertheless, such a source could present a great problem for the researcher, who is looking for 'first-person narration'. This phenomenon shows us the importance of keeping the form of the document, instead of free expression. I believe, though, that fragments can be found where the testator's voice breaks through the power of form. I speak in this place about all decisions in testaments, made by the testator, concerning the disposal of the estate and particularly the moments where this succession is argued.

The above remarks on the testamentary form do not mean, though, that the document did not alter for more than 200 years. The character of the testament changes over time, as well as the people writing it. The dynamically developing municipal culture was comprising more and more spheres of citizens, changing their attitudes towards social life, religion and even themselves. It should be mentioned that while analysing the testaments we have the possibility of observing the process of individualisation that was coming in that society, causing it to become more and more diversified.

The analysis of fourteenth-century testaments is quite difficult compared with the later testaments because of the abbreviated forms used in the records, however, it is easy to notice that in these records religious motivations were dominant. On the contrary, the fifteenth- and sixteenth-century testaments found in the Cracow 'Liber testamentorum' are far more complex. The main motivation at this time seems to be the will to prevent possible conflicts between relatives concerning the inheritance. As an example, Margret Czipser, born in 1501, formulated the reason for writing her last will in such a way: 'volens ut post mortem suam inter pueros eius, nulla esset dissensio et controversia'. The whole of the large estate, worth several hundred florins, was divided among Czipser's eight children and her third husband. For the salvation of her soul, this woman bequeathed a mere 40 florins.[18]

The testaments of the second half of the fifteenth century differ from the previous ones in their content. The major issue in them is regarding financial accounts among the obligee and debtors, trade partners and relatives, and is not the attempt to make a pact with God for one's salvation. Out of 190 testaments from the fifteenth century in the 'Liber testamentorum', there were 108 testaments (57%) with pious bequests.[19]

---

18. LT, 165-166.
19. E. Piwowarczyk and P. Tyszka, 'Przyczynek do pobożności mieszczan krakowskich na podstawie XV – wiecznych legatów w *Liber testamentorum* (rkps 772)', *Nasza Przeszłość*, 105 (2006), 10.

Despite that, at the end of the period discussed, period the idea of bequeathing some amount for the Catholic Church is still quite common. This phenomenon proves the considerable secularisation of the testamentary document during the fifteenth century.

Another fascinating aspect, which can help in the understanding of the changes of the late medieval city and its complicated social structure, is that one can find quite a list of people eager to authenticate their last will in the Cracow city court. There are citizens of all different statuses whose testaments can be found in the 'Liber testamentorum'. As well as the testaments of burghers, there can be found the wills of rich peasants, gentry, clerics and even duchesses. The presence of such a variety of estates represented in the book is possible in law because of their ownership of immovable property. The reasons for the recording of their testaments are hidden deeper, though. This phenomenon could be explained, in my view, by the fact that the municipal culture was attractive, even for those who formally did not belong to it. This issue is without a doubt open for further research and is a clear demonstration of the inadequacy in the notion of the estates and their division in this era.

Relatives in Municipal Testaments, Close and Distant

Among the testators, there are numerous traders as well as representatives of various Cracow crafts. The analysis of the testators' occupations itself is very complicated because of that. Generally, they are either very rich or at least sufficiently well-off. Out of 108 testaments of the fifteenth century, one-third belonged to the patriciate.[20] Since there are usually no detailed inventories of the testator's property, and they were frequently married men, we analyse the amount of dower in order to establish the prosperity of the burghers. Predictably, the diversification of the estates of Cracow citizens was immense at that time. In the testaments the average medium dower is 30 marks, but in some case it is hundreds and even thousands of florins. These facts can help us to better imagine the social groups we are faced with in the research.

The testaments, in which we can find more describtion of a private character, give us unique information about the burgher's family, including its composition, number of members, and the relationships among them. While the diversity of bequests and people that appear on the pages of testaments reveal to us, to some extent, the municipal society of this time, these observations can also be projected to the majority of Cracow citizens who were rich enough to possess their own property. Commonly the family

---

20. *Ibidem*, 18.

of a rich burgher was enlarged by the group of persons who were not relatives. These were faithful servants, confessors, fellow-traders etc. In the case of Jan Sweidniczer's testament, even his principal scribe Paulo and his teacher Casper are mentioned in the bequest. They were so close to him that Sweidniczer even decided to show his gratitude by leaving them a part of his property.[21] Such people are like the big 'family' of prosperous Cracow burghers.

Testaments offer such a rich field of information that even cursory reading opens to us a lot of remarkable data concerning the burgher's family in late medieval times. First and foremost the families seem to be quite small, nuclear ones. Extended or joint families are not mentioned in testaments at this time. If one were to examine family relationships judging from the facts of the property division upon succession, it could be confirmed that bequests took place to the third generation of blood and affined relatives at the furthest. The property was usually bequeathed to spouses, children and grandchildren, as well as their family and offspring. However, typically only a few heirs are mentioned in each testament. A family like that of Margaret Czipser, who had three husbands and eight children, was the exception to the general rule.[22]

The detailed analysis of fifty testaments from the 'Liber testamentorum' shows that in just twenty-three of them did the testator have offspring to whom he or she could have been bequeathed the property (sons are the beneficiaries in only twelve of them). This superficial examination leads us to the conclusion that about half of married couples remained childless and in three-quarters of families there were no male descendants. This fact proves, and helps us to understand the belief about, the immense infant mortality and low birth rates even in elite families.

Therein lies the cause of the special care for the future fate of the offspring. Testators who had no children at the time of making the testament still hoped to have them in the future. On the other hand, the families who were blessed with children were also afraid of losing them. That is why Sylvester Sweidnicher provides the dower and inheritance for his wife, but also mentions that if they should ever have a child, then he would inherit their house and stall. In case they do not have progeny, it should be sold and the proceeds divided between his niece and certain pious bequests.[23]

There are also numerous testaments which make provision in case of the death of heirs. The reality of death, an important part of people's lives, also becomes vivid in the clause usually included in testaments, 'if the heir is still alive'. It seems, in the face of the average life span of around 30

---

21. LT, 39-45.
22. LT, 165-166.
23. LT, 28-29.

years and not rare cases of infant mortality, that the consciousness that death is near and can happen to everyone in any moment of life was present, especially concerning children.[24]

This attitude led the burghers to legal acts which guaranteed, in some way, the preservation of the family, its estate and its social position. An example is the obligation placed on Kathrin, the widow of Sigmund, the village mayor, by the Cracow Supreme Court applying German law. Sigmund bequeathed both of his houses to Kathrin's daughter Dorothy and son Ulrich on the condition that they should have children of their own. If one of them should be childless, the house will pass to the other. In the event that both Dorothy and Ulrich fail to have offspring, houses are to be sold and the profit should go to the foundation of one of the Cracow church altars.[25] Today such farsighted, meticulous and provident plans concerning the estate may seem slightly exaggerated, however, for Kathrin, who was granted by God to have offspring, the death of her childless children was a great threat.

The matter of having children and bequeathing the estate to them did not solve the problem for testators of planning the future fate of the family after their own death. Even if the family was large and prosperous, it could still come to a bad end in case of arguments and disputes among its members. As I have mentioned earlier, it was the potential for these family disagreements that caused the writing and formal recording of testaments. For example, the goldsmith Jan the Polish left his house to his wife Sophia and its stall to his brother Martin. Maybe with an inclination to the difficult character of both his relatives, or to the possible conflicts that might arise among them, Jan decided that in case of dispute, his brother should leave the stall and Sophia would be obliged to buy him another place for trade in the city.[26]

The claims of blood relatives could also be the reason for the threat that the property collected during the testator's whole life time would be despoiled. The small nuclear families usually had distant relatives somewhere in other cities and by customary law they also had the right for the part of the estate in case the decedent did not have male heirs. Because a wife, daughter or siblings could be foreced to give away a part of the property to distant relatives, it caused the appearance of disinheritance of them in testaments. It means that no other blood relative could inherit any part of the estate except those mentioned in the document. The right of the testator to disinherit potential heirs was preserved for a long time. It was mainly used for family reasons. Without a doubt, this was also a way to

---

24. L. Stomma, A jeśli było inaczej... Antropologia historii (Kraków: 2008), 27.
25. LT, 8.
26. LT, 32.

punish relatives that disappointed the testator. This, I suppose, explains the testament of Nicholas Barszcz who decided to leave his 'vagabond' daughter nothing of the property he had gathered over his life. He bequeathed his estate, the value of which was only 15 marks, to his brother Peter and nephew Gregory.[27]

Moreover, from my observations the most popular and intelligible motivation of testators, which we can divine from the testaments, is the will to support the future life of the spouse. Sometimes even children are set aside. Since the majority of testators are male, this tendency applies to widows. It is they who usually inherit the biggest part of the estate, not only as the matter of dower (called *morgen gobe* or *dos seu dotalicium*). That bequest also included immovable property, although it was beyond traditional law and, what is more, the dower itself could be enlarged in the testament. Hannus Lode, for example, had bequeathed in his first testament of 1446 part of his property to two heirs; his wife Margret and his brother Nicholas. Other relatives were excluded from the succession. Margret was supposed to receive 50 florins and Nicholas 10. Ten years later Hannus Lode, probably before a trade trip to Turkey, decided to rewrite his testament, so that his wife would inherit 100 florins and his brother 10 florins, as in the previous testament.[28] There is a great number of similar examples of the testator's great care of the spouse. The typical solution of that problem was the other popular and easy testament form, so-called 'spousal reciprocal bequest', which holds the mutual obligation of husband and wife, that in case one of them dies, the survivor shall receive the whole inheritance.

Testament as the Social Process Displayed

Almost every historian can find in these testaments something for their research. As a source for specialists interested in the history of family relationships, the history of society or the history of mentalities, testaments can scarcely be overestimated. They often contain astonishingly detailed information on the private life of medieval citizens.

The Cracow burgher's family, from the testaments analysed, is a small family, which fights for its social status as well as survival in the next generation. A strong influence on that fact is the constant movement of that society, the representatives of which often came to Cracow from distant lands. It seems we can talk here about the common notion of alienation in the big city, dealing with which was the purpose of such specific urban

---

27. LT, 13.
28. LT, 37.

institutions as confraternities, and craft or trade guilds. These were somehow replacing old family, neighbourhood and parish ties, which were lost irrevocably because of moving from the original place of residence. Testaments appeared in that environment and were soon widely adopted, as in the large scale they enabled 'the uprooted life'. The traditional system of bequests did not always suit the reality of that time and, what is more, it often limited the rights of burghers, who were used to controlling and administering their property. This explains why the will of the citizen was to be in charge of his property (and family) even after his death. The testament and its significance could be treated as an indicator of changes in the social structure.

PRIVATE CITIZENS BETWEEN LAW AND POLITICS IN A TUSCAN TOWN

Siena from the Early Thirteenth Century to the Early Fourteenth Century

Mario Ascheri

Introduction

This chapter covers the period from the beginning of the thirteenth century to the beginning of the fourteenth century: a very 'long century' for the law, which is impossible to consider in all its aspects. So, I will necessarily select certain aspects to give an idea of the general framework.

That century runs indeed from the first broad development of the university system to the firmly established system of degrees and the idea of the *Studium generale*, including the completion of the *Corpus iuris canonici* and of the vulgate version of the *Corpus iuris civilis* and the '*glossae ordinariae*'.[1] In the same century there was an incredible development of the local statute law, the urban *iura propria*,[2] usually to be connected with the learned '*ius commune*' – but not without problems, as we will see later.

These developments happened also in the Tuscan city we are now considering, Siena, south of Florence along the *Francigena* road to Rome.

---

1. See, for instance, my survey in *I diritti del medioevo italiano (secoli XI-XV)*, (Rome 2000), forthcoming in English translation from Brill.
2. A general statement in my recent 'Statutory Law of Italian Cities from Middle Ages to Early Modern', *Von der Ordnung zur Norm: Statuten in Mittelalter und Früher Neuzeit*, ed. Gisela Drossbach (Paderborn: 2010), 201-216.

There, already during the first half of the thirteenth century,[3] many *podestates* – public leading officers of the city – came from Bologna (among other cities) to hold temporary offices, and rooms for teaching by university professors were being rented by the city administration by 1240. Some years later, the Portuguese scholar Petrus Hispanus, the author of the *Thesaurus pauperum* and of the *Summulae logicales* who is better known as Pope John XXI, taught in Siena. University salaries were certainly paid by the commune as early as the mid-thirteenth century, as they were paid to other school teachers.[4]

The city was said by its *consules* to live 'tota secundum legem romanam' since 1179 and the first preserved *Statutenbuch*, published in 1262[5], spoke openly of laws administered by lay civic courts in this way. Foreigners – i.e., all people coming from outside the city walls – were granted the respect of the *iura communia*, except the application of other rules in force by special agreements, while the *constitutum* – as the local statutory law book was called in Siena, as in Pisa –, was additionally granted to citizens as the first source of law.

At this time the Lombard and Salic laws, earlier partly applied in this territory, were largely abandoned in favour of Roman law, although in Florence some rules lasted longer (e.g., concerning the '*mundium*' on females). At the beginning, the changes adopted were mainly reforms of procedure, but some Roman law rules were also openly contradicted. That happened for the *turbata possessio*, the *ius testandi* for capital sentences, the *ius testandi* of females, *inaedificatio*, or for specific or newly introduced institutions (*satisdatio tutorum*, born from mixed marriage with a *servus* or *serva*). For all these subjects some research has already been done,[6] especially on marriage (detailed research on *sponsalia per verba de presenti* and so on is now available), dowry and *exclusio propter dotem*, widows, wills – but here we can not discuss these items in detail.[7]

---

3. For a general survey, see my *Siena nella storia* (Cinisello Balsamo: 2001), and now, useful mainly for an introduction to the sources, Paolo Cammarosano, *Siena* (Spoleto: 2009).
4. General introduction in *L'Università di Siena. 750 anni di storia* (Milan 1991).
5. *Il constituto del Comune di Siena dell'anno 1262*, ed. Lodovico Zdekauer (Milan: 1897, reprint Bologna: 1974).
6. For all was said above, see Giuliana Giannelli, 'Il diritto privato nelle fonti senesi del sec. XIII', *Bullettino senese di storia patria* 33-34 (1926-1927), 213-322, 35-36 (1928-1929), 28-59.
7. It is sufficient to quote Samuel K. Cohn Jr, *Death and Property in Siena, 1205–1800* (Baltimore and London: 1988), and Gianna Lumia, 'Morire a Siena. Devoluzione testamentaria, legami parentali e vincoli affettivi in età moderna', *Bullettino senese di storia patria* 103 (1996), 103-285.

To Live a Private Life in Siena

For the legal conditions of private people in that period, first it is necessary to determine whether they were citizens or not (citizens reached the full legal capacity when 25 years old – except in cases of earlier *emancipatio* of course). Foreigners could also hold different statuses according to the contemporary relationship of Siena with the city of origin of the foreigner – political submission was common for the people of the surrounding villages and castles, times of war or *treuga*, alliance and so on. A foreigner could be hosted in the city, having a house and paying taxes, just to gain citizenship generally within a short period.[8]

Other ways to become a citizen included birth in Siena or a special individual privilege granted by the government. This generally was an award given in recognition of a political and/or military alliance. At the end of our period, the trend was against free immigration. The polemics of citizens were also increasing: they complained that the foreigners were advantaged in the face of the heavy taxation![9]

Many private individuals were excluded from the city, beginning with the '*banniti*', the citizens condemned for having refused to appear in a criminal court. Others were crippled people, lepers and excommunicates. Prostitutes, more fitting with the masculine *publica utilitas*, were permitted to remain – of course, at some distance from the churches – and later paying a special tax, but even their services could not avoid a large number of women being the victims of *stuprum*, of being raped etc.[10] An unfaithful spouse could be banned, but then forgiven if he or she returned home begging for pardon. This treatment, even in favour of the women, one century ago led a good historian[11] to think that only a shortage of females in the population – perhaps because of many deaths during childbirth – could explain this. However, for Siena as for other cities, there are well documented cases of powerful widows who could operate with great freedom in their legal affairs.[12]

---

8. For the thirteenth century, see *Il constituto*, ed. Zdekauer, ad indicem: 'cittadinaticum' and 'cives Senenses'; for the late thirteenth century and the first half of the fourteenth century, see William Bowsky, *A Medieval Italian Commune. Siena under the Nine, 1287–1355* (Berkeley, CA: 1981), ad ind.
9. For the precise official statement on 1338, see Mario Ascheri, *Siena nel Rinascimento. Istituzioni politiche e sistema politico* (Siena: 1985), 116.
10. Always precious is Lodovico Zdekauer, *La vita privata dei Senesi nel Dugento* (Siena: 1896, reprint Bologna: ca. 1970).
11. Lodovico Zdekauer, 'Per la storia del divorzio. Una separazione all'amichevole in piazza del Campo (1363 – 3 luglio)', *Bullettino senese di storia patria* 5 (1898), 279, commenting on the statutory law of 1262, *distinctio* V, chapter 25-26.
12. A research study by B. J. van Damme (NYU) is forthcoming on this subject.

The thirteenth century was a time of important works for the construction of walls and fountains, the underground water system, and new churches and lay buildings, private and public.[13] This was beginning to decline at time of the Dante's death (1321), because of the first important famines which prepared the way for the catastrophic Black Death in the mid-fourteenth century. The population within the walls before the crisis could be estimated at around forty thousand (today the population of residents within the walls is less than ten thousand!), but it is impossible to compare this with the population at the beginning of the thirteenth century. If we look only at the various extensions of the walls that it was necessary to build up to mid-fourteenth century, we could say that the population had increased by three or even four times!

The rate of growth of the population must have been very high, since the abandonment of children was a crime punished only with a small fine by the end of the thirteenth century. For the year 1298, still during a period of probably rapid demographic development, it is said that about 300 children were secretly abandoned at night. They were left at the main hospital of Saint Mary of the Stairs, in front of the cathedral,[14] which had been established some centuries earlier by the canons of the Sienese church.

The '*gittatelli*' – literally the 'thrown' children, i.e., left to the public charity – grew up serving the institution, either at the hospital in town (famous for its Renaissance frescoes, still well preserved) or in one of the many fortified farms it owned, and their *fratres*, who governed it. Thanks to the testamentary bequests of citizens who died in the Black Death, the hospital became the main estate owner in the Sienese territory.[15] This included, at the mid-fourteenth century, almost the southern third of all the Tuscan territory. The huge hospital, thanks to generous tax privileges, entered under official communal protection and control by the beginning of the fourteenth century after long lawsuits, but still with its own statutes and its corporate jurisdiction.

Poor families were offered the opportunity of giving themselves as oblates to the hospital. It was a kind of '*accommendatio*' which guaranteed them something like social security. It implied also the transfer of their own houses to the hospital, which generally left the donors the '*usus*' of the apartment for their lifetime, or until they were in good health. The coat of

---

13. See Mario Ascheri, 'Le più antiche norme urbanistiche del Comune di Siena', *La bellezza della città. Stadtrecht und Stadtgestaltung im Italien des Mittelalters und der Renaissance,* eds. Michael Stolleis and Ruth Wolff (Tubingen: 2004), 241-267.
14. Zdekauer, 'La vita privata', 75.
15. Stephan R. Epstein, *Alle origini della fattoria toscana. L'ospedale della Scala di Siena e le sue terre (metà '200-metà '400)* (Florence: 1986).

arms of the hospital, put on the façades of the houses as symbols of ownership, can be still seen along the roads of the historic town.

Health services and assistance for pilgrims were complementary works for the hospital. During their stay at the hospital, pilgrims could also deposit – as with a bank – their goods and money before continuing their journey to Rome.[16]

The assistance to poor people, daily luncheon included, was very important because of the large immigration motivated by the opportunities of employment in the building industry for workers coming from farms of the countryside. A *misericordia*, among other charitable associations, was operating in Siena at the beginning of the fourteenth century.[17]

Most of the poor people at the beginning of our period were serfs in the countryside, called in the sources *servi adscriptici*, what means that they were legally included in the property of the land. They fled to the city looking for work and the freedom granted by urban residence. The government, always partly representative of, or forced to listen to, the nobles who possessed estates in the countryside, attempted to be sensitive in controlling the immigration. Instead of enacting a general legislation giving freedom to the peasants, as happened in Bolognese and Florentine territory, Siena issued the rule of 'unus de tribus per massaritiam'. In other words, the law allowed that one peasant in three could legally leave the same farm.[18] But how many continued to enter and stay within the walls *contra legem*, or how many were already inside when the law was enacted? The number of '*gittatelli*' shows the difficulty of the registration of the new born. Only at the end of the fourteenth century did the registration of the new born with the city administration become mandatory: probably for the purpose of levying taxes and for political purposes.

The celebration of baptism was held only twice a year, on Easter and Pentecost Saturdays, according to the rules included in episcopal orders of 1224, and it seems that sometimes also adults were presented. It is curious to note the prohibition, during baptism, of the use of oil or of wine! Those

---

16. Gabriella Piccinni and Lucia Travaini, *Il Libro del pellegrino (Siena, 1382-1446). Affari, uomini, monete nell'Ospedale di Santa Maria della Scala* (Naples: 2003).
17. See the recent volume: *La Misericordia di Siena attraverso i secoli: dalla Domus Misericordiae all'Arciconfraternita di Misericordia*, eds. Mario Ascheri and Patrizia Turrini (Siena: 2004).
18. Paolo Cammarosano, 'Le campagne senesi dalla fine del secolo XII agli inizi del Trecento: dinamica interna e forme del dominio cittadino', *Contadini e proprietari nella Toscana moderna*, vol. I (Florence: 1979), 153-222.

episcopal regulations also forbade the presence of minstrels in the church and clerics wearing red and green clothes: those beloved by the lay people.[19] The religious culture of marriage and the legal prescriptions certainly met with difficulties in becoming established through practical application. A notarial document[20] provides evidence, for instance, of a practice that looks something like a temporary marriage, for a term of five years ('et plus si mihi videbitur', says the husband, and only the husband!). This case occurred in 1237, with a *donatio inter vivos* by the temporary husband, who promised his help to support any offspring if the mother would like to keep them at the end of the term of the relationship ('si contigerit te filios vel filias habere... cuncta necessaria... si illos volueris retinere finito tempore predicto'). What is of the greatest interest is that the offer of help is called 'consuetudo' in the document: 'dabo tibi, quod consuetudo seu consuetum est'! How widely used was this arrangement, in reality? And how 'sanctum' was this marriage for the contemporary clergy, the relatives and public opinion?

Some Changes

Certainly, however, laws concerning private life changed profoundly during this long period, just like the urban enviroment, which took the basic structure still preserved now only at the end of our period. That means that there were deep changes both in daily life, concerning material possibilities and comforts, and in cultural life.

From a legal point of view, in general it is probably possible to say that there was only a slow spread of the religious doctrines, as for marriage, and a growing use of legislation concerning the law of private affairs. It is wrong – considering the Italian urban legal practice of that century – to consider only university legal doctrines or the customary law, as well as the procedure.[21] Against the prohibition of bigamy, sanctioned in Siena's statutory criminal law (only with a fine, anyway), it is known that husbands often lived with '*amasiae*' (girlfriends), or that the notarial '*transactio*'

---

19. Rich information and texts in Michele Pellegrini, *Chiesa e città. Uomini, comunità e istituzioni nella società senese del XII e XIII secolo* (Rome: 2004).
20. In Zdekauer, *La vita privata*, 94.
21. I look at this issue in 'Dottrine universitarie, pensiero politico e istituzioni comunali: alcuni problemi', *Science politique et droit public dans les facultés de droit européennes (XIIIe-XVIIIe)*, eds. Jacques Krynen and Michael Stolleis (Frankfurt a.M.: 2008), 283-298.

between the spouses 'ut non remaneat cum ea et e contra' was but lightly punished.²²

Moreover, a second marriage was sometimes recognized just to close the first one. There is a notarial document of some decades later than Dante's death, just at the end of our period, to be quoted. In 1363, in the main square, in front of witnesses, a lady showed a document as proof of her marriage and dowry and said also that 'nunc habet alium virum', which was recognized as clearly 'contra ius civile et canonicum', but not cause for imposing a punishment. It was held just because 'unus alteram et altera alterum in pristinum statum relassavit, ut quilibet eorum ante presens matrimonium erat'²³.

Anyway, during the thirteenth century, the new religious wave of mendicant orders complicated the private daily lives of the people. They began, for instance, to choose burial in the friars' church without any respect for the traditional parish – causing deep conflicts which required lay intervention such as a fine proportional to the amount of the estate in the deceased's will.²⁴ Moreover, strong contradictions were created by the exceptional and new urban welfare, and by the new lay culture, both of the new chivalry and of rich merchants and craftsmen.

Siena offers the splendid example of Cecco Angiolieri, 'poete maudit' *ante litteram*, who died in Rome on 1312, living in the mode of Dante's 'brigata spendareccia' (*Hell*, 29.130). This was the famous club of dissipation operating at the same time as the *fratres gaudentes* (*Hell*, 23.103), the *militia Virginis* established in 1261 which quickly gained a bad reputation ('*capponi di Cristo*'). Cecco poured ridicule on the popes just because he knew the ecclesiastical world very well: his father had been Gregory IX's official *campsor* – but other Sienese merchants were dealing even earlier with important men of the Church. For instance, in 1198, in Rome, some of them gave a loan of 1250 silver marks to the bishop of Utrecht.²⁵

---

22. *Il constituto*, ed. Zdekauer, *distinctio* V, chapter 28 (the edition in the volume stops at *dist*. IV, chap. 72; the same editor published the last part of the statute, *dist*. IV-V, from other manuscripts: see Lodovico Zdekauer, 'Il frammento degli ultimi due libri del più antico Constituto senese (1262-1270)', *Bullettino senese di storia patria* 1 (1894), 131-154, 271-284; 2 (1895), 137-144, 315-322; 3 (1896) 79-92; the numbers of chapters continue those of the book; we refer to them).
23. Zdekauer, 'Per la storia del divorzio', 282.
24. A Sienese case in *La chiesa di S. Pietro alla Magione nel Terzo di Camollia a Siena. Il monumento – l'arte – la storia*, ed. Mario Ascheri (Siena: 2001).
25. Important business documents in Lodovico Zdekauer, *Il mercante senese nel Dugento* (Siena: 1925).

The will of Iacoppus, Cecco's brother, survives from 1259.[26] It concentrates on the *restitutio usurarum* and *male ablata*, as listed 'in libro rationum mearum quem manualiter do fratri Ugoni monaci Sancti Galgani (to whom he left his rights) et in libro societatis mee' – at least 25 communes and churches of France are listed! There were also his partners of the trade companies, with record of another 'liber societatis mee qui est in Francia'. He owned, among many other goods and estates, twelve golden rings, two horses whose saddles were made of red Cordoba leather, a red coat covered with white fur and boots made of iron. Two doctors who cared for his health had guaranteed for their salaries 'unum nappum argenti' ('quem habent pignoratum').

Around the end of twelfth century and the beginning of the thirteenth, the Champagne fairs were the place where the banking skills of the Sienese – often generally confused with 'Lombards' – came to prominence. The Sienese had the advantage of a very good silver coin, thanks to the mines of the territory which was the object of a feud with the very rich bishop of Volterra.[27] From France, the Sienese introduced back in their home town beds called 'French style', with other cloths and embroideries. A will written in 1232 records as the object of a 'legatum pro uxore' a very expensive red coat ordered but still awaited from France. Notarial '*imbreviaturae*', written ten years before and concerning mainly 30 contracts related to French cloths, are preserved and give ideas of the commercial law of that time. Other documents speak of companies with partners giving only money – so-called 'commendae' – and of letters of exchange at short term – also *ad mensem* or *ad septimanam*[28] – while the city's law included rules for the proctors, distinguishing those *citra mare* or *ultra mare*.[29] Sons were often emancipated and therefore fathers should have guarantees from them, as in some documents written in Paris in 1261[30].

Rules enacted in 1262, or present in the *statutum curie placiti*, the traditional court for wardship and other family problems, certify that *filiifamilias* were gaining greater freedom from *patresfamilias*[31] and they were becoming natural partners of companies – which were now steady, and that conferred reputation to them. We 'qui sumus socii de illa societate que

---

26. Zdekauer, *Il mercante*, 36-40.
27. What follows is from Mario Ascheri, 'Per la storia del tessuto a Siena: qualche aspetto', *Drappi, velluti, taffettà et altre cose. Antichi tessuti a Siena e nel suo territorio*, ed. Marco Ciatti (Siena: 1994), 239-244.
28. Zdekauer, *Il mercante*, 19 nt 1.
29. *Il constituto*, ed. Zdekauer, *distinctio* II chapter 82.
30. Zdekauer, *Il mercante*, 41-42.
31. *Il constituto*, ed. Zdekauer, *distinctio* II, chapter 100-101.

apellatur societas filiorum Buonsignoris': so was written in 1258 in a contract with the hospital of St Mary of the Stairs.[32]

Communal rules were often issued on commercial matters, integrating or correcting the customary law of merchants, the general *lex mercatoria* and the local law produced by the House of Merchants (*Mercanzia*), where a court was held by consuls of the merchants.[33] This happened especially towards the end of our period for dealing with the bankruptcies of bankers connected with the Florentine banks – implying interventions for the dowries of the bankers' wives and rules for the administration of the banks for the protection of their creditors.[34] The current idea of a customary commercial law and no other is certainly wrong for Italian medieval cities.[35]

Guilds of merchants and craftsmen are relatively well documented as powerful institutions from this time onwards. Therefore the city government was obliged to improve the security of the roads and to sign trade agreements with other communes, princes and feudal lords, or lead an aggressive politics including expensive wars whenever possible.

For Siena that meant an aggressive politics in all directions, except north-east towards the powerful Florence. First represented by the so-called 'consules utriusque mercantiae', the merchants also gained recognition of their special local law: at least in the earliest known Sienese *Statutenbuch* from 1262.

The beautiful coinage and advanced banking became characters of Sienese civilization even earlier than its well known artistic legacy, and lasted a long time. In the mid-fourteenth century a branch of the Sienese Salimbeni family, famous local bankers, worked in Lubeck for two decades to introduce the mint and produce the first gold florin in Germany.[36] This was possibile because of a long tradition. In the mid-thirteenth century, when Florence began to mint the gold florin which gave the city the financial primacy in Europe, the so-called Great Table of Orlando Bonsignori was possibly the greatest financial company in Europe: the Bonsignori have been rightly called the Rothschilds of the thirteenth century. The Guelph triumph after 1269 made easier the cooperation of

---

32. Zdekauer, *Il mercante*, 21 nt. 2.
33. Ascheri, *Siena nel Rinascimento*, 109-137.
34. Edward D. English, *Enterprise and Liability in Sienese Banking, 1250–1350*, (Cambridge, MA: 1988).
35. Ascheri, 'Statutary Law', 207-208.
36. Thomas Szabó, 'Gli stranieri nelle città tedesche del Medioevo', *Dentro la città. Stranieri e realtà urbane nell'Europa dei secoli XII-XVI* ed. Gabriella Rossetti (Naples: 1999), 69-93 (at 79).

Florentine and Sienese bankers, until the bankruptcies of the early fourteenth century.[37]

At this point, in the mid-thirteenth century, Siena was rich enough to be the main urban centre in central Italy for the heir of Frederick II, Manfred king of Sicily, and for the Ghibelin alliance against Florence and the other towns supporting the papal primacy. Siena had the primacy in Tuscany for a few years after the great victory of Montaperti against Florence in 1260.[38]

Soon defeated and forced to the papal obedience by excommunication and the Angevin military hegemony, the Sienese people strengthened their identity and their love for the city as a whole. Urban beauty became a public concern connected with the '*honor civitatis*' more than ever before. Art and architecture achieved important results that were enhanced by the institutions; the competition among citizens was stimulated by the city-state.

The law was a necessary tool for these goals, summarized at that time by the political theology under the concept of '*bonum commune*', as is well known.[39] What did it mean from our point of view, that of private people?

The Golden Period: The Government of the People

Private life became more and more involved in legal problems and in statutes. That meant that the political life and its continuing contests became more important and more onerous than ever.

The governmental provisions could affect private life as never before. Up to the beginning of the thirteenth century there was no conflict in the division within the urban people between the '*milites*', who paid no tax because of their obligation to perform military service with expensive horses, and the other citizens, who served in the city army as infantrymen.[40] Now, more than before, success or defeat in wars or in planning public buildings, and so on, involved everybody, and even clerics could be asked to contribute to public expenses – opening harsh contests with local churches and the papacy for the so-called '*libertates ecclesiae*'.

---

37. See English, *Enterprise*.
38. *Montaperti. Per i 750 anni dalla baltaglia. Atti dell'incontrio italo-danese*, ed. Mario Ascheri (Florence: 2010).
39. Bibliography in my 'Die andere Gewalt: Der italienische Stadtstaat und der Fall Siena', *Gewalt und ihre Legitimation im Mittelalter*, ed. Gunther Mensching (Würzburg: 2003), 81-112.
40. See, in general, Jean-Claude Maire Vigueur, *Cavaliers et citoyens. Guerre, conflits et société dans l'Italie communale, XIIe-XIIIe siècles* (Paris: 2003).

For private people the need for *'aequalitas'* – among males, of course – became the first concern and many legal fields were involved, while the traditional private law continued absorbing quickly the learned doctrines coming from the universities and the notarial culture.

With the introduction of the new idea of the people, limited only to the most active part of the citizenship, constitutional law changed profoundly. The political primacy of the traditional *milites* with their *'consules civitatis'* was over. Merchants and craftsmen felt themselves the true authors of the new welfare, and therefore they asked for direct taxation proportional to their revenues and estates, but they should become a political subject for ensuring this revolutionary idea. In 1257 the taxation even of *'bona mobilia'* was finally introduced, because – it is said[41] – 'numquam actenus divites et potentes fuerint iuxta formam bonorum eorum allibrati prout alii populares'.

The people finally made the commune their own with the help of the Guelph party at the end of the 1260s. Within a few years, the conditions of some private people changed profoundly because of certain legal interventions.

In 1277 there was the first law which listed the 'magnate' families, creating a nobility by local law depending on the social and political point of view of the majority of citizens, in fact, of the party: the organized 'People'. Society was therefore divided in two parts, into legal estates with well differentiated rights and status. Magnates, regarded as potent, oppressive and arrogant, were therefore excluded from the main political office of the city and their crimes were punished more heavily than those of the *populares*. Even the sumptuary law, already existing at that time and enacted earlier with few rules, and mainly for religious or economic reasons, now acquired a new meaning.[42] It was still possible to be rich and powerful, of course, but it was not legitimate to show that condition openly. Men and women could have still public marriages and burials, but with a rigid observance of rules that were continuously revised. They restricted the kind of jewellery to be worn, the length of clothes even for dressing in the church for burials, the number of invitations and of courses for dinners... The only exceptions were foreseen for university professors (jurists and

---

41. Lodovico Zdekauer, *La vita pubblica dei Senesi nel Dugento* (Siena: 1897, reprint Bologna: c. 1970), 88 n 1.
42. *Disciplinare il lusso. La legislazione suntuaria in Italia e in Europa tra Medioevo ed Età moderna*, a cura di Maria Giuseppina Muzzarelli and Antonella Campanini (Rome: 2003).

medical doctors) and their wives, and for knights – at that time an award also granted by the commune itself.[43]

Of course, the magnates still remained powerful, even from a political point of view, having seats in the general council of the city. They continued to build important palaces in town and to own many castles scattered in the countryside. But the cultural importance of the legislation against them should not be underestimated, even if in Siena it did not forbid the intermarriage of *populares* and magnates, as other Italian 'popular' communes did.[44]

The laws against magnates showed that there were no 'natural' and eternal positions of power within the city. Moreover it showed that private people were not under the same law, but the law discriminated by introducing 'positive actions' against the social differences – while poor people were helped, for instance, by an *'advocatus pauperum'* or help when imprisoned.[45]

There was a widespread hope for these changes, space for the possibilities excluded elsewhere, which created the unstable situations we all know. But the widespread political participation also created another reason for a deep love for the city, spreading the consciousness that it was not possible to live completely in one's own privacy, avoiding any care for public problems.

Public and private affairs were interconnected in the city as never before. This became clear, for instance, in criminal matters, where over the century the inquisitorial system, even in lay courts, and the political use of the judicial system increased. It is easy to understand the presence in Siena as judge, at the end of thirteenth century, of Albertus Gandinus, the author of the first important *Tractatus criminum*.[46]

Private life should be lived carefully, also the ecclesiastical one, since the city accepted the papal and imperial constitutions against heresy. In the field of judicial proofs, at least still in 1257, a judicial duel was held in the 'Campo', the new main square of the city under construction. Also, not

---

43. The Sienese case is illustrated in Maria A. Ceppari Ridolfi and Patrizia Turrini, *Il mulino delle vacnaità. Lusso e cerimonie nella Siena medievale* (Siena: 1993).
44. A good case study is still Gina Fasoli, 'La legislazione antimagnatizia a Bologna fino al 1292', *Rivista di storia del diritto italiano*, 6 (1933), 351-392, continued by 'La legislazione antimagnatizia nei Comuni dell'alta e media Italia', *Rivista di storia del diritto italiano*, 13 (1939), 86-133, 230-309.
45. For details on the development of this Sienese legislation, see my 'Législation italienne du bas Moyen Age: le cas de Sienne (ca. 1200-1545)', *« Faire bans, edictz et statuz ». Légiférer dans la ville médiévale*, ed. Jean-Marie Cauchies and Eric Bousmar (Brussels : 2001), 51-83.
46. M. Vallerani, 'Il giudice e le sue fonti. Note su inquisitio e fama nel Tractatus de maleficiis di Alberto da Gandino', *Rechtsgeschichte* 14 (2009), 40-61.

considering the burning at the stake for homicide, heresy, and forgery in coinage, the punishments were heavy, with corporeal mutilations and frequent death penalties – as was usual everywhere at that time. The exact application of penalties under statutory law is documented,[47] but the commutation of penalties – mainly reducing the very high fines against the magnates – and amnesties were frequent.[48] There was also control by the city council of the trend for the criminal prosecutions to be held by the lay courts.[49]

The independence of the foreign judges was not absolute and political influences could push their prosecuting efforts in some directions instead of others. Exactly this could happen in the management of the communal treasure. Private citizens who suffered loss or damage because of war or fire, or from the expropriations for the public utility, were granted money by the commune, but in turn their political position could help in gaining favours – such as in lending money to the commune, which began to create its public debt[50], or in the amount of direct taxation.

Again, politics sought influence in the legal world and private people always had to be careful about it. Moments of relaxation were given, for instance, allowing free access to the city to everybody (even to debtors) during the time of fairs, or for playing games in the square, especially the *'pugna'*, a feud among groups of young people whose name calls for no explanation, or for the *'palio'* celebrations of mid-August dedicated to Our Lady. It is also interesting to stress that a law provided that the main square should be kept clean not because of religious or other official services, but because it should be pleasant for the free time and amusement of the citizens.

The rights of citizens could be endangered, however, by the arrogance of public officers and judges. Confusion of public officers could be great considering that, of the sixty *'messi'*, the messengers going around with a

---

47. Enzo Mecacci, *Condanne penali nella Siena dei Nove tra normativa e prassi*, (Siena: 2000).
48. Peter Pazzaglini, *The Criminal Ban of the Sienese Comune, 1225–1310* (Milan: 1979).
49. 'Assemblee, democrazia comunale e cultura politica: dal caso della Repubblica di Siena (secc. XIV-XV)', *Contributi alla storia parlamentare europea (secoli XIII-XX)*. Etudes présentées à la Commission internationale pour l'histoire des assemblées d'Etats, ed. Maria Sofia Corciuolo (Camerino : 1996), 77-99.
50. William Bowsky, *The Finance of the Commune of Siena, 1287–1355* (Oxford: 1970).

red hat, only three were the official town-criers riding for the public reading of any order along the road and in the churches.[51]

It was also provided that statutory law should be written in '*littera grossa*', in order to be read easily, and the written statutes were kept, tied by a chain, in a public office open to consultation by anybody. More, by the end of the thirteenth century, the citizens were also guaranteed access to the deeds of the commune, notaries and merchants, just to avoid any confusion or prevarication.

At the beginning of the fourteenth century, in 1309-10, another important step of popular culture was reached. The statutory law book was translated into the local vernacular – the future Italian language – with a declared reason that seems incredible to us: to be read even by 'poor' people without knowledge of Latin language, and they were also authorized to have copies of particular texts. The two big volumes are preserved and they are also the most ancient urban law book in the Italian language, and probably the largest medieval text in Italian. Finally recognized for these qualities, it has been celebrated during its seventh centenary (2009-10).

But why this so exceptional translation? The official reason is difficult to accept, since the 'clochards' certainly had no good reason to waste their time in communal offices reading boring legal texts. There is something deeper. We must remember that, from the beginning of the thirteenth century, it was clear that the new learned jurists and judges were complicating legal life. Their interpretations, already forbidden by Justinian, were obscuring the legal rules. In the statutory book of 1262, the interpretation in cases of doubt was still a competence of the bishop, but a few years later, in 1280, it was reserved to the government. This solution was ambiguous indeed, because at same time the judge was authorized in criminal cases to use analogy – as everywhere, however.

It was important overall to save the powers of the government and the prestige of the commune. Indeed the '*res iudicatae*' by the court of the merchants had no appeal to communal courts, and no Sienese could be a defendant in a court outside the city, no citizen could transfer to a cleric his rights, and no debtor could be called into the episcopal court.[52] At the end of the thirteenth century there was also a strong contest because the ecclesiastical courts wished to prosecute lay citizens; many years passed before it was possible to reach an agreement between the two powers.

---

51. For the details in this page, see again my 'Législation italienne du bas Moyen Age', and now Mario Ascheri and Cecilia Papi, *Il Costituto del Comune di Siena in volgare (1309-1310). Un episodedo de storia della giustizia?* (Florence: 2009).
52. *Il costituto del Comune di Siena volgarizzato nel MCCCIX-MCCCX*, ed. Mamoud Salem Elsheikh, I-IV (Siena: 2002), vol. I, *distinzione* I, chapter 492.

Around the year 1300 the commune was very close to a modern state, with its '*princeps*': the government, in which selected citizens deliberated what was necessary for the city. But at this moment it was impossible to avoid foreign judges because the communal tradition was too strong, and it was also impossible to avoid the many notaries necessary for legal transactions. The law concentrated in the Italian statute book of 1309-10[53] gives the excuses of the government: we governors know that you are damaged by legal operators (judges obscure the law and justice!) and there are too many officers... Therefore we will try to save your money with this or that provision...

Judges and notaries were regarded as an organized group that was too strong, a guild whose members were very jealous of their privileges. Therefore they were excluded from the government, like the magnates. In this context the Italian text could also be understood as a tool for better comprehension, an aid given to everybody to understand the law and avoid being cheated by legal professionals. The Italian statute book of 1309-10 shows a conflict within the leading group of the city and, moreover, between two different cultures; the traditional one, hegemonic, steady and strong, and the other one, of merchants who would govern themselves without legal '*subtilitates*' and therefore would get rid of the lawyers.[54] Private citizens could be sure, in any event. They could operate quietly knowing that the governments of the 'popular middle class' were working for them, reforming what was wrong and trying to avoid any prevarication: the bulk of the republican communal ideals.[55]

No wonder we read that the government will get rid of the officers without 'clean hands' – exactly as was said in the recent history of the Italian judiciary. Like the Roman emperor, in Siena the city government showed itself as providential, the tutor of the law, of the poor and vulnerable. No problem, it will work for you. There is something of the modern, of *déjà vu*, in that old legal, political and rhetorical context: at least for people like we are today, just private people believing in generous ideas.

We could also complain about the gap between theory and practice if we did not suffer the same gap today. There is a difference, however. Those far-off Sienese citizens could at least find the right painter for their ideology and for the frescoes of their (believed) God, Government.

---

53. *Il costituto*, ed. Salem Elsheikh.
54. I am summarizing Ascheri and Papi, *Il Costituto del Comune di Siena*.
55. I tried to explain this context in my 'Die andere Gewalt'.

MARITAL CASES OF TOWN INHABITANTS IN THE CHURCH COURTS OF MEDIEVAL POLAND

Łukasz Truściński

Introduction

The marriage of townspeople in the late Middle Ages is an issue that has been explored very little in Polish historiography. In general, the historical sources seldom go into detail with regard to medieval marriages. Therefore, particular attention should be paid to the sources of jurisprudence: registers from bishops' courts, called at the time Consistories, which include a considerable number of records of proceedings between spouses.

In the first few centuries of Christianity in Poland, ecclesiastical jurisdiction was subordinate to the monarch's authority. It was only when secular power declined during the provincial division of Poland (in the twelfth and thirteenth centuries) that the Church managed to gain a certain degree of independence in judicial matters. Jurisdictional immunity regarding Church properties was obtained in the thirteenth and fourteenth centuries (this excludes the execution of the so-called *blood penalty*) and *privilegium fori*, which meant that the clergy could be tried only by ecclesiastical courts, in the thirteenth century.[1] Therefore, in the fifteenth century, which is the period that I will discuss in this essay, the competence and organisation of church courts was already established.

---

1. W. Rymarz, *Kompetencje sadow koscielnych w Polsce przedrozbiorowej* (Warsaw: 1970), 196.

Since the number of cases at the time was so great that the bishop could not handle them himself, he delegated his authority to an official.[2] One could not appeal to the bishop against the official's judgment, but only to the archbishop (who had his own official), who represented a higher authority. The officialties had their own chancelleries, which from the end of the fourteenth century kept registers, the *acta officialia*, which is the source that I have analysed for my presentation. The official could not handle all the incoming cases either, therefore an institution of District Officialties had to be established. One could appeal against their judgment to General Officials.

The Marital Cases

The registers I have examined are from the chancelleries of the Cracow General Officialty and Lublin District Officialty. In the nineteenth century Boleslaw Ulanowski published in print 222 records of marital court cases from these registers.[3] They include 59 cases which concern residents of the region's largest cities.[4] The earliest was dated 7 March 1410 and the final one was recorded under the date of 27 August 1489.[5]

The clergy were subordinate to the Consistories, whereas laymen were summoned only in spiritual cases, *causae spirituales*, or if someone breached regulations relating to ecclesiastical cases, *causae spiritualibus*

---

2. Ibidem, 221. In the Polish sources, officials are first mentioned in the middle of the thirteenth century.
3. *Praktyka w sprawach malzenskich w sadach duchownych diecezji krakowskiej w wieku XV*, ed. B. Ulanowski, 5, Archiwum Komisji Historycznej (Krakow: 1889), 87-187. The source is also published online:
http://dir.icm.edu.pl/pl/Scriptores_Rerum_Polonicarum/Tom_13/87.
4. My choice of towns is based on the classification of towns created by H. Samsonowicz, M. Bogucka and H. Samsonowicz, *Dzieje miast i mieszczanstwa w Polsce przedrozbiorowej* (Wroclaw: 1986), 105-123, who have divided them into four categories. This paper is part of my research on societies of the largest Polish medieval towns, which is why I decided to focus on towns included in the first two categories, since the ones belonging to the third and fourth categories are more like villages in terms of their economic importance, the number of inhabitants and their lifestyle.
5. J. Flaga, 'Sprawy i ludzie sadzeni w konsystorzu lubelskim w latach 1452 – 1466', *Historia et Ius*, ed. A. Debinski and G. Gorski (Lublin: 1998), 43-52. Jerzy Flaga states that in the Lublin consistorial records alone there are a number of notes which were not published by Ulanowski in his edition of consistorial books. While this may be true, I think that these records are sufficient to make some general conclusions.

annexae. Some marital issues were considered to be of ecclesiastical character.

What was important for the Church were those marital pathologies which could threaten the soul's salvation. Marriage had been regarded as one of the sacraments since the Synod of Verona in 1184. It united two people in an eternal and indissoluble bond, therefore anyone contravening it committed a serious sin. Divorce was impossible, although it was possible to annul a marriage, in other words to declare it null and void.

The content of consistorial registers reflects the Church's stance on marital matters. The vast majority of the cases were commenced because one of the parties did not keep the marital oath. Almost as often the problem of bigamy appears, as well as various obstacles preventing the continued existence of matrimony. It is worth taking a closer look at the marital cases which were submitted to the Consistory. The most frequent are suits concerning breach of the marital oath and separation from the spouse; altogether 28 out of 48 suits are of this kind.[6]

The marriage was usually established *per verba de presenti*, 'through words about the present', the vows between the two parties from then on to live together as husband and wife. In the case of an average resident of a medieval town such a ritual was fairly straightforward, more like the conclusion of a trade agreement rather than a ceremony of religious character.[7] It could take place at home or at an inn, not necessarily in church. On the other hand, quite often it was demanded that the marriage contract be made before a priest. This was a custom taken from the bourgeois and noble elites, although the consistorial registers seem to indicate that in the fifteenth century it was quite widespread also among the poorer strata of society inhabiting Polish towns.

A marital contract *per verba de futuro* was a promise of the parties to marry in the future. In practice, it was difficult to establish the difference between such a form of contracting a marriage, and an engagement, *sponsalia*, which despite certain difficulties and financial consequences could be broken off.[8] What is more, before the Council of Trent the presence of a priest at the wedding was not obligatory (although the analysis of sources indicates that it was considered of great importance), and theologians and experts on canon law still had not decided whether a marriage became binding as a result of the vow (the consensual theory) or

---

6. There are 59 notes concerning the problems of town inhabitants, but part of them deal with the same cases and people.
7. It is possible that both parties gave each other some kind of a written confirmation that the marriage had taken place. Record 59 from 1453 mentions some kind of document confirming the marriage of Dorota and Bartosz.
8. For example, notes 160 and 161.

only upon its consummation by sexual intercourse (the coital theory). The practice of consistorial courts proves that physical love, or lack of, was an important factor for both the parties and judges in deciding whether the marriage was valid or not.

The parties in these cases did not keep the marital oath for various reasons: a husband's impotence or wife's infertility were frequent grounds stated. The motivation for invoking such an argument is obvious as it ranks among the few grounds for the annulment of a marriage before a church court. It was also possible to invoke prohibited degrees of kinship between spouses, or to claim that the marital oath was taken against one's own will.9 For social, cultural and purely pragmatic reasons, the need to have children was very strong, therefore the annulment of a marriage due to infertility quite frequently had real grounds.

How important it was for contemporaries to have progeny is proved in a case dating from 2 April 1443. The judge granted Waclaw the right to join in another marriage since his wife, Helena, proved infertile, which was confirmed under oath by unspecified 'righteous women' as a result of an examination conducted by them.10 Another record mentions the examination of impotence in a certain man. Unfortunately no details of this procedure were disclosed, only that the outcome was more favourable to the man than to the aforementioned Helena.11

Furthermore, those summoned to court for not keeping the marriage oath were often accused of bigamy. Since the institution of divorce in our present-day understanding did not exist at the time, some people resorted to running off from their legitimate spouse to another town, where they got married again. The reason for moving to another town was to keep one's reputation intact by joining a new local community, as well as in the eyes of a new spouse, who very often claimed before a court that they did not know about their spouse's previous relationship. Even if such a person did not apply for a town privilege in their new place of residence (the requirements concerning town citizenship were fairly rigorous), it was important to have a good reputation among the neighbours. One of the insults most frequently used by medieval residents of Kraków was to accuse someone of a dubious past or questionable descent, as the fifteenth-century mayoral registers show.12

---

9. A significant example of forced marriage is mentioned in records 34 and 35.
10. Note 41.
11. Note 122.
12. H. Zaremska, 'Krakowska ksiega wojtowska z 1442 roku. Bojki i obelgi', *Cracovia, Polonia, Europa. Studia z dziejow sredniowiecza ofiarowane Jerzemu Wyrozumskiemu* (Krakow: 1995), 93-100.

Not all cases of bigamy were fully intentional. An interesting and not isolated case is that of Jachna and Stefan from Lublin, dating from 1453.13 Stefan accused his wife of contracting an illegal marriage with Stanislaw from Kurow while Stefan was out of town, and he demanded that she be separated from her new husband and return to him. Jachna admitted that Stefan was her first husband, but he had disappeared for eleven years and she had heard rumours that he was dead. Therefore she considered herself a widow, married Stanislaw, and had three children with him. The most curious aspect in this case is the sentence passed by the Lublin official. He ordered Jachna to return to her first husband and executed the partition of property: feminine clothes (*habitum muliebrum*) and bedding were assigned to Jachna, whereas all other belongings, immovables and children, to Stanislaw, the second husband. This source mentions several other similar instances, which suggest that ecclesiastical judges were extreme legalists, who did not take into consideration any other circumstances, however exceptional, and tried to put everything in order at any price, so that reality conformed to the rules of canonical law.

There are 58 women and 54 men mentioned in the recorded cases – either the parties or those directly involved, such as the second husband or wife in the case of bigamy. All the names are almost always disclosed, family relations as well, although less frequently.

In a patriarchal model of a family the father is the head of the family and in the situation where surnames were not yet widespread it was his name that was used to identify the whole family. Having married, after some time a woman was named not by her relation with her father but with her husband. This is the reason why several records provide us with the information on whose widow a woman was.14 The name of a mother or any other relative was mentioned only as an exception, usually when such a piece of information was significant to the whole case,15 or was for some reason distinctive.16 With regards to men, usually their occupation was also recorded.

A list of the occupations mentioned in the cases allows us to define roughly the social strata from which the parties came. Usually they were moderately wealthy and the less affluent residents of towns, the most

---

13. Note 60.
14. Notes 110, 139, 141, 159 and 165.
15. Notes 184 and 185, 195, 220. The mother and her relatives want to marry off her daughter.
16. In records 34 and 35, Magdalena's mother is called iudea, but it is not certain whether she was a Jew or whether it was some kind of a nickname. It is certain that her husband was a Christian. Notes 80 and 81 mention that the woman's brother, named Jan, was a rector.

common being craftsmen such as tailors, cobblers, furriers, bakers and butchers, as well as apprentices and servants. A few occupations stand out; a bachelor,[17] a scribe[18] and a musician called *citharista*.[19]

In accordance with the then prevailing view on the division of roles in a family, most of the women appearing in the source were housewives. Only a few cases mention women in paid jobs, and usually these were servants working as domestic helpers.[20] Perhaps their relatively frequent presence in the source results from the fact that they were usually young women, getting married for the first time, and servants for the bourgeois households were usually recruited from this age group. What is striking is the lack of representatives of the wealthiest social strata of medieval towns, as well as merchants and town council members. This can probably be explained by their wealth and their somewhat different approach to the institution of marriage. Among the highest classes of society, marriage was always a studiously discussed and long-prepared contract between two families, whereas among poorer people it was in general done on impulse, without any prior preparation, as in a case from 1452: Mikolaj, a tailor's apprentice from Lublin, testified that during his stay in Kazimierz (on Vistula) Malgorzata called him to her father's house and asked if he wanted to be her husband, to which he immediately agreed.[21] During the hearing Malgorzata denied everything – possibly she was influenced by her father Jan, who was present at the trial and who was reprimanded by the judge for trying to affect the testimony with his shouting. In the end they did not marry, the marriage vows between them were treated as an engagement and therefore could be legally dissolved.

Of course not all marriages were contracted in such an irresponsible way. For instance, there is the case brought in 1476 by Waclaw, a cropper of cloth from Kraków.[22] From his testimony it becomes clear that a year earlier, before dinner, at the inn belonging to Anna Nyemcowa, Anna had married off her daughter Zofia to him. Since the daughter was still a minor under the age of twelve, this marriage was only permitted by Anna's special consent. The oath which was taken was treated by both parties as an engagement, and, as a confirmation of the contract, Waclaw gave Zofia a ring, a fur coat, a gaudy coif and several other gifts. After a year of waiting Waclaw seems to have run out of patience, as he demanded that the court

---

17. Notes 34, 35.
18. Note 123.
19. Note 141.
20. There are seven examples in notes 33, 107, 119, 122, 157, 179, 220. They include Latin words for a female servant: ancilla, famula, serva.
21. Note 54.
22. Notes 184, 185.

force Zofia to marry him in the church the following week, at the very latest.

The testimony of Zofia's mother explained the problem; the agreement between them included one reservation, that the girl was supposed to stay with her until she reached the age of twelve. Children younger than this age were prohibited to marry by both civic and canon law. It is clearly visible that the contract which was concluded determined certain details of the whole affair, although later some form of disagreement seems to have occurred, which is why Waclaw took the case to court. Such kinds of contracts are mentioned in the source several times.

The source usually mentioned the place of residence as well. Most often these people were residents of Kraków or its suburbs,[23] and less frequently of the region in and around Lublin. There were also several people from Bochnia and Wieliczka, towns which in medieval times played a major economic role within the region. There are descriptions of people who, before these legal proceedings, had lived in one of the cities or were married to someone from there.

Therefore these people were clearly active travellers, and changed their places of residence frequently. This migration involved not only movement from the countryside and small towns to cities but also the other way round. Similarly, there is no rule about the distances they travelled. They moved to Kraków not only from small villages surrounding the capital but also from much more remote regions of the Kingdom of Poland, as well as from beyond its borders.

The reasons for moving were first and foremost economic, although some examples from the consistorial registers indicate that cities also attracted people who wanted to benefit from the anonymity that they offered. An example is Stachna, who used to live in the village of Wiktorowice, several kilometres away from Kraków.[24] She was sued by her legitimate husband Mikolaj, a peasant from Wiktorowice, because after a year and a half of married life she ran off to Kraków away from him and lived there with a certain Jan in the bath-house on Szpitalna street, probably working there with him. The abandoned husband claimed his rights after five years, perhaps because only then did he manage to find out where Stachna lived.

---

23. I decided to include inhabitants of Kazimierz, Stradom and Kleparz, small towns located near the walls of Cracow, as citizens of Cracow, despite the fact that Kazimierz had its own municipal council and rights. This is because inhabitants of small towns neighbouring Cracow were as strongly connected with Cracow as its residents.
24. Note 122.

Concluding Remarks

I have tried to present the most interesting cases and conclusions which I have come up with while studying the consistorial registers. Undoubtedly many of the issues I have discussed should be further elaborated, and examined in more detail with the use of comparative methods. Research into those consistorial registers which have not yet been printed should be conducted, which would allow us to confirm some hypotheses and revise others. The material is very rich and opens new perspectives for research on residents of towns in medieval Poland.

CONTRIBUTORS

PER ANDERSEN is Associate Professor at the Department of Jurisprudence at the Law School, Aarhus University. His main research interests are legal change in Denmark and Europe in the twelfth and thirteenth century, especially concerning legal procedure, and the interaction between learned law and local lawmaking.

MARIO ASCHERI is Full Professor of Legal History at the School of Law, University of Rome 3. His research concentrates on the history of Italian courts during the Middle Ages and Renaissance, as well as on the institutions of a typical commune with a republican tradition: Siena. His collected essays are published in *Giuristi e istituzioni dal Medioevo all'Et moderna (secc. XI-XVIII)* (Keip Verlag, Stockstadt: 2009).

BJØRN BANDLIEN is Academic Librarian and Postdoctoral Fellow at the Institute of Archaeology and Historical Studies at the Faculty of Humanities, University of Oslo. His main research topics are gender relations, ethnic and national identities, and the legitimising of feud and warfare in medieval Norway and Iceland.

CHIARA BENATI is Assistant Professor of Germanic Philology at the University of Genoa, Italy, where she teaches both Old High German language and literature and Scandinavian Language History. Her current research interests include Middle High German literature, Middle Low German–Scandinavian language contact, German law books and their lexicon, Faroese language and literature and specialised terminology in the earliest German surgical treatises.

BRUCE C. BRASINGTON is Professor of History in the Department of History and Geography of West Texas A&M University, Canyon, TX. He teaches courses and seminars in a variety of subjects ranging from the ancient world to World War I. His research principally concerns canon law down to the Fourth Lateran Council, with emphasis on the canonical collections attributed to Bishop Ivo of Chartres (†1115).

HENDRIK CALLEWIER is Archivist at the Belgian State Archives and the Katholieke Universiteit Leuven Campus Kortrijk. His main research topic is the secular clergy of medieval Flanders in the fifteenth century.

HELGE DEDEK is Assistant Professor at the Faculty of Law at McGill University in Montreal, Canada. He holds a doctoral degree from the University of Bonn, Germany (2006) and an LLM degree from Harvard Law School as a Langdon H. Gammon Fellow (2004). At McGill, Helge Dedek teaches courses on comparative and private law, legal history and Roman law. His research focuses on the intellectual history of the reception of Roman law in Continental Europe.

HARRY DONDORP is Lecturer of European Legal History at the VU University Amsterdam and member of the Ius Commune Research School. He has published on the historical development of concepts of both private and public law. His latest publications are on the history of third party benefit contracts (especially in medieval canon law) and the right to specific performance.

RICHARD H. HELMHOLZ is the Ruth Wyatt Rosenson Distinguished Service Professor of Law at the University of Chicago. He is a student of the *ius commune* and the jurisdiction of the English ecclesiastical courts from their inception in the thirteenth century to their (temporary) abolition in the seventeenth. His principal contribution has been to show the importance of his subject to the overall development of the law of England.

FREDERIK KEYGNAERT is finishing a PhD at the University of Leuven, which deals with the origins and development of the local interdict up to the twelfth century. His research focuses on church penalties as instruments of conflict resolution, covering early medieval France in general and the archdiocese of Rheims in particular.

MIA MÜNSTER-SWENDSEN is Associate Professor at the Saxo Institute, Department of History, University of Copenhagen. Her main publications deal with the European intellectual milieus (c. 900–1220) with special regard to social structures within these milieus. Her current research focuses on the social and political impact of learned doctrine and ideas in northern Europe – especially on processes of legislation.

FREDERIK PEDERSEN is Senior Lecturer in History at the University of Aberdeen, Scotland, and president of 'Church, Law and Society in the Middle Ages' (CLASMA), a research network funded by the British Arts and Humanities Research Council. His research focuses mainly on the interaction between the rules of canon law, the practice of the courts and the reception of canon law among the medieval laity. He also publishes on Scandinavian history. A Polish translation of his jointly-authored monograph *Viking Empires* (Cambridge University Press 2005) is scheduled for publication in the near future.

CHRISTOF ROLKER is Postdoctoral Scholar at the University of Constance, Germany. He is currently working on late medieval social history, especially family and marriage. Other research topics include pre-Gratian medieval canon law, high-medieval letter collections and wills.

KIRSI SALONEN is Docent in Medieval History at the Department of History and Philosophy, University of Tampere, Finland. Her current research position is Finnish Academy Research Fellow. Her main research interests are papal and civil justice in the late Middle Ages, the Apostolic Penitentiary and Sacra Romana Rota.

ŁUKASZ TRUŚCIŃSKI currently works as an archivist in the Central Archives of Historical Records in Warsaw. He is mainly interested in the social history of towns in the fourteenth and fifteenth centuries and is now working on his doctoral degree at the University of Warsaw. The main topics of his recent research are various aspects of marriage of townspeople in medieval Poland.

HELLE VOGT is Associate Professor in Legal History at the Faculty of Law, University of Copenhagen. Her main research topics are Nordic legal history and the interaction between local law and learned Christian legal ideology.

STEPHEN D. WHITE is the Candler Professor of Medieval History at Emory University, Atlanta, USA, and, in 2009-10, was a visiting scholar in Medieval History at the University of St Andrews, Scotland. His current research interests include medieval legal and cultural history and the Bayeux Tapestry.

JAKUB WYSMUŁEK is Researcher at the Department of History at the University of Warsaw. His main research field is the social and cultural history of cities in the Middle Ages, and he is currently working on the late medieval wills of Cracow.